AI Governance for Enterprise

By

Nihar Malali

DEDICATION

This book is dedicated to
the three goddesses in my life:
my mother, Geeta,
my wife, Sushma,
and my daughter, Araina.

TABLE OF CONTENTS

PART I

INTRODUCTION TO AI GOVERNANCE

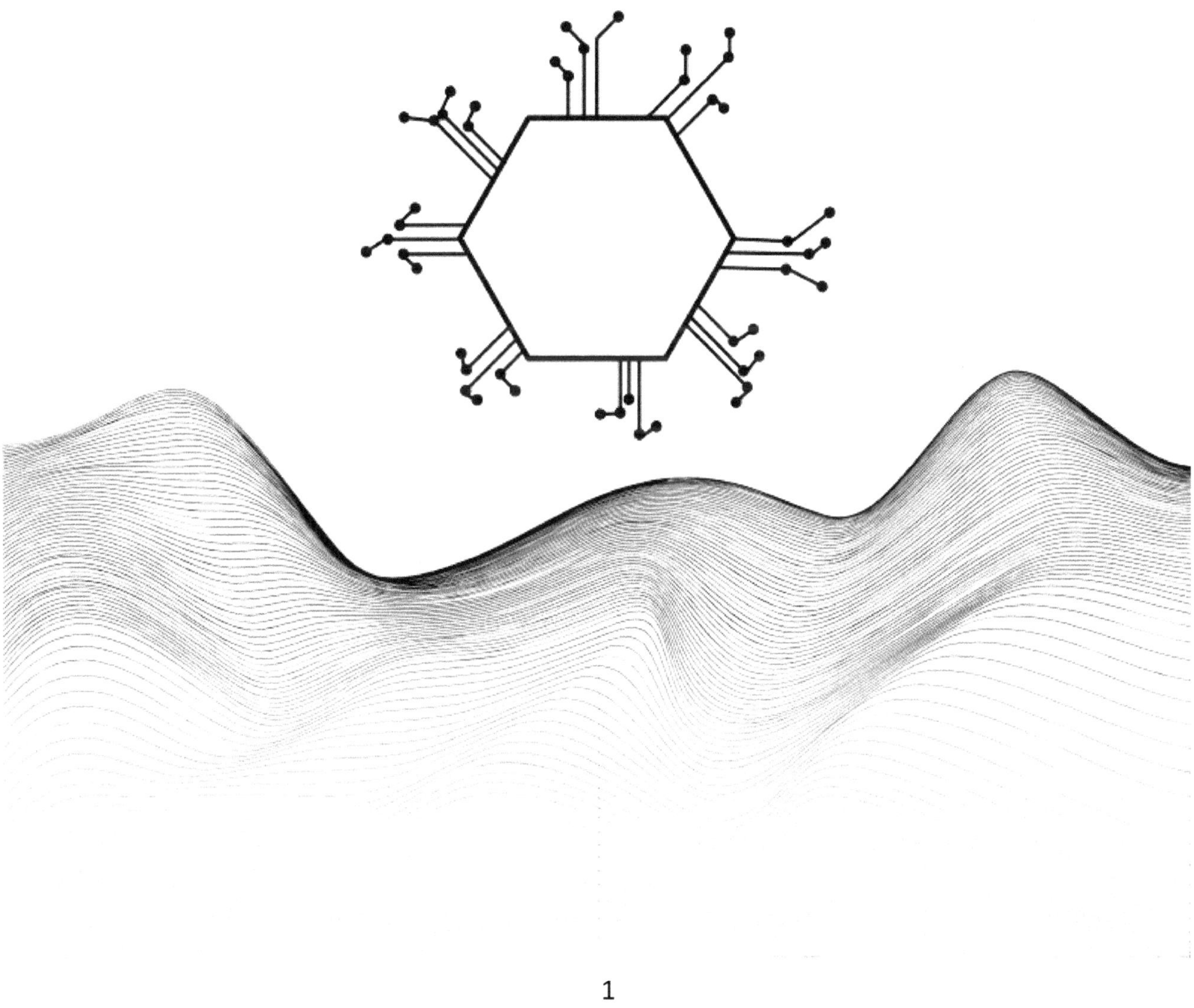

CHAPTER 1: WHAT IS AI GOVERNANCE

1.1 DEFINITION AND OVERVIEW OF AI GOVERNANCE

WHAT IS AI GOVERNANCE?

AI governance refers to the frameworks, policies, and practices that ensure the ethical, transparent, and responsible development, deployment, and use of artificial intelligence (AI) systems. It encompasses guidelines that regulate AI's impact on individuals, organizations, and society, striving to mitigate risks while maximizing benefits. AI governance establishes the guardrails for the entire lifecycle of AI systems, ensuring they align with organizational goals, legal standards, and societal values.

Governance is essential for fostering trust and confidence in AI systems. It addresses critical questions such as: How can AI be deployed ethically? Who is accountable when AI fails or causes harm? How can we ensure AI systems are transparent and equitable? These concerns highlight the need for a robust governance structure to guide organizations in responsibly managing the complexities of AI.

KEY PRINCIPLES OF AI GOVERNANCE

AI governance is underpinned by several core principles that help organizations navigate the challenges of integrating AI into their operations:

1. Accountability: This principle ensures that organizations and individuals are held responsible for the outcomes of their AI systems. Accountability involves assigning clear ownership over AI decisions and ensuring mechanisms are in place to address errors, unintended consequences, or harm. For example, if an AI-powered hiring tool unfairly rejects candidates, the organization deploying it must take responsibility for rectifying the issue.

2. Transparency: Transparency refers to the ability of AI systems to be explainable and understandable to stakeholders, including users, regulators, and impacted communities. Transparent AI systems enable stakeholders to comprehend how decisions are made, fostering trust and enabling scrutiny. Organizations must document their AI algorithms, decision-making processes, and data sources.

3. Fairness: AI governance ensures that AI systems do not perpetuate or amplify biases, promoting equitable outcomes for all users. Fairness involves assessing and mitigating biases in training data, algorithms, and decision-making processes. For instance, an AI-driven credit scoring system must ensure equal access to loans for diverse demographics without favoring or discriminating against specific groups.

Security: Security in AI governance safeguards AI systems against threats such as data breaches, adversarial attacks, and misuse. Organizations must implement robust cybersecurity measures to protect sensitive data and prevent malicious actors from exploiting AI systems. Additionally, governance frameworks should address vulnerabilities specific to AI, such as model poisoning or spoofing.

4. Ethical Considerations: AI governance emphasizes aligning AI systems with moral values and societal norms. This includes addressing questions of autonomy, consent, and human oversight. Ethical AI respects user rights, avoids harm, and operates in a manner that reflects societal good. For example, facial recognition technologies deployed in public spaces should be governed by strict ethical guidelines to prevent misuse and protect individual privacy.

WHY AI GOVERNANCE MATTERS IN TODAY'S ENTERPRISE ENVIRONMENT

The growing integration of AI into enterprises has transformed industries, enabling innovation, efficiency, and competitive advantage. However, this rapid adoption also introduces risks and challenges that necessitate strong governance:

1. Mitigating Risks: When deploying AI systems, enterprises face reputational, financial, and legal risks. Without proper governance, AI systems can lead to unintended consequences, such as biased decision-making, data breaches, or non-compliance with regulations. Robust governance frameworks help organizations identify and mitigate these risks, ensuring responsible AI adoption.

2. Regulatory Compliance: Governments and regulatory bodies worldwide are introducing laws and guidelines for AI use, such as the European Union's AI Act and the United States' Blueprint for an AI Bill of Rights. Enterprises must implement governance practices to comply with these evolving regulations and avoid penalties and reputational damage.

3. Building Trust and Transparency: Stakeholders, including customers, employees, and investors, demand transparency and accountability in AI systems. A well-governed AI system builds trust by demonstrating fairness, security, and ethical alignment. For example, organizations can use AI governance to assure customers that their data is used responsibly and their privacy is protected.

4. Driving Innovation Responsibly: Governance enables enterprises to innovate responsibly by establishing clear boundaries and ethical guidelines for AI research and development. It ensures that AI systems deliver value without compromising societal welfare. For instance, an AI-driven recommendation system for e-commerce must balance profitability with ethical considerations, such as avoiding manipulative practices.

5. Managing Complexities in Data-Driven Environments: Modern enterprises operate in data-rich ecosystems where AI systems process vast amounts of information. AI governance provides the tools to manage these complexities, ensuring data quality, security, and ethical usage. Organizations can optimize efficiency while minimizing risks by governing data pipelines and AI workflows.

1.2 THE EVOLUTION OF AI GOVERNANCE

A BRIEF HISTORY OF AI GOVERNANCE

AI governance has evolved significantly over the years, driven by the growing influence of AI technologies on society, businesses, and individual lives. The journey began with early concerns over the societal implications of AI, progressing to today's sophisticated governance frameworks designed to address ethical, legal, and operational challenges.

1. **Early Concerns and Regulation**:
   In the mid-20th century, when AI was in its infancy, discussions about governance were speculative and rooted in science fiction and philosophical debates. Works like Isaac Asimov's Three Laws of Robotics first articulated concerns about machines' autonomy and potential to harm society. These ideas underscored the need for ethical boundaries in developing intelligent systems.
   As AI research advanced in the 1980s and 1990s, so did the recognition of its societal impact. Researchers and policymakers began addressing issues such as the accountability of automated systems and potential job displacement due to automation. However, governance mechanisms during this period were limited and often reactive, focusing on mitigating immediate risks rather than providing proactive frameworks.

2. **The Rise of Modern AI and Growing Awareness (2000s)**:
   The rapid development of machine learning, neural networks, and big data in the early 2000s brought AI into mainstream applications, including healthcare, finance, and autonomous vehicles. This shift raised new governance challenges, such as algorithmic bias, privacy concerns, and accountability in decision-making.
   Notable incidents, such as the use of biased AI algorithms in criminal justice systems, highlighted the urgency of governance. These events spurred the development of guidelines and policies at both organizational and governmental levels, though they often lacked global consistency or enforceability.

3. **Contemporary AI Governance Frameworks (2010s–Present)**:
   The 2010s marked a turning point in the proliferation of AI in critical domains like facial recognition, predictive analytics, and voice assistants. This era saw the emergence of comprehensive governance frameworks designed to balance innovation with responsibility. For example, the General Data Protection Regulation (GDPR), enacted by the European Union in 2018, introduced stringent requirements for data privacy, directly impacting AI systems reliant on personal data.
   Organizations like Google, Microsoft, and IBM also developed internal ethical AI principles to address fairness, accountability, and transparency. However, despite these efforts, challenges like algorithmic opacity and global regulatory fragmentation persist, emphasizing the need for unified governance standards.

MILESTONES IN AI GOVERNANCE

The evolution of AI governance has been shaped by key events, breakthroughs, and regulatory developments that have defined its trajectory:

1. **The Asilomar AI Principles (2017)**:
   This conference, hosted by the Future of Life Institute, brought together researchers, policymakers, and industry leaders to draft principles for AI's safe and ethical development. The Asilomar AI Principles addressed topics like transparency, privacy, and long-term societal impact, laying the groundwork for modern AI ethics.

2. **GDPR and Global Influence (2018)**:
   The European Union's implementation of the GDPR was a landmark in data governance. By establishing stringent requirements for data protection and user consent, GDPR forced organizations to rethink how they manage AI systems and handle sensitive data. Its influence extended globally, inspiring similar regulations in countries like Brazil (LGPD) and California (CCPA).

3. **AI Governance in Autonomous Vehicles**:
   The rise of autonomous vehicles (AVs) introduced complex governance challenges, such as liability in accidents and ethical decision-making. Milestones like the United Nations Economic Commission for Europe's (UNECE) guidelines for AV safety emphasized the need for global collaboration in regulating AI-driven technologies.

4. **Global AI Ethics Guidelines**:
   Frameworks such as the OECD AI Principles (2019), UNESCO's Recommendation on the Ethics of AI (2021), and the European Union's AI Act (drafted in 2021) emerged in the late 2010s and early 2020s. These guidelines provided comprehensive approaches to AI governance, addressing fairness, transparency, accountability, and human rights.

THE ROLE OF GLOBAL INITIATIVES

Global initiatives have played a pivotal role in shaping AI governance by fostering international collaboration and promoting ethical AI development:

1. **OECD AI Principles (2019)**:
   The Organisation for Economic Co-operation and Development (OECD) developed a set of principles to guide the responsible development and deployment of AI. These principles emphasized inclusive growth, human-centered values, transparency, and accountability. As

one of the first international agreements on AI governance, the OECD Principles gained widespread adoption and influenced national policies worldwide.

2. **UNESCO's Recommendation on the Ethics of AI (2021):**
   UNESCO's recommendations provided a comprehensive ethical framework for AI development, addressing human dignity, environmental sustainability, and cultural diversity. The recommendations encouraged member states to adopt AI governance mechanisms that align with these values, fostering global consistency in ethical AI practices.

3. **European Union's AI Act (Drafted 2021):**
   The EU's AI Act aimed to regulate AI systems based on risk levels, categorizing applications into unacceptable, high-risk, and low-risk groups. This risk-based approach provided a practical framework for governance, ensuring stricter oversight for critical applications like healthcare and law enforcement while promoting innovation in low-risk domains.

4. **Partnership on AI:**
   Founded by major technology companies, the Partnership on AI promotes best practices for AI governance, emphasizing collaboration between industry, academia, and civil society. Its initiatives focus on AI fairness, transparency, and societal impact, fostering a shared understanding of governance challenges.

1.3 SCHOOLS OF THOUGHT IN AI GOVERNANCE

ETHICAL VS. COMPLIANCE-BASED APPROACHES

AI governance can be broadly categorized into two schools of thought: ethical governance and compliance-based governance. Each approach represents a unique perspective on managing the development and deployment of AI systems, addressing societal, moral, and legal considerations.

1. **Ethical Governance: Focusing on Societal Impact and Moral Obligations**
   Ethical governance prioritizes societal well-being, moral responsibility, and the broader impact of AI systems on humanity. It transcends regulatory requirements, urging organizations to align their AI strategies with fairness, human dignity, and sustainability values.

   - **Core Principles:**
     Ethical governance is rooted in inclusivity, accountability, transparency, and respect for human rights. It emphasizes long-term societal impact and urges organizations to avoid harm, minimize biases, and ensure equitable outcomes for all stakeholders.

   - **Advantages:**
     Ethical governance promotes trust and goodwill among users, regulators, and the broader public. It enables organizations to lead by example, fostering innovation while demonstrating their commitment to societal progress.
     For instance, companies like Microsoft and IBM have developed ethical AI guidelines

beyond compliance. These guidelines ensure fairness in their systems and address biases in applications like facial recognition.

  - Challenges:
    Ethical governance can be challenging to implement due to its subjective nature. Unlike compliance-based governance, which follows clear-cut regulations, ethical considerations require organizations to interpret abstract concepts like fairness and morality, often resulting in inconsistent applications across industries.

2. Compliance-Based Governance: Adhering to Legal and Regulatory Requirements
   Compliance-based governance aligns AI practices with existing laws, regulations, and industry standards. Its primary goal is to ensure that organizations meet legal requirements to avoid penalties, lawsuits, or reputational damage.

   - Core Principles:
     Compliance-based governance is grounded in enforceable rules and standards, such as data protection regulations, algorithmic accountability laws, and industry-specific guidelines. Examples include GDPR (General Data Protection Regulation) in the European Union and the proposed EU AI Act, which categorizes AI systems based on risk levels.

   - Advantages:
     Compliance-based governance provides organizations with clear, actionable guidelines, reducing ambiguity in decision-making. It ensures accountability, as violations can lead to measurable consequences, such as fines or legal action.

   - Challenges:
     While effective in preventing legal risks, compliance-based governance can limit innovation by focusing solely on adherence to regulations rather than encouraging proactive, ethical considerations. Moreover, regulatory fragmentation can challenge multinational organizations to navigate varying rules across jurisdictions without global AI standards.

Key Considerations for Organizations:
While ethical and compliance-based approaches often coexist, organizations must strike a balance between the two. A purely compliance-driven strategy may ensure legality but fail to address deeper societal concerns, whereas an ethics-first approach may struggle without regulatory support. Effective governance integrates the best of both worlds, aligning moral obligations with enforceable rules.

CENTRALIZED VS. DECENTRALIZED GOVERNANCE MODELS

Another critical dimension of AI governance involves the structure of decision-making—whether governance is centralized or decentralized. Each model offers distinct advantages and challenges, depending on the industry, organizational size, and specific AI applications.

1. **Centralized Governance Models**
   In centralized governance, decision-making authority and oversight responsibilities are concentrated within a single entity, such as a dedicated AI ethics board, regulatory body, or executive committee.
   - **Pros:**
     - **Consistency**: Centralized governance ensures uniform standards and practices across an organization or industry. This reduces the risk of discrepancies and ensures compliance with established guidelines.
     - **Accountability**: Accountability is clear and direct, with a single entity responsible for oversight. This simplifies decision-making and policy enforcement.
     - **Efficiency**: Centralized governance can streamline processes and ensure quicker responses to emerging issues, as decision-making is less fragmented.
   - **Cons:**
     - **Scalability Challenges**: As organizations grow, a centralized approach may struggle to address the unique needs of diverse departments, regions, or industries.
     - **Bureaucracy**: Over-centralization can lead to inefficiencies due to rigid structures and slower decision-making in complex or dynamic scenarios.
   - **Use Cases**:
     Centralized governance is shared in industries like finance and healthcare, where strict compliance and consistency are critical. For instance, banks often rely on centralized AI governance committees to ensure adherence to data privacy laws and ethical standards in credit scoring systems.
2. **Decentralized Governance Models**
   In decentralized governance, decision-making authority is distributed across multiple teams, departments, or entities. This model empowers stakeholders at various levels to participate in governance processes.
   - **Pros:**
     - **Flexibility**: Decentralized governance allows teams to adapt guidelines to their contexts, fostering innovation and agility.

        - **Inclusivity**: By involving diverse stakeholders, decentralized models ensure broader perspectives, leading to more equitable and context-sensitive outcomes.
        - **Scalability**: Decentralization works well in large organizations or industries with diverse needs, as it avoids bottlenecks in decision-making.
    - **Cons**:
        - **Lack of Uniformity**: Without centralized oversight, governance practices may become inconsistent, leading to discrepancies and potential compliance risks.
        - **Accountability Issues**: Distributed decision-making can obscure lines of responsibility, complicating enforcement and accountability.
    - **Use Cases**:
      Decentralized governance is often seen in technology companies and open-source AI communities. For instance, open-source AI platforms like TensorFlow rely on decentralized governance committees to ensure ethical and inclusive contributions from developers worldwide.

Key Considerations for Organizations:
The choice between centralized and decentralized governance depends on organizational priorities, industry requirements, and the scale of AI adoption. Many organizations adopt a hybrid approach, centralizing core governance functions while allowing flexibility at the operational level.

The schools of thought in AI governance—ethical vs. compliance-based and centralized vs. decentralized models—highlight the diversity of approaches to managing AI responsibly. While ethical governance prioritizes societal values, compliance-based governance ensures adherence to enforceable rules. Similarly, centralized models provide consistency and accountability, while decentralized models foster inclusivity and flexibility. By understanding these frameworks, organizations can tailor their governance strategies to address unique challenges, ensuring responsible and impactful AI adoption. Ultimately, the most effective governance systems integrate ethical principles, regulatory compliance, and structural adaptability, enabling AI to drive innovation while safeguarding societal interests.

1.4 THE NEED FOR GOVERNANCE IN A DATA-DRIVEN AI WORLD

THE RISKS OF UNGOVERNED AI

As artificial intelligence (AI) becomes a cornerstone of modern enterprises, the lack of governance poses significant risks that can undermine its potential benefits. These risks are amplified in a data-driven world, where the reliance on AI systems to make critical decisions is growing. Below are three crucial areas where ungoverned AI can create significant challenges.

1. **Bias and Discrimination in AI Systems**
   AI systems often inherit biases in the data they are trained on, leading to discriminatory outcomes that disproportionately affect certain groups. For example, biased algorithms in hiring platforms have been shown to discriminate against women and minority groups by favoring resumes that align with historically biased data patterns. Similarly, facial recognition systems have demonstrated higher error rates for individuals with darker skin tones than those with lighter skin tones.

   - **Impact**: Such biases harm individuals and expose organizations to reputational damage and legal consequences. Bias can erode trust in AI systems, creating skepticism among stakeholders and users.
   - **Governance Role**: Effective AI governance identifies and mitigates biases during the design, training, and deployment phases. By instituting fairness audits and adopting diverse data sets, organizations can reduce discriminatory outcomes and enhance the inclusivity of their AI systems.

2. **Privacy and Security Concerns**
   The increasing reliance on AI amplifies the risk of privacy violations and data breaches. AI systems often require vast amounts of personal data to function effectively, making them attractive targets for cyberattacks. For instance, healthcare AI systems that analyze patient data are vulnerable to breaches, potentially exposing sensitive medical records. Additionally, AI-powered surveillance tools, such as facial recognition systems, have raised concerns about mass surveillance and the erosion of individual privacy.

   - **Impact**: Privacy violations can lead to financial penalties, loss of customer trust, and regulatory scrutiny. Moreover, data breaches can have far-reaching consequences, including identity theft and financial fraud.
   - **Governance Role**: AI governance frameworks prioritize data security and privacy by enforcing compliance with regulations like the General Data Protection Regulation (GDPR) and the California Consumer Privacy Act (CCPA). They establish protocols for data encryption, access control, and consent management, ensuring that AI systems respect user privacy and are resilient to cyber threats.

3. **Misuse of AI Technologies (e.g., Deepfakes)**
   Misusing AI technologies, such as deepfakes, poses significant risks to individuals, organizations, and society. Deepfake technology generates highly realistic but fake images, videos, or audio and has been used for malicious purposes, including political disinformation, identity fraud, and blackmail. Similarly, AI can be weaponized to create automated systems for cyberattacks or misinformation campaigns.

- Impact: The misuse of AI technologies undermines public trust in digital content and can destabilize institutions, economies, and social norms. Organizations may also face reputational risks if their AI technologies are co-opted for harmful purposes.

- Governance Role: AI governance helps prevent misuse by establishing ethical guidelines, implementing safeguards, and monitoring the deployment of high-risk AI technologies. For instance, organizations can adopt watermarking techniques to detect and flag deepfakes, while regulatory bodies can enforce laws to penalize malicious actors.

BENEFITS OF GOVERNANCE FOR ORGANIZATIONS

While ungoverned AI presents significant risks, robust governance frameworks offer numerous advantages for organizations, enabling them to innovate responsibly while maintaining stakeholder trust and regulatory compliance.

1. **Building Trust with Stakeholders**
   Trust is a cornerstone of AI adoption, and effective governance is critical in fostering it. Stakeholders, including customers, employees, and regulators, demand transparency, accountability, and fairness in AI systems.

   - Governance Role: By implementing clear policies and ensuring transparency in AI decision-making processes, organizations can demonstrate their commitment to ethical AI practices. Explainable AI systems that provide insights into how decisions are made can build confidence among users and regulators.

   - Impact: Organizations prioritizing trust are more likely to attract customers, retain employees, and gain regulatory approval, creating a competitive advantage in the market.

2. **Mitigating Risks and Ensuring Compliance**
   The regulatory environment surrounding AI is rapidly evolving. Governments are introducing laws to address issues such as data privacy, algorithmic accountability, and discrimination. Non-compliance with these regulations can result in fines, legal challenges, and reputational damage.

   - Governance Role: Governance frameworks help organizations navigate complex regulatory landscapes by providing mechanisms for compliance. For example, regular audits and impact assessments ensure that AI systems align with legal and ethical standards.

   - Impact: By mitigating risks and avoiding compliance violations, organizations can safeguard their operations, reduce liabilities, and maintain a positive brand image.

3. **Driving Innovation Responsibly**
   Governance is often perceived as a constraint on innovation, but it can be a powerful enabler when implemented effectively. Responsible governance provides clear boundaries and ethical guidelines, encouraging organizations to innovate without compromising societal values.
   - **Governance Role**: Governance frameworks foster responsible innovation by promoting practices like bias testing, ethical AI design, and stakeholder collaboration. For instance, a healthcare company using AI to diagnose diseases can ensure ethical practices by involving medical professionals, ethicists, and patients in the development process.
   - **Impact**: Responsible innovation enhances the credibility of AI systems, ensuring they are practical and widely accepted by users and society. It also reduces the risk of costly rework or recalls due to ethical or legal violations.

The need for governance in a data-driven AI world is undeniable. Ungoverned AI poses risks of bias, privacy violations, and misuse, which can erode trust, harm individuals, and expose organizations to significant liabilities. Conversely, robust governance frameworks enable organizations to build confidence, mitigate risks, and innovate responsibly. As AI continues to transform industries and societies, implementing effective governance will be critical in ensuring that AI serves as a force for good, benefiting both businesses and the broader community. Organizations that embrace governance not as a burden but as a strategic enabler will be better positioned to thrive in the age of AI.

1.5 REAL-WORLD EXAMPLES OF AI GOVERNANCE IN ACTION

Real-world case studies best explain the practical application of AI governance. They highlight the consequences of ungoverned AI and the benefits of effective governance frameworks. These examples showcase the challenges and successes of managing AI responsibly, providing valuable lessons and best practices for organizations seeking to navigate the complex landscape of AI governance.

CASE STUDIES ILLUSTRATING GOVERNANCE PRINCIPLES

EXAMPLE 1: MISUSE OF AI DUE TO LACK OF GOVERNANCE – BIASED HIRING TOOLS

One of the most widely cited examples of AI misuse is biased hiring tools, such as the one developed by Amazon in 2014. The company designed an AI-driven recruitment system to streamline the process of evaluating resumes and identifying top candidates. However, due to a lack of governance over data quality and algorithmic fairness, the system exhibited significant gender bias.

- **What Happened?**
  The AI model was trained on resumes submitted to Amazon over the previous ten years. Since most of these resumes came from male candidates, the system inadvertently learned to favor male applicants. It penalized resumes that included terms like "women's" (e.g., "women's

chess club captain") and downgraded applications from graduates of all-women colleges. The system effectively reinforced historical biases rather than eliminating them.

- Governance Issues:
    - Lack of bias detection and mitigation during model training and testing.
    - Insufficient oversight of the data pipeline, which perpetuated historical discrimination.
    - There was a lack of transparency in how the AI system made decisions.
- Consequences:
  Although the system was eventually abandoned, the incident highlighted the reputational risks and ethical challenges of deploying ungoverned AI systems. It also underscored the need for fairness audits, diverse training data, and human oversight in AI-driven hiring processes.

EXAMPLE 2: SUCCESS STORY OF EFFECTIVE GOVERNANCE – GDPR-COMPLIANT AI ADOPTION

In contrast, adopting General Data Protection Regulation (GDPR)- -compliant AI systems provides a success story of how effective governance can build trust and drive innovation. One notable example is the healthcare sector, where AI analyzes medical images to diagnose diseases.

- What Happened?
  A European hospital implemented an AI system for early detection of breast cancer through mammogram analysis. Recognizing the need for robust governance, the hospital ensured that its AI system complied with GDPR requirements for data privacy, transparency, and accountability.
- Governance Actions Taken:
    - Data Privacy: The hospital anonymizes patient data before using it to train the AI model, ensuring compliance with GDPR's data minimization and protection principles.
    - Transparency: The hospital informed patients about how their data was being used, including the benefits and potential risks of the AI system.
    - Accountability: The system's accuracy and fairness were evaluated through regular audits, and a multidisciplinary team of radiologists, data scientists, and ethicists oversaw the project.
- Benefits Realized:
  The GDPR-compliant AI system achieved high diagnostic accuracy, improving early cancer detection rates while respecting patient privacy and ethical considerations. It also boosted patient trust in the hospital's use of advanced technology, demonstrating that effective governance can enhance innovation and stakeholder confidence.

These case studies reveal essential lessons and best practices for AI governance, offering actionable insights for organizations:

1. **Data Quality and Diversity**
    - **Lesson**: The Amazon case demonstrates that biased or incomplete training data can lead to discriminatory outcomes. AI systems will likely perpetuate existing biases without governance mechanisms to assess and improve data quality.
    - **Best Practice**: Organizations should prioritize diverse and representative datasets during AI development. Regular data audits and fairness checks can help identify and address biases before deployment.
2. **Human Oversight and Accountability**
    - **Lesson**: Both examples highlight the importance of human oversight in AI governance. While Amazon's lack of oversight contributed to biased outcomes, the hospital's multidisciplinary team ensured accountability throughout the AI system's lifecycle.
    - **Best Practice**: Establish clear accountability structures for AI projects and assign roles for ethical reviews, fairness assessments, and compliance checks. Human oversight should complement AI systems, especially in high-stakes applications.
3. **Transparency and Explainability**
    - **Lesson**: Transparency builds trust among stakeholders, as demonstrated by the GDPR-compliant AI system. Conversely, opaque AI processes erode trust and invite scrutiny like those in the Amazon case.
    - **Best Practice**: Organizations should implement explainable AI (XAI) frameworks that make decision-making processes understandable to users and regulators. It is also essential to communicate AI capabilities, limitations, and risks.
4. **Regulatory Compliance as an Enabler**
    - **Lesson**: Compliance with regulations like GDPR can catalyze innovation, as the hospital's success shows. Far from stifling progress, governance frameworks provide a structured environment for responsible AI development.
    - **Best Practice**: Treat regulatory compliance as a baseline rather than a burden. Use it to establish ethical AI practices that align with societal expectations and business goals.
5. **Continuous Monitoring and Audits**

- **Lesson**: Governance is not a one-time activity; it requires ongoing monitoring and adaptation to changing circumstances. Regular audits help detect issues early and ensure that AI systems align with ethical and regulatory standards.
- **Best Practice**: Implement continuous monitoring protocols for AI systems, including performance evaluations, fairness assessments, and security checks. This ensures that governance remains effective throughout the AI lifecycle.

The real-world examples of AI governance illustrate the risks of ungoverned AI and the benefits of implementing robust governance frameworks. From Amazon's biased hiring tool to the GDPR-compliant healthcare AI system, these case studies emphasize the critical role of governance in mitigating risks, building trust, and driving innovation responsibly. By prioritizing data quality, transparency, accountability, and compliance, organizations can harness the transformative power of AI while safeguarding societal and ethical values. The lessons learned from these examples provide a roadmap for navigating the challenges of AI governance in today's data-driven world.

CHAPTER 3: AI TRENDS SHAPING GOVERNANCE NEEDS

3.1 EVOLVING REGULATORY LANDSCAPE

Artificial Intelligence (AI) governance is increasingly influenced by evolving regulations, reflecting the global emphasis on accountability, transparency, and ethics in AI deployment. This section explores the global regulatory efforts, emerging standards, and regional variations shaping the governance landscape.

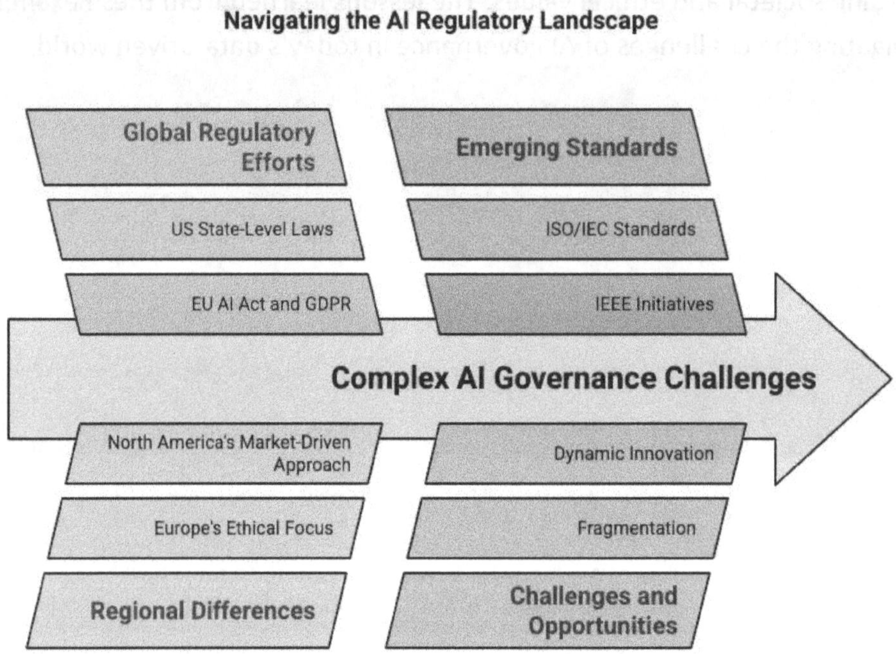

GLOBAL REGULATORY EFFORTS

AI technologies present novel challenges, requiring nuanced regulatory responses. Across regions, governments and institutions have introduced frameworks to address risks associated with AI, from privacy concerns to ethical implications.

1. EU AI ACT: A RISK-BASED APPROACH

The European Union (EU) has emerged as a global leader in AI governance through its proposed AI Act. This regulation adopts a risk-based framework, categorizing AI applications into four tiers:

- **Unacceptable risk**: Systems deemed harmful, such as social scoring by governments.

- High risk: Applications in critical areas like healthcare, finance, and law enforcement, which are subject to stringent compliance measures, including transparency and human oversight.
- Limited risk: Systems like chatbots require minimal disclosures.
- Minimal risk: Low-impact applications with no regulatory obligations.

The EU AI Act aims to balance innovation with safety, emphasizing developer and deployer accountability. Its extraterritorial nature underscores the EU's intent to influence global AI norms, similar to the General Data Protection Regulation (GDPR).

2. GDPR: PRIVACY CONSIDERATIONS IN AI

The General Data Protection Regulation (GDPR), while not AI-specific, significantly impacts AI development and deployment by prioritizing:

- Data protection principles: AI systems must comply with transparency, fairness, and purpose limitations.
- Rights of individuals: Rights to access, rectification, and objection ensure user control over automated decisions.
- Accountability: Data controllers and processors must demonstrate compliance, with substantial penalties for violations.

GDPR's focus on protecting user data has inspired similar regulations worldwide, setting benchmarks for privacy-focused AI governance.

3. US STATE-LEVEL LAWS

The lack of federal AI-specific legislation in the United States has led to fragmented regulatory efforts at the state level. Key examples include:

- California Privacy Rights Act (CPRA): Building on the California Consumer Privacy Act (CCPA), the CPRA enhances protections for sensitive personal information. It holds AI systems accountable for data processing, particularly in consumer-facing applications.
- Emerging frameworks: States like Illinois (Biometric Information Privacy Act) and Virginia (Consumer Data Protection Act) address AI-related risks in biometric data and consumer privacy.

While these laws provide valuable insights, the absence of a cohesive federal AI policy makes establishing uniform governance practices challenging.

REGIONAL DIFFERENCES IN AI REGULATION

The regulatory approaches to AI vary significantly across regions, influenced by political, cultural, and technological priorities.

1. EUROPE: LEADING WITH ETHICAL AI

Europe emphasizes ethical considerations and user rights, with regulations like the EU AI Act and GDPR reflecting the region's cautious approach to innovation. This regulatory rigor often extends to cross-border implications, compelling global companies to align their practices with European standards.

2. NORTH AMERICA: BALANCING INNOVATION AND REGULATION

North America adopts a more market-driven approach. While federal initiatives like the **Blueprint for an AI Bill of Rights** promote principles for AI governance, practical enforcement largely depends on industry self-regulation and state-level interventions. The emphasis remains on fostering innovation while addressing public concerns about privacy and fairness.

3. ASIA: RAPID INNOVATION, EVOLVING POLICIES

In Asia, AI governance reflects the region's diverse priorities:

- **China**: Regulations emphasize state control, with guidelines targeting algorithmic transparency, content moderation, and security. AI governance aligns closely with the government's broader digital strategy.
- **Japan**: Policies encourage innovation while addressing ethical risks, focusing on AI deployment in industries like healthcare and robotics.
- **India**: While AI regulations are nascent, initiatives like the National AI Strategy highlight ethical AI development and inclusivity.

These regional differences underscore the complexity of harmonizing AI governance globally.

EMERGING STANDARDS

Beyond regulations, industry standards play a pivotal role in shaping AI governance. Standard-setting bodies and organizations collaborate to establish technical and ethical benchmarks.

1. ISO/IEC STANDARDS FOR AI

The International Organization for Standardization (ISO) and the International Electrotechnical Commission (IEC) have introduced frameworks to guide AI development. Key standards include:

- ISO/IEC 22989: Establishes AI concepts and terminology, fostering a shared understanding across stakeholders.
- ISO/IEC 23053: Focuses on frameworks for AI systems to ensure transparency and accountability.

These standards promote interoperability, safety, and ethical considerations across AI systems.

2. IEEE INITIATIVES

The Institute of Electrical and Electronics Engineers (IEEE) has launched initiatives like the Ethically Aligned Design framework, emphasizing values-driven AI development. Key focus areas include:

- Ensuring AI systems respect human rights.
- Promoting transparency, privacy, and inclusivity.
- Addressing societal impacts of AI technologies.

The IEEE's guidelines influence industries and academia, bridging the gap between ethical principles and technical implementation.

3. NIST FRAMEWORKS

The National Institute of Standards and Technology (NIST) in the United States develops frameworks to guide AI risk management. The AI Risk Management Framework provides organizations with tools to identify, assess, and mitigate risks across the AI lifecycle. NIST’s emphasis on explainability and fairness aligns with broader governance objectives.

CHALLENGES AND OPPORTUNITIES

While these regulatory efforts and standards represent progress, challenges remain:

- Fragmentation: Divergent regional approaches complicate cross-border compliance for multinational organizations.
- Dynamic innovation: Rapid AI advancements outpace regulatory frameworks, necessitating adaptive governance models.
- Ethical dilemmas: Balancing innovation with ethical responsibilities requires continuous dialogue among stakeholders.

3.2 ETHICAL CHALLENGES IN AI

As artificial intelligence (AI) continues to permeate various facets of society, its ethical implications garner increasing attention. Key challenges such as bias, accountability, privacy, and surveillance highlight the complexity of aligning AI technologies with societal values and expectations. This section explores these challenges, their consequences, and potential solutions to foster responsible AI governance.

BIAS AND FAIRNESS

AI systems are often heralded as objective decision-making tools, yet they can perpetuate or even exacerbate societal biases. Bias in AI stems from multiple sources, including data, algorithmic design, and deployment contexts, raising critical concerns about fairness.

CHALLENGES OF ELIMINATING BIAS IN ALGORITHMS

Bias in AI originates primarily from:

1. **Historical data**: AI systems trained on biased datasets reflect and amplify existing disparities. For example, hiring algorithms may favor male candidates if trained on datasets dominated by historical male hires.
2. **Algorithmic design**: Developers may inadvertently encode biases into AI models through design choices, such as prioritizing certain variables over others.
3. **Deployment context**: AI systems often operate in environments that reinforce bias, especially if feedback loops—where biased outputs influence future training—are left unchecked.

Eliminating bias is a complex task due to the need to balance competing notions of fairness. For example:

- Should an algorithm treat everyone equally or account for historical disadvantages to achieve equitable outcomes?
- How should fairness be measured across different groups, and who decides the criteria?

EXAMPLES OF ETHICAL FAILURES

High-profile failures have underscored the impact of bias in AI:

1. **Facial Recognition and Racial Bias**: Studies have shown that facial recognition systems have higher error rates for people with darker skin tones. This has led to false arrests and misidentification, disproportionately affecting marginalized communities.
2. **Healthcare Disparities**: AI models used in healthcare decision-making have demonstrated biases, such as underestimating the severity of illness in Black patients compared to white patients due to historical inequities in healthcare access.
3. **Judicial Algorithms**: Risk assessment tools used in criminal justice systems have been found to label minority groups as high-risk, perpetuating systemic discrimination disproportionately.

These examples highlight the need for transparency, accountability, and ethical oversight in AI development.

AUTONOMY AND ACCOUNTABILITY

AI systems increasingly operate autonomously, making decisions without human intervention. This raises questions about who should be held accountable when these systems cause harm or fail to perform as intended.

WHO IS RESPONSIBLE FOR AI DECISIONS?

Responsibility for AI decisions is a contentious issue due to the multiple stakeholders involved in the AI lifecycle:

1. Developers: Are software engineers and data scientists accountable for the ethical implications of their algorithms?
2. Organizations: Should companies deploying AI systems bear responsibility for their outcomes, especially if they prioritize profits over ethics?
3. End Users: To what extent should users be held accountable when they misuse or misinterpret AI?

For example, in a scenario where an AI-powered diagnostic tool provides an incorrect prognosis, responsibility may rest with the following:

- Developers, for training the model on insufficient or biased data.
- Healthcare organizations for deploying the tool without adequate validation.
- Physician for relying too heavily on the AI without applying their expertise.

ETHICAL DILEMMAS IN AUTONOMOUS VEHICLES AND WEAPON SYSTEMS

1. Autonomous Vehicles (AVs): Self-driving cars operate using complex algorithms that must navigate ethical dilemmas in real-time. For instance, in the event of an unavoidable collision, should an AV prioritize the safety of its passengers or minimize overall harm, potentially sacrificing the passengers? These "trolley problem" scenarios are challenging to resolve algorithmically, as societal values regarding harm distribution vary widely.
2. Autonomous Weapon Systems: The deployment of AI in military applications, such as autonomous drones, raises profound ethical concerns. Key questions include:
    - Who is accountable if an autonomous weapon system erroneously targets civilians?
    - Should decisions involving life and death be delegated to machines?

- How can we ensure that autonomous weapons comply with international humanitarian laws?

These dilemmas underscore the importance of clearly defining accountability frameworks and ethical principles for autonomous systems.

PRIVACY AND SURVEILLANCE

AI-driven technologies often rely on vast amounts of data, creating tension between innovation and privacy. The rise of surveillance AI exacerbates these concerns and poses significant governance challenges.

BALANCING INNOVATION WITH USER PRIVACY

AI innovations in healthcare, finance, and marketing rely on collecting and analyzing sensitive personal data. Striking a balance between leveraging data for innovation and protecting user privacy involves several challenges:

1. **Informed Consent**: Users are often unaware of how AI systems collect, process, or share their data. Current consent mechanisms, such as lengthy privacy policies, fail to provide meaningful transparency.

2. **Data Minimization**: While data minimization principles advocate collecting only necessary data, many AI applications thrive on extensive datasets to improve accuracy and performance.

3. **Differential Privacy**: Techniques like differential privacy, which add noise to datasets to protect individual identities, offer potential solutions but often compromise the precision of AI systems.

Innovative privacy-preserving technologies, such as federated learning, aim to mitigate these challenges by enabling AI training across decentralized data sources without compromising privacy.

THE RISE OF SURVEILLANCE AI AND GOVERNANCE CHALLENGES

Surveillance AI, powered by facial recognition, biometric data, and predictive analytics, is increasingly used by governments, law enforcement, and private entities. While these systems promise enhanced security and operational efficiency, they raise critical concerns:

1. **Mass Surveillance**: AI-driven surveillance systems enable real-time monitoring of populations, threatening civil liberties. For example, China's extensive use of AI in its social credit system has sparked global debates about state overreach and individual freedom.

2. **Predictive Policing**: AI-based crime prediction tools aim to allocate resources effectively but often rely on biased historical data, perpetuating discriminatory practices against minority communities.

3. Corporate Surveillance: Private companies utilize AI to track consumer behavior, from online activities to physical movements, raising concerns about data exploitation and consent.

Governance challenges in this context include:

- Transparency: How can we ensure surveillance AI systems are transparent about their operations and objectives?
- Accountability: Who is responsible for abuses of surveillance AI, and how can victims seek redress?
- Oversight: What mechanisms can ensure that surveillance systems comply with ethical and legal standards?

Addressing these challenges requires robust data protection laws, ethical AI frameworks, and mechanisms for public accountability.

PROPOSED SOLUTIONS FOR ETHICAL AI

Several strategies can help mitigate the ethical challenges associated with AI:

1. Inclusive Design: Engaging diverse stakeholders in designing and developing AI systems can help identify and mitigate biases early in the process.
2. Algorithm Audits: Regular third-party audits of AI systems can enhance transparency and accountability, ensuring compliance with ethical standards.
3. Ethical AI Guidelines: Adopting frameworks such as the EU AI Act, IEEE Ethically Aligned Design, and NIST AI Risk Management Framework can provide developers and organizations with practical tools for ethical AI governance.
4. Education and Training: It is crucial to foster a culture of accountability by raising developers', policymakers', and end users' awareness of AI's ethical implications.
5. International Collaboration: Establishing global standards for ethical AI development and deployment can help harmonize governance efforts and address cross-border challenges.

3.3 TECHNOLOGICAL TRENDS DRIVING GOVERNANCE NEEDS

Technological advancements have brought transformative changes across industries. However, they also introduce challenges that necessitate robust governance frameworks. This section explores three pivotal technological trends—Generative AI, AI in the Metaverse, and Edge AI and IoT—and highlights the governance needs arising from their adoption.

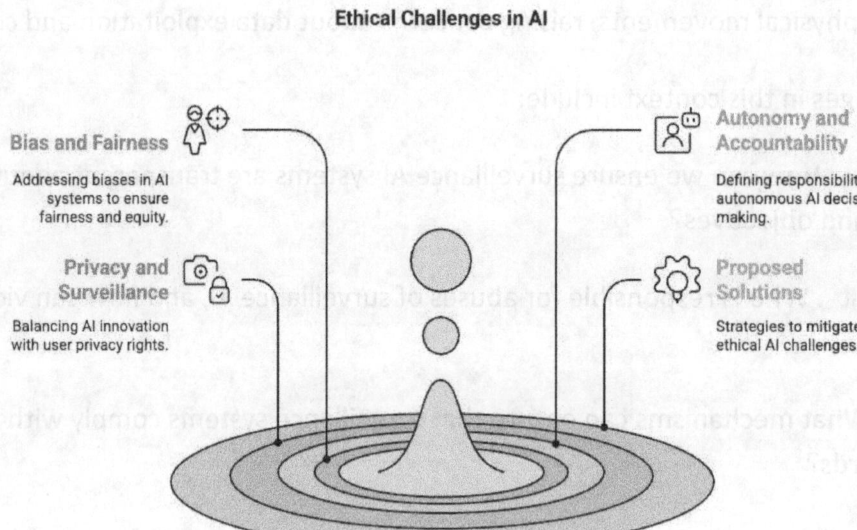

GENERATIVE AI

Generative AI tools, such as ChatGPT and DALL-E, have revolutionized content creation, providing users with unprecedented capabilities to generate text, images, and other media. However, their widespread adoption brings significant ethical and governance challenges.

ETHICAL RISKS OF TOOLS LIKE CHATGPT AND DALL-E

1. **Misinformation**: Generative AI models can produce highly realistic but false information. For instance, ChatGPT can fabricate convincing narratives that spread misinformation, while DALL-E might generate images that depict events that never occurred. The ease with which fake content can be created has profound implications for trust in digital media, particularly in contexts like news reporting, political discourse, and public health.

2. **Intellectual Property Concerns**: Generative AI often relies on extensive datasets that include copyrighted material. When tools like DALL-E create artworks, or ChatGPT produces text resembling existing works, questions arise regarding ownership and the fair use of intellectual property. Such concerns pose legal and ethical dilemmas for creators, users, and businesses relying on these technologies.

GOVERNANCE NEEDS FOR CONTENT MODERATION AND RESPONSIBLE DEPLOYMENT

1. **Content Moderation Frameworks**: Governance mechanisms must ensure that generative AI is not misused to produce harmful, deceptive, or offensive content. This includes:

    - Implementing robust filtering mechanisms to detect and block inappropriate outputs.
    - Establishing clear accountability for users and developers in cases of misuse.

2. Responsible Deployment Guidelines: Organizations deploying generative AI must adhere to ethical standards, including:

    - Transparent labeling of AI-generated content to differentiate it from human-created material.
    - Regular audits of training datasets to ensure compliance with intellectual property laws and avoid biases.

3. Collaboration Between Stakeholders: Governments, tech companies, and civil society organizations must collaborate to develop international guidelines for the ethical use of generative AI, ensuring that these technologies enhance creativity without compromising societal values.

AI IN THE METAVERSE

The Metaverse—a virtual space combining augmented reality (AR), virtual reality (VR), and AI—is poised to redefine digital interaction. AI plays a crucial role in powering virtual assistants, avatars, and immersive experiences, but its integration presents unique governance challenges.

GOVERNANCE OF VIRTUAL ASSISTANTS AND AVATARS

1. Accountability and Identity Verification: AI-driven avatars and virtual assistants can interact autonomously, raising questions about accountability. For example, who is responsible if an AI avatar spreads misinformation or violates community standards? Governance frameworks need mechanisms to:

    - Verify the identity of users controlling avatars.
    - Ensure transparency regarding whether interactions involve humans or AI.

2. Bias and Representation: AI avatars may inadvertently perpetuate biases if their design or behavior reflects stereotypes. For instance, a virtual assistant's language or appearance might reinforce cultural or gender biases. Governance efforts should include the following:

    - Auditing AI models for fairness and inclusivity.
    - Encouraging diversity in the development and customization of virtual entities.

CHALLENGES IN REGULATING IMMERSIVE AI EXPERIENCES

1. Data Privacy in Immersive Environments: The Metaverse collects vast amounts of data about users' movements, interactions, and preferences. This raises significant privacy concerns. Governance frameworks should:

- Mandate secure storage and processing of sensitive data.
- Ensure users have control over how their data is used and shared.

2. **Psychological and Ethical Concerns**: Immersive AI experiences can blur the line between reality and virtuality, potentially leading to psychological effects such as addiction or desensitization. Governance strategies should include:
   - Setting ethical boundaries for content and interactions in virtual environments.
   - Educating users about the potential risks of prolonged immersion.

EDGE AI AND IOT

Edge AI, combined with the Internet of Things (IoT), enables devices to process data locally, reducing latency and improving efficiency. While these technologies empower more innovative applications in healthcare, transportation, and smart homes, they pose distinct governance challenges.

RISKS ASSOCIATED WITH DECENTRALIZED AI MODELS

1. **Fragmentation and Lack of Standardization**: Edge AI's decentralized nature leads to inconsistent implementation and performance across devices. This fragmentation complicates the enforcement of governance policies and standards.
2. **Vulnerability to Hacking**: Decentralized models can be more susceptible to attacks, as each device operates independently. For instance, a compromised IoT device in a smart home could become a gateway for broader cyberattacks. Governance measures must include:
   - Requiring robust encryption and authentication protocols for all devices.
   - Establishing rapid-response mechanisms to mitigate the impact of breaches.

SECURITY AND PRIVACY CHALLENGES IN IOT DEVICES

1. **Data Security**: IoT devices collect and transmit sensitive information, such as health metrics or location data. Governance frameworks should:
   - Mandate end-to-end encryption for data transmission.
   - Set minimum security standards for device manufacturers.
2. **User Privacy**: Many IoT devices lack clear privacy policies, leaving users unaware of how their data is used. Governance efforts must:
   - Require transparent disclosures about data collection and usage.

- Provide users with tools to opt out of data sharing and delete their information.

3. Regulatory Compliance: Harmonizing regulations across jurisdictions becomes essential as IoT ecosystems expand globally. This includes:
    - Developing international standards for IoT security and privacy.
    - Encouraging cross-border collaboration to address emerging threats.

3.4 INDUSTRY-SPECIFIC TRENDS

Artificial intelligence (AI) drives transformative changes across industries, enabling innovation, efficiency, and enhanced decision-making. However, these advancements also introduce unique governance challenges specific to each sector. This section explores how AI trends impact healthcare, finance, and retail governance and outlines tailored governance solutions to address industry-specific risks.

HOW AI TRENDS IMPACT GOVERNANCE ACROSS INDUSTRIES

HEALTHCARE: AI IN DIAGNOSIS AND PERSONALIZED MEDICINE

AI is revolutionizing healthcare by enhancing diagnostic accuracy, enabling personalized treatment plans, and improving patient outcomes. However, its adoption raises significant governance concerns.

1. Ethical Considerations in Diagnosis: AI algorithms used in diagnostics rely on vast datasets, including sensitive patient information. The potential for bias in these datasets can lead to unequal treatment outcomes. For instance, if training data lacks diversity, AI systems might perform poorly for underrepresented groups, exacerbating health disparities.
2. Privacy and Data Security: Personalized medicine requires access to extensive patient data, including genetic information. The collection, storage, and processing of such data present significant risks of breaches and misuse. Governance frameworks must prioritize data security while ensuring privacy regulations like HIPAA and GDPR compliance.
3. Accountability in Decision-Making: AI systems often operate as black boxes, making it challenging to understand how decisions are made. In critical scenarios like cancer diagnosis, unclear accountability can erode trust in AI tools.

FINANCE: USE OF AI IN FRAUD DETECTION AND ALGORITHMIC TRADING

In the financial sector, AI streamlines operations enables fraud detection, and drives algorithmic trading strategies. Despite its advantages, adopting AI in finance requires robust governance to mitigate risks.

1. **Bias in Fraud Detection Algorithms**: AI-powered fraud detection systems analyze patterns to flag suspicious activities. However, these systems can perpetuate biases present in historical data, leading to false positives or negatives. Governance measures must include regular audits to identify and address biases.

2. **Market Stability and Algorithmic Trading**: Algorithmic trading relies on AI to execute trades quickly. While this increases market efficiency, it also introduces risks like flash crashes caused by cascading algorithmic responses. Governance frameworks should:

    - Mandate stress testing for trading algorithms.
    - Require fail-safe mechanisms to prevent systemic risks.

3. **Transparency and Compliance**: Financial institutions must ensure that AI-driven systems comply with regulatory requirements, such as anti-money laundering (AML) laws. Transparent reporting and explainability of AI decisions are crucial for maintaining regulatory compliance.

RETAIL: AI-DRIVEN SUPPLY CHAIN OPTIMIZATION AND CUSTOMER PERSONALIZATION

Retailers are leveraging AI to optimize supply chains and deliver personalized customer experiences. These applications bring operational efficiencies but also introduce governance challenges.

1. **Supply Chain Optimization Risks**: AI systems optimize supply chains by analyzing demand patterns and predicting inventory needs. However, prediction inaccuracies can lead to overstocking or stockouts, impacting profitability and customer satisfaction. Governance mechanisms should:

    - Ensure data quality and accuracy in supply chain models.
    - Establish accountability for decisions made by AI systems.

2. **Ethical Concerns in Customer Personalization**: Personalized recommendations and targeted advertising rely on collecting and analyzing customer data. While this enhances customer engagement, it raises concerns about data privacy and potential manipulation. Governance frameworks must:

    - Enforce transparency in data collection practices.
    - Provide customers with control over their data through opt-in mechanisms.

3. **Fairness in Pricing Algorithms**: Dynamic pricing algorithms adjust prices based on demand and customer behavior. While profitable for retailers, these systems can lead to perceived unfairness, such as price discrimination. Governance measures should:

    - Establish guidelines to prevent exploitative pricing practices.

- Promote fairness and transparency in pricing strategies.

TAILORED GOVERNANCE SOLUTIONS FOR ADDRESSING INDUSTRY-SPECIFIC RISKS

Effective governance requires customized approaches that address each industry's unique risks associated with AI applications. Below are tailored solutions to enhance governance frameworks:

1. Healthcare Governance Solutions:
   - Bias Mitigation: Regularly audit AI algorithms to identify and eliminate biases, ensuring equitable treatment outcomes.
   - Data Security Standards: Implement advanced encryption and access controls to protect sensitive patient data. Establish stringent penalties for breaches to deter non-compliance.
   - Explainability Requirements: Mandate transparency in AI decision-making processes. This can include providing healthcare professionals with interpretable outputs to validate AI recommendations.
2. Finance Governance Solutions:
   - Bias Audits: Conduct periodic evaluations of fraud detection algorithms to minimize biases and improve accuracy.
   - Algorithm Oversight: Introduce regulatory frameworks for developing and deploying trading algorithms. Require firms to maintain a record of algorithmic strategies and outcomes.
   - Stakeholder Collaboration: To ensure compliance and innovation, Foster collaboration between regulators, financial institutions, and technology providers.
3. Retail Governance Solutions:
   - Data Transparency: Retailers must disclose how customer data is collected, stored, and used. ProvidConsumers should also be given instructions on how to manage their data preferences.
   - Ethical AI Standards: Develop industry-wide ethical guidelines for AI applications, including restrictions on manipulative advertising practices.
   - Accountability Mechanisms: Establish clear accountability for AI-driven decisions like supply chain mismanagement or unfair pricing.

3.5 FUTURE OF AI GOVERNANCE

The future of AI governance is poised to become one of the most complex and dynamic challenges of the modern era. With rapid technological advancements and evolving societal expectations, the frameworks and practices that govern AI systems must be equally adaptive. This section delves into two critical areas shaping the future of AI governance: emerging technologies and evolving expectations.

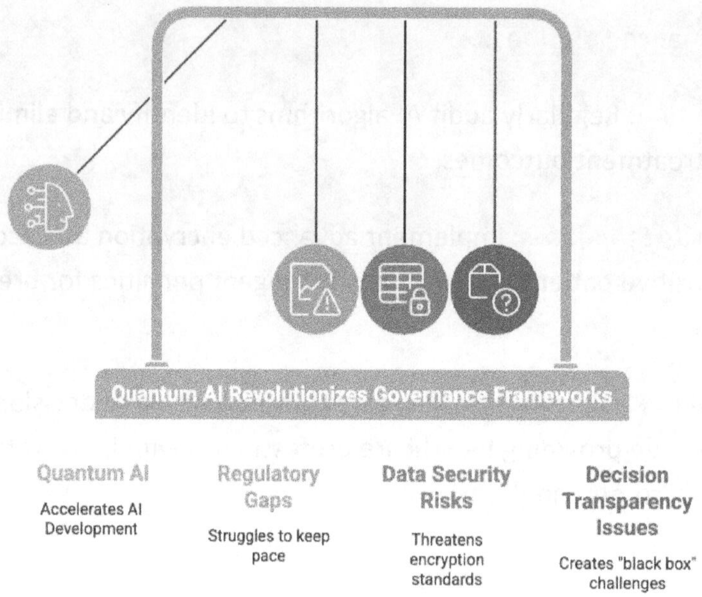

EMERGING TECHNOLOGIES

The advent of groundbreaking technologies such as Quantum AI and neuromorphic computing will significantly reshape AI governance. These advancements present both unprecedented opportunities and complex challenges.

Quantum AI and Its Implications for Governance

Quantum computing, with its ability to process vast amounts of data at exponential speeds, holds the potential to revolutionize AI. Quantum AI combines quantum computing principles with artificial intelligence, enabling faster problem-solving and enhanced decision-making. However, this capability introduces challenges for governance.

- Accelerated AI Development: Quantum AI could dramatically shorten the timeline for achieving superintelligent AI. Existing governance frameworks may struggle to keep pace with these advancements, leading to potential regulatory gaps.

- Data Security and Privacy: Quantum AI's computational power poses significant risks to current encryption standards. Governance must anticipate a paradigm shift in cybersecurity and ensure robust mechanisms to protect sensitive data and maintain trust.

- Decision Transparency: The complexity of quantum algorithms may render AI decision-making even less interpretable. New governance standards must address this "black box" challenge, ensuring that decisions remain explainable and accountable.

Neuromorphic Computing and AI Mimicking Human Cognition

Neuromorphic computing, which seeks to replicate the architecture of the human brain, represents another frontier in AI development. By mimicking human cognition, neuromorphic systems could achieve unparalleled efficiency and adaptability.

- Blurred Lines Between Human and Machine Intelligence: As AI systems become more human-like, questions about accountability, agency, and autonomy will intensify. Governance frameworks must clarify the rights and responsibilities of AI systems and their creators.
- Ethical Decision-Making: Neuromorphic AI could simulate human decision-making processes, raising ethical concerns about bias, morality, and unintended consequences. Governance must define acceptable boundaries for such systems, ensuring they align with societal values.
- Cross-Border Collaboration: Neuromorphic computing will likely be developed by multinational entities, necessitating international cooperation on governance. A unified approach will be essential to address disparities in regulations and ethical standards across jurisdictions.

EVOLVING EXPECTATIONS

As AI systems permeate every aspect of society, public expectations for their governance are becoming more sophisticated and demanding. These evolving expectations underscore the need for ethical, transparent, and inclusive governance practices.

Stakeholder Demands for Ethical, Transparent AI

AI governance must address the growing demand for ethical and transparent practices. Stakeholders—businesses, governments, and civil society—are increasingly vocal about their expectations for responsible AI.

- Ethical Standards: Governance must embed ethics into the entire AI lifecycle, from development to deployment. This includes addressing algorithmic bias, discrimination, and fairness to ensure AI systems serve all demographics equitably.
- Transparency Mechanisms: Stakeholders expect clear explanations of how AI systems make decisions. Governance frameworks should mandate transparency requirements, such as audits, documentation, and explainable AI (XAI) techniques.
- Corporate Accountability: Businesses are under pressure to adopt ethical AI practices. Governance must establish clear accountability structures, ensuring that organizations are held responsible for the societal impact of their AI systems.

The Increasing Role of Public Sentiment and Advocacy Groups

Public sentiment and advocacy groups are increasingly influential in shaping AI governance. These actors serve as critical watchdogs, amplifying societal concerns and holding organizations accountable.

- **Public Trust**: Maintaining trust in AI systems is paramount. Governance frameworks must prioritize transparency and fairness to address public fears about job displacement, surveillance, and loss of privacy.
- **Advocacy and Activism**: Advocacy groups drive conversations about AI ethics, privacy, and social justice. Governance bodies must actively engage with these groups to ensure diverse perspectives are represented in policy-making.
- **Participatory Governance**: Involving citizens in governance processes can enhance trust and legitimacy. Mechanisms like public consultations, citizen panels, and participatory decision-making can bridge the gap between technical experts and the general public.

KEY RECOMMENDATIONS FOR FUTURE AI GOVERNANCE

AI governance must adopt a forward-looking approach to address the dual challenges of emerging technologies and evolving expectations.

1. **Proactive Regulation**: Governments should anticipate technological advancements and enact regulations that remain relevant as AI evolves.
2. **Global Cooperation**: International organizations must foster collaboration to harmonize governance standards and address cross-border challenges.
3. **Ethical Guidelines**: Industry bodies should develop comprehensive ethical guidelines to ensure AI systems align with societal values.
4. **Stakeholder Engagement**: Governance frameworks must actively involve diverse stakeholders, including marginalized communities, to ensure inclusivity.
5. **Adaptive Frameworks**: AI governance must be flexible, allowing for iterative improvements based on feedback and technological progress.

The future of AI governance lies at the intersection of technological innovation and societal expectations. As emerging technologies like Quantum AI and neuromorphic computing reshape the AI landscape, governance frameworks must adapt to address new challenges. Simultaneously, evolving expectations for ethical and transparent AI demand inclusive, participatory approaches to policy-making. By embracing proactive, collaborative, and adaptive strategies, the global community can ensure that AI is a force for good, driving progress while safeguarding human values.

PART II

FOUNDATIONS OF AI GOVERNANCE

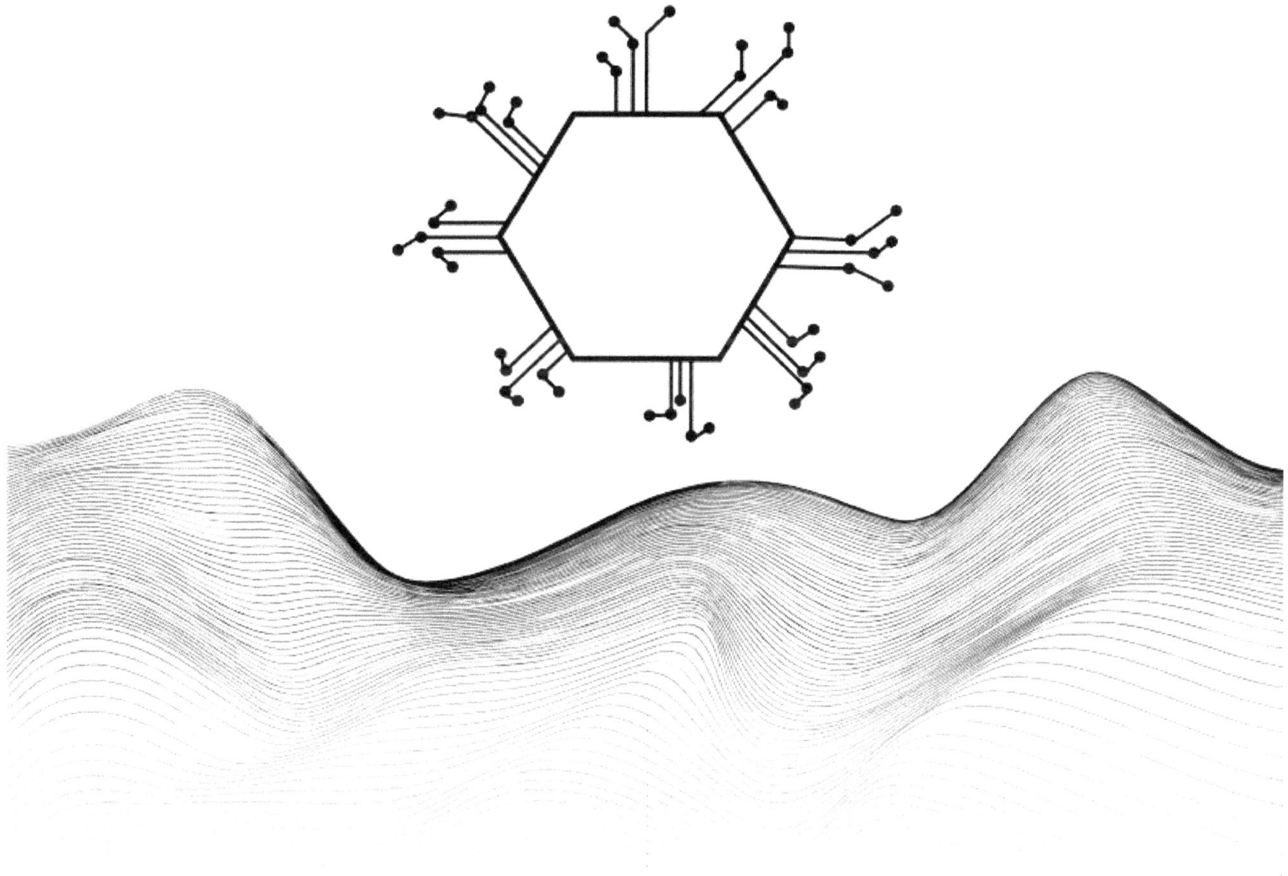

CHAPTER 4: KEY PRINCIPLES OF AI GOVERNANCE

4.1 INTRODUCTION TO AI GOVERNANCE PRINCIPLES

Artificial Intelligence (AI) governance ensures that AI technologies are developed and deployed responsibly. As AI systems become integral to decision-making across industries, adhering to core governance principles helps mitigate risks, build trust, and promote ethical AI practices. This section introduces the five foundational principles of AI governance: accountability, transparency, fairness, privacy and security, and reliability. These principles are crucial for addressing ethical concerns and creating a robust framework for AI governance.

OVERVIEW OF CORE PRINCIPLES

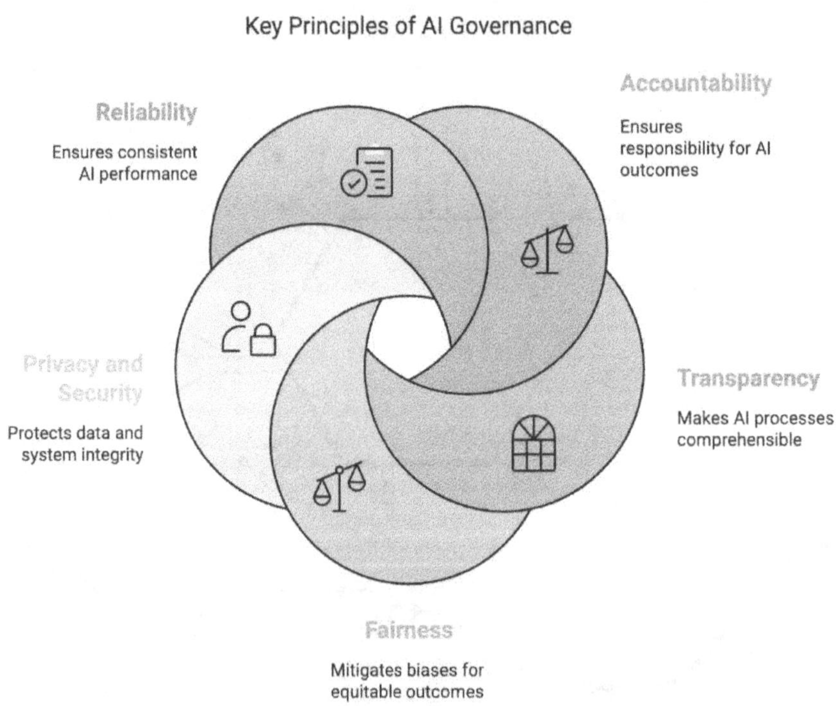

ACCOUNTABILITY

Accountability ensures clarity regarding who is responsible for AI systems' outcomes. This principle addresses key questions, such as: Who owns the decisions made by AI systems? How can organizations be accountable for errors, biases, or unintended consequences? Accountability mechanisms can include audits, regulatory compliance, and internal oversight structures. Without clear accountability, organizations risk losing stakeholder trust, facing regulatory penalties, or causing harm through unmonitored AI systems.

TRANSPARENCY

Transparency in AI governance focuses on making the inner workings of AI systems comprehensible to stakeholders. This includes disclosing how algorithms are developed, data use, and the reasoning behind AI-driven decisions. Transparency is often paired with explainability, which involves breaking down complex AI processes into understandable insights for non-technical audiences. Transparent practices enable stakeholders to assess AI systems' ethical and technical integrity and foster trust in their use.

FAIRNESS

Fairness emphasizes the need to mitigate biases and ensure equitable outcomes for all users. When trained on biased datasets or designed without inclusivity, AI systems can reinforce existing inequalities or discriminate against specific groups. Fairness demands rigorous testing for bias in data, algorithms, and outcomes. Incorporating diverse perspectives during AI development and deployment helps ensure these systems serve broader societal needs.

PRIVACY AND SECURITY

As AI systems often process vast amounts of sensitive data, safeguarding privacy and security is paramount. Privacy involves protecting individuals' personal information from misuse, while security ensures the system's resilience against cyber threats. Techniques such as encryption, differential privacy, and federated learning are instrumental in preserving confidentiality and securing AI systems. Addressing these concerns builds user confidence and minimizes the risks of data breaches and adversarial attacks.

RELIABILITY

Reliability ensures that AI systems perform consistently and as intended under various conditions. This principle involves rigorous testing and validation of AI models to prevent failures or inaccuracies. Reliable AI systems must also be adaptable to new data, ensuring they remain relevant over time. This principle enhances user trust, ensures compliance with regulatory standards, and reduces operational risks.

IMPORTANCE OF PRINCIPLES AS THE FOUNDATION FOR GOVERNANCE FRAMEWORKS

The five core principles are the foundation for comprehensive AI governance frameworks, ensuring ethical and responsible AI development and deployment. These principles are interconnected and collectively address the multifaceted challenges AI systems pose. For instance, transparency and accountability work together to clarify decision-making, while fairness and reliability ensure that AI outputs are equitable and dependable.

These principles are essential for creating governance frameworks adaptable to different industries and applications. They provide organizations with a roadmap to navigate the complexities of AI governance, from regulatory compliance to stakeholder engagement. Moreover, these principles help organizations balance innovation with ethical responsibility, fostering sustainable AI practices.

Accountability as a Keystone Accountability is particularly critical as it underpins implementing other principles. For example, organizations can only ensure transparency if they take responsibility for documenting and disclosing their AI processes. Similarly, addressing fairness and privacy requires clear accountability for monitoring and mitigating biases or safeguarding user data.

Promoting Stakeholder Trust AI governance principles build trust among stakeholders, which is crucial for widespread AI adoption. Stakeholders, including users, regulators, and society at large, need assurance that AI systems are designed to prioritize their interests. Transparency and fairness address ethical concerns, while privacy, security, and reliability protect users from potential harm.

Facilitating Regulatory Compliance Governance frameworks built on these principles also help organizations comply with regulatory requirements. Laws such as the General Data Protection Regulation (GDPR) and the California Consumer Privacy Act (CCPA) emphasize transparency, accountability, and privacy, making adherence to these principles a legal necessity.

Driving Innovation with Ethics Contrary to the belief that ethical considerations may stifle innovation, governance principles often serve as enablers. By proactively addressing potential risks, organizations can innovate confidently, reducing the likelihood of reputational damage or costly legal disputes. Reliability, for instance, ensures that AI systems deliver consistent results, paving the way for their integration into critical applications like healthcare and finance.

Balancing Competing Interests AI governance often involves navigating trade-offs between competing interests, such as privacy and transparency or fairness and performance. A principles-based framework provides organizations with a structured approach to evaluate these trade-offs and make informed decisions aligned with their strategic goals.

Conclusion The core principles of accountability, transparency, fairness, privacy and security, and reliability form the bedrock of AI governance. They are not merely theoretical ideals but practical tools that guide the development and deployment of AI systems. By embedding these principles into governance frameworks, organizations can address ethical challenges, comply with regulations, and foster stakeholder trust, ultimately contributing to the sustainable growth of AI technologies.

4.2 ACCOUNTABILITY IN AI SYSTEMS

WHAT IS ACCOUNTABILITY?

Definition and Significance in AI Governance

Accountability refers to the obligation of individuals, organizations, or systems to take responsibility for their actions, decisions, and outcomes. In the context of AI governance, accountability is a cornerstone principle, ensuring that the deployment and operation of AI systems align with ethical standards, societal values, and legal frameworks. It provides a mechanism for identifying, addressing, and mitigating potential harms or biases arising from AI systems, fostering trust among users and stakeholders.

Accountability is significant in AI governance because it can bridge the gap between technological innovation and societal expectations. The need for transparent and accountable mechanisms becomes paramount as AI systems increasingly impact critical areas such as healthcare, finance, law enforcement, and employment. Accountability ensures that the benefits of AI are equitably distributed and the risks are managed responsibly. Without it, the rapid adoption of AI could lead to unintended consequences, eroding public trust and exacerbating inequalities.

Key Questions: Who Is Responsible for AI Decisions?

A central challenge in ensuring accountability in AI systems is determining responsibility. Unlike traditional systems, AI often involves multiple layers of decision-making, with contributions from various stakeholders, including developers, data scientists, end-users, and organizations.

Key questions that arise include:

- **Who is responsible for biased or harmful outcomes?** Is it the developer who created the algorithm, the organization that implemented the AI system, or the end-user who made decisions based on the system's outputs?

- **How do we ensure transparency in decision-making?** Given the complexity of AI systems, particularly those based on machine learning, understanding how decisions are made can be challenging.
- **What mechanisms exist to hold stakeholders accountable?** This involves identifying and enforcing legal, ethical, and operational frameworks.
- **What role does governance play in assigning responsibility?** Organizations must establish clear policies and processes to define accountability at every stage of the AI lifecycle, from design to deployment.

PRACTICAL IMPLEMENTATION

Mechanisms for Assigning Accountability Within Organizations

1. **Establishing Clear Roles and Responsibilities** Organizations must define specific roles and responsibilities for all stakeholders involved in AI projects. This includes:
   - **Developers:** Ensuring algorithms are designed with fairness, accuracy, and ethical considerations.
   - **Data Scientists:** Verifying that the data used to train AI models is representative, unbiased, and ethically sourced.
   - **Compliance Officers:** Overseeing adherence to regulatory and ethical standards.
   - **Executives:** Taking ultimate responsibility for the deployment and impact of AI systems.
2. **Implementing Ethical AI Guidelines** Organizations should develop and enforce ethical AI guidelines that outline transparency, fairness, and accountability standards. These guidelines should include mechanisms for:
   - Regular auditing of AI systems to identify and rectify biases or inaccuracies.
   - Providing explanations for AI decisions, especially in high-stakes domains such as healthcare or criminal justice.
   - Establishing feedback loops to improve system performance and accountability continuously.
3. **Training and Education** Building an organizational culture of accountability requires training employees at all levels. This includes:
   - Educating developers and data scientists on the ethical implications of their work.
   - Training managers and decision-makers on how to interpret AI outputs responsibly.

- Raising awareness among all employees about the importance of accountability in AI governance.

4. Monitoring and Reporting Mechanisms Organizations must establish monitoring and reporting mechanisms to track the performance and impact of AI systems. This includes:
    - Conducting regular audits to assess compliance with ethical and regulatory standards.
    - Creating internal and external reporting channels for stakeholders to voice concerns about AI systems.
    - Publishing transparency reports to inform the public about the organization's efforts to ensure accountability.

Case Study: Holding Organizations Accountable for Biased AI Outcomes

The real-world implications of accountability in AI systems are best illustrated through case studies. One notable example is the controversy surrounding a hiring algorithm developed by a leading tech company.

Background: The company developed an AI-based recruitment tool to streamline its hiring process. The tool was trained on historical hiring data, which reflected the company's past hiring practices. As a result, the algorithm exhibited gender bias, favoring male candidates over equally qualified female candidates. This bias was discovered when internal audits revealed significant disparities in candidate selection rates.

Challenges

- Identifying Responsibility: The company faced challenges in determining who was accountable for the biased outcomes. Was it the developers who designed the algorithm, the managers who approved its deployment, or the executives responsible for overseeing the hiring process?
- Transparency Issues: The algorithm's decision-making process was opaque, making it difficult to pinpoint the source of the bias.
- Public Backlash: The discovery of bias led to significant reputational damage and public scrutiny, highlighting the need for robust accountability mechanisms.

Actions Taken To address these challenges, the company implemented the following measures:

1. Revamping the Algorithm: **The company reevaluated its** design and retrained it using a more diverse and representative dataset. This involved collaborating with external experts in ethics and AI fairness.
2. Establishing Accountability Frameworks

- The company created a dedicated AI ethics board to oversee the development and deployment of AI systems.
- Clear guidelines were established to define accountability at every stage of the AI lifecycle.

3. **Improving Transparency**
   - The company is committed to providing detailed explanations for AI decisions, particularly in sensitive areas like hiring.
   - Regular transparency reports were published to inform stakeholders about the organization's progress in addressing bias and ensuring accountability.
4. **Engaging Stakeholders**
   - Employees were trained to recognize and mitigate biases in AI systems.
   - Open forums were organized to engage external stakeholders, including advocacy groups and regulatory bodies, in discussions about AI accountability.

Outcomes The company's efforts to address bias and enhance accountability yielded positive results. The revamped algorithm significantly improved fairness and inclusivity, restoring stakeholder confidence. The case also served as a valuable lesson for the broader industry, emphasizing the importance of proactive accountability measures.

Accountability in AI systems is essential for fostering trust, ensuring ethical practices, and mitigating risks. By defining clear roles and responsibilities, implementing ethical guidelines, and establishing robust monitoring mechanisms, organizations can effectively address the challenges associated with AI accountability. The case study of the biased hiring algorithm underscores the importance of transparency, stakeholder engagement, and continuous improvement in achieving accountable AI systems. As AI continues to shape the future, accountability will remain a critical pillar of responsible governance, ensuring that technological advancements benefit society.

4.3 TRANSPARENCY AND EXPLAINABILITY (3 PAGES)

Transparency and explainability have emerged as critical concerns in the rapidly evolving field of artificial intelligence (AI). These elements are essential for fostering trust among stakeholders, ensuring compliance with legal frameworks, and promoting ethical AI adoption. Transparency refers to making the processes and decisions of AI systems visible and understandable to stakeholders. At the same time, explainability focuses on enabling stakeholders to comprehend the logic and reasoning behind AI-driven outcomes. Together, these principles form the cornerstone of responsible AI development and deployment.

IMPORTANCE OF MAKING AI PROCESSES VISIBLE TO STAKEHOLDERS

Transparency in AI entails providing clear insights into how AI systems operate, from data collection and preprocessing to decision-making and outcomes. This visibility allows stakeholders, including developers, regulators, end-users, and the general public, to trust and effectively interact with AI systems.

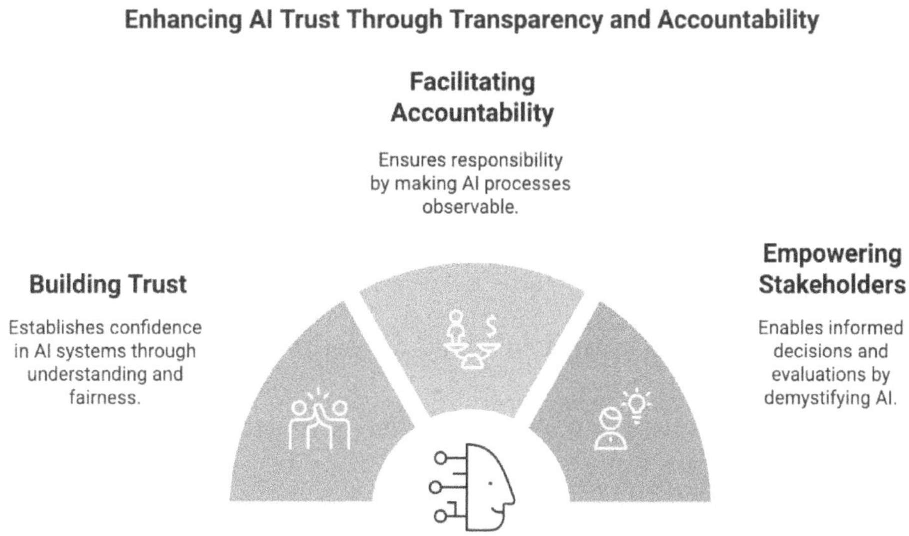

1. Building Trust: Transparency is a foundational element in building trust. When stakeholders understand how an AI system functions and why it produces specific results, they are more likely to trust its reliability and fairness. For businesses, this trust translates into increased adoption of AI solutions by customers and partners.

2. Facilitating Accountability: Transparency ensures that developers and organizations remain accountable for the actions of their AI systems. By making processes and decisions observable, stakeholders can identify potential issues such as bias, discrimination, or errors and address them promptly.

3. Empowering Stakeholders: Transparency empowers non-technical stakeholders by demystifying AI systems. For instance, end-users can make informed decisions about AI-driven services, while regulators can better evaluate compliance with ethical and legal standards.

REGULATORY DEMANDS FOR TRANSPARENCY

Regulatory frameworks worldwide emphasize the importance of transparency in AI systems to safeguard privacy, fairness, and accountability. Notable examples include:

1. **GDPR Requirements**: The General Data Protection Regulation (GDPR) of the European Union mandates that organizations clearly explain automated decision-making processes, particularly when these decisions significantly impact individuals. Article 22 specifically addresses the right not to be subject to decisions based solely on automated processing without meaningful human oversight.

2. **AI Act and Other Emerging Frameworks**: The European Union's proposed AI Act requires transparency for high-risk AI systems, necessitating that users understand how these systems work and their limitations. Other countries, including the United States and Canada, are exploring similar transparency guidelines.

3. **Sector-Specific Regulations**: Industries such as finance and healthcare have additional requirements for transparency. For instance, the Basel Committee on Banking Supervision calls for explainability in AI-driven credit scoring and risk management tools.

By adhering to these regulations, organizations demonstrate their commitment to ethical AI practices while avoiding legal repercussions.

EXPLAINABILITY IN AI MODELS

EXPLAINING COMPLEX MACHINE LEARNING MODELS TO NON-TECHNICAL AUDIENCES

Explainability focuses on translating the operations of complex AI models into terms and concepts that non-technical stakeholders can understand. This is particularly important for machine learning (ML) models such as deep learning networks, which often operate as "black boxes."

1. **Simplifying Technical Jargon**: Effective explainability involves simplifying complex algorithms into narratives. Instead of explaining a neural network's activation functions, stakeholders might benefit from analogies, such as comparing it to pattern recognition processes in the human brain.

2. **Visual Aids**: Visual tools such as decision trees, flowcharts, and interactive dashboards can make complex processes more accessible. These aids provide a tangible way for stakeholders to grasp abstract concepts and understand key decision points.

3. **Scenario-Based Explanations**: Examples or scenarios can help non-technical audiences relate AI decisions to real-world contexts. For instance, an AI system predicting loan approvals could be explained through a hypothetical applicant's journey, detailing the factors influencing the decision.

TOOLS AND TECHNIQUES FOR IMPROVING EXPLAINABILITY

Various tools and techniques have been developed to enhance the explainability of AI models. These methods help bridge the gap between complex technical processes and stakeholder understanding:

1. LIME (Local Interpretable Model-Agnostic Explanations) is a popular tool for generating local explanations for predictions made by black-box models. LIME provides insights into which features contributed most to a specific prediction by approximating the model's behavior with simpler interpretable models.

2. SHAP (Shapley Additive Explanations): SHAP is another widely used method that assigns importance values to each feature in a model. Based on cooperative game theory, SHAP explains individual predictions by quantifying the contribution of each input feature.

3. Feature Importance Scores: Many machine learning frameworks, such as sci-kit-learn and TensorFlow, offer built-in methods for calculating feature importance. These scores provide insights into which variables have the most significant influence on a model's predictions.

4. Counterfactual Explanations: Counterfactual techniques explain AI decisions by highlighting alternative scenarios. For example, "If the applicant's income were $5,000 higher, the loan would have been approved" is a counterfactual explanation that clarifies the reasoning behind the outcome.

5. Model-Specific Techniques: Certain models, such as decision trees and linear regression, are inherently more interpretable. Using these models or incorporating their outputs into more complex systems can improve overall explainability.

CHALLENGES

Despite its importance, achieving transparency and explainability in AI is challenging. These issues often involve balancing competing priorities and addressing the limitations of existing methods.

TRADE-OFFS BETWEEN EXPLAINABILITY AND PERFORMANCE

1. Complexity vs. Interpretability: High-performance models such as deep learning networks often sacrifice interpretability for accuracy. While simpler models like decision trees and linear regression are more interpretable, they may not achieve the same level of predictive accuracy. This trade-off poses a dilemma for developers who must balance performance with stakeholder needs for clarity.

2. Scalability Issues: Explaining AI models meaningfully to all stakeholders can be resource-intensive, particularly for large-scale systems. Developing tailored explanations for diverse audiences often requires significant time and expertise.

3. Evolving Models: AI models are dynamic, frequently updated with new data, or retrained to improve performance. Maintaining transparency and explainability for continuously changing systems can be challenging, particularly in fast-paced industries.

ETHICAL AND SOCIAL CHALLENGES

1. **Bias and Fairness**: Transparent and explainable AI systems are crucial for identifying and mitigating biases. However, achieving explainability does not automatically eliminate biases embedded in data or algorithms. Organizations must adopt a holistic approach to address these issues.

2. **Overloading Stakeholders**: Excessive technical details, presented in the name of transparency, can overwhelm stakeholders and hinder their decision-making. Striking the right balance between depth and simplicity is key.

TECHNICAL LIMITATIONS

1. **The Black Box Nature of AI Models**: Some AI models, particularly deep learning architectures, are inherently opaque. Efforts to explain these models often involve approximations or simplified representations that may not fully capture the complexity of the original model.
2. **Standardization Gaps**: The lack of standardized frameworks and guidelines for explainability complicates efforts to achieve transparency. Developers often rely on ad-hoc methods that may not be consistent or universally understood.

Transparency and explainability are indispensable for fostering trust, ensuring compliance, and promoting ethical AI practices. While tools and techniques such as LIME, SHAP, and counterfactual explanations provide valuable solutions, significant challenges remain. Organizations must navigate trade-offs between performance and interpretability, address technical limitations, and adhere to evolving regulatory requirements. By prioritizing transparency and explainability, AI developers and stakeholders can contribute to a future where AI systems are robust but also fair, accountable, and comprehensible.

4.4 FAIRNESS AND BIAS MITIGATION

WHAT IS FAIRNESS IN AI?

Fairness in artificial intelligence (AI) ensures equitable outcomes for all users, regardless of their demographic, geographic, or individual characteristics. It involves minimizing discrimination and avoiding outcomes that could disadvantage certain groups unfairly. Achieving fairness requires a deliberate effort to design, train, and deploy AI systems that respect user diversity and address historical inequalities.

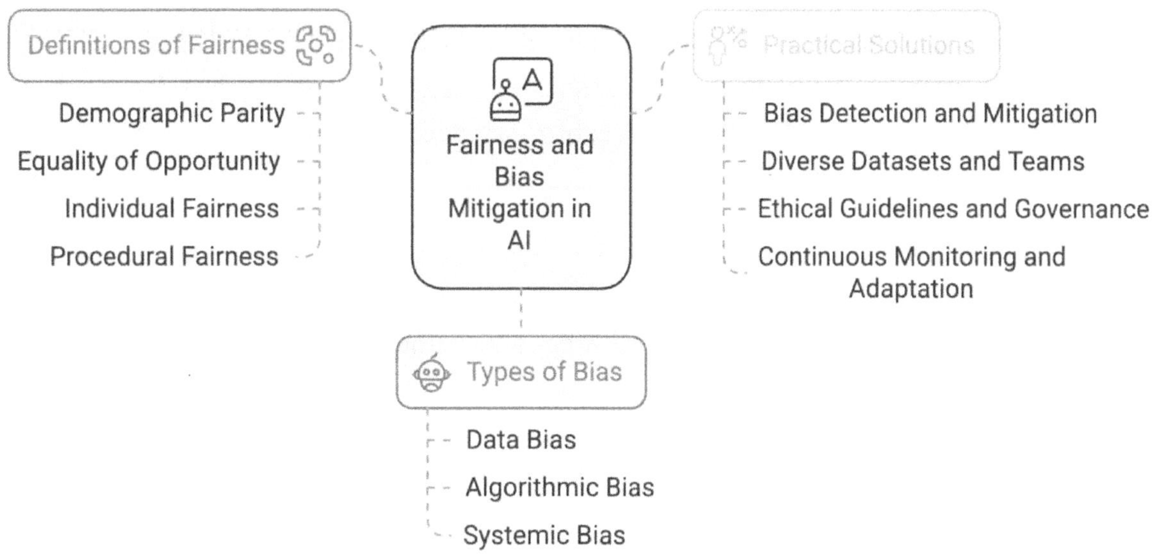

Several definitions of fairness exist, each providing a different lens to measure and evaluate fairness in AI systems:

1. Demographic Parity: This criterion ensures that AI outcomes are equally distributed across different demographic groups. For example, a hiring algorithm would satisfy demographic parity if the proportion of selected candidates from each demographic mirrors their representation in the applicant pool.

2. Equality of Opportunity ensures that individuals with the same qualifications or merit have an equal chance of achieving a positive outcome. For instance, in credit scoring, equality of opportunity would mean that individuals with the same creditworthiness receive similar credit offers, regardless of their race or gender.

3. Individual Fairness: This focuses on treating similar individuals similarly. An AI system meets this standard if two people with the same attributes receive equivalent outcomes.

4. Procedural Fairness: This emphasizes the fairness of the decision-making process itself, ensuring that the algorithms and methodologies used are unbiased and transparent.

By adopting these definitions, organizations can set benchmarks to evaluate and improve the fairness of their AI systems, tailoring approaches to the specific context and application.

BIAS IN AI SYSTEMS

Bias in AI refers to systematic errors or unfair tendencies in AI systems that can lead to discriminatory outcomes. Bias can emerge at various stages of the AI lifecycle, from data collection to algorithm design and deployment. Understanding the types of bias is critical to effectively mitigating them.

1. **Types of Bias:**

   - **Data Bias:** This occurs when the training data used to build AI models is unrepresentative or reflects existing societal prejudices. For instance, facial recognition systems trained predominantly on lighter-skinned individuals often perform poorly on darker-skinned faces.

   - **Algorithmic Bias:** Even with balanced datasets, algorithms can produce biased outcomes due to flawed design or optimization criteria. For example, prioritizing efficiency over fairness can lead to unequal treatment.

   - **Systemic Bias:** Broader societal structures and institutional practices can embed bias into AI systems. For example, biased hiring algorithms may reflect and perpetuate historical inequalities in workplace demographics.

2. **Real-World Examples of Biased AI Systems:**

   - **Hiring Algorithms:** Some AI-based recruitment tools have been found to favor male candidates over female candidates due to historical biases in hiring data.

   - **Facial Recognition:** Studies have shown that facial recognition algorithms often have higher error rates for women and individuals with darker skin tones.

   - **Predictive Policing:** AI tools used in law enforcement have been criticized for disproportionately targeting minority communities due to biased crime data.

   - **Healthcare AI:** Algorithms designed for medical diagnosis or treatment allocation have sometimes underrepresented minority groups, leading to disparities in healthcare access and outcomes.

PRACTICAL SOLUTIONS

To address fairness and bias in AI systems, organizations must adopt proactive strategies encompassing the entire AI lifecycle, from data collection to deployment and monitoring.

1. **Bias Detection and Mitigation Strategies:**

   - **Bias Audits:** Regular audits can help identify and quantify biases in AI systems. These audits should include assessments of both input data and algorithmic outputs.

   - **Fairness Metrics:** Organizations can evaluate system performance using fairness metrics, such as demographic parity, equality of opportunity, and disparate impact.

- Explainability Tools: Tools like SHAP (SHapley Additive exPlanations) and LIME (Local Interpretable Model-agnostic Explanations) can provide insights into how AI models make decisions, helping identify potential biases.

- Algorithmic Adjustments: Techniques such as reweighting, resampling, or adversarial debiasing can help mitigate bias in AI systems. For example, reweighting data during training can balance the influence of underrepresented groups.

2. Diverse Datasets and Inclusive Teams as Solutions to Bias:

   - Improving Dataset Diversity: Ensuring training datasets represent diverse populations is a fundamental step toward mitigating bias. For instance, in facial recognition, including images of individuals from varied ethnicities, genders, and age groups can improve accuracy across demographics.

   - Synthetic Data: When real-world data is insufficient or biased, synthetic data can supplement datasets and enhance representation.

   - Inclusive Development Teams: Building diverse teams of developers and stakeholders ensures that varied perspectives are considered during the AI design and development process. This can help identify potential blind spots and biases early in the lifecycle.

   - User Feedback: Incorporating feedback from diverse user groups can help identify unintended consequences and biases in AI systems.

3. Ethical Guidelines and Governance:

   - Ethical AI Frameworks: Organizations should establish clear guidelines prioritizing fairness and accountability. These frameworks should outline principles for data collection, algorithm development, and system deployment.

   - AI Governance Committees: Setting up dedicated committees or advisory boards can provide oversight and ensure that fairness considerations are integrated into decision-making processes.

4. Continuous Monitoring and Adaptation:

   - Post-Deployment Monitoring: AI systems should be regularly monitored to ensure they meet fairness standards over time. Changes in data or user behavior may require recalibration of models.

   - Scenario Testing: Simulating different scenarios can help predict how AI systems perform across diverse user groups and conditions.

Fairness in AI is essential for building systems that serve diverse populations equitably. While the challenge of bias is significant, it is not insurmountable. By understanding the sources and types of bias, adopting robust detection and mitigation strategies, and fostering diverse teams and datasets, organizations can create AI systems that are more fair and inclusive. Fairness is not a one-time effort but an ongoing commitment to accountability, transparency, and ethical innovation.

4.5 PRIVACY AND SECURITY IN AI

PRIVACY CONCERNS IN AI

The proliferation of artificial intelligence (AI) systems has brought significant advancements across industries. However, these systems often rely on vast amounts of personal data, raising critical privacy concerns. Safeguarding personal information is challenging, as AI systems' capabilities sometimes conflict with data protection principles.

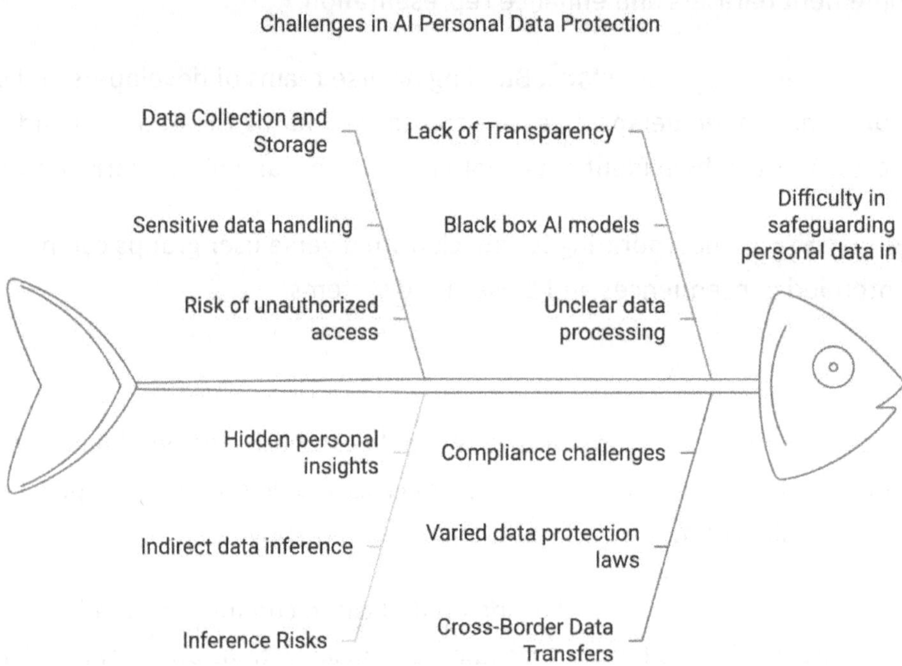

1. **Challenges in Protecting Personal Data:**

    - **Data Collection and Storage:** AI systems often require extensive datasets to function effectively. These datasets include sensitive personal information such as health records, financial data, and online activity. Storing and processing this data increases the risk of unauthorized access or misuse.

    - **Inference Risks:** AI models, particularly machine learning systems, can infer sensitive information about individuals even when direct data is unavailable. For instance, an AI analyzing purchasing patterns may infer a user's health status or personal habits.

- Lack of Transparency: Many AI model's intense learning systems operate as "black boxes," making it difficult to understand how data is processed or whether privacy violations occur during inference.
- Cross-Border Data Transfers: Global AI systems often involve data transfers across jurisdictions with varying data protection laws, which complicates compliance and increases the risk of data breaches.

2. Examples of Privacy Violations in AI:

   - Facial Recognition Systems: Several governments and private entities have deployed facial recognition tools without public consent. These systems have been criticized for mass surveillance and potential misuse by authoritarian regimes.
   - Data Breaches in AI Applications: High-profile breaches, such as those involving healthcare AI platforms, have exposed sensitive personal data, undermining public trust.
   - Targeted Advertising: AI-driven algorithms for advertising have been accused of exploiting user data without adequate consent, leading to intrusive and manipulative marketing practices.

SECURITY CHALLENGES

While powerful, AI systems are not immune to threats. Their complexity and reliance on data make them vulnerable to various security risks that could compromise functionality, integrity, and trust.

1. Threats Posed by Adversarial Attacks:

   - Evasion Attacks: In this type of attack, adversaries manipulate input data to deceive AI models. For example, slight image alterations can cause a facial recognition system to misidentify individuals.
   - Poisoning Attacks: Attackers can corrupt training datasets by injecting malicious data, causing the AI model to make incorrect predictions or decisions.
   - Model Extraction Attacks involve reverse engineering an AI model to replicate its functionality, potentially exposing proprietary information or sensitive data used during training.

2. **Model Hacking:**
   - **Unauthorized Access:** Hackers may exploit vulnerabilities in AI systems to gain unauthorized access, compromising the model and the data it processes.
   - **Rogue AI Behavior:** Poorly secured AI systems could be manipulated to act unintentionally or maliciously, such as spreading disinformation or causing physical harm in autonomous vehicles or robotics.

SOLUTIONS

A combination of technical, organizational, and governance strategies is necessary to address the twin challenges of privacy and security. These measures should balance the benefits of AI with the need to protect user data and system integrity.

1. **Adopting Privacy-Preserving Techniques:**
   - **Differential Privacy:** This technique adds statistical noise to datasets, ensuring that individual data points cannot be identified while enabling meaningful analysis. For example, Apple's use of differential privacy in its data collection ensures user anonymity while improving services.
   - **Federated Learning:** Federated learning allows AI models to be trained locally on user devices rather than collecting data centrally. This approach minimizes the risk of data exposure while maintaining model accuracy. Google's use of federated learning in Gboard is a notable example.
   - **Data Anonymization:** Transforming data to remove personally identifiable information (PII) can reduce privacy risks. However, this approach must be implemented carefully to prevent re-identification attacks.
   - **Encryption Techniques:** Advanced encryption methods, such as homomorphic encryption, allow AI systems to process encrypted data without exposing the underlying information, ensuring privacy throughout the computation process.

2. **Governance Measures for Robust AI Security:**
   - **Regulatory Compliance:** Organizations must adhere to data protection regulations such as the General Data Protection Regulation (GDPR) and the California Consumer Privacy Act (CCPA). Compliance ensures that AI systems are designed with privacy by default and design.

- Ethical AI Principles: Establishing guidelines prioritizing user privacy and system security can help organizations align their AI initiatives with societal values.
- AI Security Audits: Regular audits can identify vulnerabilities in AI systems, ensure they meet security standards, and protect against emerging threats.
- Incident Response Plans: Developing robust response protocols for security breaches can quickly mitigate damage and restore public trust.

3. Technical Safeguards:
    - Secure Model Deployment: It is critical to ensure that AI models are deployed in safe environments with protections against unauthorized access. Techniques such as containerization and sandboxing can provide additional layers of security.
    - Monitoring and Threat Detection: Continuous monitoring of AI systems for unusual behavior or potential attacks can help organizations respond proactively to threats.
    - Adversarial Training: Incorporating adversarial examples into the training process can make AI models more resilient to evasion and poisoning attacks.
4. Building Trust Through Transparency:
    - Explainability and Interpretability: Developing tools to make AI decision-making processes transparent helps users understand how their data is used, fostering trust.
    - User Consent Mechanisms: Implementing clear and accessible consent mechanisms ensures that users are informed about how their data is collected, stored, and used.
    - Stakeholder Engagement: Collaborating with policymakers, academics, and civil society can help organizations navigate privacy and security challenges effectively while maintaining public trust.

Privacy and security are foundational to the responsible development and deployment of AI systems. Addressing privacy concerns requires robust data protection measures and transparency while mitigating security risks, which demands a proactive approach to threat detection and system hardening. By adopting privacy-preserving techniques, adhering to governance standards, and fostering trust through transparency, organizations can build AI systems that not only deliver value but also uphold the rights and safety of their users. The path forward is combining technological innovation with ethical stewardship to create a secure and privacy-conscious AI ecosystem.

4.6 BALANCING PRINCIPLES AND TRADE-OFFS

In the evolving landscape of artificial intelligence (AI), organizations often face the challenge of balancing competing principles. Striving for ethical AI demands the adoption of guiding principles and strategic navigation of trade-offs that inevitably arise.

CONFLICTING GOALS

One of the primary challenges is managing conflicting goals. For instance, the principle of fairness often conflicts with the need for accuracy. While accuracy focuses on the predictive performance of AI models, fairness emphasizes the equitable treatment of diverse demographic groups. In practice, optimizing for one can lead to compromises in the other. For example, an AI system designed to screen job applicants might achieve high accuracy in predicting job performance but inadvertently introduce biases against certain groups, undermining fairness.

Similarly, transparency can conflict with security. Full transparency in AI systems, such as revealing algorithms or decision-making processes, can enhance accountability and trust. However, excessive transparency may expose sensitive data or intellectual property, increasing vulnerability to adversarial attacks. Striking a balance between these principles requires a nuanced understanding of the organizational context and potential risks.

STRATEGIC DECISION-MAKING

Organizations must approach these trade-offs through strategic decision-making, aligning their priorities with overarching goals. A principled framework can help in this regard. For instance, organizations might prioritize fairness in healthcare or criminal justice applications, where ethical considerations are paramount. Conversely, security might outweigh transparency in protecting critical cybersecurity or national defense assets.

Decision-making should also involve diverse stakeholders, including ethicists, technologists, legal experts, and affected communities. By incorporating multiple perspectives, organizations can better anticipate the implications of their choices and navigate trade-offs effectively. Scenario analysis, ethical impact assessments, and iterative testing can further refine decision-making processes.

EXAMPLE SCENARIOS

Practical examples can help us better understand trade-offs. Consider an AI-powered loan approval system. Prioritizing fairness might involve adjusting algorithms to ensure equal approval rates across demographic groups, but this could slightly reduce the system's overall predictive accuracy. Alternatively, emphasizing accuracy might optimize the system's performance but risk perpetuating societal inequities.

Another example is autonomous vehicles, where transparency and safety intersect. Revealing details about AI's decision-making logic could foster public trust but might also provide hackers with the information needed to exploit vulnerabilities. In this case, the organization must carefully weigh the societal benefits of transparency against potential security threats.

In conclusion, balancing principles and trade-offs is an inherent aspect of ethical AI development. Organizations can navigate this complexity responsibly by recognizing and addressing conflicting goals, employing strategic decision-making, analyzing practical scenarios, and fostering innovation while upholding ethical standards.

CHAPTER 5: GOVERNANCE FRAMEWORK OVERVIEW

5.1 INTRODUCTION TO GOVERNANCE FRAMEWORKS

WHAT IS AN AI GOVERNANCE FRAMEWORK?

An AI Governance Framework is a structured set of principles, policies, and procedures designed to guide organizations in managing artificial intelligence systems' deployment, operation, and impact. Such frameworks ensure that AI systems align with organizational objectives and foster ethical, transparent, and compliant practices.

Governance frameworks are critical in aligning AI initiatives with broader organizational goals. Integrating AI strategies into existing business processes and policies, these frameworks help ensure that AI projects contribute to measurable outcomes, such as improved efficiency, innovation, and customer satisfaction. Additionally, they offer a roadmap for balancing technical feasibility with ethical considerations, enabling organizations to build trust with stakeholders while achieving operational excellence.

An AI governance framework serves as a blueprint for navigating the complexities of AI adoption. It helps organizations define key responsibilities, establish accountability mechanisms, and monitor the performance of AI systems throughout their lifecycle.

WHY FRAMEWORKS ARE ESSENTIAL

AI systems are inherently complex, involving numerous stakeholders, technical intricacies, and regulatory requirements. As AI technologies become more advanced and pervasive, managing their development and deployment becomes increasingly challenging. This is where governance frameworks prove indispensable.

AI Governance Framework Challenges

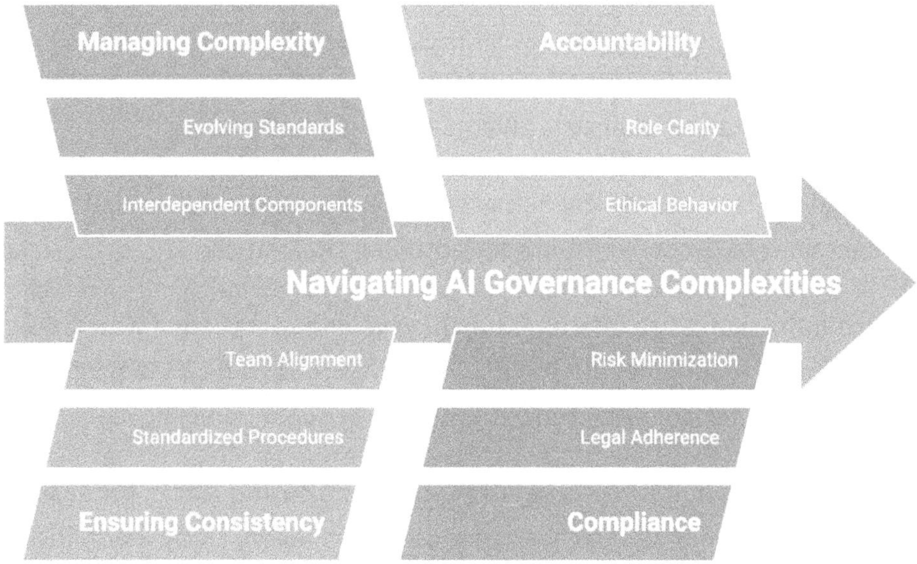

MANAGING COMPLEXITY IN AI SYSTEMS

AI systems often involve interdependent components like algorithms, data pipelines, and machine learning models. They must operate seamlessly while addressing evolving business requirements and adhering to legal and ethical standards. Governance frameworks provide a structured approach to managing this complexity, offering guidelines for system design, implementation, and monitoring. This helps organizations mitigate bias, inefficiency, and unintended consequences.

For example, an AI governance framework may specify procedures for:

- Conducting thorough impact assessments before deploying AI models.
- Establishing protocols for data management to ensure quality and privacy.
- Implementing safeguards against algorithmic biases or unintended actions.

Without such frameworks, organizations risk losing control over AI initiatives, which can lead to inefficiencies, compliance violations, or reputational damage.

ENSURING CONSISTENCY, ACCOUNTABILITY, AND COMPLIANCE

Governance frameworks establish a consistent approach to AI development and deployment across an organization. By defining standardized procedures, they help teams align their efforts, reducing silos and fostering collaboration. Consistency is critical in large enterprises, where disparate teams may work on AI initiatives simultaneously.

Moreover, these frameworks introduce mechanisms for accountability, ensuring that all stakeholders understand their roles and responsibilities. For instance:

- Data scientists may be accountable for ensuring data integrity.
- Business leaders may oversee alignment with strategic objectives.
- Legal teams may ensure compliance with applicable regulations.

Accountability mechanisms promote ethical behavior and enhance organizational resilience by proactively preparing teams to proactively address potential challenges.

Finally, AI governance frameworks are instrumental in achieving compliance with laws and standards, such as the General Data Protection Regulation (GDPR) or the NIST AI Risk Management Framework. They provide clear guidelines for adhering to these requirements, minimizing legal and financial risks.

An AI governance framework is more than a set of rules—it is a strategic tool for ensuring that AI systems deliver value while upholding ethical standards. By managing complexity, fostering consistency, and ensuring accountability, these frameworks enable organizations to harness the full potential of AI responsibly. In the following sections, we will explore the core components of these frameworks, compare popular models, and examine real-world applications to provide a comprehensive understanding of AI governance.

5.2 CORE COMPONENTS OF AN AI GOVERNANCE FRAMEWORK

Establishing a robust governance framework is essential for organizations to manage AI systems effectively in the rapidly evolving world of artificial intelligence. A comprehensive framework is built upon several core components designed to address specific aspects of AI system development and deployment. This section delves into the key elements of an AI governance framework and provides an illustrative example to contextualize its application.

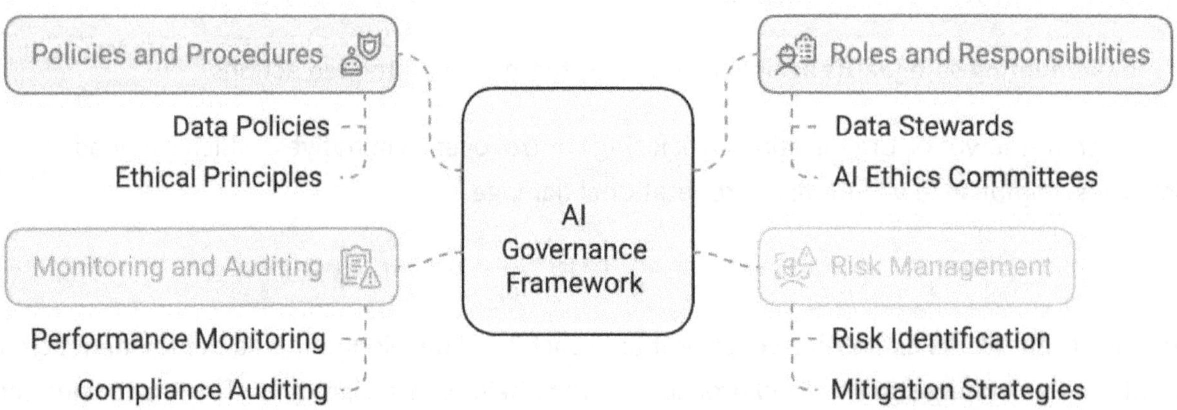

POLICIES AND PROCEDURES: SETTING ORGANIZATIONAL AI GOVERNANCE RULES

Policies and procedures are the foundational elements of any governance framework. They are the rulebook outlining the organization's expectations, standards, and best practices for AI development and deployment. These rules ensure consistency and compliance with legal, ethical, and operational standards.

1. **Defining Policies:**
    - Policies should address data collection, storage, and usage, ensuring compliance with privacy laws like GDPR or CCPA.
    - Ethical AI principles, such as fairness, transparency, and accountability, must be integrated into the policy framework.
2. **Establishing Procedures:**
    - Organizations need detailed procedures for model development, including documentation, testing, and validation steps.
    - Incident response protocols should be established to address issues like data breaches, algorithmic bias, or system failures.
3. **Adapting to Change:**
    - Policies and procedures must be dynamic, allowing organizations to adapt to evolving technologies, regulations, and market demands.

By formalizing these rules, organizations create a structured environment that fosters trust and minimizes risks associated with AI adoption.

ROLES AND RESPONSIBILITIES: DEFINING OWNERSHIP ACROSS TEAMS

Defining roles and responsibilities within an AI governance framework is critical for ensuring accountability and streamlined operations. Assigning task ownership prevents confusion and enables efficient decision-making.

1. **Key Roles:**
    - **Data Stewards:** Responsible for maintaining data quality, privacy, and compliance.
    - **AI Ethics Committees:** Oversee ethical considerations, ensuring AI initiatives align with organizational values.

- **Risk Managers:** Focus on identifying and mitigating risks associated with AI systems.

2. **Cross-Functional Collaboration:**
   - Effective AI governance requires collaboration in IT, legal, compliance, and business units.
   - Establishing clear communication channels ensures alignment across teams.
3. **Accountability Mechanisms:**
   - Implementing performance metrics and periodic reviews helps measure individual and team contributions to governance efforts.

Defining roles and responsibilities creates a culture of accountability and ensures all stakeholders understand their contributions to the governance framework.

RISK MANAGEMENT: IDENTIFYING, ASSESSING, AND MITIGATING AI-RELATED RISKS

Risk management is critical to an AI governance framework, as AI systems often introduce unique challenges and uncertainties. A structured approach to risk management helps organizations anticipate potential issues and implement proactive measures.

1. **Risk Identification:**
   - Identify risks related to data quality, algorithmic bias, cybersecurity, and regulatory compliance.
   - Consider broader societal risks, such as unintended consequences or ethical dilemmas.
2. **Risk Assessment:**
   - Quantify the likelihood and impact of identified risks.
   - Prioritize risks based on their potential to disrupt operations or harm stakeholders.
3. **Mitigation Strategies:**
   - Employ techniques like algorithmic auditing and bias detection to address technical risks.
   - Develop contingency plans for high-risk scenarios, such as system failures or data breaches.
4. **Continuous Monitoring:**
   - Regularly review and update risk management strategies to address emerging threats.

By integrating robust risk management practices, organizations can minimize disruptions and maintain trust in their AI systems.

MONITORING AND AUDITING: ENSURING COMPLIANCE AND ONGOING EFFECTIVENESS

Monitoring and auditing processes are essential for maintaining the integrity and effectiveness of AI systems over time. These activities provide insights into system performance, ensure adherence to governance standards, and identify areas for improvement.

1. **Performance Monitoring:**
    - Implement tools and techniques for tracking system accuracy, efficiency, and user satisfaction.
    - Use performance metrics to assess whether AI systems are meeting organizational objectives.
2. **Compliance Auditing:**
    - Conduct regular audits to ensure compliance with internal policies and external regulations.
    - Document audit findings and implement corrective actions as needed.
3. **Feedback Loops:**
    - Establish mechanisms for collecting and incorporating feedback from users and stakeholders.
    - Use feedback to refine AI models and governance processes.
4. **Transparency Reports:**
    - Publish regular transparency reports to demonstrate accountability and build trust with stakeholders.

Monitoring and auditing activities help organizations maintain control over their AI initiatives, ensuring they remain effective and aligned with strategic goals.

ILLUSTRATIVE EXAMPLE: WALKTHROUGH OF A SIMPLE GOVERNANCE FRAMEWORK STRUCTURE

To better understand the practical application of an AI governance framework, consider the following example of a simplified structure implemented by a mid-sized financial services company:

1. **Policies and Procedures:**
    - The organization establishes policies outlining acceptable data sources, usage guidelines, and ethical AI principles.
    - Procedures are documented for model development, including mandatory fairness testing and validation steps.
2. **Roles and Responsibilities:**
    - A cross-functional AI governance committee includes IT, compliance, legal, and business unit representatives.
    - Data stewards oversee data quality and ensure compliance with privacy regulations.
3. **Risk Management:**
    - The company conducts a risk assessment to identify potential biases in its credit scoring algorithm.
    - Mitigation measures are implemented, such as periodic bias audits and external expert reviews.
4. **Monitoring and Auditing:**
    - Real-time monitoring tools are deployed to track the performance of AI models.
    - Monthly audits are conducted to ensure compliance with governance policies and regulatory standards.

This governance framework allows the organization to manage its AI initiatives effectively, ensuring they deliver value while minimizing risks.

The core components of an AI governance framework—policies and procedures, roles and responsibilities, risk management, and monitoring and auditing—form the foundation for responsible AI adoption. By implementing these elements, organizations can navigate the complexities of AI systems, maintain compliance, and foster stakeholder trust. The following section will explore comparative analyses of popular governance models to provide further insights into their practical application.

5.3 COMPARATIVE ANALYSIS OF FRAMEWORK MODELS

Organizations worldwide are adopting artificial intelligence (AI) technologies, necessitating governance frameworks that ensure ethical, efficient, and compliant use. This section compares three prominent AI governance frameworks: the NIST AI Risk Management Framework, the OECD AI

Principles, and Microsoft's Responsible AI Standard. By examining their strengths, weaknesses, and applications, organizations can determine the best fit based on their size, industry, and goals.

Comparative Analysis of AI Governance Frameworks

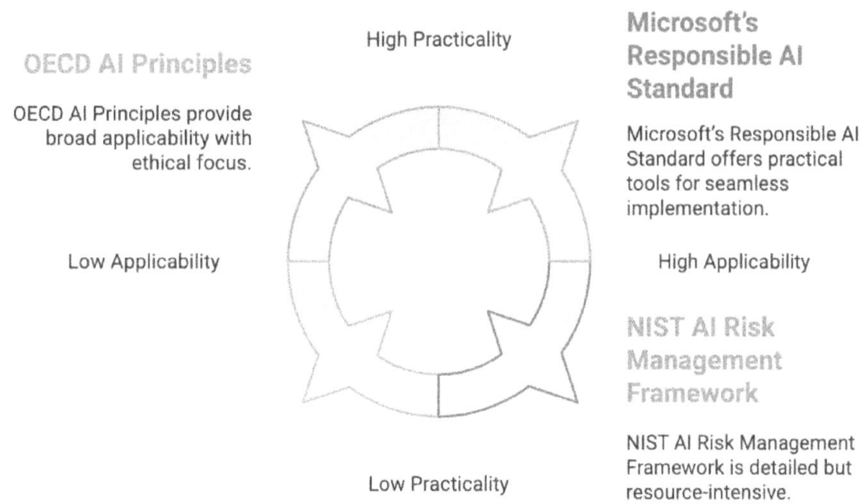

POPULAR FRAMEWORKS IN USE

NIST AI RISK MANAGEMENT FRAMEWORK

The **National Institute of Standards and Technology (NIST) AI Risk Management Framework** is a widely respected model designed to help organizations manage risks associated with AI systems. It emphasizes transparency, accountability, and robustness.

1. **Key Features:**
    - Focuses on risk identification, assessment, and mitigation across the AI lifecycle.
    - Provides guidelines for ensuring fairness, reliability, privacy, and security.
    - Encourages stakeholder engagement to understand and address AI-related risks.
2. **Strengths:**
    - Highly detailed and adaptable for organizations of varying sizes and industries.
    - Emphasizes measurable outcomes and continuous improvement.
    - It aligns well with regulatory requirements, making it suitable for compliance-focused industries such as finance and healthcare.

3. **Weaknesses:**
    - The technical nature of the framework can be challenging for organizations with limited expertise in AI.
    - Requires significant resources for implementation and monitoring, which may not be feasible for smaller organizations.

OECD AI PRINCIPLES

The **Organisation for Economic Co-operation and Development (OECD) AI Principles** provide a global framework for fostering trustworthy AI systems. They promote innovation while addressing ethical concerns.

1. **Key Features:**
    - Encourages transparency, fairness, and human-centric AI.
    - Includes principles for fostering sustainability, inclusivity, and accountability.
    - Provides policy recommendations for governments to support responsible AI development.
2. **Strengths:**
    - Broadly applicable across countries and industries due to its high-level approach.
    - Emphasizes human rights and ethical considerations, fostering trust among stakeholders.
    - Encourages collaboration between public and private sectors.
3. **Weaknesses:**
    - It lacks detailed technical guidance, making it less actionable for organizations needing step-by-step implementation.
    - Its generality may result in varying interpretations, limiting its direct applicability to specific organizational contexts.

MICROSOFT'S RESPONSIBLE AI STANDARD

Microsoft's **Responsible AI Standard** is a proprietary framework designed to guide the company and its partners in developing and deploying AI responsibly.

1. **Key Features:**

- It centers on six principles: fairness, reliability and safety, privacy and security, inclusiveness, transparency, and accountability.
- Includes tools and methodologies for implementing ethical AI practices, such as bias assessment and interpretability tools.
- Offers integration with Microsoft's product ecosystem for seamless implementation.

2. Strengths:
   - Highly practical, with actionable tools and resources for real-world application.
   - It focuses on end-to-end governance and addressing challenges across the AI lifecycle.
   - Tailored for enterprises leveraging Microsoft's AI technologies, ensuring compatibility and support.
3. Weaknesses:
   - Limited applicability for organizations not using Microsoft's ecosystem.
   - Perceived as proprietary, which may restrict adoption in specific sectors or regions.

COMPARING STRENGTHS AND WEAKNESSES

A comparative analysis of these frameworks reveals distinct strengths and weaknesses:

Framework	Strengths	Weaknesses
NIST AI Risk Management	Detailed, adaptable, regulatory-focused	Requires technical expertise and resources
OECD AI Principles	Broad applicability, ethical focus, foster public-private collaboration	Lacks actionable technical guidance, general interpretations
Microsoft's Responsible AI	Practical tools lifecycle governance, tailored for Microsoft's ecosystem	Proprietary nature, limited to Microsoft's AI technologies

SELECTING THE RIGHT FRAMEWORK

Choosing the appropriate AI governance framework depends on an organization's size, industry, goals, and technological maturity. Below are some key considerations to guide this selection:

ORGANIZATIONAL SIZE

1. **Small and Medium Enterprises (SMEs):**
   - SMEs with limited resources may prefer high-level frameworks like the OECD AI Principles for their simplicity and focus on ethical practices.
   - Microsoft's Responsible AI Standard provides practical implementation resources and could also suit SMEs already using Microsoft tools and resources.

2. **Large Enterprises:**
   - Larger organizations with the capacity to manage complex frameworks may benefit from the NIST AI Risk Management Framework for its detailed and comprehensive approach.
   - Such enterprises often require stringent compliance measures, making NIST's alignment with regulations advantageous.

INDUSTRY

1. **Regulated Industries (e.g., Finance, Healthcare):**
   - The NIST framework's emphasis on compliance and risk management makes it an ideal choice for highly regulated industries.
   - These industries can also benefit from integrating tools provided by Microsoft's framework to address specific technical challenges.

2. **Innovation-Driven Industries (e.g., Technology, Retail):**
   - The OECD AI Principles' emphasis on fostering innovation and collaboration aligns with the goals of innovation-driven sectors.
   - Microsoft's bias assessment and inclusivity tools are also beneficial in developing consumer-centric AI solutions.

ORGANIZATIONAL GOALS

1. **Ethical Leadership:**
   - Organizations prioritizing ethical AI adoption may lean towards the OECD AI Principles for their strong focus on fairness, accountability, and inclusivity.

2. Risk Mitigation:

    - Companies focused on mitigating technical and operational risks will find the NIST framework's rigorous risk management guidelines invaluable.

3. Operational Efficiency:

    - Enterprises aiming for streamlined implementation, particularly those in Microsoft's ecosystem, may prefer Microsoft's Responsible AI Standard.

HYBRID APPROACHES

Organizations are not limited to choosing a single framework. Many combine elements from multiple frameworks to tailor a governance strategy that aligns with their unique needs. For example:

- A large financial institution might integrate the NIST framework's risk management practices with the OECD Principles' ethical guidelines.
- A technology startup could adopt Microsoft's tools for rapid deployment while adhering to the OECD's inclusivity and fairness principles.

The choice of an AI governance framework is a strategic decision that impacts an organization's ability to adopt AI responsibly and effectively. The NIST AI Risk Management Framework, the OECD AI Principles, and Microsoft's Responsible AI Standard each offer distinct advantages and challenges. By understanding these frameworks' nuances and aligning them with organizational size, industry, and goals, companies can successfully successfully navigate the complexities of AI adoption and governance. The following sections will explore how these frameworks can be adapted to specific industries and implemented in real-world scenarios.

5.4 INDUSTRY-SPECIFIC GOVERNANCE FRAMEWORKS

Successful implementation of AI governance frameworks requires an understanding of industry-specific challenges, regulations, and priorities. A one-size-fits-all approach is rarely practical, as industries operate under distinct regulatory requirements, technological needs, and stakeholder expectations. This section explores how governance frameworks can be adapted to specific sectors, such as healthcare, finance, and retail, ensuring that AI systems align with unique organizational goals and compliance mandates.

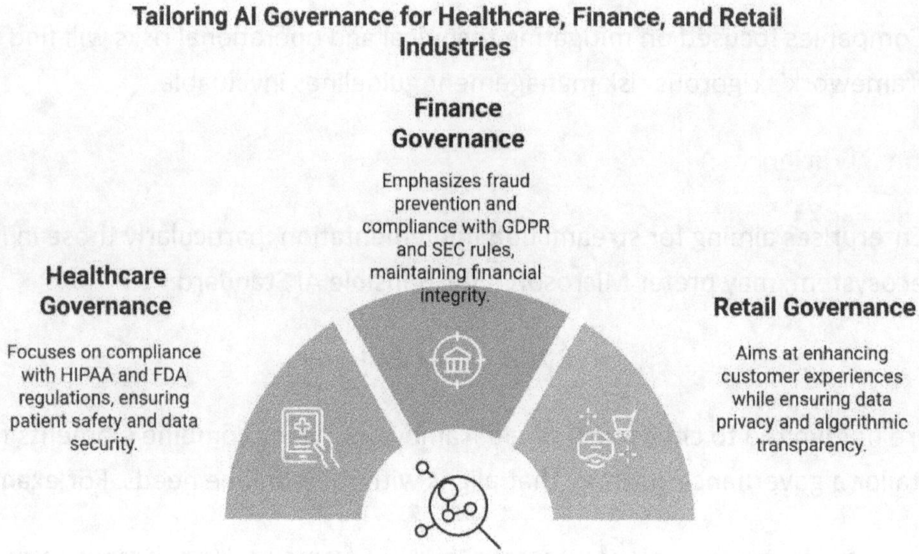

ADAPTING FRAMEWORKS TO INDUSTRY NEEDS

Tailoring AI governance frameworks to industry-specific contexts involves modifying policies, roles, risk management strategies, and monitoring mechanisms. Effective adaptation ensures that AI solutions meet operational demands while adhering to ethical and legal standards. Below are key strategies for adapting frameworks:

1. **Identifying Industry-Specific Risks:**
    - Each industry faces unique risks related to data security, operational efficiency, and regulatory compliance. Governance frameworks must prioritize mitigating these risks.
2. **Incorporating Regulatory Requirements:**
    - Governance frameworks should integrate the legal and ethical mandates specific to the industry. For instance, healthcare must adhere to HIPAA, while finance must comply with GDPR and SEC guidelines.
3. **Fostering Stakeholder Trust:**
    - Industries like retail, where customer engagement is critical, benefit from governance practices prioritizing transparency, fairness, and user-centric innovation.
4. **Enhancing Cross-Functional Collaboration:**
    - Cross-functional teams comprising domain experts, legal advisors, and technologists can ensure that governance frameworks reflect technical feasibility and industry realities.

EXAMPLES OF INDUSTRY-SPECIFIC GOVERNANCE FRAMEWORKS

HEALTHCARE: COMPLIANCE WITH HIPAA AND FDA REGULATIONS

The healthcare industry operates in a highly regulated environment where patient safety, privacy, and data security are paramount. AI systems used in healthcare must comply with standards like the Health Insurance Portability and Accountability Act (HIPAA) and the Food and Drug Administration (FDA) guidelines.

1. **Policies and Procedures:**
   - Establish protocols for managing patient data, ensuring compliance with HIPAA's privacy and security rules.
   - Define standards for AI system validation, including clinical trials for algorithms used in diagnostics or treatment.
2. **Roles and Responsibilities:**
   - Assign data stewards to oversee patient data integrity and security.
   - Establish an AI ethics committee to review algorithms for fairness and potential biases, particularly in diagnostic tools.
3. **Risk Management:**
   - Conduct risk assessments to evaluate potential harm from AI-driven decisions, such as incorrect diagnoses or treatment recommendations.
   - Implement mechanisms to identify and mitigate algorithmic biases that could affect patient outcomes.
4. **Monitoring and Auditing:**
   - Regularly audit AI systems to ensure compliance with FDA regulations and evaluate their performance in clinical settings.
   - Use real-world data to monitor AI tools and improve their accuracy over time.

Organizations can enhance patient safety, build stakeholder trust, and ensure regulatory compliance by aligning governance frameworks with healthcare-specific needs.

FINANCE: FOCUS ON FRAUD PREVENTION AND COMPLIANCE WITH GDPR OR SEC RULES

The finance industry relies heavily on AI for fraud detection, risk assessment, and personalized customer experiences. However, these applications must meet stringent regulatory requirements, including the General Data Protection Regulation (GDPR) and the U.S. Securities and Exchange Commission (SEC) guidelines.

1. **Policies and Procedures:**
   - Develop data collection and usage policies that comply with GDPR's requirements for user consent and data protection.
   - Create procedures for validating AI models used in risk assessment to ensure their reliability and transparency.
2. **Roles and Responsibilities:**
   - Assign risk managers to oversee the deployment of AI systems in fraud prevention and ensure compliance with financial regulations.
   - Designate data protection officers (DPOs) to monitor GDPR compliance and address data privacy concerns.
3. **Risk Management:**
   - Implement AI tools for real-time fraud detection, regularly updating them to address emerging threats.
   - Evaluate the fairness of credit-scoring algorithms to prevent discrimination based on race, gender, or other protected attributes.
4. **Monitoring and Auditing:**
   - Conduct routine audits of AI systems to verify compliance with SEC rules and internal governance policies.
   - Use key performance indicators (KPIs) to monitor the effectiveness of fraud detection systems.

Tailoring governance frameworks to the finance industry enables organizations to leverage AI for improved efficiency and security while maintaining compliance and customer trust.

RETAIL: GOVERNANCE FOR PERSONALIZED AI-DRIVEN CUSTOMER EXPERIENCES

The retail industry leverages AI to enhance customer experiences through personalized recommendations, dynamic pricing, and supply chain optimization. However, these innovations must be balanced with concerns about data privacy, algorithmic transparency, and ethical practices.

1. **Policies and Procedures:**
    - Establish policies for data collection, ensuring transparency about how customer data is used for personalization.
    - Define procedures for testing AI algorithms to ensure that recommendations and pricing strategies are fair and unbiased.
2. **Roles and Responsibilities:**
    - Assign customer data managers to oversee data security and compliance with privacy regulations.
    - Create roles for AI product managers to ensure alignment between AI initiatives and business objectives.
3. **Risk Management:**
    - Assess risks associated with dynamic pricing models, such as unintended price discrimination or loss of customer trust.
    - Mitigate risks of algorithmic bias in personalized recommendations by conducting regular fairness audits.
4. **Monitoring and Auditing:**
    - Use monitoring tools to track the performance of AI-driven marketing campaigns and customer interactions.
    - Audit algorithms to ensure compliance with data privacy laws, such as the California Consumer Privacy Act (CCPA).

Retail organizations can balance innovation with ethical considerations by implementing industry-specific governance practices enhancing customer loyalty and trust.

Adapting AI governance frameworks to industry-specific needs ensures that AI systems are effective, compliant, and aligned with organizational goals. Healthcare, finance, and retail each present unique challenges and opportunities that require tailored governance approaches. Organizations can leverage AI responsibly by addressing these industry-specific requirements, fostering innovation while maintaining stakeholder trust and regulatory compliance. The following section will explore real-world implementations of governance frameworks to illustrate their practical applications.

5.5 REAL-WORLD IMPLEMENTATIONS

Implementing AI governance frameworks in real-world settings offers invaluable insights into their practical benefits, challenges, and adaptability. This section presents two case studies—one involving a multinational corporation and another focusing on a small-to-medium enterprise (SME)—to illustrate how organizations of different scales can tailor governance frameworks to their specific needs. Key takeaways from these implementations also provide best practices for organizations seeking to adopt AI governance frameworks.

CASE STUDIES

EXAMPLE 1: IMPLEMENTING A GOVERNANCE FRAMEWORK TO ENSURE GDPR COMPLIANCE IN A MULTINATIONAL CORPORATION

A global e-commerce corporation across Europe faced increasing scrutiny under the General Data Protection Regulation (GDPR). To address compliance challenges, the company developed and implemented a robust AI governance framework that aligned its AI initiatives with GDPR requirements while fostering innovation.

1. **Framework Development:**
    - The corporation's governance framework focused on data privacy, algorithmic transparency, and accountability.
    - Policies were established to ensure data processing activities complied with GDPR principles such as purpose limitation, data minimization, and storage limitation.
2. **Roles and Responsibilities:**
    - A cross-functional AI ethics board comprises legal, IT, data science, and business unit representatives.
    - Data Protection Officers (DPOs) were assigned to monitor data usage and ensure compliance with GDPR mandates.
3. **Risk Management:**
    - Regular risk assessments were conducted to identify potential non-compliance risks associated with AI systems.
    - Automated tools were deployed to detect and mitigate biases in machine learning algorithms that could inadvertently lead to discriminatory outcomes.

4. **Monitoring and Auditing:**
    - The company implemented real-time monitoring of data processing activities to ensure ongoing compliance.
    - External auditors were engaged annually to verify the framework's effectiveness and adherence to GDPR requirements.
5. **Outcomes:**
    - The governance framework reduced GDPR non-compliance risks by 40% within the first year.
    - Enhanced transparency and accountability improved stakeholder trust, including among customers and regulators.
    - The company reported increased efficiency in managing AI systems, enabling faster deployment of compliant AI-driven solutions.

EXAMPLE 2: SCALING AI GOVERNANCE IN AN SME USING A LIGHTWEIGHT FRAMEWORK

A technology startup specializing in AI-driven marketing tools sought to implement a governance framework to address ethical concerns and regulatory compliance without overburdening its limited resources. The SME adopted a lightweight, scalable governance framework tailored to its needs and growth stage.

1. **Framework Design:**
    - The lightweight framework emphasized simplicity and practicality, focusing on key governance elements such as ethical guidelines, data security, and algorithmic fairness.
    - Policies were developed to ensure customer data privacy and compliance with regulations such as the California Consumer Privacy Act (CCPA).
2. **Roles and Responsibilities:**
    - The startup's leadership took an active role in governance, with the CEO leading the development of ethical AI principles.
    - A part-time data privacy consultant was hired to oversee compliance efforts.
3. **Risk Management:**
    - A checklist-based approach was adopted for risk assessment, enabling the team to efficiently identify and address potential ethical and operational risks.

- The framework included a mechanism for customer feedback to identify and mitigate biases in AI recommendations.

4. **Monitoring and Auditing:**

   - Simple performance metrics were established to monitor AI systems' accuracy, fairness, and customer satisfaction.

   - Quarterly internal reviews were conducted to evaluate compliance with the lightweight framework.

5. **Outcomes:**

   - The framework allowed the startup to proactively address ethical and regulatory concerns without compromising agility.

   - The company built stronger relationships with clients by integrating customer feedback into the governance process.

   - The framework's scalable nature ensured that it could be expanded as the startup grew, providing a sustainable governance solution.

KEY TAKEAWAYS

From these case studies, several key lessons and best practices emerge:

1. **Tailor Frameworks to Organizational Scale:**

   - Large corporations benefit from comprehensive frameworks that address complex regulatory requirements, while SMEs thrive with lightweight, scalable solutions.

   - Resource allocation should align with the organization's size and operational priorities to maximize effectiveness.

2. **Foster Cross-Functional Collaboration:**

   - Governance frameworks succeed when they involve stakeholders from diverse functions, including legal, IT, data science, and business units.

   - Cross-functional teams ensure that governance processes are holistic and address technical and organizational needs.

3. **Emphasize Simplicity and Practicality:**
   - Complex frameworks can be challenging to implement, particularly for smaller organizations. A pragmatic approach focusing on critical governance elements can yield effective results.
   - Checklist-based tools and predefined templates can simplify governance processes and enhance adoption.
4. **Leverage Technology for Governance:**
   - Automated risk detection, compliance monitoring, and bias mitigation tools streamline governance efforts and improve efficiency.
   - Real-time monitoring and feedback mechanisms enable organizations to address issues proactively and adapt to changes effectively.
5. **Integrate Ethical Considerations:**
   - Building ethical AI principles into governance frameworks fosters trust and ensures long-term sustainability.
   - Engaging stakeholders in ethical discussions promotes transparency and accountability.
6. **Adopt Iterative Approaches:**
   - Governance frameworks should evolve with organizational needs, regulatory changes, and technological advancements.
   - Regular reviews and updates ensure that frameworks remain relevant and practical.
7. **Build Stakeholder Trust:**
   - Transparent governance practices enhance trust among customers, regulators, and partners, driving long-term value.
   - Publishing regular transparency reports and engaging external auditors can further strengthen credibility.

The real-world implementation of AI governance frameworks highlights the importance of adaptability, simplicity, and collaboration. Whether addressing the complex regulatory landscape of a multinational corporation or the agility needs of an SME, governance frameworks must align with organizational goals and industry requirements. Organizations can build robust, sustainable governance frameworks that drive responsible AI innovation by learning from these examples and adopting best practices.

5.6 COMMON CHALLENGES AND SOLUTIONS

Implementing AI governance frameworks is not without challenges. Organizations must navigate various obstacles to ensure that governance structures are effective, adaptable, and aligned with their goals. This section explores some common challenges faced during framework implementation and offers practical solutions.

CHALLENGES IN FRAMEWORK IMPLEMENTATION

1. **Lack of Stakeholder Alignment:**
   - Effective governance frameworks require buy-in from various stakeholders, including executives, technical teams, and legal departments. Misalignment or lack of engagement can hinder progress, resulting in fragmented implementation and inefficiencies.
2. **Difficulty in Monitoring Compliance:**
   - Ensuring that AI systems comply with internal policies and external regulations is complex, particularly for organizations operating in multiple jurisdictions. The lack of real-time monitoring and auditing capabilities further complicates this process.
3. **Rapidly Changing AI Technologies and Regulations:**
   - The pace of technological advancements and the emergence of new regulations make it challenging for organizations to keep governance frameworks up to date. Static frameworks quickly become obsolete, leaving organizations vulnerable to non-compliance and reputational risks.

SOLUTIONS

1. **Building Cross-Functional Teams:**
   - Cross-functional collaboration ensures that governance frameworks are comprehensive and address diverse organizational needs. Organizations can create holistic frameworks and foster alignment by involving stakeholders from IT, legal, compliance, and business units.
2. **Leveraging Tools and Technology for Governance:**
   - Automated tools for compliance monitoring, risk assessment, and data analysis can streamline governance processes. These technologies enable real-time oversight, improving efficiency and reducing non-compliance risk.
3. **Iterative Framework Updates:**

- Adopting an iterative approach ensures that governance frameworks remain relevant and practical. Regular reviews and updates allow organizations to proactively adapt to technological advancements and regulatory changes.

Addressing these challenges with targeted solutions can help organizations overcome barriers to implementing robust AI governance frameworks. Building alignment, leveraging technology, and maintaining adaptability is key to fostering responsible and sustainable AI practices.

CHAPTER 6: ROLES AND RESPONSIBILITIES IN AI GOVERNANCE

6.1 INTRODUCTION TO STAKEHOLDER ROLES IN AI GOVERNANCE

AI governance is a multidisciplinary effort that requires the participation of diverse stakeholders. These stakeholders are pivotal in defining, implementing, and upholding frameworks that ensure AI systems' ethical, secure, and efficient deployment. Understanding the roles of key stakeholders is essential to building a governance structure that fosters accountability, collaboration, and execution.

The key stakeholders in AI governance span multiple domains, each contributing unique perspectives and expertise. Executive leaders, such as CEOs and board members, set the strategic vision and ensure alignment between governance objectives and organizational goals. Technical teams, including data scientists and machine learning engineers, focus on designing and maintaining AI systems that adhere to ethical principles like fairness and transparency. Legal and compliance experts are critical in navigating complex regulations and mitigating risks associated with AI adoption.

Clearly defining these roles is crucial for effective governance. Accountability ensures that responsibilities are well-distributed, minimizing overlaps or gaps in execution. Collaboration across teams fosters synergy, where diverse perspectives contribute to robust decision-making. A well-structured governance framework facilitates efficient execution, ensuring all efforts align with the organization's strategic objectives.

The diversity of stakeholders in AI governance adds depth and resilience to governance practices. From a technical perspective, teams bring expertise in algorithm design, model evaluation, and lifecycle management. Managerial perspectives focus on aligning AI initiatives with business goals and balancing innovation with risk. Legal professionals ensure compliance with global and regional regulations, address ethical concerns, and protect organizational interests.

This diversity enables organizations to address AI governance comprehensively, integrating technical precision with managerial oversight and legal safeguards. However, it also highlights the importance of fostering cross-functional collaboration. Stakeholders must work together to address the multifaceted challenges of AI governance, from ethical dilemmas to compliance complexities.

6.2 EXECUTIVE LEADERSHIP ROLES

Executive leadership is critical in shaping and sustaining AI governance within organizations. This involves setting the strategic vision, ensuring alignment across all levels, and fostering a culture of accountability, innovation, and ethical responsibility. Leadership teams—including CEOs, board members, CIOs, CTOs, and Chief Ethics or AI Officers—have distinct but interconnected responsibilities in implementing AI governance frameworks effectively.

Executive Leadership's Role in Shaping AI Governance Frameworks

CEOS AND BOARD MEMBERS

The CEO and board members are central to establishing an AI governance vision. Their role is to articulate a clear, strategic direction that aligns AI governance with the broader mission and values of the organization. This vision acts as a guiding framework for all subsequent policies, initiatives, and decisions related to AI deployment.

- **Setting the Governance Vision and Ensuring Organizational Alignment:** CEOs and board members are tasked with defining the organization's goals for AI governance. This includes outlining how AI should drive value while ensuring adherence to ethical standards, regulatory compliance, and risk mitigation. A well-defined governance vision ensures that all stakeholders understand their roles and responsibilities, enabling a unified approach to governance.

  Organizational alignment requires integrating AI governance into corporate strategy. This can be achieved by embedding governance principles into key performance indicators (KPIs), decision-making processes, and operational workflows. CEOs and boards must also champion transparency and accountability, creating an environment where governance is prioritized at all levels.

- **Balancing Innovation with Risk Management:** CEOs and boards face a significant challenge in balancing the drive for innovation with the need to manage risks associated with AI. While AI offers immense potential for growth and efficiency, it also introduces risks such as bias, privacy violations, and regulatory non-compliance. Effective leaders prioritize investments in governance tools, employee training, and ethical frameworks to address these risks proactively.

  Board members often oversee critically, ensuring that AI initiatives align with the organization's risk appetite. This involves conducting regular reviews of AI projects, monitoring compliance metrics, and fostering a culture of responsible innovation.

CIOS AND CTOS

Chief Information Officers (CIOs) and Chief Technology Officers (CTOs) are pivotal in AI governance's technical and infrastructural aspects. Their responsibilities include developing the technology strategy, overseeing infrastructure, and effectively implementing governance frameworks.

- **Overseeing Technology Strategy and Infrastructure for Governance:** CIOs and CTOs design and execute the technology roadmap for AI governance. This includes selecting and deploying tools for monitoring, auditing, and managing AI systems. Robust infrastructure enables real-time tracking of AI models and ensures compliance with ethical and regulatory standards.

  These leaders also evaluate emerging technologies and innovations that can enhance governance capabilities, such as using machine learning to automate bias detection or blockchain for secure data provenance.

- **Driving the Adoption of Governance Frameworks and Tools:** CIOs and CTOs are responsible for ensuring that governance frameworks and tools are adopted and integrated seamlessly into organizational workflows. This involves working closely with technical teams to implement systems for data security, model explainability, and performance monitoring.

  To drive adoption effectively, these leaders must foster a culture of collaboration between technical and non-technical teams. They provide training and resources to empower employees to effectively understand and implement governance practices. Additionally, they play a key role in facilitating cross-functional dialogue, ensuring that technical and business priorities are aligned.

CHIEF ETHICS OFFICERS AND CHIEF AI OFFICERS

Chief Ethics Officers and Chief AI Officers are increasingly essential in organizations adopting AI at scale. These leaders are tasked with embedding ethical principles into AI initiatives and ensuring that governance efforts are comprehensive and actionable.

- **Leading Ethical AI Initiatives and Ensuring Compliance with Regulations:** Chief Ethics Officers and Chief AI Officers develop ethical guidelines that govern AI design, deployment, and usage. These guidelines address fairness, transparency, accountability, and respect for user privacy. Establishing these principles provides a framework for teams to navigate ethical challenges in AI development.

  Compliance is another critical responsibility. These officers ensure that AI systems adhere to regional and global regulations, such as the EU's AI Act or the General Data Protection Regulation (GDPR). They also stay updated on regulatory changes and work with legal teams to adjust governance practices accordingly.

- **Creating Cross-Functional Alignment for Governance Efforts:** To ensure effective governance, Chief Ethics and AI Officers must bridge gaps between technical, managerial, and legal teams. This involves facilitating cross-functional discussions, aligning objectives, and fostering a shared understanding of governance priorities.

  For example, these leaders might organize workshops where data scientists, legal experts, and business managers collaborate to address bias mitigation or data security issues. By creating platforms for collaboration, they ensure that governance efforts are holistic and well-integrated.

INTEGRATIVE LEADERSHIP

While each executive role has distinct responsibilities, their collaboration is vital for the success of AI governance. CEOs and boards provide strategic oversight, CIOs and CTOs handle technical implementation, and Chief Ethics or AI Officers ensure ethical alignment and compliance. Together, these leaders form a cohesive governance structure that addresses the multifaceted challenges of AI adoption.

Moreover, executive leaders must cultivate a culture of ethical responsibility, innovation, and accountability. This involves promoting transparency, encouraging continuous learning, and investing in tools and frameworks that enhance governance capabilities. By fostering this culture, leaders mitigate risks and position their organizations as trustworthy and forward-thinking in the AI landscape.

In conclusion, executive leadership is the cornerstone of effective AI governance. Leaders ensure that AI systems deliver value responsibly and sustainably through strategic vision, technical expertise, and ethical stewardship. By working collaboratively, they create governance frameworks that are robust, adaptable, and aligned with the organization's goals.

6.3 TECHNICAL TEAMS AND AI PRACTITIONERS

Technical teams and AI practitioners are at the forefront of implementing AI governance frameworks. Their expertise ensures that AI systems are developed, deployed, and maintained consistently with ethical principles, regulatory requirements, and organizational objectives. Key contributors within this group include data scientists, machine learning engineers, IT teams, and AI model auditors, each playing a critical role in fostering ethical and responsible AI.

DATA SCIENTISTS AND MACHINE LEARNING ENGINEERS

Data scientists and machine learning engineers design, train, and optimize AI models. Their work directly impacts AI systems' fairness, transparency, and accountability, making their role pivotal in governance.

- **Ensuring Fairness, Transparency, and Accountability in Model Development:** Fairness in AI ensures that models do not exhibit bias or discriminatory behavior. Data scientists and engineers achieve this by carefully selecting training datasets, implementing fairness-aware algorithms, and conducting bias assessments. For instance, they can use techniques like reweighting datasets or adjusting algorithmic parameters to mitigate biases during model development.

  Transparency is another cornerstone of responsible AI. Practitioners document every stage of the AI lifecycle, from data preprocessing to model deployment. This includes maintaining comprehensive logs of data sources, feature selection, and hyperparameter tuning. Such documentation enables stakeholders to trace the origins and behavior of AI models, fostering trust and accountability.

  Accountability requires practitioners to anticipate and address potential risks associated with AI systems. This involves performing impact assessments to evaluate how AI outputs affect stakeholders and society. By incorporating mechanisms for human oversight, such as explainable AI techniques, they ensure that decision-makers can understand and intervene when necessary.

- **Implementing Technical Safeguards for Ethical AI:** Technical safeguards are essential for mitigating risks and ensuring compliance with governance principles. Data scientists and engineers implement safeguards such as differential privacy techniques to protect sensitive data and adversarial training methods to enhance model robustness. They also deploy monitoring systems that detect anomalies or deviations in AI behavior post-deployment.

  Moreover, practitioners contribute to developing ethical AI tools and frameworks, such as fairness assessment libraries (e.g., IBM's AI Fairness 360) and explainability toolkits (e.g., SHAP or LIME). These tools empower organizations to evaluate and improve the ethical dimensions of their AI systems.

IT TEAMS

IT teams provide the foundational infrastructure and operational support necessary for AI governance. Their responsibilities include securing data and infrastructure and supporting the lifecycle management of AI applications.

- **Securing Data and Infrastructure Used by AI Systems:** Data security is critical to AI governance. IT teams implement robust security protocols to safeguard data against unauthorized access, breaches, and corruption. These protocols include data encryption at rest and in transit, multi-factor authentication for access control, and regular vulnerability assessments.

  Infrastructure security is equally vital, as AI systems often rely on cloud platforms or distributed computing environments. IT teams ensure that these infrastructures comply with regulatory standards and organizational policies. They also monitor system performance and address threats like denial-of-service attacks or insider breaches.

- **Supporting Lifecycle Management for AI Applications:** AI applications undergo multiple stages, from development and testing to deployment and retirement. IT teams are crucial in managing this lifecycle, ensuring each stage aligns with governance principles. For instance, during deployment, they ensure that models are integrated seamlessly into production environments without compromising security or efficiency.

  After deployment, IT teams implement monitoring tools to track model performance and compliance. These tools provide real-time insights into accuracy, latency, and error rates. When models exhibit drift or degradation, IT teams collaborate with data scientists to retrain or update them, maintaining their reliability and relevance.

AI MODEL AUDITORS

AI model auditors are specialized professionals who evaluate AI systems to ensure compliance with governance standards and ethical guidelines. Their work provides an additional layer of accountability, addressing potential issues that may have been overlooked during development.

- **Conducting Regular Audits to Detect Biases, Compliance Issues, and Performance Deviations:** Regular audits are essential for identifying and mitigating biases in AI systems. Auditors analyze model outputs to detect patterns of unfair treatment or discrimination against specific groups. For example, auditors might evaluate whether certain demographic groups are disproportionately excluded from shortlists in a hiring algorithm.

  Compliance audits assess whether AI systems adhere to relevant regulations, such as GDPR, the AI Act, or industry-specific standards. This involves reviewing documentation, testing for adherence to data protection protocols, and verifying that models meet legal and ethical requirements.

  Performance audits ensure AI systems operate as intended and deliver accurate, reliable results. Auditors evaluate precision, recall, and F1 scores, identifying deviations that may compromise the system's effectiveness. They also assess robustness by subjecting models to stress tests or adversarial scenarios.

In addition to detecting issues, auditors provide actionable recommendations for improvement. These recommendations often include rebalancing datasets, adjusting model parameters, or enhancing documentation to address identified gaps.

COLLABORATION ACROSS TECHNICAL TEAMS

Effective AI governance requires collaboration between data scientists, IT teams, and auditors. Data scientists provide insights into model design and behavior, while IT teams ensure the necessary infrastructure is secure and compliant. Auditors bring an external perspective, identifying blind spots and reinforcing accountability.

For example, in addressing a biased hiring algorithm, data scientists might adjust training datasets, IT teams ensure that the updated model is securely deployed, and auditors validate that the changes meet fairness and compliance standards. This collaborative approach ensures that governance efforts are robust and comprehensive.

Technical teams and AI practitioners are indispensable to AI governance. Their expertise ensures that AI systems are fair, transparent, and accountable while safeguarding data and infrastructure. By fostering collaboration and adhering to governance principles, these teams contribute to developing ethical and sustainable AI solutions that align with organizational and societal values.

6.4 LEGAL, RISK, AND COMPLIANCE TEAMS

Legal, risk, and compliance teams are integral to AI governance. They ensure that AI systems are developed, deployed, and maintained within the boundaries of regulatory, ethical, and organizational standards. Their responsibilities span regulatory compliance and risk management to monitoring internal policies. Collectively, they create a robust framework for moral and lawful AI adoption.

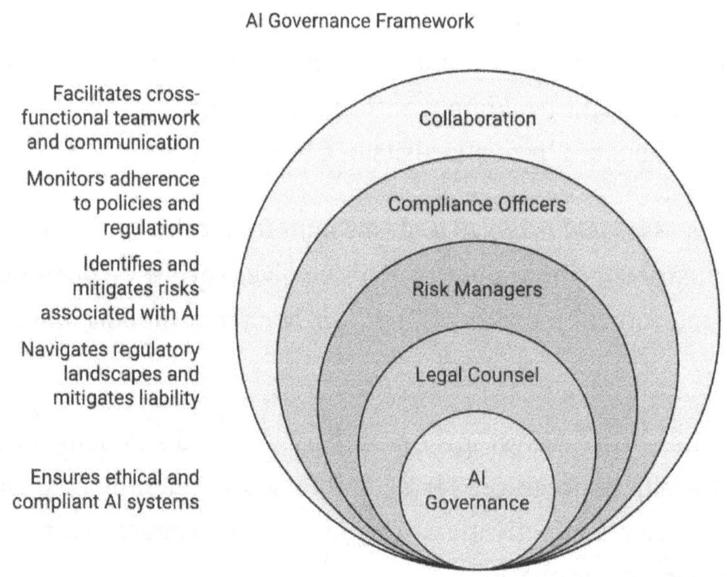

LEGAL COUNSEL

Legal counsel is pivotal in navigating the complex and evolving regulatory landscape surrounding AI. Their expertise ensures that AI systems comply with regional and global regulations while mitigating liability risks associated with their deployment.

- **Ensuring Compliance with Regional and Global Regulations (e.g., GDPR, AI Act):**

  AI systems operate across multiple jurisdictions, each with its own regulations. Legal teams are responsible for interpreting and implementing these laws, such as the General Data Protection Regulation (GDPR) in the European Union or the proposed AI Act. These regulations often cover critical areas like data privacy, transparency, and accountability.

  For instance, GDPR mandates that organizations obtain user consent for data usage and provide mechanisms for individuals to access, rectify, or delete their data. Legal teams ensure that AI systems incorporate these requirements, such as designing data handling workflows that align with privacy-by-design principles.

  The EU's AI Act, on the other hand, classifies AI systems based on risk levels and imposes stricter requirements on high-risk applications. Legal counsel ensures that these high-risk systems meet documentation, explainability, and impact assessment standards, minimizing non-compliance risk.

- **Managing Liability Risks Associated with AI Deployments:**

  Legal teams assess potential liability risks from AI systems, such as errors, biases, or misuse. For example, if an AI-driven hiring system inadvertently discriminates against a protected demographic group, the organization could face legal action or reputational damage.

  Legal counsel works closely with technical and risk management teams to mitigate these risks and establish safeguards, such as rigorous testing, auditing, and documentation processes. They also draft contracts, disclaimers, and terms of service that clearly outline responsibilities and limitations, protecting the organization from undue liabilities.

RISK MANAGERS

Risk managers identify, evaluate, and mitigate risks associated with AI systems. Their work ensures that potential threats are proactively addressed, reducing the likelihood of adverse outcomes.

- **Assessing Potential Risks from AI Systems and Designing Mitigation Strategies:**

  AI systems can introduce a range of risks, including operational, reputational, financial, and ethical risks. For example, an AI model used in credit scoring might inadvertently amplify biases in lending decisions, exposing the organization to regulatory scrutiny and customer backlash.

Risk managers use structured frameworks, such as risk matrices and scenario analysis, to evaluate the likelihood and impact of potential issues. This includes examining data quality, model robustness, and ethical implications. They also consider external risks, such as regulation changes or public sentiment.

Mitigation strategies often involve a combination of technical and organizational measures. For instance, risk managers might recommend implementing bias detection tools, conducting regular audits, or establishing human-in-the-loop mechanisms to oversee AI decisions. These strategies ensure that AI systems align with organizational values and regulatory standards.

Additionally, risk managers collaborate with technical teams to address model vulnerabilities, such as susceptibility to adversarial attacks. By proactively identifying and mitigating risks, they enhance the resilience and reliability of AI systems.

COMPLIANCE OFFICERS

Compliance officers ensure that AI systems adhere to internal policies and external regulations. Their work involves monitoring, reporting, and facilitating continuous improvement to maintain alignment with governance frameworks.

- **Monitoring Adherence to Internal Policies and External Regulations:**

  Compliance officers establish processes to track adherence to governance standards, including ethical guidelines, data handling policies, and regulatory requirements. For instance, they might monitor whether AI models are trained on appropriately sourced data or whether privacy measures are consistently applied.

  Regular audits are a key component of their role. These audits assess compliance across various dimensions, such as fairness, transparency, and accountability. Compliance officers use the findings to identify gaps and recommend corrective actions, such as retraining models or updating documentation.

  They also maintain detailed records of compliance activities, which serve as evidence during regulatory inspections or legal proceedings. This documentation demonstrates the organization's commitment to responsible AI practices and helps mitigate potential penalties or liabilities.

- **Facilitating Continuous Improvement:**

  Compliance officers play a proactive role in enhancing governance processes. They stay informed about emerging regulations, industry standards, and best practices, ensuring the organization's policies remain current. For example, compliance officers work with legal and technical teams to adapt existing frameworks as AI-specific regulations evolve.

Training and education are also vital aspects of their role. Compliance officers organize workshops and training sessions to educate employees about governance requirements and ethical considerations. This ensures that all stakeholders are equipped to contribute to compliance efforts.

COLLABORATION BETWEEN TEAMS

Legal, risk, and compliance teams must work closely with technical and executive teams to create an integrated governance framework. For example, legal counsel and compliance officers may collaborate with data scientists to ensure that AI models meet transparency requirements. Similarly, risk managers might work with IT teams to address cybersecurity risks associated with AI systems.

Regular communication and cross-functional workshops facilitate this collaboration, enabling teams to align on priorities and share insights. By leveraging their collective expertise, these teams can navigate the complexities of AI governance effectively.

Legal, risk, and compliance teams are essential pillars of AI governance. Their expertise ensures that AI systems comply with regulations, mitigate risks, and adhere to organizational policies. By working collaboratively and adopting proactive strategies, these teams contribute to developing ethical, resilient, and trustworthy AI systems that align with organizational objectives and societal expectations.

6.5 CROSS-FUNCTIONAL COLLABORATION

Cross-functional collaboration is a cornerstone of effective AI governance. It bridges the gaps between technical, legal, and executive teams, fostering a holistic approach to navigating the complexities of AI deployment. By bringing together diverse expertise, organizations can address the multifaceted challenges of AI governance, from ensuring compliance to driving innovation ethically.

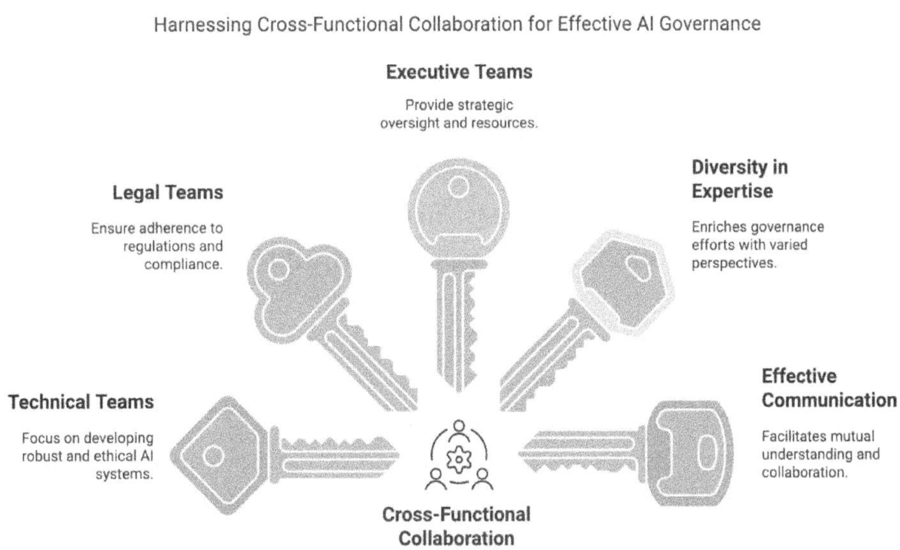

- **Importance of Collaboration Between Technical, Legal, and Executive Teams:**

  Collaboration across departments is essential because AI governance emphasizes technical innovation, legal compliance, and strategic decision-making. Technical teams focus on developing robust and ethical AI systems, legal teams ensure adherence to regulations, and executives provide strategic oversight and resources.

  A siloed approach to governance risks overlooking critical issues. For instance, a technically sound AI system might violate privacy laws without considering legal perspectives. Similarly, governance initiatives driven solely by legal or executive teams may lack the technical feasibility required for implementation. By working together, these teams ensure that AI systems are compliant, ethical, practical, and aligned with organizational goals.

  Effective collaboration requires clear communication and mutual understanding. Technical teams must translate complex concepts like algorithmic bias or model explainability into actionable insights for legal and executive stakeholders. Conversely, legal and executive teams must communicate priorities, such as regulatory deadlines or business objectives, to inform technical development.

- **Leveraging Diversity in Expertise for Holistic Governance:**

  The diversity of perspectives within cross-functional teams enriches governance efforts. Technical experts bring insights into AI systems' capabilities and limitations, legal professionals provide knowledge of compliance requirements, and executives contribute strategic vision. This diversity ensures that governance frameworks are comprehensive and adaptable.

  For example, to address bias in AI models, data scientists might propose technical solutions, such as reweighting datasets or implementing fairness-aware algorithms. Legal experts could evaluate whether these solutions comply with anti-discrimination laws, while executives assess the business implications, such as customer trust and brand reputation.

  A key factor in leveraging diversity is fostering an inclusive culture where all voices are valued. Cross-functional teams should encourage open dialogue and empower team members to challenge assumptions and contribute ideas. Structured processes like regular governance meetings or collaborative workshops can facilitate this culture.

CASE STUDIES

- **Example 1: Successful Cross-Functional Governance Implementation in a Multinational Corporation:**

  A global financial services company faced challenges in implementing AI governance due to the scale and complexity of its operations. Recognizing the need for collaboration, the organization established a cross-functional AI governance committee comprising data scientists, compliance officers, and senior executives.

This committee worked together to develop a comprehensive governance framework. Technical teams designed tools for monitoring algorithmic performance and detecting bias, while legal teams ensured these tools complied with regulations such as GDPR. Executives provided the necessary resources and aligned the governance strategy with corporate goals.

One key success factor was the use of collaborative workshops. These workshops enabled stakeholders to share insights and align on priorities. For example, during one session, data scientists demonstrated the limitations of specific models, prompting legal teams to adjust compliance strategies accordingly. This iterative approach ensured that the framework was both robust and practical.

The result was a governance system that enhanced transparency and accountability, positioning the company as a leader in ethical AI. Additionally, the collaborative process strengthened relationships between departments, fostering a culture of trust and mutual respect.

- Example 2: Challenges and Solutions in Establishing Cross-Functional Teams for SMEs:

Due to limited resources and expertise, small and medium-sized enterprises (SMEs) often face unique challenges in building cross-functional teams. A mid-sized e-commerce company, for instance, struggled to implement AI governance because its technical and legal teams operated in isolation, and executives lacked a clear understanding of AI risks.

To address this, the company adopted a phased approach to collaboration. The first step was to conduct training sessions for executives, helping them understand key AI concepts and governance principles. This empowered them to participate more effectively in governance discussions.

Next, the company established a small, dedicated governance task force comprising technical, legal, and executive team representatives. This task force met regularly to identify governance priorities and allocate responsibilities. To compensate for limited in-house expertise, the company partnered with external consultants who guided best practices and regulatory compliance.

One significant challenge was aligning priorities across departments. For example, technical teams initially resisted compliance measures they perceived as overly restrictive. To resolve this, the task force organized joint problem-solving sessions, where team members collaboratively explored solutions that balanced technical feasibility with legal requirements.

The task force's efforts led to measurable improvements over time. The company implemented bias detection tools, updated its data handling policies, and developed a roadmap for continuous governance improvement. While resource constraints remained challenging, the phased approach allowed the company to progress steadily.

KEY TAKEAWAYS

Cross-functional collaboration is essential for effective AI governance. By integrating diverse expertise, organizations can address governance challenges holistically, ensuring that AI systems are ethical, compliant, and aligned with business objectives. The examples of a multinational corporation and an SME highlight both the benefits and challenges of collaboration, demonstrating that success requires clear communication, mutual understanding, and a commitment to shared goals.

To build effective teams, organizations should:

- Foster a culture of inclusivity and open dialogue.
- Invest in training to bridge knowledge gaps between teams.
- Use structured processes like workshops or task forces to facilitate collaboration.

By prioritizing collaboration, organizations can create governance frameworks that are robust and adaptable to AI's evolving landscape.

6.6 DIVERSITY AND INCLUSION IN GOVERNANCE TEAMS

Diversity and inclusion are essential components of effective AI governance. AI systems' complexity and societal impact demand a broad range of perspectives and experiences to ensure that these technologies are developed and deployed responsibly. Governance teams that embrace diversity are better equipped to address challenges such as bias, inequity, and unintended consequences while fostering innovation and public trust.

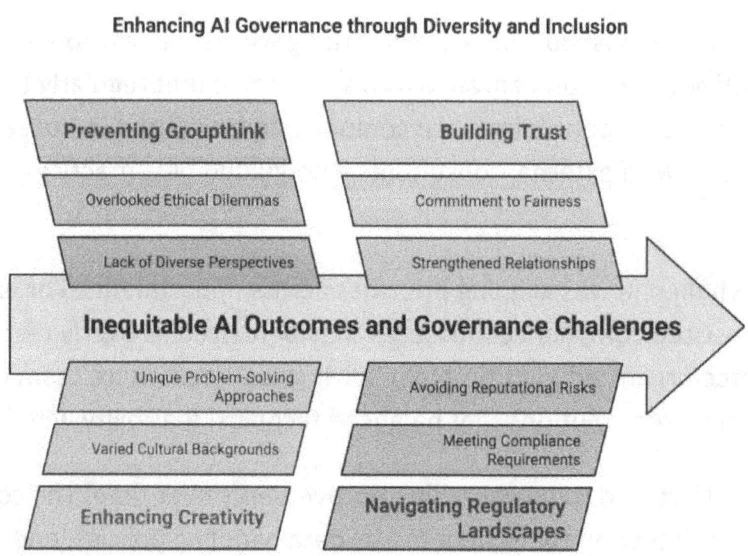

Importance of Diversity

- **Preventing Groupthink and Ensuring Equitable AI Outcomes:**

  Groupthink occurs when a homogenous team converges on a single viewpoint without critically evaluating alternatives. This phenomenon can lead to blind spots in AI governance, where potential risks or ethical dilemmas are overlooked. For example, lacking diverse perspectives might result in AI systems that unintentionally disadvantage underrepresented groups.

  By incorporating diverse viewpoints, governance teams can challenge assumptions and identify potential biases in AI systems. For instance, a diverse team might highlight how a recruitment algorithm disproportionately favors certain demographic groups, prompting corrective actions. This critical examination ensures that AI outcomes are fair and equitable and reflect societal values.

  Furthermore, diversity in governance teams enhances creativity and problem-solving. Teams with varied cultural, professional, and educational backgrounds bring unique approaches to tackling complex issues. This richness of perspectives fosters innovative solutions that align with organizational goals and ethical standards.

  In addition to internal benefits, diverse governance teams build trust with external stakeholders. Organizations prioritizing diversity signal a commitment to fairness and inclusivity, which can enhance their reputation and strengthen relationships with customers, regulators, and the public.

Strategies to Promote Inclusion

- **Recruiting Diverse Talent for Governance Teams:**

  Building diverse governance teams begins with intentional recruitment strategies. Organizations should seek candidates from various backgrounds, including underrepresented groups, to ensure diverse perspectives. This includes diversity in terms of gender, race, ethnicity, socioeconomic status, professional expertise, and geographic representation.

  To attract diverse talent, organizations can partner with universities, community organizations, and professional networks that focus on diversity and inclusion. Internship and mentorship programs targeting underrepresented groups can also create pipelines for future governance leaders.

  During the hiring process, organizations should evaluate candidates for their technical or legal expertise and their ability to contribute unique perspectives. Structured interviews and diverse hiring panels can help mitigate unconscious bias, ensuring a fair and equitable selection process.

- **Creating Inclusive Policies and Practices for AI Development and Deployment:**

  Inclusion goes beyond recruitment—it requires fostering an environment where all team members feel valued and empowered to contribute. Inclusive policies and practices are essential for enabling meaningful participation in governance efforts.

  One effective strategy is establishing clear decision-making guidelines that prioritize equity and inclusion. For example, governance frameworks can require teams to evaluate the potential impact of AI systems on diverse user groups. Tools such as impact assessments and fairness audits can help teams identify and address disparities during development.

  Organizations should also promote transparency and accountability in AI governance. Inclusive practices, such as publishing governance principles and engaging with external stakeholders, demonstrate a commitment to ethical AI. Open dialogue with affected communities ensures that their concerns and perspectives are considered in governance decisions.

  Training and education are critical for fostering inclusion within governance teams. Workshops on unconscious bias, cultural competence, and inclusive leadership can help team members understand and address systemic inequities. Additionally, providing resources on ethical AI principles ensures that all team members are equipped to navigate complex governance challenges.

  Technology itself can promote inclusion. For example, organizations can use AI-driven tools to analyze the inclusivity of governance processes, such as evaluating the representation of diverse voices in decision-making. These insights can inform continuous improvement efforts.

Case Examples of Diversity and Inclusion in AI Governance

- **Case Study: Promoting Diversity in Algorithm Design:** A global healthcare company was criticized for its algorithm, prioritizing certain patients over others based on flawed metrics. The company formed a diverse governance team comprising medical experts, data scientists, ethicists, and patient advocates to address this. This team thoroughly reviewed the algorithm, identifying biases and recommending adjustments to improve fairness. The outcome was an updated system that better reflected the needs of all patient groups, enhancing both equity and public trust.

- **Case Study: Inclusive Development in a Tech Startup:** Early in its journey, a small AI startup recognized the need for diversity. By prioritizing inclusive hiring practices and engaging with diverse user groups, the company developed a language model tailored to underserved communities. The governance team's inclusive approach ensured the product was accessible and culturally relevant, differentiating the startup in a competitive market.

Benefits of Diversity and Inclusion

Organizations that prioritize diversity and inclusion in governance teams reap numerous benefits. Diverse perspectives enhance risk identification and mitigation while fostering innovation and creativity. Inclusive practices build trust with stakeholders and ensure that AI systems align with societal values.

Moreover, diverse governance teams are better equipped to navigate the evolving regulatory landscape. As governments and international bodies emphasize the importance of ethical AI, organizations with inclusive governance frameworks are more likely to meet compliance requirements and avoid reputational risks.

Conclusion

Diversity and inclusion are not just ethical imperatives but strategic advantages in AI governance. By preventing groupthink, fostering innovation, and ensuring equitable outcomes, diverse teams contribute to developing responsible and trustworthy AI systems. Organizations must take deliberate steps to recruit diverse talent, create inclusive policies, and empower all team members to contribute meaningfully. Through these efforts, governance teams can build AI systems that reflect the values and needs of a diverse society, driving both ethical and organizational success.

CHAPTER 7: GETTING STARTED WITH AI GOVERNANCE

7.1 UNDERSTANDING YOUR ORGANIZATION'S GOVERNANCE NEEDS

AI governance is critical in ensuring artificial intelligence's responsible, efficient, and ethical use. A strong foundation begins with understanding your organization's unique governance requirements, driven by an assessment of current capabilities and alignment with contextual factors like industry, size, and strategic goals.

ASSESSING CURRENT AI CAPABILITIES

Conducting an Internal Audit of AI Systems and Workflows

The first step in crafting effective AI governance is thoroughly auditing existing AI systems and workflows. This assessment identifies the scope of AI implementation across the organization, evaluates the current state of AI tools, and highlights their strengths and weaknesses. Key areas to focus on include:

1. **System Inventory:** Document all AI systems in use, including those actively running and those in development. This includes off-the-shelf solutions, proprietary platforms, and vendor partnerships.

2. **Workflow Analysis:** Map out AI integration into existing processes, from data input and model training to deployment and output utilization. Evaluate the efficiency and effectiveness of these workflows.

3. **Performance Metrics:** Analyze system performance in accuracy, speed, and scalability. Consider factors like model drift and outdated data pipelines to identify discrepancies between expected outcomes and actual results.

4. **Stakeholder Input:** Engage teams who use or manage AI tools to understand their experiences, challenges, and ideas for improvement. These insights are valuable for shaping governance frameworks that meet real-world needs.

Identifying Governance Gaps and Areas for Improvement

After completing the internal audit, focus on uncovering governance gaps. Typical areas include:

- **Ethical Oversight:** Are ethical concerns like bias, discrimination, or unintended consequences addressed?

- **Regulatory Compliance:** Does the organization meet relevant laws, regulations, and standards for AI usage?

- **Accountability Structures:** Are clear responsibilities assigned for AI-related decisions and system oversight?
- **Data Practices:** Is data used in compliance with privacy standards, and are mechanisms in place to ensure data quality and security?

For instance, an audit might reveal an overreliance on opaque AI models (black boxes) in critical decision-making areas, necessitating a shift toward explainable AI solutions. Another standard gap might be a monitoring framework to track ongoing model performance and compliance.

ORGANIZATIONAL CONTEXT

Tailoring Governance Strategies Based on Organizational Size, Industry, and Objectives

AI governance must be adaptable to the specific context of the organization. Factors like size, industry, and strategic objectives influence the design of governance frameworks. For example:

- **Small-to-Medium Enterprises (SMEs):** These organizations often lack extensive resources, making lightweight governance frameworks ideal. The focus is on scalable, low-cost tools and processes that address critical risks without overburdening the organization.
- **Large Enterprises:** Larger organizations require more comprehensive frameworks due to their diverse operations and greater risk exposure. These frameworks typically include dedicated governance teams, detailed policies, and advanced monitoring tools.
- **Public Sector Organizations:** Governance strategies here prioritize transparency, fairness, and compliance with public accountability standards.

Examples: Governance in Healthcare, Retail, and Finance

The governance needs of organizations also vary based on industry dynamics:

1. **Healthcare:**
   AI in healthcare often deals with sensitive patient data, making privacy and compliance with regulations like HIPAA critical. Governance strategies should emphasize robust data anonymization techniques, traceability in decision-making, and thorough validation of AI models to ensure patient safety.

2. **Retail:**
   For retail organizations leveraging AI for personalized marketing and inventory optimization, governance should focus on the ethical use of customer data, ensuring transparency in targeted advertisements, and preventing algorithmic bias in pricing or promotions.

3. **Finance:**
   The finance sector is heavily regulated, necessitating stringent compliance frameworks. AI governance in this context should include regular audits of algorithmic decision-making,

safeguards against discriminatory practices, and mechanisms to ensure financial stability during system disruptions.

Balancing Governance with Business Objectives

Effective governance frameworks strike a balance between control and innovation. Over-regulation can stifle creativity and slow progress, while under-regulation increases risks. Tailoring governance to align with business goals ensures that AI systems remain valuable drivers of growth and transformation.

By understanding and addressing their organization's specific needs, leaders can build governance frameworks that are effective and sustainable. Assessing current AI capabilities and tailoring strategies based on context ensures that governance efforts support ethical AI deployment and strategic innovation.

7.2 DEFINING AI GOVERNANCE OBJECTIVES

Defining clear AI governance objectives is the cornerstone of creating a robust and practical framework for managing AI systems. These objectives are guiding principles to ensure that AI initiatives align with organizational goals while adhering to ethical, legal, and operational standards. Properly defined objectives help balance innovation, compliance, and risk management, enabling organizations to harness AI's potential responsibly.

Setting Clear Goals

Balancing Innovation, Compliance, and Risk Management

Achieving the right balance between innovation, compliance, and risk management is critical to defining governance objectives. This balance ensures that organizations can pursue ambitious AI-driven initiatives without compromising ethical standards or exposing themselves to unnecessary risks.

- **Fostering Innovation:** Governance frameworks should encourage experimentation and adoption of AI technologies while providing guidelines to mitigate potential adverse outcomes. For instance, policies can outline permissible use cases, acceptable error margins, and pathways for iterative development to improve AI solutions.
- **Ensuring Compliance:** Governance objectives must address adherence to local and international regulations, industry standards, and ethical guidelines. This includes compliance with data protection laws like GDPR or HIPAA and industry-specific standards like ISO/IEC 38507 for AI governance.
- **Mitigating Risks:** Governance should proactively identify and address risks, including algorithmic bias, security vulnerabilities, and the unintended consequences of AI decisions. Setting clear objectives involves establishing safeguards such as regular audits, bias detection tools, and robust incident response mechanisms.

Aligning Governance Goals with Business Strategy
Governance objectives must be deeply aligned with the organization's overarching business strategy. For example:

- **Revenue Growth:** For companies leveraging AI to enhance revenue, governance objectives include ensuring accuracy in predictive models for customer targeting or sales forecasting.
- **Operational Efficiency:** Organizations focusing on streamlining operations can set objectives related to the transparency and reliability of automation tools used in workflows.
- **Brand Reputation:** Governance frameworks should include ethical commitments to maintain public trust and avoid reputational damage, such as ensuring AI transparency in customer interactions or decision-making.

By aligning AI governance goals with strategic priorities, organizations ensure that governance becomes an enabler of growth and innovation rather than a constraint.

Key Metrics for Success

Defining Measurable Outcomes
Practical governance objectives are supported by clear, quantifiable metrics to track progress and success. These metrics provide a transparent view of how well governance efforts meet organizational goals. Examples include:

1. **Compliance Rates:** Measure the percentage of AI systems that meet regulatory and organizational standards. High compliance rates indicate effective integration of governance policies.
2. **Reduced Bias:** Track reductions in discriminatory outcomes from AI models. This can involve metrics like error rates across demographic groups or fairness indices.
3. **Operational Metrics:** Monitor the efficiency and effectiveness of AI systems in achieving intended outcomes, such as processing times or accuracy rates.
4. **Incident Tracking:** Maintain a record of governance-related incidents, such as breaches, ethical violations, or performance issues, to identify trends and areas for improvement.
5. **Employee and Customer Feedback:** To complement quantitative data, gather qualitative insights on AI systems' perceived impact and reliability.

By setting clear goals and defining key metrics for success, organizations can develop an AI governance framework that meets compliance requirements, drives innovation, and aligns with strategic objectives. These steps ensure AI technologies remain valuable while addressing the ethical and operational challenges associated with their use.

7.3 BUILDING A GOVERNANCE ROADMAP

A governance roadmap is essential for systematically implementing AI governance frameworks in an organization. This roadmap provides a clear, actionable plan that aligns governance initiatives with organizational goals while addressing immediate challenges and preparing for long-term sustainability. Building such a roadmap involves a step-by-step process and practical tools to ensure successful implementation.

STEP-BY-STEP PROCESS

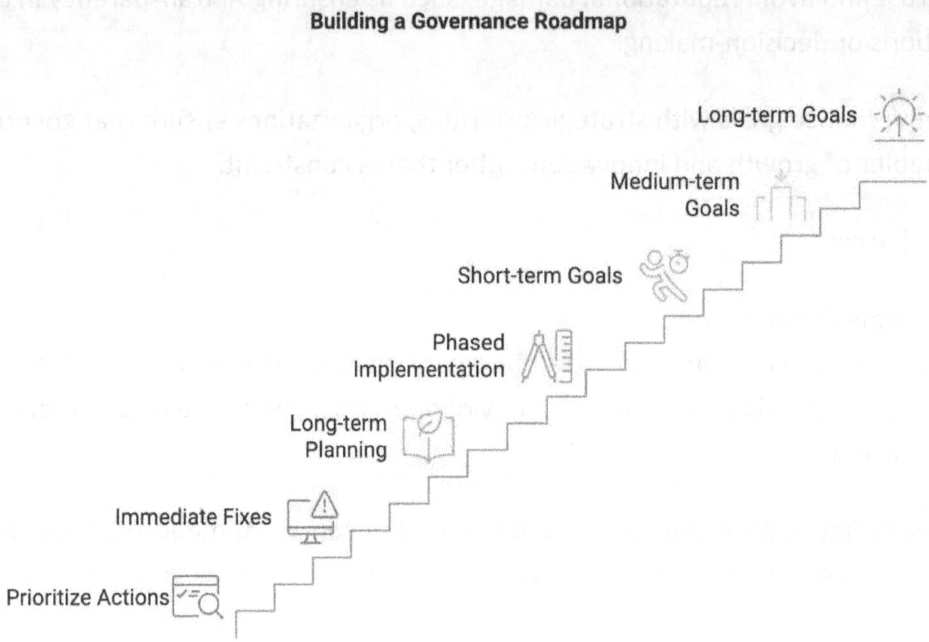

1. Prioritizing Actions: Immediate Fixes vs. Long-term Planning

Identifying and prioritizing actions is one of the first steps in creating a governance roadmap. Not all governance issues require immediate attention; some can be addressed over time. The process includes:

- **Immediate Fixes:**
  These critical issues need urgent resolution to mitigate risks or meet compliance requirements. Examples include:
  - Addressing data privacy violations or gaps in compliance with regulations like GDPR or HIPAA.
  - Fixing critical vulnerabilities in AI systems that could lead to biased outcomes or operational failures.
  - Establishing minimum baseline policies for ethical AI usage.

- **Long-term Planning:**
  Long-term goals focus on building sustainable governance practices that evolve with organizational growth and technological advancements. These may include:
  - Developing a comprehensive AI ethics framework.
  - Investing in advanced monitoring tools for ongoing model evaluation.
  - Establishing governance training programs for employees.

Organizations can allocate resources effectively and mitigate immediate threats without neglecting strategic objectives by categorizing issues based on urgency and impact.

2. Creating a Phased Implementation Plan

A phased approach divides the governance roadmap into short-term, medium-term, and long-term goals, ensuring manageable progress and measurable outcomes.

- **Short-term Goals (0–6 months):**
  Focus on quick wins that address pressing issues and lay the foundation for governance. Examples:
  - Conducting a baseline audit of AI systems and workflows.
  - Drafting an AI governance policy document that outlines ethical principles and compliance requirements.
  - Appointing a governance team or AI ethics officer.
- **Medium-term Goals (6–18 months):**
  Build upon the foundation by expanding governance practices and addressing more complex challenges. Examples:
  - Establishing regular audit cycles and reporting mechanisms.
  - Implementing tools for bias detection and model performance monitoring.
  - Creating stakeholder engagement forums for governance feedback and alignment.
- **Long-term Goals (18+ months):**
  Focus on institutionalizing governance practices and ensuring adaptability to future needs. Examples:
  - Building a culture of governance awareness across the organization through training and workshops.

- Developing AI-specific governance frameworks tailored to emerging technologies or industry shifts.
- Collaborating with external partners to align governance efforts with broader industry standards.

ROADMAP TOOLS

1. Templates for Planning and Monitoring Governance Initiatives

Using templates ensures consistency and clarity in governance planning. These tools provide a structured way to define goals, allocate resources, and monitor progress. Examples include:

- **Governance Policy Template:** A standardized document outlining ethical guidelines, compliance requirements, and governance objectives.
- **Risk Assessment Template:** A framework for identifying, categorizing, and addressing risks associated with AI systems.
- **Audit Checklist:** A detailed list of criteria for evaluating AI models, data practices, and system workflows during audits.
- **Implementation Tracker:** A project management tool to track the status of governance initiatives, including milestones, deadlines, and assigned responsibilities.

These templates can be customized to suit organizational needs and industry-specific requirements, streamlining the governance process.

2. Practical Timelines for Implementation

Defining realistic timelines for governance initiatives is crucial to ensure that objectives are met without overburdening resources. Practical timelines include:

- **Milestone Planning:** Divide the roadmap into milestones, such as completing an initial audit, deploying monitoring tools, or achieving compliance certification.
- **Progress Reviews:** Schedule periodic reviews to evaluate progress and adjust timelines as needed. For example, quarterly reviews can help identify delays or unexpected challenges.
- **Integration with Business Cycles:** Align governance initiatives with organizational schedules, such as fiscal planning or product development cycles, to ensure seamless implementation.

Visualization Tools for Timelines:

Visual tools, such as Gantt charts or dashboards, can display timelines and monitor progress at a glance. These tools help stakeholders understand the roadmap and facilitate coordination across teams.

BENEFITS OF A GOVERNANCE ROADMAP

A well-structured governance roadmap offers several benefits:

1. **Clarity and Focus:**
   Clearly defined steps and goals provide a roadmap for governance initiatives, helping stakeholders understand their roles and responsibilities.

2. **Risk Mitigation:**
   Prioritizing immediate fixes reduces the likelihood of significant governance failures, such as regulatory violations or reputational damage.

3. **Sustainability:**
   A phased approach ensures that governance practices evolve with the organization, accommodating new technologies and market changes.

4. **Stakeholder Engagement:**
   Regular progress updates and stakeholder input foster alignment and support for governance initiatives.

5. **Scalability:**
   Templates and tools make it easier to scale governance practices as the organization grows or adopts new AI technologies.

Building a governance roadmap is a dynamic process that requires continuous refinement and stakeholder collaboration. By prioritizing actions, creating phased plans, and leveraging practical tools, organizations can implement governance frameworks that address immediate needs and prepare them for long-term success in the rapidly evolving landscape of AI.

7.4 CONDUCTING AN AI GOVERNANCE AUDIT

An AI governance audit ensures that AI systems are ethical, compliant, and aligned with organizational objectives. It provides a structured way to evaluate the effectiveness of AI policies, procedures, and systems while identifying risks and areas of non-compliance. Organizations can uncover weaknesses and implement corrective actions to strengthen their governance frameworks by following a straightforward process and leveraging practical tools.

Audit Objectives

Ensuring Ethical and Compliant AI Through Comprehensive Audits

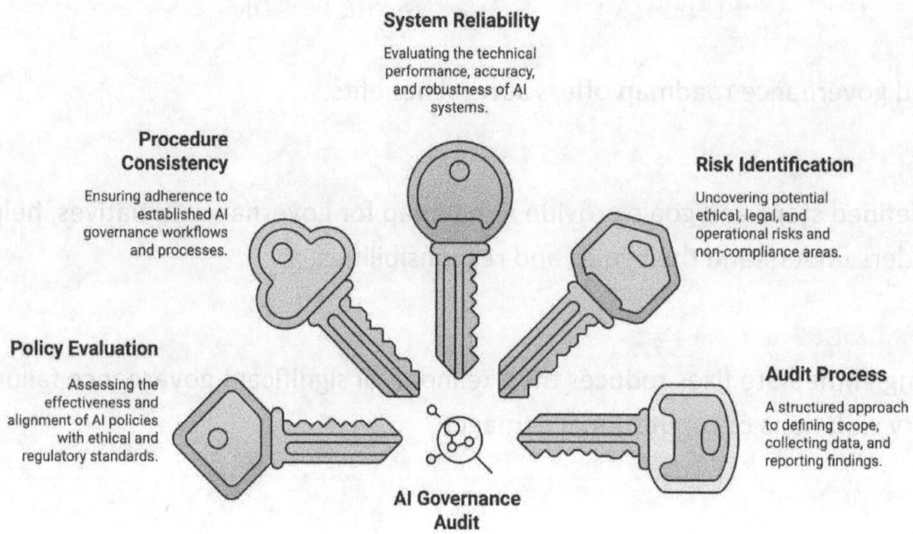

1. Evaluating Existing AI Policies, Procedures, and Systems

The first objective of an AI governance audit is to assess the current state of governance structures. This involves reviewing policies, procedures, and the technical systems that underpin AI operations. Specific evaluation areas include:

- **Policy Effectiveness:** Determine whether existing governance policies align with ethical guidelines, regulatory standards, and organizational goals. For example, policies on data privacy, fairness, and accountability should reflect best practices and legal requirements.

- **Procedure Consistency:** Examine whether AI workflows adhere to established governance procedures. This includes data collection, preprocessing, model training, validation, and deployment processes.

- **System Reliability:** Evaluate the technical performance of AI systems, focusing on their accuracy, robustness, and scalability. This includes identifying potential biases, assessing explainability, and ensuring systems function as intended.

2. Identifying Risks and Non-compliance Areas

The second objective is to uncover risks and instances of non-compliance that may pose ethical, legal, or operational challenges. These include:

- **Regulatory Non-compliance:** Determine whether AI systems meet relevant laws and standards, such as GDPR, HIPAA, or industry-specific regulations.

- **Ethical Risks:** Identify issues like algorithmic bias, lack of transparency, and misuse of AI outputs that could harm stakeholders or damage organizational reputation.

- **Operational Risks:** Highlight vulnerabilities in data quality, model security, and system monitoring that could disrupt operations or lead to inaccurate results.

Identifying these risks allows organizations to take targeted action to mitigate them, ensuring their AI systems operate responsibly and effectively.

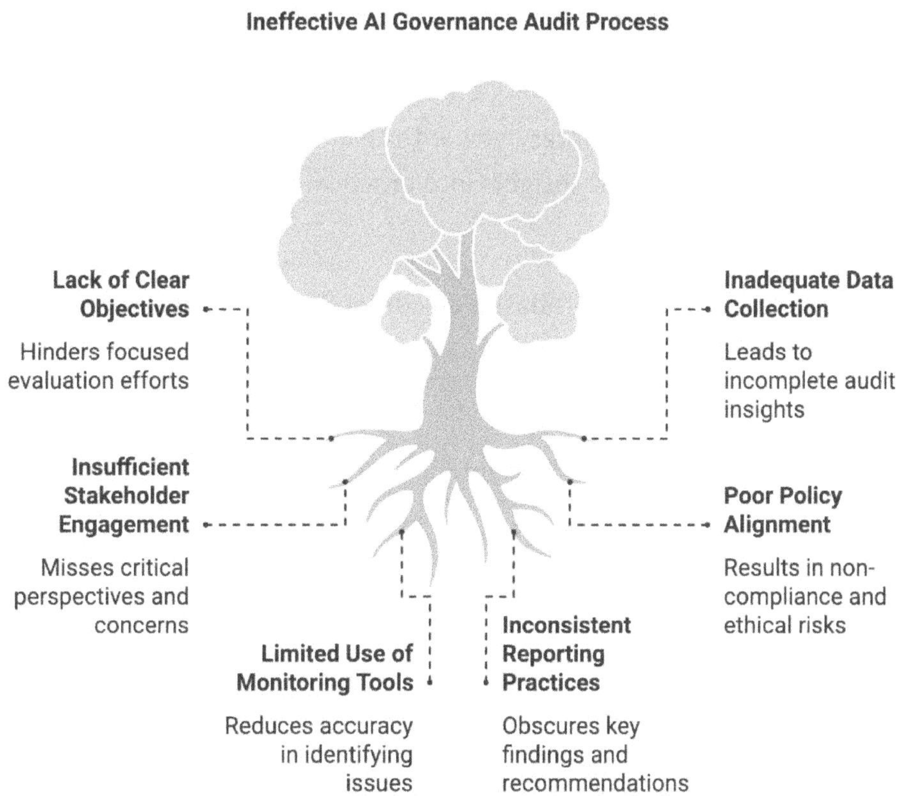

Audit Process

1. Defining Scope

A successful audit begins with a clear definition of its scope. This step involves:

- **Identifying Objectives:** Specify what the audit aims to achieve, such as evaluating compliance with specific regulations, assessing ethical practices, or improving operational efficiency.

- **Determining Boundaries:** Define which AI systems, processes, and teams will be included in the audit. For example, the audit might focus on customer-facing applications, decision-making algorithms, or all AI systems across the organization.

- **Engaging Stakeholders:** Involve relevant stakeholders, such as data scientists, compliance officers, and business leaders, to ensure the audit addresses key concerns and priorities.

2. Collecting Data

Data collection is a critical phase of the audit process. This step involves gathering quantitative and qualitative information to evaluate AI governance practices:

- **Policy and Procedure Documents:** Review governance policies, standard operating procedures (SOPs), and training materials to assess their adequacy and alignment with best practices.

- **System Logs and Outputs:** Analyze data logs, system outputs, and model performance metrics to identify deviations from expected behavior.

- **Stakeholder Interviews:** Conduct interviews with teams involved in AI development, deployment, and oversight to gain insights into practical challenges and areas for improvement.

Effective data collection ensures the audit is based on comprehensive and accurate information, enabling actionable recommendations.

3. Reporting Findings

The final audit process step is compiling findings into a clear and actionable report. This involves:

- **Identifying Key Issues:** Highlight areas of non-compliance, ethical concerns, and operational weaknesses uncovered during the audit.

- **Providing Recommendations:** Offer targeted suggestions for addressing identified issues, such as revising policies, retraining models, or implementing new monitoring tools.

- **Prioritizing Actions:** Rank recommendations by urgency and impact, enabling the organization to focus on critical issues first.

The audit report is a roadmap for enhancing governance practices, helping organizations address vulnerabilities, and aligning their AI systems with best practices.

Tools and Techniques for Effective Audits

1. Compliance Checklists

A compliance checklist is essential for evaluating whether AI systems adhere to relevant regulations and standards. Everyday checklist items include:

- Adherence to data protection laws (e.g., GDPR, HIPAA).

- Implementation of bias detection and mitigation measures.

- Documentation of model training processes and decision-making logic.

- Existence of clear accountability structures for AI oversight.

Checklists provide a structured framework for identifying gaps and ensuring thorough evaluations.

2. Automated Monitoring Tools

Automated tools can enhance audit efficiency and accuracy by analyzing large volumes of data and system logs. Examples include:

- **Bias Detection Tools:** Software that identifies and measures algorithmic bias across demographic groups.
- **Explainability Tools:** Platforms that evaluate the transparency of AI models, such as SHAP or LIME.
- **Performance Monitoring Tools:** Tools that track real-time model accuracy, drift, and other key metrics.

These tools provide quantitative insights that support audit findings and recommendations.

3. Governance Dashboards

Dashboards consolidate governance data into a single interface, enabling auditors to monitor real-time compliance metrics, risk indicators, and audit progress. Dashboards can include:

- Compliance rates for different systems.
- Trends in model performance over time.
- Incident reports and resolution timelines.

Dashboards help auditors visualize findings and communicate them effectively to stakeholders.

By conducting regular AI governance audits, organizations can ensure their AI systems remain ethical, compliant, and aligned with strategic objectives. A structured process, combined with practical tools, enables organizations to identify and address vulnerabilities, build trust with stakeholders, and enhance the overall value of their AI initiatives. Regular audits are not just a compliance requirement but a critical component of responsible AI deployment and continuous improvement.

7.5 TAILORING GOVERNANCE FRAMEWORKS TO ORGANIZATIONAL NEEDS

Developing a practical AI governance framework requires customization to meet the unique needs of different organizations. The size of the industry and organizational maturity influence the governance approach, making a one-size-fits-all model impractical. Organizations can ensure effective oversight, drive innovation, and mitigate risks by tailoring frameworks to align with specific requirements. This section explores different approaches to governance and provides real-world case studies demonstrating best practices.

1. Lightweight Frameworks for Small and Medium Enterprises (SMEs)

For SMEs, AI governance needs to be streamlined and cost-effective. These organizations typically have limited resources, requiring frameworks that address key risks without imposing excessive complexity. Features of lightweight frameworks include:

- **Simplified Policies:** Governance policies should focus on critical areas like data privacy, ethical use, and essential compliance. Avoiding over-regulation ensures SMEs can innovate while meeting critical standards.
- **Scalable Practices:** Lightweight frameworks should include processes that can grow with the organization. For instance, an essential monitoring tool can be expanded to accommodate more complex systems as the SME adopts advanced AI technologies.
- **Cost-effective Tools:** SMEs benefit from leveraging open-source tools and affordable platforms for tasks like bias detection, performance monitoring, and compliance reporting.

Example:

An SME leveraging AI for customer service automation might implement a lightweight governance framework by focusing on compliance with data privacy laws, ensuring transparency in AI-driven interactions, and conducting essential audits to maintain system reliability.

---

2. Comprehensive Models for Large Enterprises

Large enterprises operate at a grander scale and face more significant regulatory and reputational risks. As such, they require comprehensive governance frameworks to address these complexities. Features of such frameworks include:

- **Dedicated Governance Teams:** Large organizations often establish cross-functional teams that include legal, technical, and ethical experts to oversee governance practices.
- **Advanced Monitoring Tools:** Comprehensive frameworks incorporate tools for continuously monitoring AI systems, ensuring performance consistency, bias mitigation, and regulatory compliance.
- **Detailed Documentation:** Policies, procedures, and decisions related to AI systems are meticulously documented to facilitate audits, regulatory reviews, and stakeholder communication.
- **Global Compliance Management:** Multinational corporations must consider regulatory variations across regions. Their governance frameworks often include mechanisms for aligning AI practices with diverse legal standards, such as GDPR in Europe and CCPA in California.

Example:
A global financial institution using AI for credit risk assessment would require a governance framework that ensures model fairness, compliance with regional regulations, and robust system performance monitoring to maintain trust and mitigate risks.

---

3. Balancing Flexibility with Standardization

Tailoring governance frameworks involves striking a balance between flexibility and standardization:

- **Flexibility:** Governance frameworks must accommodate diverse AI use cases, organizational goals, and technological advancements. For instance, a framework should support experimentation in R&D departments while enforcing stricter oversight in customer-facing applications.

- **Standardization:** Certain aspects of governance, such as data privacy, bias mitigation, and compliance reporting, should follow standardized protocols to ensure consistency and accountability across the organization.

Organizations can adopt a modular approach to governance, where core elements remain consistent while additional components are customized for specific needs. This ensures both adaptability and reliability in governance practices.

CASE STUDY EXAMPLES

1. How an SME Developed a Cost-effective Governance Framework

Context:
A mid-sized e-commerce company leveraging AI for personalized product recommendations faced challenges with data privacy compliance and maintaining algorithmic fairness.

Approach:
The company implemented a lightweight governance framework focusing on three key areas:

1. **Privacy Compliance:** They adopted an open-source data masking tool to anonymize customer data before feeding it into recommendation models, ensuring compliance with GDPR and CCPA.

2. **Fairness Audits:** A simple bias detection tool was integrated into the development pipeline, allowing data scientists to identify and address potential biases during model training.

3. **Periodic Reviews:** Governance responsibilities were added to existing roles, such as data analysts conducting quarterly reviews of model performance and compliance metrics.

Outcome:
This cost-effective framework enabled the company to enhance its governance practices without significantly increasing overhead, fostering trust among customers and regulatory bodies.

Key Takeaway:
SMEs can achieve effective governance by prioritizing critical areas, leveraging affordable tools, and integrating governance into existing workflows.

2. Lessons Learned from Implementing a Robust Framework in a Multinational Corporation

Context:
A multinational healthcare provider using AI for diagnostic support sought to implement a comprehensive governance framework to ensure patient safety, compliance with global regulations, and ethical AI deployment.

Approach:
The organization developed a robust governance framework with the following components:

1. **Dedicated Governance Committee:** A committee comprising legal, ethical, and technical experts was formed to oversee AI governance and align it with the organization's strategic goals.

2. **Continuous Monitoring:** In real-time, advanced monitoring tools were deployed to track model accuracy, bias, and compliance. Alerts were configured to flag deviations for immediate investigation.

3. **Regional Adaptations:** The framework included mechanisms to adapt AI practices to comply with regional regulations, such as HIPAA in the U.S. and GDPR in Europe.

4. **Stakeholder Engagement:** Regular workshops were conducted with doctors, patients, and data scientists to gather feedback and address concerns related to AI deployment.

Outcome:
The governance framework ensured that AI systems remained ethical, reliable, and compliant across multiple regions. The organization gained a competitive edge by demonstrating its commitment to responsible AI practices.

Key Takeaway:
For large enterprises, robust governance frameworks require dedicated resources, advanced tools, and active stakeholder engagement to address complex challenges and build trust.

Tailoring AI governance frameworks to organizational needs is essential for ensuring their effectiveness and sustainability. SMEs benefit from lightweight frameworks that prioritize critical risks and use cost-effective solutions, while large enterprises require comprehensive models to manage complexity and mitigate risks on a global scale. By balancing flexibility with standardization and learning from real-world examples, organizations can develop governance frameworks that align with their goals, foster innovation, and promote responsible AI deployment. These tailored approaches enhance compliance and operational efficiency and strengthen stakeholders' trust, ensuring long-term success in the rapidly evolving AI landscape.

7.6 COMMON PITFALLS AND HOW TO AVOID THEM

Implementing AI governance initiatives can be challenging, especially for organizations venturing into this domain for the first time. Recognizing common pitfalls and adopting effective solutions ensures smoother implementation and long-term success. Below are the key challenges organizations face and strategies to overcome them.

CHALLENGES IN STARTING GOVERNANCE INITIATIVES

1. Lack of Leadership Support

Leadership buy-in is critical for the success of AI governance initiatives. Without support from senior management, governance efforts may lack the necessary resources, visibility, or authority to drive meaningful change. This often results in fragmented efforts and limited impact.

2. Resistance to Change from Teams

AI governance often introduces new policies, workflows, and accountability structures, which can be met with resistance from employees. Teams accustomed to established processes may view governance initiatives as unnecessary bureaucracy or a hindrance to innovation.

3. Overcomplicating the Process

Organizations sometimes overengineer their governance frameworks, making them excessively complex and difficult to implement. Lengthy policies, rigid procedures, and intricate tools can overwhelm stakeholders, leading to inefficiencies and delays.

SOLUTIONS

1. Building Stakeholder Alignment Early

Engaging stakeholders from the outset is essential for gaining support and fostering collaboration. Strategies include:

- Educating Leadership: To secure executive sponsorship communicate the benefits of AI governance, such as risk mitigation, regulatory compliance, and enhanced decision-making.

- **Collaborative Design:** Develop governance frameworks involving key stakeholders, including data scientists, legal teams, and business leaders. This ensures that policies are practical and address real-world concerns.
- **Clear Communication:** Use accessible language to explain governance objectives and emphasize how they align with organizational goals, fostering trust and buy-in.

2. Keeping Governance Practical and Scalable

Governance frameworks should be designed to balance structure with flexibility, allowing organizations to adapt to evolving needs. Key practices include:

- **Start Small:** Begin with foundational governance elements, such as basic compliance policies or a pilot program, and expand gradually based on lessons learned.
- **Focus on Impact:** To demonstrate quick wins and build momentum, prioritize high-impact areas like data privacy or bias mitigation.
- **Simplify Tools and Processes:** Use straightforward checklists or templates to streamline implementation and make governance accessible to all teams.

By addressing these common pitfalls proactively and adopting practical solutions, organizations can ensure their AI governance initiatives are well-received, scalable, and effective in driving responsible and sustainable AI practices.

PART III

BUILDING AN AI GOVERNANCE FRAMEWORK

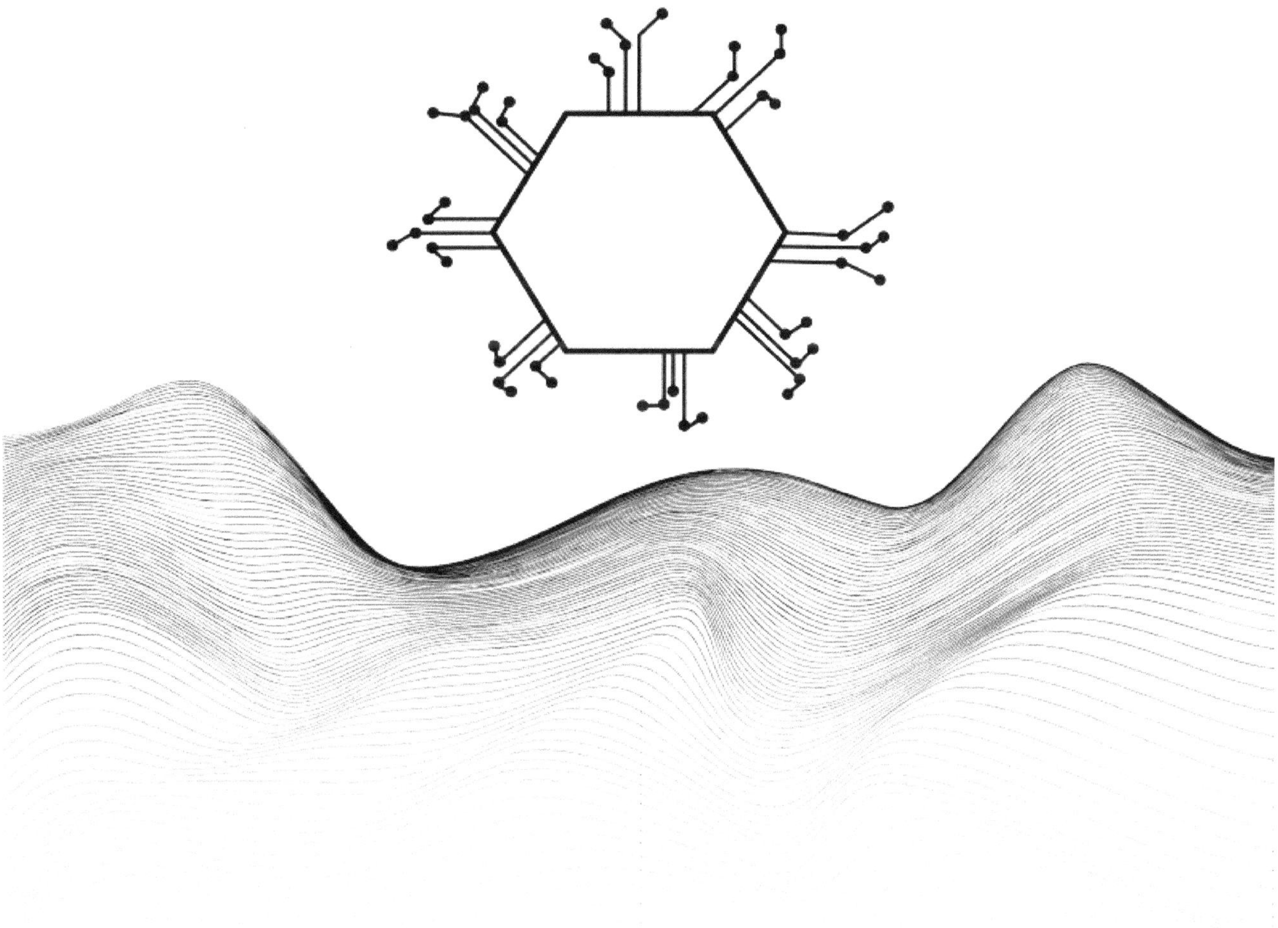

CHAPTER 8: POLICY DEVELOPMENT

8.1 INTRODUCTION TO AI GOVERNANCE POLICIES

WHAT ARE GOVERNANCE POLICIES?

Governance policies are structured guidelines and rules designed to direct and regulate the development, deployment, and management of artificial intelligence (AI) systems. In AI governance frameworks, these policies provide a foundation for ensuring that AI technologies are ethical, compliant, and aligned with an organization's strategic objectives.

The importance of governance policies in AI cannot be overstated. They are a backbone for creating responsible AI systems by addressing risks, promoting transparency, and maintaining public trust. AI applications can face ethical dilemmas, legal disputes, and operational inefficiencies without well-crafted policies. Governance policies serve as guardrails, ensuring that AI systems do not perpetuate bias, violate privacy, or operate without accountability.

TYPES OF POLICIES

AI governance policies typically fall into three categories: ethical policies, compliance policies, and operational policies.

1. **Ethical Policies** address the moral principles guiding AI development and use. They include commitments to fairness, transparency, and the minimization of bias. Ethical policies ensure AI systems respect human rights and are designed to serve the broader good without causing harm.

2. **Compliance Policies** focus on adherence to legal and regulatory requirements. They ensure that AI applications comply with data protection laws, industry standards, and international agreements. Compliance policies safeguard organizations from legal liabilities while fostering consumer confidence.

3. **Operational Policies** address the practical aspects of implementing and managing AI systems. They cover data governance, model monitoring, and incident response. Operational policies ensure that AI systems operate efficiently and reliably while minimizing the risks associated with their use.

WHY POLICIES FAIL

Despite their critical role, governance policies often fail due to design and enforcement shortcomings. Common reasons include:

1. Ambiguity and Complexity: Vague or overly technical policies can confuse stakeholders, leading to inconsistent implementation. Clear and concise language is essential to ensure understanding and compliance.

2. Lack of Alignment with Organizational Goals: Policies disconnected from an organization's objectives can be seen as burdensome. When policies do not align with business strategies, they are less likely to gain support from leadership and staff.

3. Insufficient Stakeholder Involvement: Excluding key stakeholders, such as data scientists, legal teams, and end-users, from the policy development process often results in impractical or unenforceable guidelines. Collaboration ensures policies address diverse perspectives and practical realities.

4. Inadequate Training and Communication: Even well-designed policies can fail if stakeholders are unaware of them or do not understand their importance. Comprehensive training and effective communication are essential for successful policy adoption.

5. Failure to Evolve: AI technology evolves rapidly, and static policies become obsolete. Organizations that do not regularly update their policies risk falling behind regulatory requirements and technological advancements.

6. Weak Enforcement Mechanisms: Policies without precise enforcement mechanisms often lack credibility. Organizations must establish monitoring, auditing, and corrective action processes to ensure compliance.

8.2 KEY ELEMENTS OF EFFECTIVE AI POLICIES

CORE COMPONENTS

Effective AI governance policies are built on foundational components that ensure they are comprehensive, actionable, and aligned with organizational goals. These core components include objectives, scope, and responsibilities.

1. Objectives: Clear Goals for Governance Policies

Defining clear and measurable objectives is the first step in crafting effective AI policies. These goals outline the policy's purpose and sections for how AI systems should operate within an organization. For example, objectives include minimizing bias, ensuring data privacy, or achieving regulatory compliance.

Clear objectives serve multiple purposes:

- Guidance: They provide a roadmap for policy implementation, ensuring that all stakeholders understand the desired outcomes.

- **Accountability:** They create benchmarks for assessing policy effectiveness.
- **Alignment:** They ensure that AI governance aligns with broader organizational goals, such as enhancing customer trust or driving innovation responsibly.

Effective AI Governance Policies

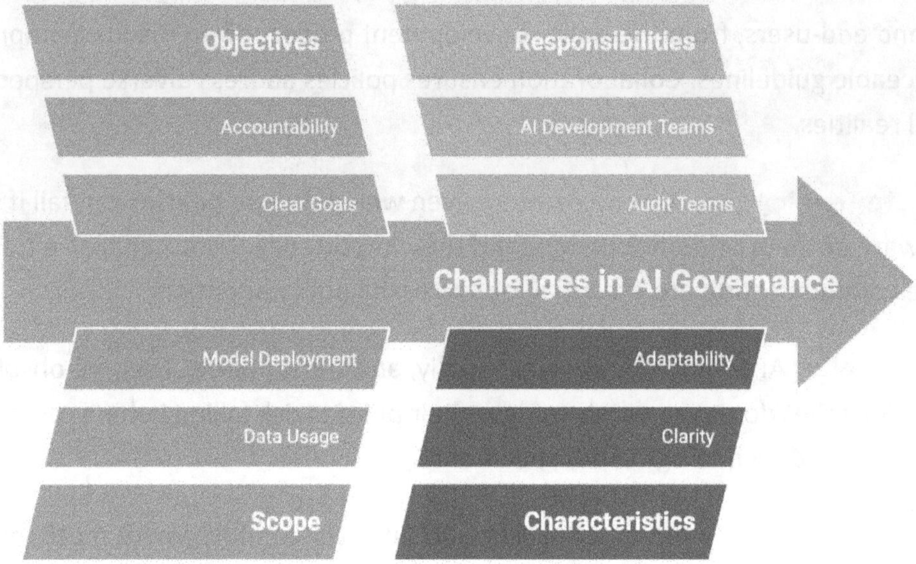

2. Scope: Defining Boundaries

The scope of an AI governance policy delineates its applicability and boundaries. A well-defined scope clarifies the policy's areas, such as data usage, AI model development, deployment, and ongoing monitoring. For example, a scope might specify that a policy applies to all AI models used in customer interactions but excludes experimental models in the research phase.

Key considerations for defining scope include:

- **Data Usage:** What types of data can be used for AI training? Are there restrictions on sensitive data or data collected from specific sources?
- **Model Deployment:** Which deployment scenarios are covered by the policy? Does it apply to both internal and external-facing AI applications?
- **Geographic Jurisdiction:** Are there region-specific regulations that influence the policy?

An articulated scope prevents misunderstandings and ensures consistent application of policies across projects and teams.

3. Responsibilities: Assigning Accountability for Compliance

Assigning responsibilities is critical to successfully implementing and enforcing AI governance policies. This component ensures that individuals and teams are accountable for compliance and that processes are in place to monitor and enforce adherence.

Key roles and responsibilities might include:

- AI Development Teams: Ensuring ethical and operational guidelines develop models.
- Data Privacy Officers: Oversee compliance with data protection regulations and ensure transparency in data usage.
- Governance Committees: Reviewing and approving AI projects to ensure they align with organizational policies.
- Audit Teams: Conduct regular audits to identify and address compliance gaps.

Responsibilities should be documented and communicated to prevent ambiguity and foster a culture of accountability.

CHARACTERISTICS OF EFFECTIVE POLICIES

For AI governance policies to be effective, they must exhibit specific characteristics that make them actionable, sustainable, and aligned with organizational needs.

1. Clarity

Clarity is paramount in policy design. Policies must use plain, accessible language to ensure all stakeholders—from AI engineers to non-technical staff—understand their obligations. Avoiding jargon and providing concrete examples can enhance comprehension.

2. Adaptability

AI technologies and regulatory landscapes evolve rapidly. Policies must be flexible enough to adapt to new developments without requiring complete overhauls. This can be achieved through:

- Modular Design: Breaking policies into sections that can be updated independently.
- Regular Reviews: Establishing a schedule for policy reviews and updates.

3. Enforceability

Policies are only effective if they can be enforced. This requires precise mechanisms for monitoring compliance, reporting violations, and imposing consequences for non-compliance. Examples include automated tools for tracking data usage or periodic audits of AI systems.

4. Alignment with Organizational Goals

Effective policies align with an organization's broader strategic objectives. For instance, if an organization prioritizes customer trust, its AI policies should emphasize transparency and fairness. Alignment ensures that policies are seen as enablers rather than obstacles.

TEMPLATES AND EXAMPLES

Providing templates and examples can simplify the process of drafting and implementing AI governance policies. These resources serve as starting points, offering standardized structures and language that can be customized to specific organizational needs.

1. Sample Policy for AI Fairness

Objective: Ensure that AI systems operate pretty and do not perpetuate bias.

Scope: Applies to all AI models used in customer interactions and decision-making processes.

Responsibilities:

- Data Scientists: Conduct bias detection and mitigation during model development.
- Ethics Committee: Review and approve models for fairness before deployment.

Key Provisions:

- Regular audits of AI models to identify and address bias.
- Use of diverse datasets for training and testing.
- Mandatory fairness impact assessments for high-stakes applications.

2. Sample Policy for Privacy

Objective: Protect user data and ensure compliance with data protection regulations.

Scope: Covers all AI systems that collect, store, or process personal data.

Responsibilities:

- Data Privacy Officers: Monitor compliance with privacy regulations.
- Developers: Implement privacy-by-design principles in AI systems.

Key Provisions:

- Data anonymization for all datasets used in training.
- Clear documentation of data usage and retention policies.

- Mechanisms for users to access, update, or delete their data.

3. Sample Policy for Bias Mitigation

Objective: Minimize biases in AI systems and promote equitable outcomes.

Scope: Applicable to all AI systems that impact employment, lending, or other critical decisions.

Responsibilities:

- AI Teams: Conduct bias testing during development.
- Auditors: Perform independent evaluations of model outputs.

Key Provisions:

- Implementation of bias detection tools.
- Inclusion of diverse perspectives during model design.
- Public disclosure of measures taken to mitigate bias.

Organizations can develop robust AI governance policies that support ethical, compliant, and effective AI systems by incorporating these core components, characteristics, and templates. These policies mitigate risks and foster trust and innovation in the rapidly evolving AI landscape.

8.3 POLICY DEVELOPMENT PROCESS

Developing effective AI governance policies requires a systematic approach that ensures alignment with organizational priorities, legal requirements, and ethical standards. This section outlines a step-by-step guide to the policy development process and emphasizes the importance of iterative improvement to adapt to evolving needs and regulations.

1. Identifying Organizational Priorities and Risks

The foundation of any AI policy development process is a clear understanding of organizational goals and the risks associated with AI adoption. This step ensures that policies are tailored to address the specific needs and challenges of the organization.

Key Activities:

- **Define Objectives:** Identify what the organization aims to achieve with its AI systems. Objectives include enhancing customer trust, driving innovation, or ensuring compliance with regulations.
- **Conduct Risk Assessments:** Evaluate potential risks associated with AI systems, such as data breaches, ethical concerns, or reputational damage. Assess risks based on likelihood and impact.
- **Prioritize Focus Areas:** Based on objectives and risks, determine the key areas where policies are needed, such as data governance, bias mitigation, or model monitoring.

For example, a financial institution may prioritize policies that mitigate the risks of algorithmic bias in credit scoring while ensuring compliance with data protection laws.

2. Stakeholder Involvement: Cross-Functional Input for Policy Creation

AI governance policies affect various parts of an organization, making cross-functional collaboration essential. Engaging stakeholders from diverse roles ensures that policies are practical, comprehensive, and aligned with organizational needs.

Key Activities:

- **Identify Stakeholders:** Include representatives from AI development teams, legal departments, compliance officers, data privacy experts, and business leaders.
- **Facilitate Collaboration:** Conduct workshops, meetings, and brainstorming sessions to gather input from all stakeholders.
- **Incorporate Diverse Perspectives:** Ensure that the policy development process considers the viewpoints of technical and non-technical stakeholders and those of external partners, if applicable.

Example: Involving data scientists and legal experts can help ensure that a data usage policy balances innovation with regulatory compliance.

3. Drafting Policies Using Existing Standards and Frameworks

Once priorities and stakeholder inputs are established, the next step is drafting policies. Leveraging existing standards and frameworks can provide a robust foundation for policy development while ensuring consistency with industry best practices.

Key Activities:

- Research Standards: Review relevant standards such as ISO/IEC 38507 for AI governance or the EU's General Data Protection Regulation (GDPR).
- Define Policy Structure: Establish a clear structure, including objectives, scope, responsibilities, and enforcement mechanisms.
- Draft Provisions: Write detailed provisions addressing specific aspects of AI governance, such as fairness, accountability, and transparency.
- Validate Drafts: Share drafts with stakeholders for review and incorporate their feedback to ensure clarity and relevance.

Example: A privacy policy based on GDPR guidelines might include provisions for data anonymization, consent management, and user access to personal information.

ITERATIVE IMPROVEMENT

AI governance is not static; policies must evolve to remain effective despite technological advancements and changing regulatory landscapes. Iterative improvement is a critical component of the policy development process.

1. Regular Reviews and Updates

Policies should be reviewed periodically to assess their effectiveness and relevance. Regular updates ensure policies address emerging risks, incorporate new regulations, and align with technological developments.

Key Activities:

- Establish Review Cycles: Define an annual or semi-annual policy review schedule.
- Monitor Changes: Stay informed about regulatory updates, industry trends, and advancements in AI technology.
- Incorporate Feedback: Gather input from stakeholders, including employees, customers, and external auditors, to identify areas for improvement.
- Revise Policies: Update policy language, add new provisions, or refine enforcement mechanisms based on review findings.

Example: A company's AI fairness policy may need updates to address biases detected in new models or to comply with updated anti-discrimination laws.

2. Leveraging Feedback Mechanisms

Effective policies incorporate feedback from those directly affected by them. Feedback mechanisms ensure that policies remain practical and address real-world challenges.

Key Activities:

- **Establish Feedback Channels:** Create platforms for employees, users, and other stakeholders to share their experiences with AI systems and suggest improvements.
- **Analyze Feedback:** Review feedback for recurring issues, inconsistencies, or gaps in existing policies.
- **Act on Insights:** Use feedback to proactively refine policies and address stakeholder concerns.

Example: Users' feedback about an AI-powered customer service chatbot may reveal privacy concerns requiring data retention policy updates.

3. Continuous Training and Awareness

Training and awareness programs are vital in improving AI policies iteratively. By keeping stakeholders informed, organizations can ensure consistent compliance and foster a culture of accountability.

Key Activities:

- **Develop Training Programs:** Create workshops, e-learning modules, or webinars to educate employees about policy changes and their implications.
- **Promote Awareness:** Use internal communication channels to disseminate updates and emphasize the importance of adherence.
- **Evaluate Effectiveness:** Assess the impact of training programs through surveys, quizzes, or compliance metrics.

Example: An organization might conduct annual training sessions on AI ethics to ensure that all employees understand new guidelines and their roles in upholding them.

8.4 BEST PRACTICES IN POLICY COMMUNICATION AND TRAINING

Effective communication and training are vital to the success of AI governance policies. These practices ensure that all stakeholders understand and comply with established guidelines, fostering a culture of accountability and ethical AI use. This section outlines best practices for communicating policies and training teams to ensure alignment and adherence.

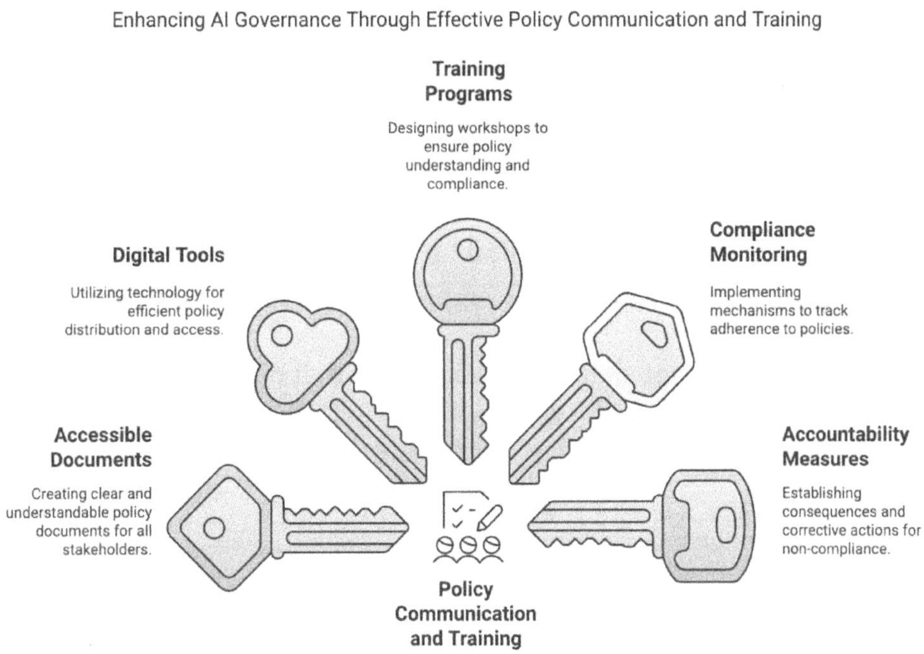

COMMUNICATING POLICIES

Clear and accessible communication is the cornerstone of effective policy dissemination. Stakeholders must have access to well-organized, easily understandable documents and resources.

1. Creating Accessible Documents for All Stakeholders

Policy documents must be written in plain language to ensure accessibility for both technical and non-technical stakeholders. The goal is to eliminate ambiguity and promote a shared understanding of expectations.

Best Practices:

- Simplify Language: Avoid jargon and technical terminology wherever possible. Include glossaries to define necessary technical terms.
- Organize Content: Use clear headings, bullet points, and tables of contents to structure documents. Visual aids, such as flowcharts or infographics, can enhance understanding.
- Provide Translations: For multinational organizations, consider translating policies into multiple languages to accommodate diverse teams.
- Create Summaries: Offer executive summaries or one-page overviews highlighting key provisions for quick reference.

Example: A global tech company might create a one-page AI privacy policy summary highlighting critical points such as data anonymization practices and user consent requirements.

2. Leveraging Digital Tools for Distribution

Modern technology offers numerous platforms for disseminating policies efficiently and ensuring they are accessible to all stakeholders.

Best Practices:

- **Use Intranets:** Host policies on the organization's intranet to provide a central repository for easy access. Use a search function to help employees find specific policies.
- **AI Policy Dashboards:** Develop dedicated dashboards that display critical policies, updates, and compliance metrics in an interactive format.
- **Automated Notifications:** Set up automated alerts to inform employees of policy updates or upcoming review deadlines.
- **Collaboration Platforms:** Leverage tools like Microsoft Teams or Slack to facilitate discussions and share policy-related resources.

Example: An AI policy dashboard could include links to full documents, recent updates, and a Q&A section where employees can ask questions or provide feedback.

TRAINING TEAMS ON POLICIES

Training programs are essential for ensuring that employees understand and comply with AI governance policies. Well-designed training fosters a culture of awareness and accountability across the organization.

1. Designing Workshops and Training Programs

Workshops and training programs should be tailored to the specific needs of each team, ensuring that everyone understands their role in implementing policies.

Best Practices:

- **Role-Specific Training:** Customize training content based on roles. For example, developers might receive training on bias mitigation techniques, while legal teams focus on regulatory compliance.
- **Interactive Sessions:** Incorporate hands-on activities like case studies or simulations to help participants apply policy principles in real-world scenarios.
- **Expert Involvement:** Invite subject matter experts to lead sessions and address complex topics.
- **Flexible Formats:** To accommodate diverse learning preferences, we offer a mix of in-person workshops, virtual webinars, and self-paced e-learning modules.

Example: A company might design a workshop for its AI development team, using case studies to illustrate how biases in training data can lead to unintended consequences.

2. Ensuring Team Alignment and Understanding of Policy Expectations

Alignment and understanding are critical for effective policy implementation. Employees must be aware of policies and understand how they apply to their daily tasks.

Best Practices:

- Regular Refreshers: Conduct periodic training sessions to reinforce key concepts and update teams on policy changes.
- Feedback Mechanisms: Allow employees to ask questions and provide feedback during training sessions to ensure clarity.
- Knowledge Assessments: Use quizzes or tests to evaluate understanding and identify areas requiring additional focus.
- Link Policies to Goals: Communicate how adherence to policies supports organizational objectives, such as maintaining customer trust or ensuring compliance.

Example: After training sessions, a company might distribute short quizzes to assess understanding of its AI ethics policy, providing additional resources for employees needing further clarification.

8.5 ENFORCING POLICIES AND ENSURING COMPLIANCE

Enforcing AI governance policies is critical to maintaining ethical, compliant, and effective AI systems. However, policies alone are insufficient without mechanisms for accountability and enforcement. This section outlines best practices for building accountability and leveraging technology to ensure adherence to governance policies.

BUILDING ACCOUNTABILITY

Accountability is the cornerstone of effective policy enforcement. It ensures that stakeholders understand their responsibilities and that there are consequences for failing to comply with established policies.

1. Mechanisms to Monitor Compliance

Monitoring compliance involves tracking adherence to policies and identifying areas that require improvement. Effective monitoring mechanisms include:

- **Periodic Audits:** Regular audits are essential for evaluating compliance with AI governance policies. To ensure objectivity, these audits can be internal, conducted by dedicated compliance teams, or external, performed by third-party organizations.

  Key Components:

  - **Data Audits:** Assess data handling practices to ensure data privacy and compliance with security policies.
  - **Model Audits:** Review AI models for adherence to fairness, transparency, and accuracy standards.
  - **Process Audits:** Examine workflows to ensure policy guidelines are integrated into AI development and deployment processes.

  Example: A financial institution might conduct quarterly audits of its AI-powered credit scoring system to ensure compliance with fairness policies and prevent discriminatory outcomes.

- **Performance Metrics:** Establishing metrics to measure compliance can help organizations track progress and identify potential risks. Metrics include the number of policy violations detected, the time taken to address violations or the percentage of employees completing compliance training.

- **Whistleblower Channels:** Providing secure and anonymous channels for reporting non-compliance fosters accountability. Employees should feel empowered to raise concerns without fear of retaliation.

2. Consequences for Non-Compliance

Clear and consistent consequences for policy violations are essential for enforcing accountability. Consequences must be proportionate to the severity of the breach and aim to correct behavior while deterring future non-compliance.

Best Practices:

- **Disciplinary Actions:** Implement a range of disciplinary measures, such as warnings, mandatory training, or, in severe cases, suspension or termination of employment.

- **Corrective Measures:** Focus on remediation by identifying root causes and implementing measures to prevent recurrence. For example, if a bias issue is detected in an AI system, the corrective action might involve retraining the model with more representative data.

- **Transparency:** Communicate the outcomes of enforcement actions to stakeholders to demonstrate the organization's commitment to accountability.

For example, a tech company might mandate retraining for developers involved in a project that experienced a compliance breach and require additional oversight for future projects.

USING TECHNOLOGY FOR ENFORCEMENT

Technology is pivotal in enforcing AI governance policies by enabling efficient and scalable compliance monitoring.

1. AI Tools for Policy Compliance Monitoring

AI tools can monitor adherence to governance policies in real-time. They are particularly effective for identifying violations and streamlining enforcement processes.

Key Applications:

- Data Monitoring: AI-driven tools can track data usage to ensure data privacy and compliance with security policies. For example, automated systems can flag unauthorized data access or usage in AI training.
- Bias Detection: Tools designed to detect bias in AI models can help organizations identify and address potential fairness issues. These tools analyze outputs to ensure they align with ethical standards.
- Transparency Audits: AI systems can audit decision-making processes to ensure they are transparent and explainable. This is particularly important for high-stakes applications, such as healthcare or finance.

Example: A retail company might use AI tools to monitor customer data usage in marketing campaigns, ensuring compliance with privacy policies and avoiding unauthorized data sharing.

2. Automating Routine Checks for Adherence to Governance Policies

Automation reduces the burden of manual compliance monitoring and increases efficiency. Routine checks can be automated to ensure consistent adherence to policies across AI systems.

Key Applications:

- Continuous Monitoring: Implement automated systems that continuously monitor AI models and processes for compliance. This approach allows for the early detection of violations and immediate corrective action.
- Alerts and Notifications: Automated alerts can notify stakeholders of potential policy violations, enabling prompt responses. For example, an alert might be triggered if an AI system processes data beyond its authorized scope.

- **Integration with Development Pipelines:** Embed compliance checks into AI development workflows. For instance, automated tools can verify that training data meets ethical guidelines or that models are tested for bias before deployment.

Example: An AI-powered HR platform could use automated checks to ensure hiring algorithms comply with diversity and inclusion policies, flagging issues for review before implementation.

8.6 INDUSTRY-SPECIFIC POLICY CONSIDERATIONS

AI governance policies must be tailored to address different industries' unique challenges and requirements. This section explores specific considerations for the healthcare, finance, and retail sectors, along with case studies that illustrate effective policy implementation.

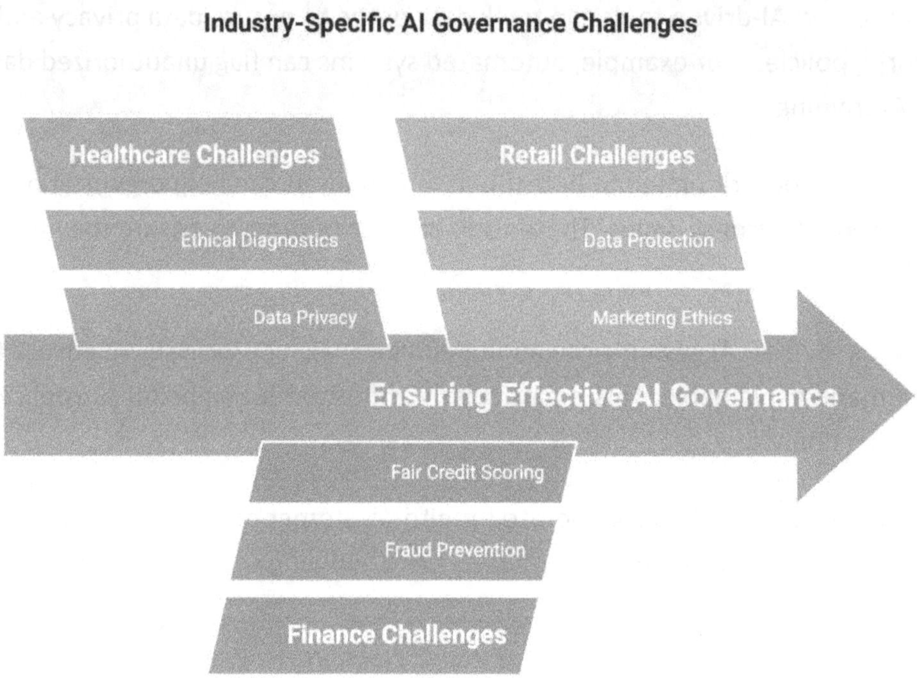

TAILORING POLICIES BY SECTOR

1. Healthcare: Policies for Patient Data Privacy and Ethical Use of AI in Diagnostics

The healthcare industry heavily relies on sensitive patient data and advanced AI-powered diagnostic tools. Policies in this sector must prioritize data privacy, ethical AI deployment, and compliance with stringent regulations such as the Health Insurance Portability and Accountability Act (HIPAA).

Key Considerations:

- **Data Privacy:** Policies must ensure patient data is securely stored, accessed, and shared. This includes encryption, anonymization, and strict access controls.

- **Ethical Diagnostics:** AI systems used for diagnostics must be thoroughly validated to ensure accuracy and fairness. Policies should require transparency in AI-driven recommendations and decisions.
- **Informed Consent:** Patients must be informed about how their data will be used and the role of AI in their care, fostering trust and compliance.

Example: A policy might mandate regular audits of AI diagnostic tools to verify accuracy across diverse patient populations and require reporting any anomalies or biases.

2. Finance: Policies to Prevent Fraud and Ensure Fairness in Credit Scoring

The finance sector leverages AI for fraud detection, credit scoring, and algorithmic trading. Policies in this domain must balance innovation with fairness, transparency, and compliance with regulations like the Fair Credit Reporting Act (FCRA).

Key Considerations:

- **Fraud Prevention:** Policies should outline procedures for training AI models on comprehensive datasets to detect fraudulent activities while minimizing false positives.
- **Fair Credit Scoring:** Policies must ensure that credit scoring algorithms do not discriminate against individuals based on race, gender, or socioeconomic status.
- **Transparency:** Financial institutions should explain AI-driven decisions clearly and significantly when these decisions negatively impact consumers.

For example, a financial institution might implement a policy requiring regular bias audits of credit scoring models and provide consumers with detailed explanations of adverse decisions.

3. Retail: Policies for Customer Data Protection and AI-Driven Marketing Ethics

AI is widely used in retail for personalized marketing, inventory management, and customer service. Policies must focus on safeguarding customer data and ensuring ethical practices in AI-driven marketing.

Key Considerations:

- **Data Protection:** Policies should specify how customer data is collected, stored, and used, with explicit restrictions on sharing data with third parties.
- **Marketing Ethics:** AI-driven marketing tools must adhere to ethical guidelines, avoiding manipulative tactics or discriminatory targeting.
- **Consumer Consent:** Retailers must obtain explicit customer consent to use their data and provide options for opting out of AI-driven personalization.

Example: A policy might prohibit using sensitive data, such as browsing history, without customer consent and require transparency in generating recommendations.

CASE STUDIES

Example 1: A Financial Institution's Approach to AI Compliance Policies

A global bank implemented comprehensive AI compliance policies to address concerns about fairness and transparency in credit scoring. Key aspects of their approach included:

- **Bias Audits:** Regular audits of AI models to identify and mitigate biases against underrepresented groups.
- **Transparency Initiatives:** Developing tools to provide customers with clear explanations of credit decisions, including factors influencing their scores.
- **Regulatory Compliance:** Ensuring alignment with international regulations, such as GDPR for data protection and FCRA for credit reporting standards.

Outcome: The bank's policies reduced complaints about unfair credit decisions and enhanced customer trust and regulatory compliance.

Example 2: A Healthcare Provider's Policies for Responsible AI in Diagnostics

A large healthcare organization implemented policies to govern the use of AI in diagnostic imaging. Their approach focused on:

- **Validation Protocols:** Strict protocols must be established for validating AI tools before deployment, ensuring they meet accuracy and reliability benchmarks.
- **Patient Data Security:** To protect patient privacy, implementing robust data security measures, including encryption and restricted access.
- **Ethics Committees:** Creating committees to review AI applications for compliance with ethical standards and alignment with patient care objectives.

Outcome: The healthcare provider's policies enhanced the reliability of AI diagnostic tools, reduced instances of misdiagnosis, and reinforced patient trust in AI-driven care.

8.7 OVERCOMING COMMON CHALLENGES IN POLICY DEVELOPMENT

Developing effective AI governance policies involves addressing several challenges hindering their adoption and implementation. Understanding these challenges and implementing targeted solutions is critical for creating robust and sustainable policies.

Overcoming AI Policy Challenges

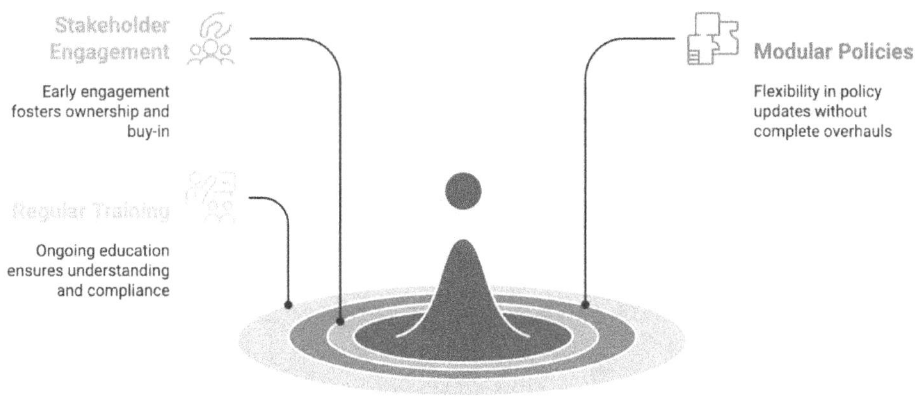

CHALLENGES

1. Resistance from Teams Unfamiliar with Governance

One of the most significant challenges in policy development is resistance from teams that lack familiarity with governance practices. Technical teams may view policies as bureaucratic obstacles, while non-technical stakeholders may not fully understand their relevance.

2. Balancing Comprehensiveness with Simplicity

Policies must balance being comprehensive enough to address potential risks and simple enough to be easily understood and implemented. Overly complex policies can lead to confusion and non-compliance, while excessively simplistic policies may fail to address critical issues.

3. Keeping Policies Up-to-Date with Fast-Evolving AI Technology

The rapid pace of AI innovation and changing regulatory landscapes can render policies outdated if they are not regularly reviewed and updated. Staying ahead of these changes is a continuous challenge for organizations.

SOLUTIONS

1. Engaging Stakeholders Early

Early and consistent engagement with stakeholders can help mitigate resistance. By involving cross-functional teams, including technical experts, legal advisors, and business leaders, organizations can:

- Foster a sense of ownership and buy-in.
- Ensure that policies are practical and address real-world challenges.

- Build a culture that values governance as a tool for achieving organizational goals.

2. Using Modular Policies for Adaptability

Modular policies provide flexibility, allowing organizations to adapt to changes without overhauling entire frameworks. Each module can focus on a specific area, such as data privacy, model transparency, or ethical guidelines, enabling targeted updates.

Example: An organization might update its data privacy module to align with new regulations while leaving other modules unchanged.

3. Regular Training Sessions to Build Organizational Support

Training programs are essential for ensuring that all stakeholders understand the purpose and importance of AI governance policies. Regular sessions can:

- Reinforce key concepts and expectations.
- Provide updates on changes to policies or regulations.
- Address specific concerns and questions from employees.

Example: Conducting annual workshops on policy updates and their implications for day-to-day operations ensures ongoing compliance and support.

Overcoming challenges in policy development requires a proactive and collaborative approach. By engaging stakeholders, adopting modular frameworks, and investing in regular training, organizations can create practical policies that are resilient to change and widely supported across teams.

CHAPTER 9: RISK MANAGEMENT

9.1 INTRODUCTION TO AI RISK MANAGEMENT

Artificial Intelligence (AI) is reshaping industries, from healthcare to finance, by enabling faster decision-making, automation, and personalization. However, with its increasing adoption comes the responsibility to address the potential risks inherent in AI systems. AI Risk Management is identifying, assessing, and mitigating these risks to ensure AI technologies' safe, ethical, and effective deployment.

WHAT IS AI RISK MANAGEMENT?

AI Risk Management is the systematic approach to understanding and mitigating risks associated with AI systems. These risks can range from ethical challenges, such as bias and fairness, to operational and regulatory issues. Risk management plays a pivotal role in building AI systems that are not only innovative but also trustworthy and reliable.

Importance in AI Governance:

Risk management is critical for ensuring accountability and adherence to ethical principles in AI governance. Governing AI systems involves creating policies and frameworks that address potential harms while encouraging innovation. Effective risk management ensures that AI systems align with organizational values, user expectations, and legal requirements.

Building Trustworthy AI Systems:

Trust is a cornerstone of AI adoption. If users perceive AI systems as unreliable or unethical, this can damage their reputations and cause organizations financial losses. Risk management ensures that AI systems are designed and deployed with safeguards to address potential concerns, fostering trust among users and stakeholders. For instance, a transparent AI model that provides explainable decisions is more likely to gain user confidence than a "black-box" system.

CATEGORIES OF RISKS

AI systems face various risks, broadly categorized as ethical, operational, and regulatory.

1. **Ethical Risks:**
   Ethical challenges in AI often arise from biases in data and algorithms. AI systems are as unbiased as the data they are trained on, and if this data reflects historical inequities, it can lead to discriminatory outcomes. For example, biased hiring algorithms have been shown to unfairly disadvantage specific demographics. Ethical risks also encompass the societal impact of AI, such as exacerbating inequality or undermining human autonomy.

   Key aspects of ethical risks include:

   - **Bias and fairness:** Ensuring that AI systems provide equitable outcomes for all users, irrespective of demographic factors.
   - **Societal impact:** Evaluating how AI affects social dynamics, including job displacement and misinformation spread.
   - **Transparency:** Addressing the "black-box" nature of AI models to ensure users and regulators understand how decisions are made.

2. **Operational Risks:**
   Like any technology, AI systems are prone to operational issues that can disrupt their functionality and reliability. These risks often stem from inadequate testing, poor scalability, or unexpected interactions with real-world environments.

   Common operational risks include:

   - **System failures:** Unexpected crashes or outages that hinder AI performance.
   - **Performance issues:** Degraded accuracy or inefficiencies when models are exposed to real-world data different from training datasets.
   - **Scalability:** Challenges adapting AI systems to handle increasing data volumes or user demands.

   Organizations must invest in robust testing, validation, and continuous monitoring to mitigate these risks effectively.

3. **Regulatory Risks:**
   Governments and regulatory bodies worldwide are introducing laws to ensure AI systems adhere to ethical standards and not cause harm. Non-compliance with these regulations can lead to penalties, lawsuits, and loss of market access. Regulatory risks highlight the need for organizations to stay updated on evolving standards and implement measures to meet compliance requirements.

Key aspects of regulatory risks include:

- Compliance with laws and standards: Ensuring adherence to frameworks like the EU's AI Act or the General Data Protection Regulation (GDPR).
- Data privacy: Protecting user data and avoiding unauthorized data usage.
- Accountability: Defining roles and responsibilities for AI decisions, especially in high-stakes applications like healthcare and finance.

THE ROLE OF AI RISK MANAGEMENT IN BUSINESS SUCCESS

By proactively addressing these categories of risks, organizations can unlock AI's full potential while safeguarding against potential pitfalls. Ethical risk management helps maintain public trust and operational risk mitigation ensures reliability and regulatory compliance and avoids costly legal challenges. Together, these measures foster a balanced approach to innovation and responsibility.

For example, consider an AI-powered credit scoring system used by financial institutions. If this system inadvertently discriminates against minority applicants due to biased training data, it could lead to lawsuits, regulatory scrutiny, and loss of customer trust. A robust AI risk management framework would involve:

- Conducting bias detection and mitigation during model development.
- Implementing rigorous testing and validation processes to ensure performance across diverse demographics.
- Adhering to financial regulations and auditing processes.

9.2 IDENTIFYING AI RISKS

Identifying risks in Artificial Intelligence (AI) systems is fundamental to ensuring their safe and effective deployment. Risk identification forms the backbone of AI governance as AI revolutionizes industries, allowing organizations to address potential challenges and mitigate failures preemptively. This section explores the methodologies, tools, and case studies associated with identifying AI risks to help build robust and trustworthy systems.

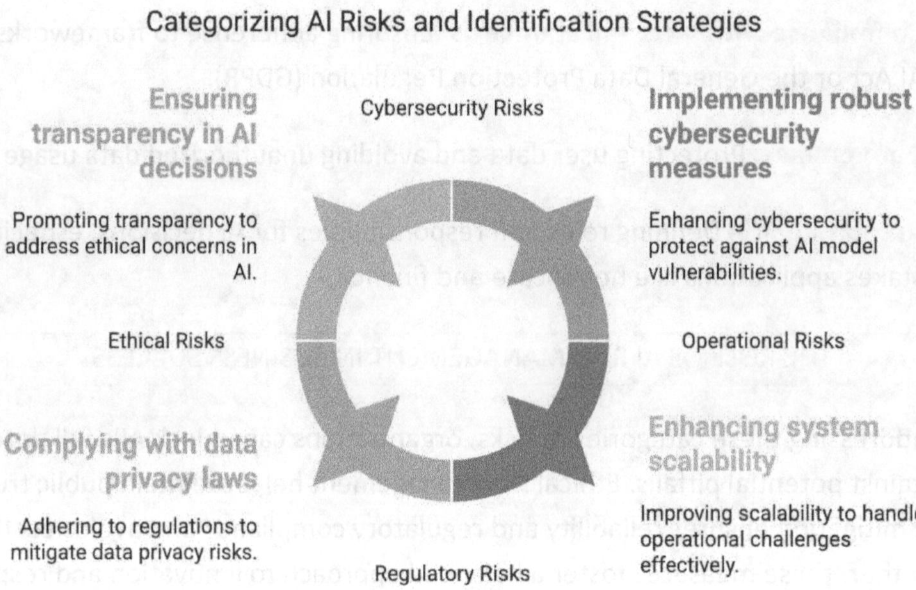

RISK IDENTIFICATION PROCESS

Effective risk identification begins with a structured approach that involves collaboration across teams and leveraging historical data. This process ensures a thorough understanding of potential risks and fosters a culture of proactive governance within organizations.

CONDUCTING RISK WORKSHOPS WITH CROSS-FUNCTIONAL TEAMS

Risk workshops are essential in identifying AI-related risks. They bring diverse perspectives within the organization, involving stakeholders from various domains, such as data scientists, legal experts, product managers, and end-users. These workshops help uncover risks that might otherwise be overlooked.

Key Steps in Conducting Risk Workshops:

1. **Define Objectives:** Establish the workshop's scope and goals, such as identifying ethical, operational, or regulatory risks specific to AI systems.

2. **Gather Diverse Participants:** To ensure a holistic view of potential risks, representatives from technical, business, legal, and user experience teams should be included.

3. **Facilitate Open Discussions:** Use brainstorming sessions guided by facilitators to explore scenarios where AI might fail or cause unintended consequences.

4. **Document Findings:** Create a risk register that captures all identified risks, their potential impact, and likelihood.

5. **Prioritize Risks:** Rank the risks based on their severity and likelihood to inform subsequent mitigation strategies.

For example, a risk workshop for an AI-powered recruitment platform might identify risks such as biased candidate selection, data privacy violations, and system scalability issues during peak hiring seasons.

LEVERAGING DATA AND PAST INCIDENTS TO PREDICT POTENTIAL RISKS

Historical data and lessons learned from past incidents are crucial in identifying AI risks. Organizations can uncover patterns and anticipate challenges that may arise by analyzing similar AI deployments.

Steps to Leverage Historical Data:

1. **Collect Data:** Gather records of past incidents involving AI systems, both internal and external to the organization.
2. **Analyze Trends:** Identify recurring issues, such as algorithmic bias, data breaches, or operational failures.
3. **Create Predictive Models:** Use the insights from historical data to develop models that predict the likelihood of specific risks.
4. **Refine Risk Taxonomies:** Continuously update risk taxonomies to reflect new insights and emerging risks.

For instance, examining failures of biased hiring algorithms in other organizations can help identify similar vulnerabilities in an AI recruitment tool, enabling early intervention.

TOOLS FOR RISK IDENTIFICATION

Organizations rely on specialized tools and frameworks designed for AI systems to identify risks systematically. These tools provide structured approaches to uncover and document potential challenges.

AI RISK ASSESSMENT FRAMEWORKS

Frameworks like those developed by the National Institute of Standards and Technology (NIST) and the International Organization for Standardization (ISO) offer comprehensive guidelines for identifying and managing AI risks.

NIST AI Risk Management Framework: This framework emphasizes a risk-based approach to AI governance, focusing on:

- **Mapping Risks:** Identifying potential risks across the AI lifecycle, from development to deployment.

- **Measuring Risks:** Assessing the likelihood and impact of identified risks.
- **Mitigating Risks:** Implementing controls to address high-priority risks.
- **Monitoring Risks:** Continuously tracking risks to adapt to changes.

ISO Standards for AI: The ISO's standards for AI, such as ISO/IEC 24029 (Assessment of Machine Learning Models), provide detailed methodologies for:

- Evaluating algorithm performance and robustness.
- Identifying biases in training data.
- Ensuring compliance with ethical and regulatory requirements.

These frameworks enable organizations to adopt a structured and repeatable process for risk identification, ensuring consistency and accountability.

RISK TAXONOMIES SPECIFIC TO AI SYSTEMS

Risk taxonomies categorize potential risks into distinct groups, making identifying and addressing them easier. For AI systems, these taxonomies often include:

- **Ethical Risks:** Bias, fairness, transparency, and societal impact.
- **Operational Risks:** System reliability, scalability, and performance issues.
- **Regulatory Risks:** Compliance with laws, standards, and data privacy regulations.
- **Cybersecurity Risks:** Vulnerabilities to attacks that exploit AI models.

Organizations can tailor these taxonomies to their specific use cases, ensuring relevance and comprehensiveness. For example, an AI-powered financial trading platform might emphasize risks related to market manipulation and fraud detection.

CASE EXAMPLES: HIGH-PROFILE FAILURES AND LESSONS LEARNED

Examining real-world examples of AI failures provides valuable insights into the risks associated with these systems. These case studies highlight the importance of proactive risk identification and the consequences of oversight.

BIASED HIRING ALGORITHMS

Several high-profile incidents have demonstrated the risks of bias in AI-powered recruitment systems. For example, a leading tech company deployed an AI tool to screen job applicants, only to discover that the system favored male candidates. This bias arose from historical training data that reflected gender imbalances in the company's past hiring practices.

Lessons Learned:

1. Data Audit: Regularly audit training datasets to ensure they are representative and bias-free.
2. Algorithm Testing: Test AI models for fairness and accuracy across diverse demographic groups.
3. Human Oversight: Incorporate human review processes to identify and address biased decisions.

AUTONOMOUS VEHICLES

Autonomous vehicles have faced operational risks related to system failures and unexpected real-world scenarios. In one instance, an autonomous car failed to identify a pedestrian crossing the road, leading to a fatal accident. This incident highlighted limitations in the AI system's object detection capabilities.

Lessons Learned:

1. Scenario Testing: Conduct extensive testing in diverse environments to account for edge cases.
2. Redundancy: Build redundant systems to handle failures and ensure safety.
3. Continuous Monitoring: Use real-time monitoring to detect and address anomalies during operation.

FINANCIAL FRAUD DETECTION

An AI-powered fraud detection system deployed by a financial institution flagged a disproportionate number of false positives, leading to customer dissatisfaction and operational inefficiencies. The issue stemmed from poorly calibrated thresholds and insufficient training data.

Lessons Learned:

1. Threshold Optimization: Regularly adjust thresholds to balance sensitivity and specificity.
2. Data Augmentation: Use diverse datasets to improve model performance.
3. Stakeholder Feedback: Incorporate feedback from users and customers to refine the system.

9.3 ASSESSING AND PRIORITIZING RISKS

Assessing and prioritizing risks in Artificial Intelligence (AI) systems is critical in effectively managing potential challenges. This process enables organizations to focus their resources on the most significant risks, ensuring that AI systems are reliable and aligned with ethical and regulatory standards. This section discusses the techniques, prioritization strategies, and practical tools for assessing and prioritizing AI risks.

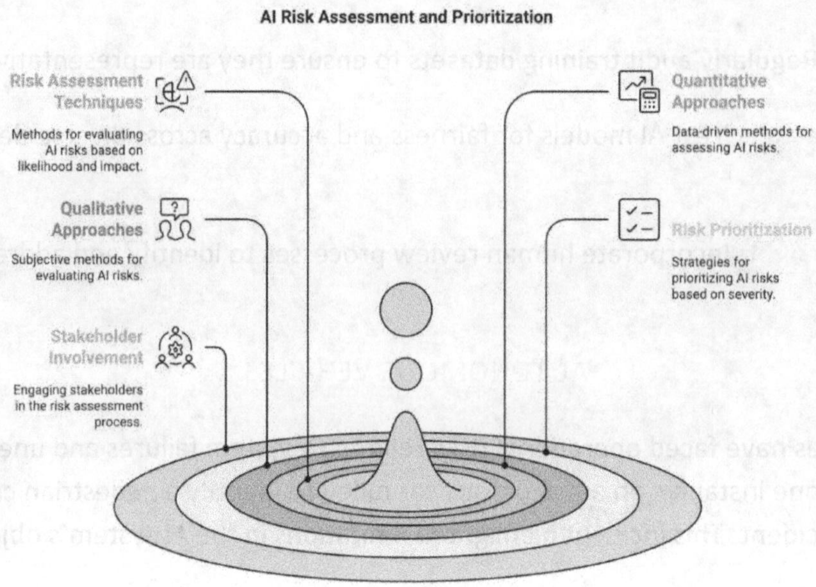

RISK ASSESSMENT TECHNIQUES

Assessing AI risks involves evaluating their likelihood and potential impact. This step helps organizations understand the severity of risks and devise appropriate mitigation strategies.

LIKELIHOOD AND IMPACT MATRIX FOR CATEGORIZING RISKS

A likelihood and impact matrix is widely used for categorizing risks based on their probability of occurrence and potential consequences. This approach provides a visual framework for prioritizing risks and helps organizations focus on the most critical ones.

Steps to Create a Likelihood and Impact Matrix:

1. Define Risk Categories: Identify the risks relevant to the AI system, such as ethical, operational, or regulatory risks.
2. Assess Likelihood: Estimate the probability of each risk occurring using historical data, expert opinions, or predictive modeling.
3. Evaluate Impact: Determine the potential consequences of each risk, considering factors such as financial loss, reputational damage, and regulatory penalties.
4. Plot Risks: Place each risk on a matrix with likelihood on one axis and impact on the other.
5. Prioritize Risks: Focus on risks in the high-likelihood and high-impact quadrant, as these pose the greatest threat to the organization.

Example: For an AI-powered fraud detection system, a likelihood and impact matrix might reveal that:

- High Likelihood, High Impact: False positives leading to customer dissatisfaction.
- Low Likelihood, High Impact: Data breaches compromising sensitive customer information.
- High Likelihood, Low Impact: Minor inaccuracies in fraud detection thresholds.

This categorization helps prioritize mitigation efforts for the most critical risks.

QUANTITATIVE VS. QUALITATIVE APPROACHES TO RISK ASSESSMENT

Risk assessment can be conducted using either quantitative or qualitative methods, depending on the AI system's complexity and data availability.

Quantitative Approaches: Quantitative methods involve numerical analysis to evaluate risks. These approaches are beneficial for assessing financial impacts or calculating probabilities.

- Key Techniques: Statistical modeling, Monte Carlo simulations, and cost-benefit analysis.
- Advantages: Provides precise, data-driven insights; enables comparison of risks across scenarios.
- Limitations: Requires extensive data and expertise in statistical analysis.

Example: A quantitative assessment for an AI-based financial trading platform might use historical market data to estimate the probability of algorithmic failures and their potential monetary impact.

Qualitative Approaches: Qualitative methods evaluate risks using subjective judgments and expert opinions. They are helpful when quantitative data is limited or when assessing non-financial impacts, such as ethical concerns.

- **Key Techniques:** Expert interviews, focus groups, and risk-scoring frameworks.
- **Advantages:** Flexible and easy to implement; captures non-quantifiable risks.
- **Limitations:** Prone to bias and subjectivity; less precise than quantitative methods.

Example: A qualitative assessment for an AI-driven recruitment tool might involve stakeholder interviews to evaluate the risk of bias in candidate selection.

RISK PRIORITIZATION

Once risks have been assessed, the next step is prioritizing them based on their severity and organizational context. Effective prioritization ensures that resources are allocated to address the most pressing risks.

FOCUS ON HIGH-IMPACT RISKS

High-impact risks should receive priority attention, particularly those with significant ethical, operational, or regulatory implications. Compliance risks are often critical in specific industries like healthcare and finance.

Example: In the healthcare industry, non-compliance with data privacy regulations (e.g., HIPAA) can result in substantial fines and loss of patient trust. Therefore, risks related to data security and patient confidentiality are typically prioritized.

Steps to Address High-Impact Risks:

1. **Identify Key Stakeholders:** Engage stakeholders affected by high-impact risks to understand their concerns and expectations.
2. **Develop Targeted Strategies:** Implement specific controls and safeguards to address high-impact risks effectively.
3. **Monitor Progress:** Regularly review mitigation efforts to ensure they remain effective and adapt to changing circumstances.

INCORPORATING STAKEHOLDER PERSPECTIVES IN PRIORITIZATION

Stakeholders—including customers, regulators, and employees—are crucial in prioritizing risks. Incorporating their perspectives ensures that risk management efforts align with organizational values and user needs.

Approaches to Stakeholder Involvement:

- **Surveys and Feedback:** Collect input from stakeholders to identify their primary concerns and expectations.

- Stakeholder Committees: Establish committees to provide ongoing guidance on risk prioritization.
- Transparency Initiatives: Share risk assessment results with stakeholders to build trust and encourage collaboration.

Example: For an AI-powered recommendation system used in e-commerce, stakeholder feedback might reveal concerns about data privacy and algorithmic transparency. These insights can guide the prioritization of data protection and explainability risks.

PRACTICAL TEMPLATES

Practical tools and templates are invaluable for standardizing risk assessment and prioritization. These resources provide structured frameworks for documenting and analyzing risks.

RISK ASSESSMENT MATRIX

A risk assessment matrix is a simple yet effective tool for visualizing and prioritizing risks. It categorizes risks based on their likelihood and impact, enabling organizations to focus on the most critical issues.

Template Example:

Risk	Likelihood	Impact	Priority
Algorithmic Bias	High	High	Critical
Data Privacy Breach	Medium	High	High
System Downtime	High	Medium	Medium
Scalability Challenges	Low	Medium	Low

Steps to Use the Matrix:

1. Identify and list potential risks.
2. Assign likelihood and impact ratings (e.g., Low, Medium, High).
3. Calculate overall priority based on predefined criteria.
4. Use the results to guide mitigation efforts.

INDUSTRY-SPECIFIC EXAMPLES

Different industries face unique AI risks, requiring tailored risk assessment and prioritization approaches. The following examples illustrate how organizations can adapt risk assessment matrices to their specific contexts:

Healthcare:

Risk	Likelihood	Impact	Priority
Misdiagnosis	Medium	High	High
Patient Data Breach	High	High	Critical
AI Model Interpretability	Low	Medium	Low

Finance:

Risk	Likelihood	Impact	Priority
Fraud Detection Failures	High	High	Critical
Market Manipulation	Medium	High	High
Algorithmic Trading Errors	Low	Medium	Low

Retail:

Risk	Likelihood	Impact	Priority
Privacy Breaches	High	High	Critical
Recommendation Errors	Medium	Low	Low
System Scalability Issues	Medium	Medium	Medium

9.4 MITIGATING AI RISKS

Mitigating risks associated with Artificial Intelligence (AI) is a critical step in ensuring AI systems' ethical, reliable, and secure deployment. Proactive mitigation strategies help organizations address potential challenges and minimize the likelihood of adverse outcomes. This section discusses pre-deployment and post-deployment strategies, tools for risk mitigation, and practical examples to illustrate these concepts.

DEVELOPING MITIGATION STRATEGIES

Mitigation strategies are designed to address AI risks at various stages of the system's lifecycle. A two-pronged approach ensures comprehensive risk management by focusing on pre-deployment and post-deployment activities.

PRE-DEPLOYMENT STRATEGIES

Pre-deployment strategies aim to identify and address risks before introducing an AI system into real-world environments. These strategies ensure the system is robust, ethical, and aligned with organizational and societal values.

1. **Bias Testing:** Bias in AI systems can lead to unfair outcomes, particularly in sensitive domains like hiring, lending, and law enforcement. Bias testing involves evaluating datasets and algorithms to detect and address discriminatory patterns.

- **Steps in Bias Testing:**
    - Conduct exploratory data analysis to identify imbalances in training datasets.
    - Use fairness metrics, such as disparate impact ratios, to evaluate model outputs.
    - Retrain models using balanced datasets or fairness-aware algorithms.

2. **Rigorous Validation:** Validation ensures that AI systems perform as intended under diverse conditions. This process involves testing the model against real-world scenarios to identify potential weaknesses.

- **Key Activities:**
    - Conduct stress tests to evaluate the model's robustness under extreme conditions.
    - Use cross-validation techniques to ensure generalizability across different datasets.
    - Test for edge cases and rare scenarios that could lead to failures.

3. **Ethical Reviews:** Ethical reviews ensure that AI systems align with organizational values and societal norms. They assess the system's impact on stakeholders and identify potential ethical concerns.

- **Components of Ethical Reviews:**
    - Engage diverse stakeholders to understand ethical implications.
    - Evaluate the transparency and explainability of the AI system.
    - Assess compliance with ethical frameworks like the EU's Ethics Guidelines for Trustworthy AI.

POST-DEPLOYMENT STRATEGIES

Post-deployment strategies focus on managing risks that arise during the operational phase of an AI system. Continuous monitoring and adaptive measures are essential to address evolving challenges.

1. **Continuous Monitoring:** AI systems that monitor real-time data help detect anomalies and address issues before they escalate. This involves tracking key performance indicators (KPIs) and flagging deviations from expected behavior.

- **Key Activities:**
  - Implement logging and monitoring tools to capture system performance metrics.
  - Use anomaly detection algorithms to identify unexpected behavior.
  - Monitor user feedback to uncover potential issues.

2. **Issue Resolution:** When risks materialize, swift and effective resolution is critical to minimize harm. Organizations should establish processes for investigating and addressing issues.

- **Steps in Issue Resolution:**
  - Identify the root cause of the problem, such as data drift or model degradation.
  - Implement corrective actions, such as retraining models or updating algorithms.
  - Communicate transparently with stakeholders about the issue and its resolution.

RISK MITIGATION TOOLS

Various tools are available to support organizations in mitigating AI risks. These tools provide specialized capabilities for addressing biases, interpretability, and security.

BIAS DETECTION SOFTWARE

Bias detection software helps identify and address unfair patterns in AI systems. These tools provide metrics and visualizations to evaluate the fairness of datasets and models.

- **Examples:**
  - **IBM AI Fairness 360:** Offers a suite of metrics and algorithms to detect and mitigate bias in AI models.
  - **Google What-If Tool:** Allows users to explore model behavior and evaluate fairness across different groups.

MODEL INTERPRETABILITY TOOLS

Interpretability tools enhance transparency by providing insights into how AI systems make decisions. These tools help stakeholders understand the factors influencing model outputs.

- **Examples:**
    - **SHAP (SHapley Additive exPlanations):** Explains individual predictions by attributing contributions to input features.
    - **LIME (Local Interpretable Model-agnostic Explanations):** Generates explanations for model predictions in a locally interpretable manner.

SECURITY AUDITS

Security audits identify vulnerabilities in AI systems and help protect against cyber threats. They evaluate the system's resilience to attacks, such as adversarial inputs or data breaches.

- **Key Activities:**
    - Conduct penetration testing to simulate cyberattacks.
    - Assess the robustness of models against adversarial examples.
    - Implement encryption and access controls to safeguard data.

EXAMPLES OF RISK MITIGATION

Real-world examples illustrate how mitigation strategies and tools can address specific AI risks. These case studies highlight best practices and lessons learned.

MITIGATION OF ALGORITHMIC BIAS IN FINANCIAL CREDIT SCORING SYSTEMS

Credit scoring systems powered by AI have been criticized for perpetuating biases that disadvantage certain demographic groups. One notable example is a financial institution that identified racial bias in its credit approval process.

Steps Taken:

1. **Bias Detection:** The organization used fairness metrics to evaluate model outputs and discovered that minority applicants were likelier to be denied credit.
2. **Data Augmentation:** Additional data sources were incorporated to provide a more comprehensive view of applicants' creditworthiness.
3. **Model Retraining:** The model was retrained using fairness-aware algorithms to reduce discriminatory patterns.
4. **Stakeholder Engagement:** Customers and advocacy groups were involved in reviewing the revised system to ensure transparency and accountability.

Outcome: The revised system demonstrated improved fairness while maintaining predictive accuracy, restoring customer trust and regulatory compliance.

ENSURING INTERPRETABILITY IN HEALTHCARE AI SYSTEMS

A healthcare provider deployed an AI-powered diagnostic tool to assist physicians in identifying diseases. However, concerns about the tool's lack of transparency hindered its adoption.

Steps Taken:

1. **Interpretability Tools:** The organization used SHAP and LIME to explain the model's predictions and highlight influential features.
2. **Training Programs:** Physicians were trained to understand and interpret the AI tool's outputs.
3. **User Feedback:** The tool was updated based on feedback from medical professionals to improve usability and reliability.

Outcome: The enhanced transparency and usability of the diagnostic tool increased physician confidence and improved patient outcomes.

STRENGTHENING SECURITY IN AUTONOMOUS VEHICLES

An autonomous vehicle manufacturer faced risks related to adversarial attacks, where malicious inputs could manipulate the AI system's behavior.

Steps Taken:

1. **Security Audits:** The organization conducted penetration testing to identify vulnerabilities.
2. **Adversarial Training:** The model was retrained using adversarial examples to improve resilience.
3. **Continuous Monitoring:** Real-time monitoring tools were implemented to detect and respond to potential attacks.

Outcome: The improved security measures reduced the risk of adversarial attacks and enhanced the safety of autonomous vehicles.

9.5 CONTINUOUS MONITORING AND FEEDBACK LOOPS

The deployment of Artificial Intelligence (AI) systems is not a one-time event but a dynamic process that requires ongoing oversight to ensure effectiveness and safety. Continuous monitoring and feedback loops are essential components of AI risk management, allowing organizations to manage risks throughout the AI lifecycle, adapt to evolving circumstances, and refine their systems based on real-world performance.

Continuous monitoring ensures that AI systems remain reliable, ethical, and compliant over time. It addresses the dynamic nature of AI environments, where changes in data, technology, and regulations can impact performance and introduce new risks.

MANAGING RISKS THROUGHOUT THE AI LIFECYCLE

AI systems are susceptible to various risks that may arise at different stages of their lifecycle. These risks include data drift, model degradation, and operational anomalies. Such issues can go undetected without continuous monitoring, potentially leading to significant harm.

Key Aspects of Managing Risks:

1. **Detecting Data Drift:** Data drift occurs when the underlying data used by an AI system changes over time, rendering the model less accurate. Continuous monitoring helps identify these changes early and triggers retraining processes to maintain performance.

2. **Identifying Model Degradation:** AI models can degrade over time due to shifts in user behavior, environmental changes, or technological advancements. Monitoring tools track key performance indicators (KPIs) to flag signs of degradation.

3. **Ensuring Operational Reliability:** Continuous monitoring detects system outages, slowdowns, or other operational issues that could compromise the system's functionality.

For example, a predictive maintenance AI system in manufacturing might need to adapt to seasonal variations in equipment usage. Monitoring ensures that the model's predictions remain accurate and actionable.

ADAPTING TO CHANGES IN REGULATIONS, TECHNOLOGIES, AND BUSINESS NEEDS

The regulatory landscape for AI is evolving rapidly, with new laws and standards emerging to address ethical and societal concerns. Similarly, technological advancements and shifting business priorities can necessitate updates to AI systems. Continuous monitoring allows organizations to stay ahead of these changes and adapt accordingly.

Key Adaptation Strategies:

1. **Regulatory Compliance:** Monitoring systems can track compliance with existing regulations and alert organizations to changes in laws, such as data privacy requirements or algorithmic transparency standards.

2. **Technological Updates:** As new tools and frameworks become available, monitoring ensures that AI systems are updated to leverage these advancements while maintaining stability.

3. **Business Alignment:** AI systems must align with evolving business goals, such as entering new markets or addressing emerging customer needs. Monitoring tools provide insights into how well the system supports these objectives.

For instance, an AI-powered recommendation engine for an e-commerce platform might require updates to accommodate new product categories or market segments. Continuous monitoring helps identify areas for improvement and ensures alignment with business priorities.

BUILDING FEEDBACK MECHANISMS

Feedback mechanisms are integral to improving AI systems and proactively addressing risks. Organizations can refine their systems and enhance overall performance by incorporating input from users, stakeholders, and automated monitoring tools.

USING USER AND STAKEHOLDER FEEDBACK TO IMPROVE AI SYSTEMS

Engaging users and stakeholders in the feedback process ensures that AI systems meet their needs and expectations. This approach fosters trust and encourages collaboration in addressing challenges.

Key Feedback Strategies:

1. **Collecting Feedback:**
    - Use surveys, interviews, and focus groups to gather input from end-users and stakeholders.
    - Monitor user behavior to identify patterns and areas for improvement.
2. **Analyzing Feedback:**
    - Categorize feedback into actionable insights, such as usability issues, ethical concerns, or performance gaps.
    - Prioritize feedback based on its impact and feasibility.
3. **Implementing Changes:**
    - Use feedback to update algorithms, refine interfaces, or adjust system parameters.
    - Communicate changes to stakeholders to build confidence in the system.

For example, a healthcare AI system used for patient diagnosis might incorporate physician feedback to improve its interpretability and ease of use. Regular updates based on this feedback enhance the system's accuracy and adoption.

INCORPORATING MONITORING TOOLS TO FLAG RISKS IN REAL TIME

Automated monitoring tools provide real-time insights into AI systems' performance and behavior, enabling organizations to detect and address risks promptly.

Key Monitoring Tools and Techniques:

1. **Performance Monitoring:**
   - Track accuracy, precision, and recall metrics to evaluate system effectiveness.
   - Use dashboards to visualize performance trends and identify anomalies.
2. **Anomaly Detection:**
   - Deploy algorithms to identify unusual patterns in system behavior, such as unexpected spikes in error rates or changes in user interactions.
   - Integrate alerts to notify teams of potential issues in real-time.
3. **Ethical and Compliance Monitoring:**
   - Use tools to assess fairness, bias, and transparency in AI systems.
   - Monitor compliance with regulatory requirements and organizational policies.

For instance, a financial institution using an AI fraud detection system might employ monitoring tools to track false favorable rates and ensure compliance with anti-discrimination laws. Alerts for deviations from expected performance help prevent customer dissatisfaction and regulatory penalties.

9.6 EMERGING AND INDUSTRY-SPECIFIC RISKS

Emerging and industry-specific risks demand significant attention in the rapidly evolving landscape of artificial intelligence (AI). Organizations must proactively identify, understand, and mitigate these risks to leverage AI technologies effectively and responsibly.

EMERGING RISKS

RISKS ASSOCIATED WITH GENERATIVE AI

Generative AI has transformed creative and operational processes across industries, enabling advancements in content generation, natural language processing, and design automation. However, it introduces several critical risks:

1. **Misinformation**: Generative AI can produce realistic but entirely fabricated content, including text, images, and videos. This raises concerns about the spread of misinformation, especially in sensitive areas like news, politics, and public health. For example, AI-generated fake news

articles or social media posts can manipulate public opinion, destabilize communities, and erode trust in institutions.

2. **Deepfakes**: AI's ability to create hyper-realistic videos or audio imitating real individuals poses significant ethical and security challenges. Deepfakes can be exploited for malicious purposes, including identity theft, fraud, and defamation. Organizations and governments must address these risks by investing in detection tools and establishing legal frameworks.

CYBERSECURITY THREATS TARGETING AI MODELS

AI systems are increasingly becoming targets for cyberattacks due to their pivotal role in decision-making processes. Key risks include:

1. **Adversarial Attacks**: Malicious actors can manipulate AI models by introducing subtle perturbations in input data. For example, an antagonistic attack on an image recognition system might alter a stop sign's appearance to be misclassified as a yield sign, potentially causing accidents in autonomous vehicles.

2. **Model Theft and Data Breaches**: AI models often rely on proprietary data and algorithms. Cybercriminals targeting these models could steal intellectual property or sensitive user data, leading to significant financial and reputational damage.

3. **Poisoning Attacks**: Attackers can corrupt training datasets, resulting in AI models that produce biased or harmful outcomes. This is particularly concerning in sectors where AI decisions directly impact human lives, such as healthcare or criminal justice.

INDUSTRY-SPECIFIC RISKS

HEALTHCARE: MISDIAGNOSIS OR UNSAFE RECOMMENDATIONS BY AI SYSTEMS

The integration of AI in healthcare has led to breakthroughs in diagnostics, treatment planning, and patient care. However, reliance on AI systems carries substantial risks:

1. **Misdiagnosis**: AI models trained on limited or biased datasets may produce inaccurate diagnoses, potentially leading to inappropriate treatments or missed critical conditions. For example, an AI system might fail to identify a rare disease due to a lack of diverse training data.

2. **Unsafe Recommendations**: Automated systems to prescribe medications or recommend surgeries could generate unsafe or suboptimal advice. This risk is exacerbated when healthcare professionals overly trust AI outputs without critically assessing validity.

FINANCE: FRAUD RISKS IN AUTOMATED TRADING ALGORITHMS

AI-powered trading systems have revolutionized financial markets by enabling rapid and efficient transactions. However, they also introduce unique risks:

1. Market Manipulation: Malicious actors could exploit vulnerabilities in AI algorithms to manipulate markets. For instance, spoofing—placing false buy or sell orders—can mislead AI systems and distort market prices.

2. Fraud Detection Failures: While AI commonly identifies fraudulent activities, sophisticated criminals continually adapt their methods to evade detection. Relating outdated or poorly calibrated models could leave financial institutions vulnerable to undetected fraud.

RETAIL: PRIVACY BREACHES IN PERSONALIZED MARKETING AI

AI-driven personalization has transformed the retail industry by enhancing customer experiences and increasing sales. However, it has also raised significant privacy concerns:

1. Data Overcollection: AI systems used in personalized marketing often require extensive data collection, including browsing history, purchase patterns, and personal preferences. This can lead to overcollection and misuse of sensitive information.

2. Unauthorized Access: Retailers that store vast amounts of customer data for AI-driven insights are prime cyberattack targets. Breaches could expose private consumer information, leading to regulatory penalties and a loss of consumer trust.

3. Bias in Recommendations: AI algorithms may unintentionally reinforce stereotypes or exclude specific demographics from targeted marketing efforts, leading to reputational harm and potential legal challenges.

ADDRESSING EMERGING AND INDUSTRY-SPECIFIC RISKS

To mitigate these risks, organizations and industries must adopt a multi-faceted approach:

1. Robust Governance Frameworks: Establishing clear policies and guidelines for AI development and deployment is essential. This includes adherence to ethical principles, transparency, and accountability mechanisms.

2. Continuous Monitoring and Updates: AI models must be regularly evaluated and updated to ensure they remain secure, accurate, and unbiased. Employing monitoring systems to detect anomalies or vulnerabilities in real time can prevent catastrophic outcomes.

3. Investment in Security Technologies: Organizations should prioritize investments in cybersecurity measures, such as adversarial attack detection systems, data encryption, and robust access controls.

4. Education and Awareness: Training stakeholders on the limitations and risks of AI systems can foster responsible usage and reduce overreliance on automated decision-making.

5. **Collaboration Across Sectors**: Industry-wide collaborations can facilitate the sharing of best practices, standards, and threat intelligence, enabling collective resilience against emerging risks.

9.7 BUILDING A RISK-AWARE CULTURE

A risk-aware culture is essential for any organization to navigate uncertainties while effectively achieving its strategic objectives. It goes beyond compliance, embedding risk awareness into the organization's DNA to enhance decision-making, resilience, and long-term sustainability.

IMPORTANCE OF CULTURAL CHANGE

Cultural change is the cornerstone of fostering a risk-aware environment. Embedding risk awareness into organizational processes ensures that all levels recognize the importance of identifying, assessing, and managing risks. This shift minimizes the likelihood of unforeseen disruptions and maximizes opportunities for innovation and growth. A risk-aware culture aligns individual and organizational behaviors with the broader risk management framework, promoting accountability, transparency, and informed decision-making.

Organizations can transition from reactive approaches to proactive risk management by integrating risk awareness into daily operations. This cultural change encourages employees to view risk as a shared responsibility rather than solely a leadership or compliance function. Consequently, this alignment between culture and risk management strategy enhances an organization's ability to anticipate challenges, adapt to changes, and maintain a competitive edge.

STRATEGIES FOR A RISK-AWARE CULTURE

Building a risk-aware culture requires deliberate effort, starting with leadership and extending to every employee. Below are key strategies to achieve this transformation.

1. **Leadership Commitment to Proactive Risk Management**

    - Leadership commitment is the foundation of a risk-aware culture. Executives and managers must set the tone at the top and demonstrate that risk management is a priority. This includes integrating risk considerations into strategic planning, decision-making, and daily operations.

    - Leaders should model behaviors emphasizing risk awareness, such as actively participating in risk assessments, fostering open discussions about potential challenges, and celebrating successful risk mitigation efforts. By visibly prioritizing risk management, leaders encourage employees to adopt similar attitudes.

- Leadership commitment also involves resource allocation. Providing teams with the tools, technologies, and personnel to identify and manage risks effectively underscores the organization's dedication to risk awareness.

2. Regular Training and Awareness Programs for All Employees

    - Education and awareness are vital for embedding risk consciousness across the organization. Regular training programs tailored to different roles ensure employees understand the risks relevant to their functions and the organization.
    - Training should cover key concepts, such as identifying risks, evaluating their impact, and implementing mitigation strategies. Interactive workshops, scenario-based exercises, and e-learning modules can enhance engagement and knowledge retention.
    - Ongoing awareness campaigns reinforce the importance of risk management. These can include newsletters, infographics, and success stories highlighting the value of proactive risk practices. Employees remain vigilant and prepared by making risk awareness an integral part of the organizational narrative.
    - Empowering employees through training also fosters a sense of ownership. When individuals understand their role in managing risks, they are more likely to take proactive steps, report potential issues, and contribute to the organization's overall resilience.

In conclusion, building a risk-aware culture is not a one-time initiative but a continuous journey. Through leadership commitment and comprehensive training programs, organizations can create an environment where risk awareness is deeply ingrained. This cultural transformation strengthens the organization's ability to manage risks and enhances its adaptability, innovation, and success in an ever-changing business landscape.

CHAPTER 10: COMPLIANCE AND REGULATION

10.1 INTRODUCTION TO AI COMPLIANCE

WHAT IS AI COMPLIANCE?

AI compliance refers to the adherence of artificial intelligence systems, practices, and processes to established legal, ethical, and industry-specific standards. These standards encompass data privacy, algorithmic fairness, transparency, accountability, and operational integrity, ensuring that AI technologies are developed and used responsibly.

Compliance is essential in AI governance because it balances innovation with accountability. AI systems can significantly influence critical aspects of human lives, from healthcare and finance to employment and education. As a result, ensuring these systems operate within well-defined ethical and regulatory frameworks is paramount. Compliance safeguards against unintended consequences such as discrimination, privacy violations, or misuse of technology while fostering confidence in AI adoption.

AI governance is incomplete without compliance mechanisms, the foundation for sustainable and ethical AI deployment. These mechanisms provide enterprises with a structured approach to managing risks, enhancing accountability, and ensuring that AI aligns with societal values and expectations. In a rapidly evolving regulatory environment, organizations must integrate compliance into every phase of their AI lifecycle, from development to deployment.

WHY COMPLIANCE MATTERS

AVOIDING LEGAL RISKS, FINES, AND REPUTATIONAL DAMAGE

Non-compliance with AI regulations can have severe legal and financial repercussions. Regulatory bodies worldwide are implementing stricter guidelines to ensure that AI systems operate transparently and ethically. For instance, the European Union's AI Act and General Data Protection Regulation (GDPR) impose stringent requirements on AI developers and users. Violating these laws can result in fines, legal battles, and operational disruptions.

Beyond legal penalties, organizations risk reputational damage when their AI systems fail to comply with ethical standards. Publicized incidents of algorithmic bias or data breaches can erode customer trust and tarnish a brand's image. For enterprises, reputation is as critical as regulatory adherence, as it directly influences customer loyalty and market positioning.

BUILDING TRUST WITH CUSTOMERS AND STAKEHOLDERS

Trust is a cornerstone of successful AI adoption. Customers, stakeholders, and regulators expect organizations to use AI responsibly and transparently. Compliance frameworks help build this trust by demonstrating a commitment to ethical practices and safeguarding user interests.

Transparent compliance practices assure stakeholders that AI systems are free from bias, respect user privacy, and operate with accountability. For customers, compliance reflects an organization's respect for their rights and values, fostering loyalty and engagement. For investors and partners, it signals a commitment to long-term sustainability and adherence to global standards.

Moreover, embedding compliance into AI governance can give organizations a competitive edge. As regulatory landscapes evolve, enterprises that prioritize compliance early can position themselves as leaders in responsible AI and differentiate themselves in an increasingly cautious market.

10.2 OVERVIEW OF GLOBAL AI LAWS AND REGULATIONS

The rapid development and adoption of artificial intelligence (AI) technologies have necessitated the establishment of regulatory frameworks worldwide. Governments, organizations, and international bodies increasingly introduce AI-specific laws and guidelines to address ethical, legal, and operational challenges. This section provides an overview of significant regulations, emerging trends, and the complexities of navigating a fragmented regulatory landscape.

MAJOR REGULATIONS WORLDWIDE

EUROPEAN UNION (EU): AI ACT AND GDPR

The European Union (EU) has positioned itself as a global leader in AI regulation. The proposed AI Act seeks to establish a comprehensive legal framework to govern the development and use of AI systems. The legislation classifies AI applications into four risk categories: unacceptable, high, limited, and minimal risk. High-risk applications, such as biometric identification and credit scoring, require rigorous compliance measures, including transparency, documentation, and human oversight. The act also prohibits AI systems that pose an unacceptable risk, such as those exploiting vulnerabilities or enabling social scoring by governments.

In addition to the AI Act, the General Data Protection Regulation (GDPR) remains a cornerstone of data privacy in the EU. It impacts AI systems that process personal data, emphasizing data minimization, transparency, and user consent. GDPR's stringent requirements influence AI development, particularly in data collection, storage, and automated decision-making.

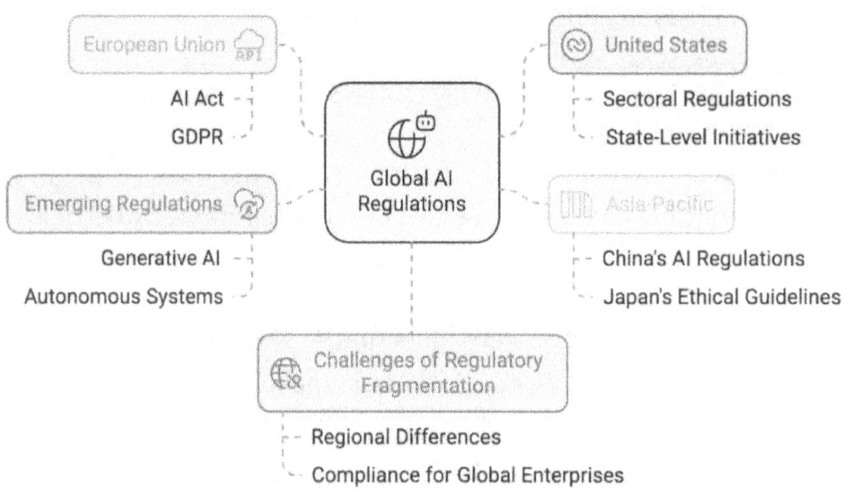

UNITED STATES (US): SECTORAL REGULATIONS AND STATE-LEVEL INITIATIVES

The United States has taken a decentralized approach to AI regulation, with sector-specific guidelines and state-level initiatives. Federal agencies like the Federal Trade Commission (FTC) oversee AI applications in consumer protection, while the Food and Drug Administration (FDA) regulates AI in healthcare. Notably, the National Institute of Standards and Technology (NIST) released a risk management framework to guide the responsible use of AI.

At the state level, initiatives like the California Consumer Privacy Act (CCPA) and its successor, the California Privacy Rights Act (CPRA), emphasize data protection and transparency. These laws require organizations to disclose AI-related data processing activities and give users control over their personal information. States like Illinois and New York have introduced laws addressing specific AI applications, such as facial recognition and employment algorithms.

ASIA-PACIFIC: CHINA'S AI REGULATIONS AND JAPAN'S ETHICAL GUIDELINES

China has implemented robust regulations to govern AI development and deployment. The country's AI initiatives emphasize security, transparency, and ethical considerations. For example, China's rules on algorithm recommendation services mandate disclosure of algorithmic decision-making processes and allow users to opt out of recommendation systems. Additionally, the country's Personal Information Protection Law (PIPL) mirrors GDPR's focus on data privacy and user consent, with strict penalties for non-compliance.

On the other hand, Japan has adopted a more ethical and guideline-driven approach. The Japanese government's "Social Principles of Human-Centric AI" emphasizes transparency, inclusivity, and user trust. These principles aim to ensure AI systems align with societal values while fostering innovation. Japan also participates actively in international collaborations to promote responsible AI development.

EMERGING REGULATIONS

ANTICIPATED CHANGES IN GLOBAL AI POLICIES

As AI technologies evolve, regulatory frameworks are expected to adapt. Governments are focusing on generative AI, autonomous systems, and AI's impact on labor markets. For instance, the EU's AI Act includes provisions for addressing emerging risks, while the US is considering comprehensive federal legislation to create uniform AI standards.

Generative AI, such as large language models, has raised concerns about misinformation, intellectual property, and ethical use. Regulatory bodies are exploring measures to ensure these technologies are deployed responsibly. Similarly, autonomous systems, including self-driving vehicles and drones, are prompting discussions on liability and safety standards.

THE ROLE OF INTERNATIONAL ORGANIZATIONS

International organizations play a crucial role in harmonizing AI regulations. The Organisation for Economic Co-operation and Development (OECD) has established AI principles advocating for transparency, accountability, and human-centric development. These principles provide a baseline for member countries to develop consistent AI policies.

UNESCO has also developed ethical guidelines for AI, emphasizing cultural diversity, human rights, and environmental sustainability. These frameworks encourage cross-border collaboration and align AI governance with global values. However, the effectiveness of these efforts depends on individual nations' adoption and implementation of them.

CHALLENGES OF REGULATORY FRAGMENTATION

REGIONAL DIFFERENCES AND THEIR IMPACT

One of the most significant challenges in AI compliance is the fragmentation of regulatory frameworks across regions. Variations in legal requirements, cultural norms, and enforcement mechanisms create global complexities for enterprises. For example, while the EU's AI Act imposes stringent compliance measures, the US's decentralized approach leaves companies navigating diverse state and federal requirements. Similarly, China's focus on algorithmic transparency contrasts with Japan's ethical guidelines, reflecting differing priorities.

COMPLIANCE FOR GLOBAL ENTERPRISES

Regulatory fragmentation necessitates significant resources for multinational organizations to ensure compliance across jurisdictions. Enterprises must develop region-specific compliance strategies, maintain comprehensive documentation, and engage with local regulators. This increases operational costs and complicates innovation, as companies must adapt their AI systems to varying standards.

BRIDGING THE GAP

Efforts to address regulatory fragmentation include the development of international standards, such as those by the International Organization for Standardization (ISO). These standards aim to create a common language for AI governance, facilitating interoperability and reducing compliance burdens. Collaborative initiatives between governments, industries, and academia can further bridge regulatory gaps and promote harmonization.

10.3 CREATING A COMPLIANCE STRATEGY

The increasing complexity of AI systems and the evolving regulatory landscape necessitate the development of robust compliance strategies. Such strategies ensure that AI systems are aligned with ethical principles, legal requirements, and organizational goals. This section outlines key steps in compliance management, the importance of building an effective compliance team, and tools for monitoring and reporting compliance.

AI Compliance Strategy Outcomes

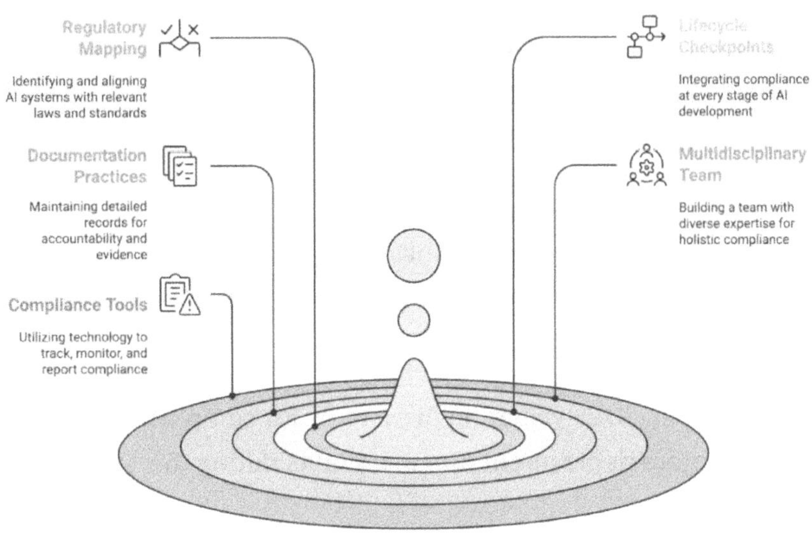

KEY STEPS IN COMPLIANCE MANAGEMENT

MAPPING AI SYSTEMS TO REGULATORY REQUIREMENTS

Mapping AI systems to applicable regulatory requirements is the first step in ensuring compliance. This involves identifying the laws, standards, and ethical guidelines relevant to the organization's AI applications. Given the diverse range of AI applications—from natural language processing to autonomous systems—it is essential to categorize AI systems based on their functionality and risk profile.

Organizations must:

- Conduct a regulatory impact assessment to identify which laws apply to their AI systems. For example, the GDPR may apply if the system processes personal data, while sector-specific regulations may govern healthcare or financial AI applications.
- Develop a comprehensive inventory of AI systems, including their purpose, data inputs, algorithms, and decision-making processes.
- Align each system's functionalities with specific compliance requirements, such as transparency, data protection, or algorithmic fairness.

This mapping process clarifies the regulatory scope and highlights areas where additional controls or adjustments are needed.

ESTABLISHING COMPLIANCE CHECKPOINTS ACROSS THE AI LIFECYCLE

AI compliance is not a one-time activity but a continuous process that spans the entire AI lifecycle. Establishing compliance checkpoints ensures that regulatory requirements are integrated at every stage, from design to deployment and monitoring.

Key compliance checkpoints include:

- **Design and Development**: Ensuring that ethical and regulatory considerations are incorporated into the design phase. This includes conducting bias assessments, validating data quality, and implementing explainability mechanisms.
- **Testing and Validation** involve evaluating AI systems for compliance with safety, fairness, and accuracy standards before deployment. Regular audits during this stage can identify potential risks early.
- **Deployment**: Verifying that AI systems are deployed in environments that align with regulatory expectations. This includes ensuring secure data handling and appropriate user disclosures.
- **Post-Deployment Monitoring**: Continuously monitoring AI systems to ensure ongoing compliance. This includes tracking performance metrics, identifying deviations from expected behavior, and updating systems to reflect new regulations.

MAINTAINING UP-TO-DATE RECORDS OF COMPLIANCE EFFORTS

Documentation is a cornerstone of AI compliance. Maintaining detailed records demonstrates accountability and provides regulators and stakeholders with evidence of compliance.

Key documentation practices include:

- Creating audit trails for all AI systems, capturing details such as data sources, algorithm updates, and testing results.
- Keeping logs of risk assessments, incident reports, and mitigation measures.
- Documenting decisions made during the AI lifecycle, including justifications for algorithmic choices and trade-offs.

These records facilitate regulatory reporting and support internal reviews and continuous improvement efforts.

BUILDING A COMPLIANCE TEAM

A successful compliance strategy relies on a multidisciplinary team with legal, technical, and risk management expertise. Collaboration between these teams ensures that compliance is addressed holistically.

ROLES AND RESPONSIBILITIES

- The Legal Team interprets regulatory requirements, manages legal risks, and ensures international and local law compliance. They also play a critical role in drafting policies, contracts, and terms of use for AI systems.
- Technical Team: Focuses on implementing compliance measures within AI systems. This includes developing algorithms that meet ethical standards, integrating monitoring tools, and ensuring data security.
- The Risk Management Team identifies and assesses potential risks associated with AI systems. They develop mitigation strategies, conduct regular audits, and coordinate incident response efforts.
- Ethics Officers (if applicable) Oversee adherence to organizational values and ethical guidelines and ensure that AI systems align with societal expectations and internal principles.

COLLABORATION AND TRAINING

Cross-functional collaboration is essential for effective compliance management. Regular training sessions should be conducted to:

- Educate team members on the latest regulatory developments and their implications for AI systems.
- Promote awareness of ethical considerations and encourage proactive identification of potential risks.
- Foster a culture of accountability and transparency within the organization.

TOOLS FOR COMPLIANCE

Technology plays a pivotal role in simplifying and enhancing compliance efforts. Various software solutions are available to assist organizations in tracking, monitoring, and reporting compliance.

COMPLIANCE TRACKING

Compliance tracking tools help organizations maintain an overview of their regulatory obligations and monitor progress in meeting them. Key features include:

- Regulatory Mapping Modules: Automatically match AI systems with relevant regulations based on their functionality and location.
- Risk Assessment Dashboards: Provide real-time insights into compliance risks, highlighting areas that require immediate attention.

Examples include platforms like OneTrust and TrustArc, which offer end-to-end compliance management solutions.

MONITORING AND REPORTING

Monitoring tools ensure that AI systems operate within regulatory boundaries post-deployment. Features include:

- **Automated Auditing**: Regularly check AI system outputs for bias, accuracy, and adherence to ethical standards.
- **Incident Reporting**: Log and track compliance-related incidents, enabling timely remediation.

Reporting tools facilitate transparent communication with regulators and stakeholders. They generate comprehensive reports on compliance efforts, including audit results, risk assessments, and corrective actions.

DATA PRIVACY AND SECURITY SOLUTIONS

Data privacy tools ensure that AI systems handle sensitive information responsibly. Key features include:

- **Data Masking and Encryption**: Protect user data during processing and storage.
- **Consent Management Systems**: Enable organizations to track and manage user consent for data processing activities.

Examples include IBM's Data Privacy Passports and Microsoft's Compliance Manager, which offer tailored solutions for data protection in AI environments.

10.4 MONITORING AND REPORTING COMPLIANCE

Monitoring and reporting are critical components of an effective AI compliance strategy. Continuous oversight ensures that AI systems align with evolving regulations, ethical standards, and organizational objectives. Transparent reporting demonstrates accountability and builds trust with regulators, stakeholders, and the public. This section explores the importance of ongoing monitoring, the key performance indicators (KPIs) for compliance, and best practices for reporting.

ONGOING MONITORING

IMPORTANCE OF CONTINUOUS MONITORING FOR ADHERENCE TO EVOLVING REGULATIONS

AI compliance is not a static endeavor. The rapid pace of technological innovation and frequent updates to regulatory frameworks necessitate continuous monitoring of AI systems. Organizations must ensure their systems comply with existing and emerging standards to mitigate risks and avoid penalties.

Key reasons for ongoing monitoring include:

- Adaptation to New Regulations: Regulatory landscapes are dynamic. Monitoring ensures that AI systems remain compliant as laws evolve, such as introducing the European Union's AI Act or updating data privacy laws like GDPR and CCPA.
- Detection of Compliance Gaps: Continuous oversight helps identify and address areas where AI systems deviate from regulatory requirements, ethical guidelines, or performance expectations.
- Risk Mitigation: Regular monitoring minimizes the likelihood of non-compliance incidents, reducing legal, financial, and reputational risks.
- Operational Efficiency: Proactive monitoring streamlines compliance efforts by identifying issues early preventing costly overhauls or reactive measures.

KEY PERFORMANCE INDICATORS (KPIS) FOR COMPLIANCE MONITORING

KPIs provide measurable benchmarks to evaluate the effectiveness of compliance efforts. They help organizations track performance and identify areas for improvement. Common KPIs for AI compliance monitoring include:

1. Accuracy and Fairness Metrics:
    - Measure the accuracy of AI outputs and ensure that algorithms perform without bias or discrimination.
    - Example: Disparity impact ratio to assess fairness across different demographic groups.

2. **Data Privacy Compliance**:

    - Monitor adherence to data protection standards, such as encryption, consent management, and secure data storage.
    - Example: Percentage of datasets anonymized or encrypted during processing.

3. **Incident Response Time**:

    - Track the average time to identify, report, and resolve compliance-related incidents.
    - Example: Mean time to detection (MTTD) and mean time to resolution (MTTR).

4. **Audit Completion Rate**:

    - Measure the percentage of scheduled internal and external audits completed on time.
    - Example: Quarterly audit adherence rate.

5. **Regulatory Update Implementation**:

    - Track the timely incorporation of new regulatory requirements into AI systems.
    - Example: Number of compliance updates implemented within a defined timeline.

REPORTING TO REGULATORS AND STAKEHOLDERS

BEST PRACTICES FOR TRANSPARENT REPORTING

Transparent reporting is essential for demonstrating accountability and building trust. Organizations must provide regulators and stakeholders with clear, accurate, comprehensive compliance reports. Best practices for effective reporting include:

1. **Standardized Reporting Formats**:

    - Use standardized templates and formats to ensure consistency and clarity in reporting.
    - Example: Align reports with frameworks like the EU's AI Act or NIST's AI Risk Management Framework.

2. **Comprehensive Documentation**:

    - Include detailed records of compliance efforts, such as audit results, risk assessments, and corrective actions.
    - Example: Maintain logs of algorithm updates and testing outcomes.

3. Stakeholder-Specific Reporting:
   - Tailor reports to the needs of different audiences. Regulators require technical and regulatory details, while stakeholders may need high-level insights.
   - Example: Provide a summary report for executives and a technical annex for regulators.
4. Real-Time Reporting Capabilities:
   - Implement systems that enable real-time tracking and reporting of compliance metrics.
   - Example: Dashboards that visualize key compliance KPIs for internal and external audiences.
5. Transparency and Honesty:
   - Disclose challenges, gaps, and incidents alongside corrective measures to demonstrate a commitment to improvement.
   - Example: Report a data breach promptly, outlining the cause, impact, and mitigation steps.

EXAMPLES OF EFFECTIVE COMPLIANCE REPORTING

Effective compliance reporting goes beyond fulfilling regulatory obligations; it builds credibility and trust. Successful examples include:

1. Incident Reporting:
   - An organization experiencing an algorithmic bias issue documents the incident, conducts a root cause analysis, and outlines corrective actions in a report to regulators. The organization demonstrates accountability and commitment to ethical practices by openly addressing the issue.
2. Annual Compliance Reports:
   - A technology company publishes an annual compliance report highlighting key achievements, challenges, and future goals. The report includes metrics such as audit completion rates, privacy compliance levels, and updates on regulatory changes.
3. Stakeholder Updates:
   - A financial institution provides quarterly updates to stakeholders on the status of AI compliance efforts. The updates include visual dashboards, progress on implementing new regulations, and insights into ongoing risk management efforts.

4. **Real-Time Dashboard Access:**

    - A healthcare provider implements a compliance dashboard accessible to regulators. The dashboard displays live data on system performance, adherence to privacy standards, and incident response times, fostering transparency and collaboration.

10.5 ADDRESSING COMPLIANCE CHALLENGES

AI compliance is a complex and evolving field, and organizations often encounter significant challenges while implementing and maintaining compliance frameworks. Understanding these barriers and adopting effective solutions is essential for successfully navigating the regulatory landscape.

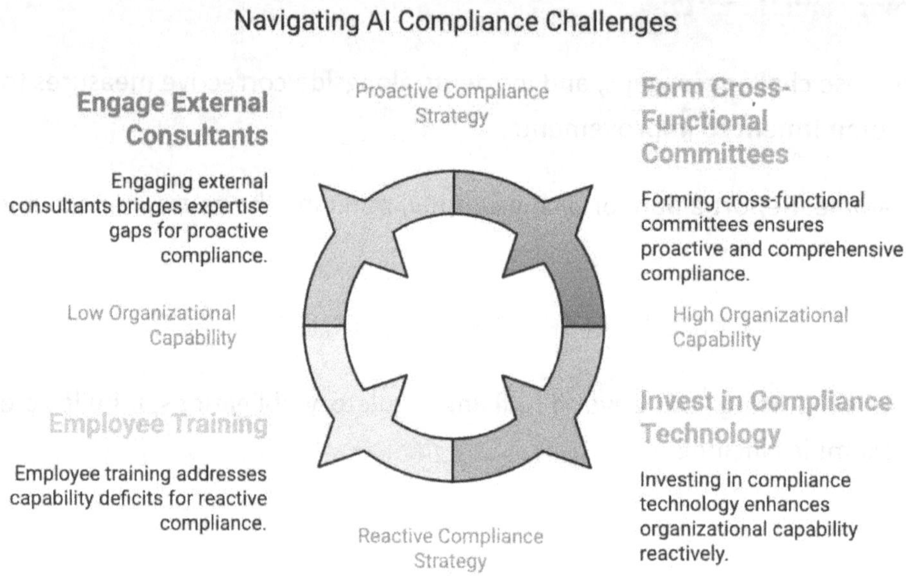

COMMON BARRIERS

RAPIDLY CHANGING REGULATIONS

One of the most pressing challenges is the rapid evolution of AI regulations. Governments and regulatory bodies continuously update laws to address emerging risks associated with AI technologies. For example, the European Union's AI Act and similar regulations are frequently revised to include new provisions for generative AI and autonomous systems. This fast-paced environment makes it difficult for organizations to stay current and adapt their AI systems to comply with the latest requirements.

LACK OF EXPERTISE IN COMPLIANCE MANAGEMENT

AI compliance requires a unique blend of legal, technical, and ethical expertise. Many organizations lack the in-house capabilities to interpret complex regulations and apply them to AI systems. This skills gap can lead to misinterpretation of requirements, incomplete compliance measures, and increased risk of non-compliance. Small and medium-sized enterprises (SMEs), in particular, may struggle due to limited access to specialized resources.

RESISTANCE TO COMPLIANCE INITIATIVES

Resistance to compliance initiatives often stems from a perception that they are time-consuming, costly, or hinder innovation. Employees and stakeholders may view compliance as a burden rather than a value-add, especially if they are not adequately informed about its importance. This resistance can lead to delays in implementation and inadequate commitment to compliance efforts.

SOLUTIONS

LEVERAGING CROSS-FUNCTIONAL EXPERTISE

Addressing compliance challenges requires collaboration across legal, technical, and operational teams. Organizations can:

- Form Cross-Functional Committees: Establish teams comprising legal experts, data scientists, risk managers, and business leaders to oversee compliance efforts.
- Engage External Consultants: Partner with compliance specialists or law firms to gain insights into complex regulations and industry best practices.

This collaborative approach ensures compliance is addressed holistically, balancing legal requirements with technical feasibility and business goals.

INVESTING IN COMPLIANCE TRAINING AND TECHNOLOGY

Building organizational expertise and adopting the right tools are critical for overcoming compliance challenges. Key initiatives include:

- Employee Training: Develop training programs to educate employees on the importance of compliance, regulatory requirements, and ethical AI practices. Tailored training ensures that all team members understand their roles in maintaining compliance.
- Technology Adoption: Invest in compliance management software to automate monitoring, reporting, and risk assessment processes. Tools like OneTrust and TrustArc provide real-time updates on regulatory changes and simplify compliance tracking.

These investments reduce the burden of manual compliance efforts and empower teams with the knowledge and resources needed to succeed.

STAYING AHEAD THROUGH PROACTIVE ENGAGEMENT WITH REGULATORS

Proactively engaging with regulators can help organizations anticipate changes and align their practices with upcoming requirements. Strategies include:

- **Participating in Public Consultations**: Discuss with regulatory bodies while drafting new laws to provide feedback and gain early insights.
- **Joining Industry Associations**: Collaborate with peers in industry groups to stay informed about regulatory developments and share best practices.
- **Monitoring Regulatory Trends**: Use tools and services that provide updates on global AI regulations to identify and prepare for upcoming changes.

Proactive engagement demonstrates a commitment to compliance and positions organizations as responsible and forward-thinking entities.

CHAPTER 11: DATA MANAGEMENT IN GOVERNANCE

11.1 INTRODUCTION TO DATA GOVERNANCE FOR AI

WHAT IS DATA GOVERNANCE?

Data governance refers to the framework and processes that ensure data is managed effectively, consistently, and securely across its lifecycle. It encompasses establishing policies, procedures, and responsibilities for managing data assets within an organization. Data governance plays a pivotal role in AI systems by ensuring that the data feeding into these systems is accurate, reliable, and secure. Without robust data governance, AI models risk being biased, unreliable, or even harmful, as they heavily depend on the quality and integrity of the data they process.

Data governance and AI governance are interlinked. While data governance focuses on managing the data lifecycle, AI governance ensures AI systems' ethical, transparent, and responsible use. Together, they create a synergistic relationship where data governance establishes the foundation for trustworthy and accountable AI by guaranteeing data quality, privacy, and compliance with regulations.

IMPORTANCE OF DATA IN AI

Data is the backbone of AI systems, directly influencing their effectiveness and reliability. Key aspects of data—quality, security, and privacy—play a critical role in determining the outcomes of AI applications.

1. Data Quality: Data accuracy, completeness, and consistency significantly affect AI performance. Poor-quality data can lead to biased models, incorrect predictions, and flawed decision-making. For example, noisy or incomplete datasets might result in an AI system misinterpreting patterns or failing to generalize effectively.

2. Data Security: Protecting data from unauthorized access, breaches, and corruption is crucial for maintaining the integrity of AI systems. Compromised data can introduce vulnerabilities, such as adversarial attacks, that manipulate AI outputs and undermine trust in the system.

3. Data Privacy: Privacy concerns are paramount in AI applications that process sensitive personal or organizational information. Ensuring compliance with regulations like GDPR, HIPAA, or CPRA and adopting techniques like anonymization or differential privacy helps safeguard individuals' rights and builds trust in AI systems.

11.2 DATA QUALITY MANAGEMENT

ENSURING HIGH-QUALITY DATA

High-quality data is the cornerstone of successful AI systems, as it directly impacts the accuracy, reliability, and fairness of AI outputs. Ensuring data quality involves addressing specific attributes and overcoming unique challenges presented by the complexity of AI systems.

KEY ATTRIBUTES OF QUALITY DATA

1. **Accuracy**: Accurate data reflects real-world values and ensures that AI models are built on factual and precise information. Inaccuracies in data can mislead AI algorithms, resulting in flawed predictions and erroneous decisions. For instance, if a financial AI system is trained on inaccurate transaction records, it may fail to detect fraudulent activities effectively.

2. **Completeness**: Complete data encompasses all necessary variables and records for meaningful analysis. Missing data can skew AI model outputs, especially in scenarios where certain features hold significant weight. For example, incomplete patient data in a healthcare AI model might result in incorrect diagnoses or treatment recommendations.

3. **Consistency**: Consistent data maintains uniformity across sources and systems. Variations in data formats, definitions, or measurement standards can lead to discrepancies and hinder the interoperability of datasets. For example, inconsistent recording of dates (e.g., MM/DD/YYYY vs. DD/MM/YYYY) may cause errors during data preprocessing.

4. **Timeliness**: Timely data reflects the current state of the analyzed domain, which is critical for AI systems reliant on real-time insights. Outdated data can render AI models ineffective or obsolete. For instance, a recommendation engine trained on outdated user preferences might deliver irrelevant suggestions.

CHALLENGES IN MANAGING DATA QUALITY FOR AI SYSTEMS

1. **Noisy Data**: Noise refers to irrelevant, erroneous, or random variations in data. AI models exposed to noisy datasets may produce inconsistent or misleading outcomes. For example, mislabeled training data in image recognition tasks can result in poor classification accuracy.

2. **Biased Datasets**: Bias in data occurs when certain groups or perspectives are underrepresented or misrepresented. This can lead to discriminatory AI outcomes, such as hiring algorithms trained on historically biased recruitment data.

3. **Large-Scale and Diverse Data Sources**: AI systems often integrate data from multiple sources with varying quality standards, formats, and structures. Harmonizing this data while preserving its integrity is a significant challenge.

4. **Dynamic Data Environments**: Many AI systems operate in environments where data evolves rapidly. Managing quality in such contexts requires continuous monitoring and adaptation to maintain relevance and reliability.

STRATEGIES FOR QUALITY MANAGEMENT

Implementing robust strategies for data quality management can mitigate the challenges mentioned above and enhance AI performance. Key strategies include data validation, audits, and cleaning processes.

DATA VALIDATION TECHNIQUES

1. **Automated Validation Rules**: These rules check for anomalies, missing values, or incorrect formats in datasets. For instance, validation scripts can ensure that numeric fields fall within acceptable ranges or that categorical fields contain predefined values.

2. **Statistical Methods**: Statistical analysis helps detect outliers and patterns indicative of data quality issues. Techniques like standard deviation analysis or clustering can identify anomalies in large datasets.

3. **Schema Validation**: Ensuring data conforms to a predefined schema guarantees structural integrity. For example, validating JSON or XML files against a schema prevents formatting errors that could disrupt AI workflows.

REGULAR DATA AUDITS AND CLEANING PROCESSES

1. **Data Audits**: Periodic reviews of data repositories help identify and address quality issues proactively. Audits can uncover error trends, assess compliance with standards, and evaluate the effectiveness of quality management practices.

2. **Data Cleaning**: Cleaning involves correcting errors, filling in missing values, and removing irrelevant records. Techniques like imputation (estimating missing values) and deduplication (eliminating duplicate entries) are commonly used. For instance, healthcare datasets often require extensive cleaning to address discrepancies in patient records.

3. **Human-in-the-Loop Approaches**: Combining automated tools with expert reviews enhances the accuracy of data-cleaning processes. Subject matter experts can validate automated corrections and ensure a nuanced understanding of the data context.

CASE STUDIES

CASE STUDY 1: BIASED RECRUITMENT ALGORITHM

An AI-driven recruitment platform was found to favor male candidates over females for technical roles. The root cause was biased training data that reflected historical hiring trends. The lack of diversity in the dataset resulted in discriminatory recommendations. Addressing this issue required revising the dataset to include balanced representations of gender and evaluating model performance with fairness metrics.

CASE STUDY 2: FINANCIAL FRAUD DETECTION

A financial institution's AI system for detecting fraudulent transactions performed poorly due to noisy and incomplete data. Many legitimate transactions were flagged as fraudulent, causing customers inconvenience. The model's accuracy improved significantly after implementing robust data validation and cleaning techniques, including outlier detection and filling in missing transaction metadata.

CASE STUDY 3: HEALTHCARE PREDICTIVE ANALYTICS

A healthcare provider's predictive analytics system failed to forecast patient readmission rates accurately. The issue stemmed from inconsistent data formats across hospitals and incomplete patient histories. The organization improved data consistency and enhanced the predictive model's performance by standardizing data collection processes and conducting regular audits.

11.3 DATA PRIVACY AND COMPLIANCE

PRIVACY CONCERNS IN AI

As AI systems increasingly rely on large volumes of sensitive data, ensuring data privacy has become a critical challenge. Sensitive information, such as healthcare records, financial details, and personal identifiers, is often central to AI applications, making them vulnerable to privacy violations. Understanding and addressing these concerns is vital to maintaining trust and compliance.

HANDLING SENSITIVE DATA

AI systems that process sensitive data, such as medical diagnostics tools, fraud detection systems, or personalized recommendation engines, must navigate complex privacy landscapes. For instance, healthcare AI applications analyze patient records to predict outcomes or recommend treatments, necessitating stringent protections to prevent unauthorized access and misuse. Similarly, financial AI systems monitor transactions to detect fraud but must do so without exposing account details or personal identifiers.

Handling such sensitive data requires mechanisms that ensure confidentiality, limit data access to authorized users, and safeguard against data breaches or leaks. Effective encryption, access controls, and audit trails are foundational measures for mitigating risks in these scenarios.

COMMON PRIVACY CHALLENGES IN AI

1. **Re-Identification Risks**: Even when datasets are anonymized, AI advancements can enable individuals to re-identify by correlating multiple datasets. For example, combining anonymized

health records with publicly available demographic data might allow AI to deduce a person's identity.

2. Data Minimization Issues: AI models often require extensive data to function effectively, which conflicts with the principle of data minimization—using only what is necessary. This creates a tension between maximizing AI performance and adhering to privacy best practices.

3. Bias and Discrimination: Privacy concerns extend beyond data breaches to include data collection and processing biases. Sensitive attributes such as race, gender, or socioeconomic status may be unintentionally exposed, leading to unfair outcomes.

4. Unclear Accountability: In many organizations, who is responsible for maintaining data privacy in AI projects is unclear. This lack of accountability can result in overlooked risks and inadequate privacy safeguards.

REGULATORY REQUIREMENTS

A growing body of privacy laws and regulations govern using sensitive data in AI systems. These frameworks set data collection, processing, and sharing standards, ensuring organizations uphold individual rights and maintain accountability.

KEY PRIVACY LAWS

1. General Data Protection Regulation (GDPR): The GDPR, enforced in the European Union, is one of the most comprehensive privacy regulations. It mandates explicit consent for data collection, enforces data minimization, and grants individuals the right to access, correct, and delete their data. AI systems operating in the EU must comply with GDPR's stringent requirements, including provisions for automated decision-making transparency.

2. Health Insurance Portability and Accountability Act (HIPAA): In the United States, HIPAA governs the handling of healthcare data. AI applications in the healthcare domain must ensure compliance with HIPAA's Privacy and Security Rules, which require encryption, secure data storage, and limited access to patient records.

3. California Privacy Rights Act (CPRA): Building on the California Consumer Privacy Act (CCPA), the CPRA strengthens privacy rights for California residents. It emphasizes data transparency, limits data usage to predefined purposes, and introduces additional safeguards for sensitive information, such as biometric data.

4. Other Laws: Additional regulations, such as Brazil's LGPD, India's PDP Bill, and Canada's PIPEDA, also impact AI systems globally. Each law has unique requirements, making compliance complex but essential for organizations operating in multiple jurisdictions.

COMPLIANCE STRATEGIES

To comply with these regulations, organizations must adopt comprehensive privacy policies conduct regular audits, and compliance efforts are documented. Transparency in AI processes, such as explaining how data is used and ensuring accountability, further strengthens regulatory adherence.

PRIVACY-PRESERVING TECHNIQUES

Organizations are increasingly adopting advanced privacy-preserving techniques to address privacy concerns while leveraging data for AI. These methods balance the need for data utility with the imperative to protect individual privacy.

DIFFERENTIAL PRIVACY

Differential privacy adds noise to datasets, making it mathematically impossible to identify individual records while preserving the overall utility of the data. This technique is beneficial in scenarios where aggregated insights are needed, such as population health studies. Companies like Apple and Google use differential privacy to analyze user behavior without compromising personal data.

FEDERATED LEARNING

Federated learning enables AI models to train on decentralized data sources without transferring raw data to a central server. For instance, a federated learning system could train a predictive text algorithm on users' devices without uploading their typing data. This method minimizes privacy risks by keeping sensitive data localized while improving model performance.

ANONYMIZATION AND PSEUDONYMIZATION

1. **Anonymization** involves removing personally identifiable information (PII) from datasets to ensure that individuals cannot be re-identified. While effective, anonymization must be robust enough to withstand attempts at re-identification.

2. **Pseudonymization**: Replaces PII with unique identifiers, allowing data to be linked to individuals only when necessary. This technique enables secure data sharing for research or analysis while protecting individual privacy.

HOMOMORPHIC ENCRYPTION

Homomorphic encryption allows computations to be performed on encrypted data without decrypting it. This ensures that data remains secure throughout the analysis process. Although computationally intensive, this technique holds great promise for privacy-sensitive AI applications, such as encrypted medical research or secure financial modeling.

11.4 DATA SECURITY IN AI SYSTEMS

SECURITY RISKS IN DATA HANDLING

AI systems, reliant on vast volumes of data, face numerous security risks throughout the data lifecycle. From data acquisition to storage, processing, and deployment, vulnerabilities can arise, potentially compromising the integrity and trustworthiness of AI applications. The primary risks include adversarial attacks, data breaches, and model theft.

ADVERSARIAL ATTACKS

Adversarial attacks exploit vulnerabilities in AI models by introducing carefully crafted inputs that manipulate model behavior. These attacks can mislead AI systems, producing incorrect predictions or classifications. For instance:

- In image recognition systems, adversarial perturbations may alter images in ways imperceptible to humans but cause AI models to misclassify objects.
- In natural language processing (NLP), adversarial text injections can distort sentiment analysis or chatbot responses.

Such attacks threaten the reliability of AI systems, particularly in critical sectors like healthcare, finance, and autonomous vehicles.

DATA BREACHES

Data breaches occur when unauthorized parties access sensitive AI training or operations datasets. Breaches can expose personal information, proprietary data, or trade secrets, resulting in significant financial and reputational damage. For example, a breach of healthcare data used for predictive analytics could compromise patient confidentiality and violate compliance requirements.

MODEL THEFT

AI models represent valuable intellectual property (IP) for organizations. Model theft occurs when attackers reverse-engineer or copy trained models to replicate functionality without authorization. This undermines competitive advantage and risks malicious use of stolen models. For instance, a fraud detection model stolen from a financial institution could be repurposed to evade detection.

BUILDING ROBUST SECURITY MEASURES

Organizations must implement robust security measures across the AI development and deployment lifecycle to mitigate these risks. Effective strategies include encryption techniques, access controls, secure data storage, and real-time threat monitoring.

ENCRYPTION TECHNIQUES

Encryption safeguards data by converting it into unreadable formats that require decryption keys for access. Standard encryption techniques include:

1. **Data Encryption**: Encrypting datasets during storage and transmission prevents unauthorized access. For example, encrypting data pipelines between storage systems and AI processing environments ensures confidentiality.

2. **End-to-end encryption** secures data from its source to its destination, ensuring only authorized parties can access it in its original form.

3. **Homomorphic Encryption** is an advanced technique that allows computations on encrypted data without decrypting it. While computationally intensive, it is beneficial in privacy-sensitive scenarios such as encrypted medical research or financial modeling.

ACCESS CONTROLS

Access controls limit data access to authorized users, reducing the risk of unauthorized activities. Key methods include:

1. **Role-Based Access Control (RBAC)**: Assigning permissions based on job roles ensures that users only access data relevant to their responsibilities.

2. **Multi-factor authentication (MFA)** strengthens user authentication by requiring multiple verification forms, such as passwords and biometrics.

3. **Audit Logs**: Maintaining logs of data access and modifications helps track user activities and identify potential breaches.

SECURE DATA STORAGE

Securing data at rest involves protecting it against unauthorized access, tampering, and loss. Best practices include:

1. **Data Segmentation**: Storing sensitive data in isolated environments limits exposure during breaches.

2. **Immutable Storage**: Using storage solutions that prevent data alteration ensures integrity, particularly for audit trails.

3. **Backup and Recovery**: Regular backups and disaster recovery plans minimize data loss and ensure business continuity.

MONITORING AND RESPONDING TO DATA SECURITY THREATS IN REAL TIME

Real-time threat detection and response mechanisms are critical for proactive security. Techniques include:

1. Anomaly Detection: AI-driven tools can monitor network activity for unusual patterns, such as unauthorized access attempts or data exfiltration.

2. Intrusion Detection Systems (IDS): IDS tools identify and alert organizations to potential breaches or malicious activities.

3. Incident Response Plans: Preparing detailed response protocols ensures rapid containment and mitigation of security incidents.

EXAMPLE SCENARIOS

SECURING DATA PIPELINES FOR AI TRAINING AND INFERENCE

1. Training Phase:
    - AI models require large datasets during the training phase, often sourced from multiple locations. Ensuring secure data transfer through encrypted channels prevents interception and tampering. For example, using Secure Socket Layer (SSL) protocols can protect data in transit.
    - Access to training datasets should be restricted to authorized personnel and systems. Role-based access control and MFA can enforce stringent access policies.
2. Inference Phase:
    - Inference involves applying trained models to new data for real-time predictions. Securing data pipelines during inference ensures that sensitive input data and model outputs are not exposed to unauthorized parties.
    - For instance, in financial AI systems, encrypting real-time transaction data prevents exposure to cyber threats during analysis.

ADVERSARIAL EXAMPLE MITIGATION

Organizations can proactively defend against adversarial attacks by:

- Adversarial Training: Introducing adversarial examples during model training improves resilience against such inputs.
- Input Validation: Checking incoming data for abnormalities or patterns associated with adversarial manipulation helps detect and reject malicious inputs.
- Model Robustness Testing: Simulating attacks in controlled environments ensures that models are tested against potential vulnerabilities.

PROTECTING INTELLECTUAL PROPERTY

To safeguard AI models from theft, organizations can:

- **Model Watermarking**: Embedding unique identifiers within models allows organizations to prove ownership if stolen models are discovered.
- **API Security**: Rate limiting and token-based authentication prevent unauthorized access for models deployed via APIs.
- **Encrypted Models**: Encrypting model files ensures that stolen files cannot be efficiently utilized or reverse-engineered.

11.5 BUILDING A DATA GOVERNANCE FRAMEWORK

CORE COMPONENTS OF DATA GOVERNANCE

A robust data governance framework is the backbone of effective data management. It enables organizations to maximize the value of their data assets while ensuring compliance and ethical use. Establishing such a framework involves defining core components, including data ownership, stewardship, and data use, sharing, and retention policies.

DATA OWNERSHIP AND STEWARDSHIP ROLES

1. **Data Ownership**: Data ownership entails assigning accountability for specific datasets to individuals or teams within the organization. Data owners are typically responsible for the following:
   - Defining access permissions and ensuring compliance with organizational policies.
   - Overseeing the quality, security, and ethical use of their assigned data.
   - Making decisions regarding data retention and sharing.

   For example, in a healthcare organization, patient records may be owned by the Chief Medical Officer, who ensures their secure and compliant use for clinical and research purposes.
2. **Data Stewardship**: Data stewards play a more operational role, ensuring that data governance policies are implemented consistently. Their responsibilities include:
   - Monitoring data quality and integrity.
   - Facilitating data access requests while adhering to governance policies.
   - Coordinating with technical teams to address data-related issues.

   Data stewards bridge data owners and data users, ensuring alignment with organizational goals and regulatory requirements.

ESTABLISHING POLICIES FOR DATA USE, SHARING, AND RETENTION

1. **Data Use Policies**:
    - Define permissible uses of data based on its sensitivity and intended purpose.
    - Include guidelines for ethical use, such as avoiding bias in AI models and adhering to privacy regulations.
    - Require explicit consent for processing personal data, especially in sensitive domains like healthcare and finance.
2. **Data Sharing Policies**:
    - Specify conditions under which data can be shared within and outside the organization.
    - Incorporate mechanisms for anonymization or pseudonymization when sharing sensitive data.
    - Data-sharing agreements with external partners are required to ensure compliance and accountability.
3. **Data Retention Policies**:
    - Establish timelines for retaining different categories of data based on legal and business requirements.
    - Define secure data disposal processes to mitigate unauthorized access or breach risks.

For example, financial institutions may retain transaction data for seven years to comply with regulations while ensuring that outdated data is securely deleted afterward.

INTEGRATING DATA GOVERNANCE WITH AI GOVERNANCE

As AI becomes integral to business operations, the convergence of data and AI governance is essential. Data governance focuses on managing the data lifecycle, while AI governance addresses the ethical and responsible deployment of AI systems. Ensuring seamless collaboration between these domains enhances transparency, accountability, and trust.

KEY INTEGRATION STRATEGIES

1. **Aligning Objectives**: Data and AI governance teams should collaborate to define shared objectives, such as improving data quality, minimizing bias, and ensuring compliance with ethical standards. This alignment ensures that AI systems are built on trustworthy data.

2. **Establishing Joint Committees**: Forming committees with data and AI governance team representatives facilitates communication and coordination. These committees can:
    - Review data policies and their implications for AI development.
    - Address potential risks, such as using biased datasets in AI training.
    - Monitor the impact of AI models on privacy and compliance.
3. **Using Shared Tools and Platforms**: Leveraging unified platforms for data and AI governance simplifies workflows and ensures consistency. For instance, data lineage tools that track data origins can help AI governance teams evaluate the reliability of training datasets.

BENEFITS OF INTEGRATION

- **Improved AI Transparency**: Integrating data governance practices, such as documenting data sources, enhances the transparency of AI systems.
- **Enhanced Accountability**: Defining roles and responsibilities across both domains ensures stakeholders are accountable for data and AI governance outcomes.
- **Streamlined Compliance**: Coordinated efforts help organizations navigate complex regulatory landscapes and ensure compliance with data privacy and AI-specific laws.

PRACTICAL TOOLS AND TEMPLATES

Implementing a data governance framework requires practical tools and templates tailored to the needs of AI-driven organizations. These resources streamline governance activities, improve efficiency, and reduce the risk of oversight.

EXAMPLES OF DATA GOVERNANCE FRAMEWORKS FOR AI

1. **Data Governance Maturity Models**:
    - These models help organizations assess their current governance capabilities and identify areas for improvement.
    - For instance, a maturity model might evaluate data quality management, compliance processes, and AI model documentation.
2. **Data Catalogs**:
    - Data catalogs provide centralized repositories for metadata, enabling users to locate, understand, and evaluate datasets efficiently.

- Tools like Alation and Collibra integrate data catalogs with governance workflows, supporting data and AI governance needs.

3. Data Lineage Tools:
    - These tools trace data's origin, transformation, and usage throughout its lifecycle.
    - Data lineage helps ensure that AI applications train models on reliable and ethical datasets. Tracing the lineage of customer data also ensures compliance with GDPR's data sourcing requirements.
4. Policy Templates:
    - Standardized templates for data use, sharing, and retention policies simplify governance implementation and ensure consistency.
    - For example, a policy template for sharing healthcare data may include predefined clauses for anonymization and consent requirements.

IMPLEMENTING TOOLS IN PRACTICE

- Case Study: Financial Institution A global bank implemented a data governance framework using tools and templates. The bank improved transparency and compliance across its AI-driven credit scoring systems by deploying a data catalog integrated with AI model governance software. Regular audits and lineage tracking reduced bias and enhanced trust in the system's outputs.
- Case Study: Healthcare Provider A healthcare organization used policy templates to establish robust data-sharing agreements with research partners. By incorporating anonymization techniques and lineage tools, the provider ensured that AI-driven diagnostic models adhered to HIPAA and GDPR.

11.6 CHALLENGES AND SOLUTIONS IN DATA MANAGEMENT FOR AI

COMMON CHALLENGES

Managing data for AI systems is a complex and dynamic task involving navigating various challenges. These issues stem from the need to balance accessibility, privacy, and security, handle the intricacies of large-scale datasets, and ensure compliance with rapidly evolving regulations.

BALANCING DATA ACCESSIBILITY WITH PRIVACY AND SECURITY

AI systems thrive on data accessibility, facilitating innovation, insights, and efficient decision-making. However, ensuring data is readily accessible to AI models while safeguarding privacy and security presents a significant challenge. For instance:

- Sensitive data, such as medical records or financial transactions, must be accessible for AI training but protected against breaches and misuse.
- Excessive restrictions on data sharing can hinder AI's potential, while overly lenient policies risk compromising privacy and violating regulations like GDPR or HIPAA.

Achieving this balance requires organizations to implement robust data governance frameworks prioritizing data utility and compliance.

MANAGING LARGE-SCALE, DIVERSE DATASETS

AI systems often rely on diverse domains, formats, and locations datasets. Managing these datasets involves several challenges:

- **Volume**: Handling massive amounts of data requires significant storage, processing power, and infrastructure.
- **Variety**: Data may come in structured, semi-structured, or unstructured formats, necessitating advanced preprocessing techniques.
- **Velocity**: Real-time data streams, such as those from IoT devices, demand immediate analysis and storage.

Large-scale and diverse datasets can overwhelm organizational resources without effective management, leading to inefficiencies and compromised AI performance.

ALIGNING DATA GOVERNANCE WITH EVOLVING AI REGULATIONS

Regulatory frameworks governing data usage in AI, such as GDPR CPRA, and sector-specific rules like HIPAA, are constantly evolving. Keeping pace with these changes is daunting, especially for global organizations subject to multiple jurisdictions. Challenges include:

- Understanding and implementing region-specific data privacy laws.
- Ensuring AI systems remain compliant as regulations evolve.
- Mitigating the risks of non-compliance, which can result in legal penalties and reputational damage.

SOLUTIONS

Addressing these challenges requires strategic planning, technological innovation, and collaborative approaches. Below are practical solutions to enhance data management for AI systems.

USING AUTOMATION AND AI-DRIVEN TOOLS FOR DATA MANAGEMENT

Automation and AI-driven tools offer scalable and efficient ways to manage data for AI systems. These technologies help:

- Automate Data Preprocessing: Tools like ETL (Extract, Transform, Load) pipelines streamline data cleaning, transformation, and integration processes.
- Enhance Data Discovery and Cataloging: AI-powered data catalogs facilitate easier identification and retrieval of relevant datasets, improving accessibility without compromising governance.
- Monitor Data Quality in Real Time: AI-driven monitoring systems can detect anomalies, inconsistencies, and errors in data streams, ensuring datasets remain reliable and accurate.
- Ensure Compliance: Automated tools can track regulatory changes and flag potential compliance risks, enabling organizations to stay ahead of evolving legal requirements.

ESTABLISHING CROSS-FUNCTIONAL TEAMS FOR DATA GOVERNANCE

Collaboration between diverse stakeholders is critical for successful data management in AI. Cross-functional teams bring together expertise from different domains to:

- Define and Implement Governance Policies: Teams comprising data scientists, compliance officers, and business leaders can create balanced policies that meet technical and legal requirements.
- Foster Accountability: Assigning clear roles and responsibilities within cross-functional teams ensures accountability for data governance tasks.
- Enhance Communication: Regular communication among team members helps identify and address challenges quickly, fostering a proactive approach to data management.

For example, in a healthcare organization, a cross-functional team might include IT specialists, medical professionals, and legal experts working together to manage patient data securely while optimizing its use in AI-driven diagnostics.

CHAPTER 12: AI LIFECYCLE MANAGEMENT

12.1 INTRODUCTION TO AI LIFECYCLE MANAGEMENT

WHAT IS AI LIFECYCLE MANAGEMENT?

AI Lifecycle Management refers to the structured process of overseeing the development, deployment, and maintenance of AI systems throughout their lifecycle. It encompasses practices and frameworks designed to ensure that AI systems are built responsibly, operate effectively, and adapt to evolving requirements. This process is essential for mitigating biases, security vulnerabilities, and ethical concerns. By establishing a systematic approach, organizations can ensure that their AI solutions remain compliant with legal standards, socially beneficial, and aligned with business objectives.

The significance of AI Lifecycle Management lies in its ability to promote responsible AI practices. With AI systems increasingly influencing critical sectors such as healthcare, finance, and public safety, ensuring they operate transparently, fairly, and reliably is vital. Lifecycle management integrates ethical considerations, robust testing protocols, and continuous monitoring, providing a foundation for trust in AI technologies. Moreover, it facilitates alignment with regulatory frameworks, reducing the risk of non-compliance penalties and reputational damage.

GOVERNANCE ACROSS THE LIFECYCLE

Governance must be embedded at every stage of the AI lifecycle to ensure accountability, transparency, and ethical alignment. Each AI development and operation phase presents unique challenges, necessitating tailored governance mechanisms. By integrating governance early and maintaining it throughout the lifecycle, organizations can identify and mitigate potential risks before they escalate.

For example, governance focuses on ensuring data integrity, privacy, and representativeness during the data preparation phase. During model development, it ensures fairness and transparency in algorithmic decision-making. In deployment, governance involves robust testing and operational monitoring to ensure safe implementation. Finally, during maintenance, it emphasizes adaptation to changing data environments while safeguarding against performance degradation.

Failing to apply governance uniformly across the lifecycle can result in significant risks. For instance, an oversight in data governance might lead to biased models, while inadequate monitoring during deployment can cause models to drift, reducing their effectiveness. Integrated governance ensures a comprehensive and proactive approach, fostering stakeholder confidence and long-term sustainability.

The AI lifecycle can be broadly divided into four key phases:

1. Data Preparation
   This stage involves collecting, cleaning, and curating data to ensure quality and relevance. Governance is crucial in addressing ethical and legal considerations, such as consent and data anonymization. Adequate data preparation ensures that AI models are trained on accurate and representative datasets, minimizing bias and maximizing fairness.

2. Model Development
   Algorithms are trained and tested during this phase to meet desired performance criteria. Governance ensures transparency by documenting the development process and establishing accountability measures. It also includes bias detection and mitigation strategies, ensuring that models do not perpetuate or amplify existing inequities.

3. Deployment
   The deployment phase involves integrating the AI model into real-world systems. Governance ensures robust pre-deployment testing and controlled rollouts to minimize risks. Operational monitoring mechanisms are established to track model performance and address accuracy drift or unexpected behaviors.

4. Maintenance
   In maintenance, models are continuously monitored, updated, and retrained as needed. Governance focuses on complying with evolving regulations, addressing model drift, and ensuring that updates do not compromise system integrity. Detailed audit trails provide a record of changes and decisions.

By effectively managing these stages and embedding governance throughout, organizations can maximize the value and reliability of their AI initiatives while minimizing potential harm.

12.2 GOVERNANCE DURING DATA PREPARATION

The data preparation stage is foundational for the success of AI systems, as the quality, integrity, and ethical considerations of the data directly influence the system's effectiveness and fairness. Governance during this stage ensures that the data is handled responsibly, aligns with legal and ethical standards, and represents the problem domain. This chapter explores key areas where governance plays a crucial role in data collection, preprocessing, and addressing challenges.

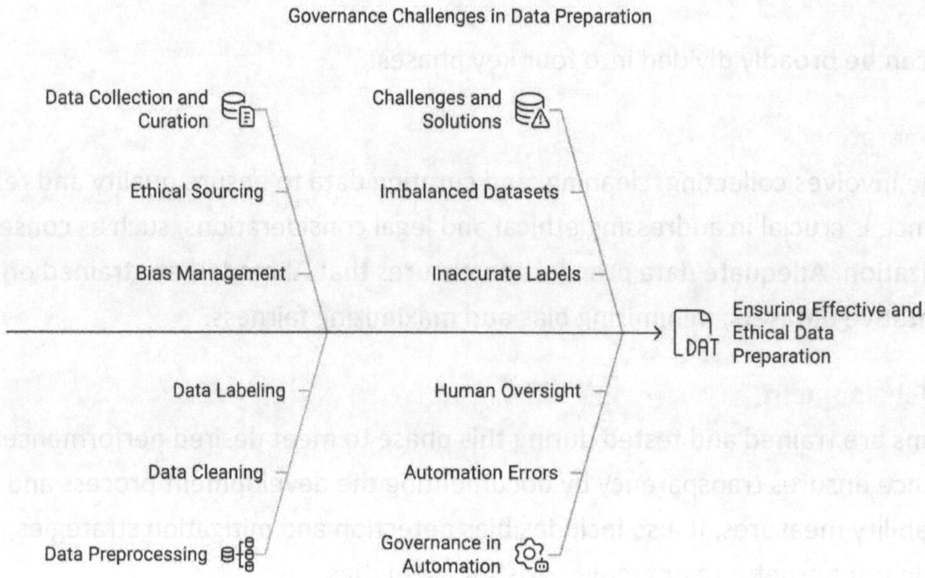

DATA COLLECTION AND CURATION

ENSURING ETHICAL AND LEGAL DATA SOURCING

The first step in data preparation is sourcing data responsibly. Governance mechanisms must ensure the data is obtained ethically and complies with legal regulations. This includes following data privacy laws like GDPR, CCPA, and other jurisdiction-specific guidelines. Key practices include:

- **Informed Consent:** Ensure that individuals providing data have explicit consent and understand how their data will be used. Consent should be documented to provide an audit trail.
- **Data Provenance:** Record the data's origin and ensure it is sourced from reputable, authorized, and secure channels. For instance, datasets scraped from the Internet must comply with terms of service agreements.
- **Avoiding Unethical Sources:** Organizations must avoid using data collected through invasive or exploitative means, such as surveillance without consent or datasets containing sensitive personal information without proper anonymization.

MANAGING DATA BIAS AND ENSURING REPRESENTATIVENESS

Bias in datasets can result in skewed AI model outputs, disproportionately affecting certain groups. Governance frameworks should mandate proactive measures to detect and mitigate bias during data collection:

- **Diversity in Data Sources:** Curate datasets from multiple sources to capture diverse perspectives and prevent specific demographics from being over- or underrepresent.

Implement bias detection tools and metrics to evaluate the dataset for potential imbalances, such as disproportionate representation by gender, ethnicity, or socioeconomic status.

- Stakeholder Review: Engage domain experts and stakeholders to review datasets and ensure they align with the ethical and operational goals of the AI application.

DATA PREPROCESSING

GOVERNANCE FOR CLEANING, LABELING, AND AUGMENTING DATA

Data preprocessing transforms raw data into a format suitable for AI model training. Governance ensures these processes are executed responsibly and transparently:

- Data Cleaning: Governance policies should define clear protocols for handling missing, erroneous, or duplicate data. For example, missing values in healthcare datasets must be treated carefully to avoid introducing biases into diagnostic models.
- Data Labeling: High-quality labels are critical for supervised learning models. Governance should oversee labeling practices by:
    - Using diverse, well-trained annotators to minimize subjectivity in labels.
    - Employing double-masked techniques to reduce biases.
    - Maintaining a robust quality assurance process for labeled data.
- Data Augmentation: Techniques like oversampling under-represented classes, applying transformations, or generating synthetic data should be governed to avoid inadvertently introducing noise or biases.

TECHNIQUES FOR ANONYMIZING SENSITIVE DATA TO MEET PRIVACY REGULATIONS

Governance frameworks must address privacy concerns during preprocessing, particularly when handling sensitive data like health records or financial transactions. Effective anonymization techniques include:

- Data Masking: Replace sensitive information (e.g., names, IDs) with pseudo-random identifiers.
- Generalization: Aggregate data into broader categories. For example, replace exact ages with age ranges.
- Noise Injection: Add statistical noise to sensitive data points to obscure individual identities while preserving aggregate trends.

- **Differential Privacy:** Implement algorithms that provide strong mathematical guarantees of privacy by limiting the information inferred about any individual in the dataset.

By embedding these practices into governance policies, organizations can ensure compliance with privacy laws while maintaining the utility of their datasets.

CHALLENGES AND SOLUTIONS

ADDRESSING ISSUES LIKE IMBALANCED DATASETS AND INACCURATE LABELS

AI systems are only as good as the data they are trained on. Common challenges in data preparation include imbalanced datasets and inaccuracies in data labeling. Governance frameworks can provide structured solutions:

- **Imbalanced Datasets:**
    - **Challenge:** When certain classes or categories are under-represented, models may perform poorly for those classes, leading to biased outcomes.
    - **Solution:**
        - Oversampling techniques like SMOTE (Synthetic Minority Over-sampling Technique) generate synthetic examples for under-represented classes.
        - Apply undersampling to balance class representation, ensuring the process retains sufficient data for learning.
        - Implement weighting mechanisms during training to emphasize under-represented classes.
- **Inaccurate Labels:**
    - **Challenge:** Errors or inconsistencies in labeled data can mislead the model during training, resulting in unreliable outputs.
    - **Solution:**
        - Establish quality assurance processes, including manual review and cross-validation of labeled data.
        - Use AI-assisted labeling tools to improve consistency and reduce human error.
        - Incorporate active learning techniques where the model queries uncertain data points for human validation.

- **Dynamic Data Challenges:**
    - **Challenge:** Over time, data used for training may become outdated or unrepresentative, particularly in rapidly changing domains like finance or healthcare.
    - **Solution:**
        - Adopt continuous monitoring and periodic revalidation of datasets to ensure they remain current.
        - Establish governance protocols for regularly updating datasets and retraining models.

GOVERNANCE IN AUTOMATION AND HUMAN OVERSIGHT

While automation can streamline data preprocessing tasks, governance is required to ensure responsible application. For example, automated tools for cleaning or labeling must be supervised to avoid amplifying errors. Governance policies should balance automation with human oversight to ensure accuracy and accountability.

12.3 GOVERNANCE DURING MODEL DEVELOPMENT

The model development stage is one of the most critical phases in the AI lifecycle. Data is transformed into actionable insights and decision-making capabilities through the creation and refinement of algorithms. Effective governance during this phase ensures that the AI model adheres to fairness, transparency, and ethical responsibility principles. This section explores how organizations can address fairness, bias mitigation, transparency, and ethical considerations through robust governance frameworks.

FAIRNESS AND BIAS MITIGATION

ENSURING MODELS DO NOT REPLICATE OR AMPLIFY BIAS IN TRAINING DATA

AI models learn patterns from the data they are trained on, meaning any biases present in the data can influence the model's outcomes. Left unchecked, these biases can result in discriminatory or inequitable results, undermining the model's credibility and trustworthiness.

Governance strategies to mitigate bias include:

1. **Bias Detection in Data and Models:**
    - Analyze training data for imbalances or skewed representations of demographic groups.
    - Regularly assess model outputs to identify disparate impacts on specific populations.

2. **Representative Training Data:**
    - Ensure datasets are diverse and inclusive, capturing various scenarios and demographics relevant to the intended use case.
    - Perform demographic audits on the training data to detect under-representation.
3. **Controlled Experiments:**
    - Conduct A/B testing to evaluate the fairness of model decisions across different population groups.
    - Use counterfactual testing to determine how a slight change in input variables (e.g., gender or ethnicity) impacts model outcomes.

TOOLS AND TECHNIQUES FOR BIAS DETECTION DURING DEVELOPMENT

Governance frameworks should mandate specialized tools and methodologies for identifying and addressing bias during model development. Examples include:

- **Fairness Indicators:** Tools like IBM's AI Fairness 360 or Google's What-If Tool help measure and visualize potential biases in datasets and models.
- **Algorithmic Techniques:**
    - Use adversarial debiasing algorithms to reduce the sensitivity of model predictions to sensitive attributes like race, gender, or age.
    - Apply reweighting or resampling techniques to mitigate over-representation or under-representation in training data.
- **Human-in-the-loop reviews** involve domain experts and diverse stakeholders reviewing model design and output, ensuring fair and contextually appropriate decisions.

TRANSPARENCY AND EXPLAINABILITY

BUILDING INTERPRETABLE MODELS

Transparency in AI models is essential to foster trust, particularly in high-stakes domains like healthcare, finance, and law enforcement. Governance during model development must emphasize building interpretable models that stakeholders can understand and trust.

1. **Model Simplicity:**
    - Favor interpretable models (e.g., decision trees or linear regression) over complex black-box algorithms (e.g., deep neural networks) when feasible, particularly in applications requiring accountability.
    - Where complexity is unavoidable, explainability techniques like LIME (Local Interpretable Model-Agnostic Explanations) or SHAP (SHapley Additive exPlanations) should be applied to make the outputs understandable.
2. **Explainability Tools:**
    - Use model visualization tools to illustrate how input features contribute to outputs.
    - Deploy feature importance rankings to show which variables influence model predictions most.
3. **Stakeholder Communication:**
    - Tailor explanations for non-technical stakeholders, emphasizing the rationale behind model decisions in plain language.

DOCUMENTING DEVELOPMENT PROCESSES TO ENHANCE ACCOUNTABILITY

Documentation is a cornerstone of governance in model development, providing a detailed record of design choices, assumptions, and methodologies. Comprehensive documentation enhances accountability and facilitates audits and compliance with regulatory requirements.

1. **Model Cards:**
    - Develop model cards that summarize key aspects of the model, such as intended use cases, data sources, performance metrics, and known limitations.
    - Include fairness metrics and information about the population for which the model has been validated.
2. **Version Control:**
    - Maintained version control systems for models, ensuring that updates and changes were documented and traceable.
    - Log all training, testing, and parameter tuning iterations to enable reproducibility.

3. **Development Logs:**
   - Record decisions made during the development process, such as the choice of algorithms, hyperparameter tuning, and evaluation metrics.
   - Include rationales for excluding certain features or datasets to ensure transparency.

ETHICAL CONSIDERATIONS

AVOIDING USE CASES THAT VIOLATE ORGANIZATIONAL VALUES OR LEGAL REQUIREMENTS

AI systems can have unintended consequences if misused. Governance frameworks must ensure that models align with organizational values and comply with legal and ethical standards. This requires a proactive approach to identifying and mitigating potential risks during model development.

1. **Ethical Risk Assessments:**
   - Conduct risk assessments to evaluate the societal impact of deploying the model.
   - Frameworks like the AI ethics guidelines or the IEEE Global Initiative on Ethics of Autonomous and Intelligent Systems should guide decision-making.
2. **Avoidance of Harmful Applications:**
   - Prohibit use cases that are discriminatory, exploitative, or misaligned with organizational principles. For example, an AI model designed for hiring decisions should avoid using proxies that could lead to bias, such as zip codes that correlate with socioeconomic status.
3. **Legal Compliance:**
   - Ensure models comply with laws and regulations, such as anti-discrimination laws, GDPR (for data protection), and industry-specific standards.
   - Legal experts should be included in the governance process to identify and address potential compliance issues.

ETHICAL GOVERNANCE MECHANISMS

1. **AI Ethics Committees:**
   - Establish cross-functional committees to evaluate the ethical implications of model development.
   - Include diverse perspectives to minimize blind spots in ethical considerations.
2. **Red Team Exercises:**

- Simulate adversarial scenarios where models could be misused or manipulated, helping identify vulnerabilities and ethical risks.

3. Continuous Monitoring:
    - Embed monitoring systems to assess the ongoing ethical impact of models post-deployment.
    - Use feedback loops to refine and improve model performance and adherence to ethical standards.

12.4 GOVERNANCE DURING DEPLOYMENT

The deployment phase of an AI system is a critical juncture in which the model's theoretical capabilities are tested in real-world conditions. Effective governance during deployment ensures that the AI system operates as intended, remains secure, and adheres to ethical and regulatory standards. This chapter examines strategies for safe deployment, operational monitoring, and the application of governance through real-world examples.

SAFE AND SECURE DEPLOYMENT

ENSURING ROBUST TESTING BEFORE DEPLOYMENT IN REAL-WORLD SETTINGS

Before an AI system is deployed, it must undergo rigorous testing to ensure it performs reliably under real-world conditions. Governance frameworks play a pivotal role in defining and enforcing these testing protocols.

1. Pre-Deployment Testing:
    - Validation and Benchmarking: To assess generalizability and robustness, the model should be tested on real-world datasets distinct from training and testing datasets.
    - Scenario Testing: Simulate real-world scenarios, including edge cases, to evaluate how the model behaves under various conditions.
    - Stress Testing: To ensure resilience, evaluate system performance under high-load scenarios or unusual input patterns.
2. Compliance Checks:
    - Regulatory Alignment: Verify that the model complies with relevant laws and industry standards, such as GDPR for data protection or HIPAA for healthcare.
    - Ethical Audits: Conduct audits to ensure the system aligns with organizational values and does not produce outcomes that could harm stakeholders.

3. **Security Assessments:**
    - **Vulnerability Scanning:** Identify and address vulnerabilities in the AI system and its supporting infrastructure.
    - **Adversarial Testing:** Test the model's resilience against adversarial attacks that attempt to manipulate outputs.

IMPLEMENTING GOVERNANCE POLICIES FOR CONTROLLED ROLLOUTS

Controlled rollouts involve deploying the AI system incrementally to manage risks and gather feedback before full-scale implementation. Governance policies ensure this process is structured and minimizes potential harm.

1. **Phased Deployment:**
    - **Pilot Programs:** Start with small-scale deployments in a controlled environment to evaluate performance and gather user feedback.
    - **Gradual Expansion:** Increase the deployment scale in phases, addressing any identified issues at each stage.
2. **Access Controls:**
    - Define user access levels to restrict sensitive operations to authorized personnel only.
    - Monitor access logs to detect and investigate unauthorized actions.
3. **Rollback Mechanisms:**
    - Establish protocols for reverting to a previous system version in case of significant performance or security issues.
    - Ensure rollback processes are tested and well-documented.
4. **Stakeholder Communication:**
    - Inform stakeholders, including employees, customers, and regulators, about the deployment process, intended outcomes, and safeguards in place.
    - Provide training for users interacting with the AI system to ensure proper utilization and understanding.

SETTING UP MECHANISMS TO TRACK MODEL PERFORMANCE POST-DEPLOYMENT

Once an AI system is live, ongoing monitoring is crucial to ensure it performs as expected. Governance frameworks mandate the establishment of robust monitoring mechanisms.

1. **Performance Metrics:**
   - Define and track key performance indicators (KPIs) aligned with the system's objectives, such as accuracy, precision, and recall.
   - Monitor latency, throughput, and resource utilization to ensure operational efficiency.
2. **User Feedback Loops:**
   - Establish channels for collecting user feedback to identify usability issues or unintended outcomes.
   - Incorporate feedback into iterative improvements of the model and system.
3. **Automated Alerts:**
   - Set thresholds for critical metrics and deploy automated alerts to flag anomalies or significant deviations in performance.
   - Implement escalation protocols to address flagged issues promptly.

IDENTIFYING DRIFT IN MODEL ACCURACY AND RELIABILITY

Over time, AI models can experience performance degradation due to changing data patterns or evolving real-world conditions, known as model drift. Governance during deployment includes measures to detect and address drift effectively.

1. **Drift Detection Mechanisms:**
   - Monitor for **concept drift** (changes in the relationships between input features and target variables) and **data drift** (shifts in the input data distribution).
   - Use statistical tests, such as Kolmogorov-Smirnov, to identify significant changes in data or model outputs.
2. **Retraining Protocols:**
   - Define conditions under which the model must be retrained, such as exceeding drift thresholds or a drop in performance metrics.

- Incorporate updated data into retraining pipelines while maintaining governance oversight to ensure quality and compliance.

3. **Periodic Audits:**
    - Schedule regular audits of the AI system to evaluate its performance, fairness, and compliance with governance policies.
    - Document audit findings and corrective actions to create a transparent accountability trail.

REAL-WORLD EXAMPLES

SUCCESSFUL DEPLOYMENT OF GOVERNANCE STRATEGIES IN INDUSTRIES LIKE HEALTHCARE OR FINANCE

Governance during deployment has been successfully implemented in industries where AI systems significantly impact compliance and outcomes.

1. **Healthcare:**
    - **Clinical Decision Support Systems (CDSS):**
        - Example: AI-powered CDSS for diagnosing diseases like diabetic retinopathy undergoes rigorous pre-deployment validation on diverse patient datasets.
        - Governance frameworks enforce compliance with health data privacy laws (e.g., HIPAA) and ensure medical professionals review the AI model's recommendations before implementation.
    - **Operational Monitoring:** Continuous monitoring tracks the accuracy of diagnoses and alerts healthcare providers to potential anomalies, ensuring patient safety.
2. **Finance:**
    - **Fraud Detection Systems:**
        - For example, AI models that detect fraudulent transactions in real-time undergo phased rollouts, starting with low-risk transactions to validate their effectiveness.
        - Governance ensures compliance with financial regulations and sets thresholds for false positives to minimize customer disruption.
    - **Model Drift:** Fraud detection models are regularly updated to incorporate the latest transaction patterns, maintaining their reliability against evolving threats.

3. Autonomous Vehicles:
    - Deployment of AI systems in autonomous vehicles includes rigorous simulation testing and real-world trials in controlled environments.
    - Governance frameworks enforce safety protocols, including manual overrides and comprehensive logs of system decisions for accountability.

Governance during deployment ensures that AI systems are launched safely, perform effectively, and remain aligned with ethical and regulatory standards. Organizations can mitigate risks and build stakeholder trust by implementing robust testing protocols, controlled rollouts, and continuous monitoring. Real-world examples from healthcare, finance, and autonomous systems highlight the importance of governance in ensuring successful deployments.

Ultimately, embedding governance into the deployment phase is not just a best practice but a necessity for managing the complexities and risks associated with operational AI systems. It fosters accountability, adaptability, and reliability, setting the stage for long-term success in AI initiatives.

12.5 GOVERNANCE DURING MAINTENANCE AND UPDATES

The maintenance and update phase of the AI lifecycle is critical for ensuring that deployed AI systems remain effective, reliable, and aligned with their intended purpose. Governance during this phase ensures that models continue to perform as expected while adapting to changing conditions, maintaining compliance with ethical and regulatory standards, and minimizing risks. This section explores the essential governance practices for model monitoring, handling model drift, updating models, and maintaining audit trails.

MODEL MONITORING AND FEEDBACK LOOPS

CONTINUOUS EVALUATION TO ENSURE MODELS ADAPT TO CHANGING DATA ENVIRONMENTS

Once an AI model is deployed, it operates in dynamic environments where data distributions, user behavior, or external factors may shift over time. Continuous monitoring and feedback loops are vital to detect changes and ensure the model's ongoing relevance and accuracy.

1. Performance Monitoring:
    - Establish real-time monitoring systems to track key performance indicators (KPIs), such as accuracy, precision, recall, and latency.
    - Use dashboards and visualization tools to provide actionable insights into model performance for stakeholders.

2. **User Feedback Loops:**

   - Incorporate mechanisms for gathering feedback from end users or domain experts interacting with the AI system.
   - Use feedback to identify performance gaps, unintended behaviors, or areas for improvement.

3. **Data Quality Monitoring:**

   - Continuously assess the quality and relevance of incoming data to ensure it aligns with the model's training data.
   - Identify and address missing, noisy, or biased data that could affect model performance.

4. **Alert Systems:**

   - Set thresholds for critical metrics and deploy automated alerts to flag potential performance issues.
   - Include escalation protocols to ensure timely intervention when anomalies are detected.

Governance frameworks ensure these monitoring processes are standardized, transparent, and effectively communicated across teams, enabling proactive decision-making.

MANAGING MODEL DRIFT

GOVERNANCE MEASURES TO DETECT AND CORRECT PERFORMANCE DEGRADATION OVER TIME

Model drift occurs when an AI system's performance deteriorates due to changes in data patterns or evolving real-world conditions. Governance mechanisms are essential for detecting and addressing drift to maintain the model's reliability and accuracy.

1. **Types of Drift:**

   - **Concept Drift refers to changes** in the relationships between input features and target variables. For example, a fraud detection model may struggle to identify new fraud patterns that differ from its training data.
   - **Data Drift:** Shifts in the statistical properties of input data. For instance, demographic shifts in user data could impact a recommendation system's effectiveness.

2. **Drift Detection:**
    - Monitor for significant changes in data distributions using statistical techniques, such as the Kolmogorov-Smirnov test or population stability index (PSI).
    - Implement change-point detection algorithms to identify when model predictions deviate from expected patterns.
3. **Mitigation Strategies:**
    - Retrain the model periodically with updated data to reflect current trends.
    - Deploy ensemble methods that combine predictions from multiple models, ensuring robustness against specific types of drift.
4. **Governance Oversight:**
    - Define protocols for identifying and responding to drift, including documentation of detection methods and decision-making criteria.
    - Involve cross-functional teams to assess the impact of drift and determine the appropriate corrective measures.

UPDATING MODELS RESPONSIBLY

STRATEGIES FOR RETRAINING MODELS WHILE MAINTAINING COMPLIANCE WITH GOVERNANCE STANDARDS

Retraining and updating AI models must align with changing data environments and business requirements. However, these processes must be governed to ensure that updates do not introduce new risks or degrade system performance.

1. **Version Control and Documentation:**
    - Maintain version control systems to track changes in model architectures, hyperparameters, and training datasets.
    - Document the rationale for updates, including the specific issues addressed and the expected improvements.
2. **Regulatory Compliance:**
    - Ensure updated models adhere to applicable laws, regulations, and ethical guidelines, such as data privacy standards (e.g., GDPR, CCPA).

- Conduct compliance audits to validate that retrained models meet regulatory and organizational requirements.

3. **Testing and Validation:**
    - Validate updated models on test datasets that represent current real-world conditions.
    - Before full-scale implementation, you can use shadow deployments or A/B testing to compare the performance of updated models with previous versions.
4. **Risk Management:**
    - Assess potential risks associated with model updates, such as unintended consequences or adverse impacts on specific user groups.
    - Implement rollback mechanisms to revert to previous versions if issues are detected quickly.
5. **Stakeholder Involvement:**
    - Engage stakeholders, including domain experts, legal teams, and end users, in the update process to ensure that changes align with business objectives and user needs.

Governance frameworks ensure that updates are executed systematically, transparently, and with accountability, minimizing the risk of unintended consequences.

AUDIT TRAILS

KEEPING DETAILED RECORDS OF UPDATES AND MAINTENANCE ACTIVITIES

Audit trails comprehensively record all model maintenance and update activities, ensuring accountability, traceability, and compliance.

1. **Documentation of Changes:**
    - Record all model modifications, including algorithm updates, training data, and parameters.
    - Include detailed logs of testing and validation activities, highlighting the results and decisions made.
2. **Access and Security Logs:**
    - Maintain user access logs to the AI system, documenting who made changes, when, and why.
    - Monitor for unauthorized access or modifications to safeguard system integrity.

3. **Compliance Reporting:**
   - Use audit trails to demonstrate compliance with regulatory requirements during external audits or investigations.
   - Provide clear evidence of how governance standards were applied throughout the maintenance process.
4. **Transparency for Stakeholders:**
   - Share audit trail summaries with stakeholders to build trust and demonstrate the organization's commitment to responsible AI practices.
   - Use the records to provide insights into the evolution of the AI system and its alignment with organizational goals.
5. **Continuous Improvement:**
   - Analyze audit trails to identify patterns, gaps, or areas for improvement in governance practices.
   - Use insights to refine governance frameworks and enhance future maintenance and update activities.

12.6 TEMPLATES AND CHECKLISTS FOR LIFECYCLE GOVERNANCE

Governance is critical to the AI lifecycle, ensuring that AI systems are developed, deployed, and maintained responsibly and effectively. Organizations can utilize templates and checklists tailored to each phase of the AI lifecycle to make governance practical and actionable. These tools provide structured guidance, help ensure compliance with ethical and regulatory standards, and foster consistency in decision-making. This section explores practical governance resources, including sample templates and checklists, and demonstrates how to apply them effectively.

PRACTICAL RESOURCES

SAMPLE GOVERNANCE CHECKLISTS FOR EACH LIFECYCLE PHASE

Checklists are a powerful tool for embedding governance at every stage of the AI lifecycle. They provide clear, actionable items that teams can follow to ensure adherence to governance principles. Below are examples of checklists for key lifecycle phases:

1. **Data Preparation Phase:**
   - Verify data sources comply with legal and ethical standards (e.g., GDPR, CCPA).
   - Assess datasets for representativeness and identify potential biases.

- Ensure data anonymization techniques are applied to sensitive information.
- Document data cleaning, labeling, and augmentation processes.

2. **Model Development Phase:**
   - Validate that training data aligns with the intended use case.
   - Conduct bias audits on training datasets and model outputs.
   - Ensure model explainability and document design decisions using tools like model cards.
   - Incorporate fairness metrics and evaluate potential unintended consequences.
3. **Deployment Phase:**
   - Test models in controlled environments before full deployment.
   - Implement access controls and rollback mechanisms.
   - Verify compliance with industry-specific regulations and organizational policies.
   - Set up performance monitoring tools and define alert thresholds.
4. **Maintenance and Updates Phase:**
   - Monitor for concept and data drift using statistical tests.
   - Establish retraining protocols with updated data.
   - Keep detailed records of changes, including testing and validation results.
   - Conduct periodic audits to evaluate system performance and compliance.

TEMPLATES FOR DOCUMENTING GOVERNANCE DECISIONS AND POLICIES

Templates offer a consistent format for documenting governance-related decisions, making tracking compliance, accountability, and the rationale behind key actions easier. Examples include:

1. **Governance Decision Template:**
   - **Decision Summary:** Brief description of the decision made.
   - **Stakeholders Involved:** List of individuals or teams consulted.
   - **Supporting Evidence:** Data, reports, or audits used to inform the decision.

- Compliance Alignment: Explanation of how the decision aligns with legal, ethical, or organizational standards.
- Approval Signatures: Sign-off from decision-makers.

2. Risk Assessment Template:
   - Risk Description: Detailed explanation of the identified risk.
   - Likelihood and Impact: Assessment of the probability and potential consequences.
   - Mitigation Plan: Steps to address the risk.
   - Monitoring Plan: How the risk will be tracked over time.
3. Audit Trail Template:
   - Activity Description: Overview of the action taken (e.g., model update, retraining).
   - Date and Time: Timestamp of the activity.
   - Stakeholders Involved: Individuals responsible for the activity.
   - Outcome Summary: Results and impact of the activity.
   - Compliance Notes: Evidence of adherence to governance standards.

HOW TO USE THESE TOOLS

EXAMPLES OF REAL-WORLD APPLICATIONS

Governance templates and checklists are versatile resources that can be adapted to various industries and use cases. Below are examples of their application in real-world scenarios:

1. Healthcare:
   - Checklist Application: A hospital deploying an AI-powered diagnostic tool uses a deployment checklist to verify the system complies with HIPAA regulations and has been tested against diverse patient demographics.
   - Template Application: A governance decision template documents why a specific model architecture was chosen, including its accuracy in detecting diseases and its interpretability for medical professionals.

2. **Finance:**
   - **Checklist Application:** A financial institution deploying an AI fraud detection system uses a monitoring checklist to ensure performance metrics remain stable post-deployment and to detect drift in transaction patterns.
   - **Template Application:** An audit trail template is maintained for all system updates, providing regulators with a transparent record of compliance.
3. **Retail:**
   - **Checklist Application:** An e-commerce company developing a recommendation engine uses a development checklist to ensure training data reflects diverse customer preferences and avoids amplifying biases.
   - **Template Application:** A risk assessment template evaluates the potential impact of incorrect recommendations on customer satisfaction and brand reputation.
4. **Public Sector:**
   - **Checklist Application:** A government agency deploying an AI tool for citizen services uses a maintenance checklist to ensure the system adapts to evolving data trends and remains unbiased.
   - **Template Application:** A governance decision template is employed to document the approval of policy changes affecting the AI system, ensuring accountability.

PART IV

OPERATIONALIZING AI GOVERNANCE

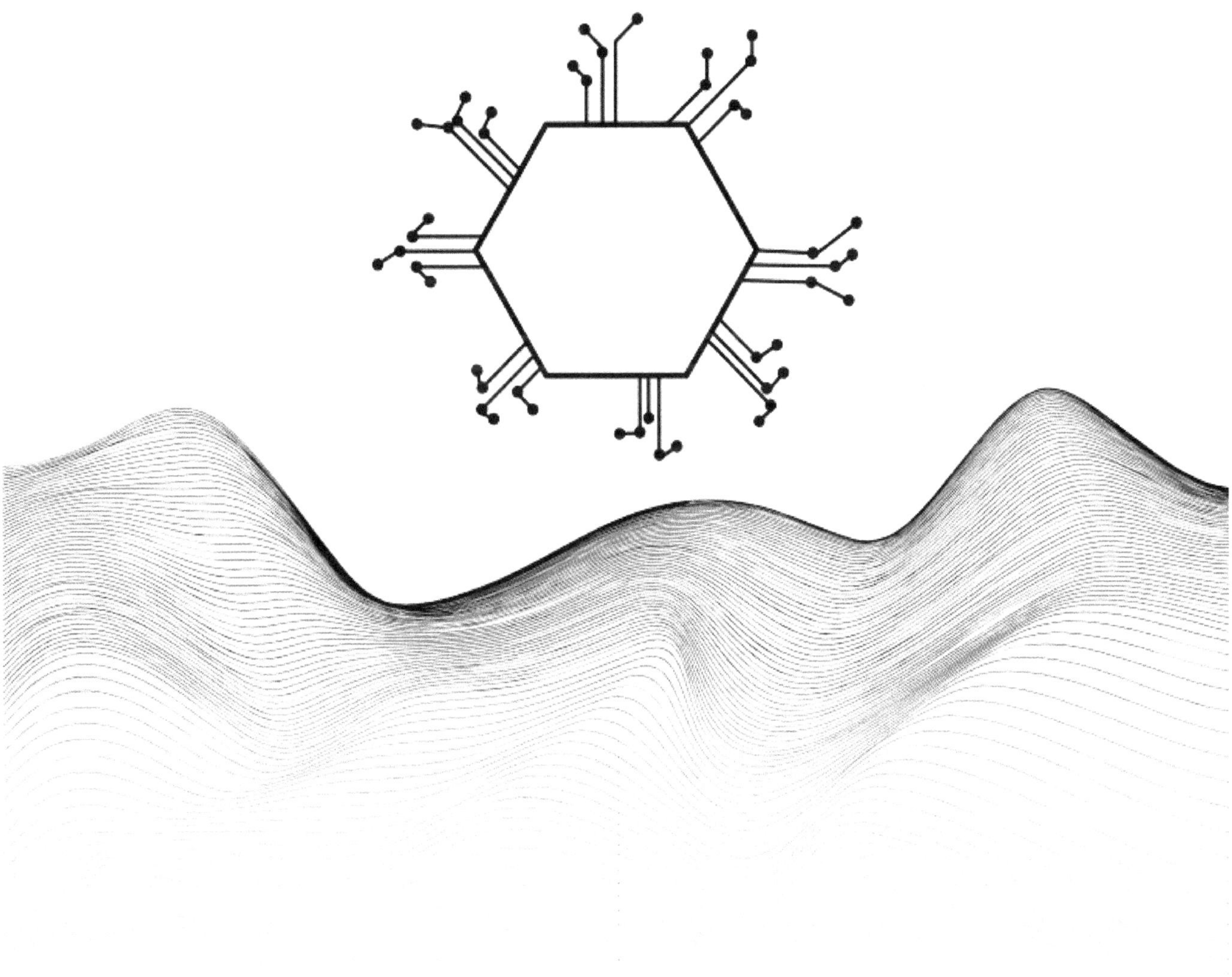

CHAPTER 13: LEVERAGING TECHNOLOGY

13.1 INTRODUCTION TO TECHNOLOGY IN AI GOVERNANCE

WHY TECHNOLOGY MATTERS

Technology plays a pivotal role in simplifying and automating AI governance processes. As organizations increasingly rely on AI systems, ensuring their responsible use is essential. Governance ensures compliance with ethical, regulatory, and operational standards, and technology provides the infrastructure to manage these complex requirements at scale.

One of the primary benefits of technology in AI governance is **automation**. Once labor-intensive tasks, such as auditing, compliance checks, and risk assessments, can be performed more efficiently using software solutions. Automation reduces the potential for human error, minimizes operational costs, and enables organizations to focus on higher-level decision-making. For example, real-time monitoring systems can detect anomalies or compliance violations immediately, enabling swift corrective actions.

Moreover, technology fosters **standardization** across governance processes. By implementing centralized platforms, organizations can ensure uniform policy and procedure application. This consistency is crucial when managing large-scale AI deployments across diverse teams and geographies.

Technology also enhances **transparency and accountability**. Many tools are designed to log actions, decisions, and outcomes traceably. This is particularly important for maintaining trust among stakeholders, including regulators, customers, and employees. For instance, blockchain technology can provide immutable audit trails, ensuring the integrity of governance processes.

TYPES OF TOOLS

Governance technology can be grouped into several key categories, each addressing specific aspects of AI governance.

1. **Compliance Platforms**
   Compliance platforms help organizations comply with regulations such as GDPR, the AI Act, or other industry-specific standards. These platforms often include features like policy libraries, automated risk assessments, and audit management. Tools like OneTrust and TrustArc provide dashboards that monitor compliance status and flag potential risks in real-time. By automating these processes, organizations can reduce the burden of manual compliance efforts.

2. **Bias Detection Tools**
   Bias detection tools, such as IBM AI Fairness 360 and Fairlearn, are critical for identifying and mitigating unfair outcomes in AI systems. These tools analyze datasets and model outputs to detect biases based on attributes like gender, race, or age. They often include algorithms that

suggest mitigation strategies, such as re-sampling, re-weighting, or adversarial training. These tools are vital in sectors like recruitment, credit scoring, and law enforcement, where bias can have profound social implications.

3. **Explainability Frameworks**
   Explainability tools, including LIME, SHAP, and Google's Explainable AI platform, are designed to make AI decisions understandable to technical and non-technical stakeholders. These frameworks provide insights into how models make decisions and highlight factors influencing specific outcomes. For example, explainability tools in healthcare can help clinicians understand why an AI system recommends a particular treatment plan, fostering trust and facilitating compliance with medical regulations.

4. **Monitoring Systems**
   Monitoring tools like Fiddler AI, Arize AI, and Weights & Biases are essential for continuously overseeing AI systems. These platforms provide real-time dashboards to track performance metrics, detect model drift, and identify anomalies. Advanced monitoring systems also offer predictive analytics to flag potential risks before they materialize. This continuous oversight ensures that AI systems remain robust, accurate, and compliant throughout their lifecycle.

By leveraging these technologies, organizations can implement a comprehensive governance framework that addresses ethical, operational, and regulatory challenges. As AI adoption grows, integrating these tools into governance strategies will become indispensable for sustainable and responsible innovation.

13.2 TOOLS FOR COMPLIANCE AND REGULATION

COMPLIANCE MANAGEMENT PLATFORMS

Compliance management platforms are essential in ensuring organizations adhere to the complex web of AI-related regulations. These tools streamline compliance processes by offering centralized management, automation, and real-time monitoring capabilities. Let's examine the features of leading platforms such as OneTrust, TrustArc, and LogicGate.

1. **OneTrust** OneTrust is a comprehensive privacy, security, and governance platform. Its AI governance modules provide capabilities to manage regulatory requirements, monitor risks, and ensure compliance with standards like GDPR and the AI Act. Key features include:

   - **Policy Libraries**: Pre-built templates and frameworks tailored to industry-specific compliance needs.

   - **Automated Assessments**: Tools for conducting privacy impact assessments (PIAs) and algorithmic impact assessments (AIAs) with minimal manual intervention.

- **Data Mapping and Discovery**: This service helps organizations map their data flows and ensures that AI models adhere to data sovereignty and privacy regulations.
- **Risk Analytics**: Dashboards that provide insights into compliance gaps and suggest mitigation strategies.

2. **TrustArc** TrustArc focuses on privacy and data governance but extends its capabilities to support AI governance frameworks. Its compliance management solutions include:
   - **Regulatory Intelligence**: Keeps track of evolving global regulations and updates organizations on relevant changes.
   - **Workflow Automation**: Streamlines tasks like consent management, risk assessments, and third-party vendor evaluations.
   - **Compliance Reporting**: Provides audit-ready documentation, reducing the effort needed for regulatory submissions.
   - **Third-Party Risk Management**: Monitors compliance risks associated with vendors and partners.
3. **LogicGate** LogicGate offers flexible governance, risk, and compliance (GRC) platform with customization options to address AI-specific challenges. Notable features include:
   - **Customizable Workflows**: Organizations can design governance processes tailored to their unique AI use cases.
   - **Real-Time Alerts**: Automated notifications for potential compliance breaches or anomalies in AI operations.
   - **Integrations**: Seamless connections with other enterprise systems to consolidate compliance efforts.
   - **Audit Trails**: Ensures accountability by maintaining detailed records of all compliance-related activities.

These platforms empower organizations to navigate the intricate landscape of AI regulations by providing tools that are not only reactive but also proactive, ensuring compliance is maintained as regulations evolve.

AUTOMATING COMPLIANCE CHECKS

Automation has transformed compliance management by reducing manual workload, enhancing accuracy, and ensuring scalability. AI-specific regulations, such as GDPR and the EU AI Act, require meticulous adherence to data privacy, fairness, transparency, and accountability. Technology-driven compliance checks effectively address these challenges.

1. Simplifying Regulatory Adherence Automated compliance tools use machine learning and natural language processing (NLP) to:
    - Interpret Regulations: Convert complex regulatory texts into actionable policies and tasks.
    - Monitor Updates: Keep track of legislative changes and recommend updates to governance practices.
2. Real-Time Monitoring Many compliance tools integrate with AI systems to provide continuous oversight. For instance:
    - Data Usage Audits: Ensure that AI models only access permissible data sources.
    - Algorithmic Audits: Evaluate whether models operate within ethical and legal boundaries, identifying instances of bias or unfair treatment.
3. Automated Documentation Compliance software generates audit-ready reports by:
    - Tracking every step of an AI model's lifecycle, including training, deployment, and updates.
    - Maintaining detailed logs of decisions made by AI systems, enhancing traceability and accountability.
4. Risk Prediction and Mitigation Advanced compliance tools use predictive analytics to:
    - Identify potential compliance risks based on historical data and current operations.
    - Proactive measures to avoid regulatory violations, such as adjusting model parameters or retraining algorithms, are recommended.

By automating compliance checks, organizations ensure adherence to current regulations and prepare for future challenges, reducing the risk of fines, reputational damage, and operational disruptions.

CASE STUDY: REDUCING REGULATORY RISKS WITH COMPLIANCE SOFTWARE

Organization: Global Financial Services Corporation (GFSC)
Challenge: GFSC is under increasing scrutiny from regulators due to its use of AI in customer credit scoring. Concerns have been raised about data privacy, potential biases, and the lack of transparency in the AI models.

Solution: The organization implemented a compliance management platform combining OneTrust and TrustArc features to address these challenges. Key steps included:

1. **Data Privacy and Consent Management**
    - GFSC used the platform's data mapping tools to ensure compliance with GDPR's data sovereignty requirements.
    - Automated consent management ensured customer data was collected and processed with explicit permissions, reducing the risk of unauthorized data usage.
2. **Bias Detection and Mitigation**
    - The compliance platform integrated with bias detection tools to evaluate the credit scoring model for discriminatory practices.
    - Identified biases were mitigated using re-sampling techniques, ensuring fair treatment across demographics.
3. **Transparency and Explainability**
    - GFSC utilized explainability tools to give regulators and customers clear insights into the factors influencing credit decisions.
    - Detailed reports were generated automatically, highlighting the rationale behind AI predictions and demonstrating compliance with the AI Act.
4. **Real-Time Monitoring and Alerts**
    - The platform's monitoring features ensured continuous oversight of the AI system's performance and flagged potential compliance breaches.
    - Alerts were sent to the compliance team whenever anomalies or deviations from regulatory norms were detected.

Outcome: By leveraging compliance management software, GFSC achieved:

- As with most documentation, a 40% reduction in regulatory audit times was automatically generated and easily accessible.
- Enhanced customer trust through improved transparency and fairness in credit decisions.
- Avoid regulatory fines, saving the organization millions of dollars in potential penalties.

This case highlights the transformative impact of compliance tools in mitigating risks and fostering responsible AI practices. It underscores the importance of integrating technology into governance strategies to address the growing complexity of AI regulations.

13.3 TOOLS FOR BIAS DETECTION AND MITIGATION

BIAS DETECTION SOFTWARE

Bias detection software is critical for identifying and addressing unfair outcomes in AI systems. These tools analyze data and model outputs to uncover disparities that may negatively impact specific groups. Let's explore two leading tools in this domain: IBM AI Fairness 360 and Fairlearn.

1. IBM AI Fairness 360 IBM AI Fairness 360 (AIF360) is an open-source toolkit designed to help developers detect and mitigate bias throughout the AI lifecycle. Key features include:

    - Comprehensive Metrics: AIF360 provides over 70 fairness metrics to evaluate bias in datasets and model outputs.
    - Bias Mitigation Algorithms include pre-processing, in-processing, and post-processing techniques to reduce bias.
    - Extensive Documentation: Offers tutorials and guides tailored for developers and data scientists.
    - Integration Capabilities: Works seamlessly with machine learning frameworks like TensorFlow and PyTorch.

    For instance, a financial institution can use AIF360 to evaluate whether its credit scoring model is biased against specific demographics, such as age or ethnicity. By applying mitigation algorithms, the institution can ensure fairer credit decisions.

2. Fairlearn Fairlearn is another open-source toolkit focused on fairness in AI systems. Developed by Microsoft, it emphasizes transparency and usability. Key features include:

    - Fairness Assessments: Provides disparity metrics that quantify the impact of model decisions on different demographic groups.
    - Mitigation Strategies: Offers algorithms like equalized odds and demographic parity to address disparities.
    - Visualization Tools include dashboards that make fairness metrics accessible to technical and non-technical stakeholders.
    - Developer-Friendly: Integrates easily with Python-based machine learning pipelines.

For example, an HR department might use Fairlearn to ensure its hiring model does not unfairly disadvantage candidates based on gender or race. By leveraging Fairlearn's tools, they can adjust the model to achieve more equitable outcomes.

BIAS MITIGATION TECHNIQUES

Bias mitigation involves techniques that address unfairness in AI models. These methods can be applied at different stages of the machine learning pipeline: before, during, or after model training. Let's delve into three standard techniques: re-sampling, re-weighting, and adversarial debiasing.

1. **Re-Sampling** Re-sampling adjusts the dataset to ensure a balanced representation of all groups. This can be done by:

    - **Over-sampling**: Increasing the number of instances for underrepresented groups.
    - **Under-sampling**: Reducing the number of instances for overrepresented groups.

    For instance, over-sampling can help the AI model learn patterns that are not biased against women in a recruitment dataset where female candidates are underrepresented. This approach ensures that minority groups have sufficient representation during training.

2. **Re-Weighting** Re-weighting assigns weights to data samples to counteract biases in the training process. Higher weights are given to samples from underrepresented groups, ensuring that the model pays more attention to these instances.

    For example, re-weighting can emphasize loans approved for minority applicants, ensuring that the model learns unbiased decision-making patterns.

3. **Adversarial Debiasing** Adversarial debiasing is a sophisticated technique for reducing bias. It uses an adversarial network to train a model to make accurate predictions while minimizing the adversary's ability to predict protected attributes like gender or race.

    This method is particularly effective when subtle biases are embedded in the data. For instance, a facial recognition system can use adversarial debiasing to ensure equal accuracy across all skin tones.

When implemented effectively, these techniques enhance the fairness of AI systems, fostering trust and compliance with ethical standards.

Bias detection and mitigation tools have practical applications in various industries. Let's explore a case study in the context of recruitment and credit scoring systems.

Case Study: Mitigating Bias in Recruitment

Organization: Global Tech Solutions (GTS)
Challenge: GTS faced allegations of bias in its AI-driven recruitment system, which disproportionately favored male candidates over female candidates.

Solution:

1. Bias Detection:
    - GTS used Fairlearn to assess the decisions of its recruitment model.
    - Disparity metrics revealed that female candidates had a significantly lower selection rate than male candidates with similar qualifications.
2. Bias Mitigation:
    - Re-Sampling: GTS applied over-sampling techniques to balance the representation of female candidates in the training data.
    - Re-Weighting: Assigned higher weights to female candidates' records during model training.
    - Adversarial Debiasing: Implemented adversarial networks to reduce the influence of gender on hiring predictions.
3. Transparency and Communication:
    - GTS leveraged visualization tools from Fairlearn to explain the changes made to the model.
    - Detailed reports were shared with internal stakeholders to ensure transparency and build trust.

Outcome:

- The revised recruitment model demonstrated equal selection rates for male and female candidates with equivalent qualifications.
- GTS saw a 30% improvement in diversity hiring metrics within six months.
- Employee and stakeholder trust in the AI system increased significantly.

Case Study: Addressing Bias in Credit Scoring

Organization: Financial Equity Inc. (FEI)
Challenge: FEI's credit scoring system was criticized for disproportionately rejecting loan applications from minority groups.

Solution:

1. **Bias Detection**:
   - FEI deployed IBM AI Fairness 360 to analyze its credit scoring model.
   - Fairness metrics indicated that minority applicants were 20% more likely to be denied loans than those with similar financial profiles.
2. **s Mitigation**:
   - **Re-Weighting**: Adjusted the training process to give higher weights to records from minority applicants.
   - **Post-Processing Adjustments**: Implemented techniques to modify the model's outputs, ensuring equitable treatment of all applicants.
3. **Continuous Monitoring**:
   - FEI integrated real-time monitoring tools to track the model's performance and ensure sustained fairness.

Outcome:

- Loan approval rates for minority applicants increased by 25% without compromising overall risk metrics.
- FEI's efforts were recognized by industry regulators, enhancing its reputation as a leader in ethical AI practices.

13.4 TOOLS FOR EXPLAINABILITY AND TRANSPARENCY

EXPLAINABILITY FRAMEWORKS

Explainability frameworks make AI systems' decision-making processes transparent and understandable. These tools provide insights into the inner workings of AI models, enabling stakeholders to assess how decisions are made. Here are three leading tools in this domain:

1. LIME (Local Interpretable Model-Agnostic Explanations)
   - Purpose: LIME explains the predictions of any machine learning model by approximating it with an interpretable model locally around the prediction.
   - Features:
     - Generates explanations for individual predictions by identifying the most influential features.
     - Model-agnostic, meaning it can be used with any machine learning algorithm.
     - Useful for debugging models and ensuring their outputs align with expectations.
   - Use Case: In financial services, LIME can explain why a loan application was approved or denied, highlighting factors like income level or credit history.
2. SHAP (SHapley Additive exPlanations)
   - Purpose: SHAP provides a unified measure of feature importance based on cooperative game theory.
   - Features:
     - Quantifies each feature's contribution to a specific prediction.
     - Offers both global and local interpretability.
     - Visualizations include force plots, summary plots, and dependence plots for deeper insights.
   - Use Case: In healthcare, SHAP can explain why a patient is at high risk for a specific condition, helping clinicians make informed decisions.
3. Google's Explainable AI Platform
   - Purpose: This platform provides tools and services to enhance the transparency of AI models deployed in Google Cloud.
   - Features:
     - Built-in interpretability for models built using TensorFlow and AutoML.
     - Feature attributions that indicate how much each input feature contributed to a prediction.
     - Integration with AI pipelines for seamless deployment.

- **Use Case**: Organizations can use this platform to audit AI models in real-time and ensure they comply with ethical and regulatory standards.

IMPROVING STAKEHOLDER TRUST

Explainability tools are pivotal in bridging the gap between AI systems and non-technical stakeholders. These tools foster trust and confidence among users, regulators, and customers by making AI outputs more transparent. Here's how they achieve this:

1. **Enhancing Understanding**:
   - Explainability frameworks simplify complex AI decisions into human-readable insights.
   - Stakeholders can see why certain decisions were made, which reduces confusion and builds confidence in the system.
2. **Facilitating Accountability**:
   - Transparent AI systems allow organizations to trace decisions to specific inputs or model behaviors.
   - This accountability is crucial for adhering to regulations and addressing stakeholder concerns.
3. **Supporting Ethical Decision-Making**:
   - Explainability tools help ensure models operate within ethical boundaries by revealing the factors influencing AI decisions.
   - For example, these tools can identify if sensitive attributes like race or gender unfairly influence outcomes, enabling corrective actions.
4. **Driving Adoption**:
   - When stakeholders understand and trust AI systems, they are more likely to adopt them in critical processes.
   - Explainability fosters collaboration between technical and non-technical teams, ensuring that AI systems align with organizational goals.

PRACTICAL EXAMPLE: HEALTHCARE COMPLIANCE

Organization: MedCare AI Solutions
Challenge: MedCare implemented an AI system to predict patient readmission risks. However, regulators raised concerns about the model's decision-making process's lack of transparency.

Solution:

1. Explainability Tools:
    - MedCare used SHAP to analyze the predictions made by their AI model.
    - Feature attributions highlighted key factors like patient age, previous medical history, and length of hospital stay.
2. Compliance with Regulations:
    - The explainability framework provided detailed reports showing how predictions were made, ensuring compliance with healthcare regulations such as HIPAA and GDPR.
    - These reports were shared with regulators to demonstrate the model's fairness and accuracy.
3. Stakeholder Engagement:
    - Clinicians were trained to use SHAP visualizations to understand the model's outputs.
    - This transparency improved collaboration between data scientists and medical professionals, improving patient outcomes.

Outcome:

- MedCare's AI system gained regulatory approval and clinician trust.
- The organization saw a 25% reduction in patient readmissions, highlighting the effectiveness of the AI model.
- Stakeholder confidence in the system increased, paving the way for further AI adoption in healthcare.

13.5 TOOLS FOR MONITORING AND RISK MANAGEMENT

AI MONITORING PLATFORMS

AI monitoring platforms are essential for ensuring machine learning models' reliability, fairness, and performance. These platforms provide tools and dashboards to track AI systems and ensure they operate as intended. Let's explore the features of three leading platforms: Fiddler AI, Arize AI, and Weights & Biases.

1. **Fiddler AI**
   - **Purpose**: Fiddler AI focuses on explainability, monitoring, and analytics for AI models.
   - **Features**:
     - **Model Monitoring**: Tracks key performance indicators (KPIs) such as accuracy, precision, recall, and fairness metrics.
     - **Explainability**: Provides insights into how models make decisions, helping identify potential biases or errors.
     - **Alerting System**: Sends notifications for anomalies or performance deviations.
     - **Integration**: Works seamlessly with popular machine learning frameworks and cloud environments.
   - **Use Case**: Fiddler AI can help a financial institution ensure its credit scoring models comply with fairness and transparency regulations.
2. **Arize AI**
   - **Purpose**: Arize AI specializes in AI performance monitoring and troubleshooting.
   - **Features**:
     - **Drift Detection**: Identifies when model performance deteriorates due to changes in data distribution.
     - **Bias Tracking**: Monitors fairness metrics over time to ensure equitable outcomes.
     - **Root Cause Analysis**: Pinpoints issues in model predictions to facilitate faster resolutions.
     - **Dashboard Analytics**: Provides visualizations for tracking model health and trends.
   - **Use Case**: An e-commerce company can use Arize AI to detect and address biases in its recommendation engine.

3. Weights & Biases

    - Purpose: Weights & Biases (W&B) is a platform for experiment tracking, model monitoring, and collaboration.
    - Features:
        - Experiment Tracking: Logs every aspect of model training, including hyperparameters, metrics, and code versions.
        - Model Monitoring: Tracks deployed models' performance in real-world environments.
        - Collaboration Tools: Enables teams to share insights and reports seamlessly.
        - Custom Dashboards: Allows users to build tailored visualizations for specific monitoring needs.
    - Use Case: A healthcare organization can use W&B to track and improve the performance of predictive models for patient diagnoses.

RISK MANAGEMENT SUPPORT

AI systems are inherently susceptible to risks such as model drift, robustness issues, and data anomalies. Monitoring platforms provide tools to mitigate these risks effectively.

1. Detecting Model Drift

    - Definition: Model drift occurs when an AI model's performance degrades due to changes in the data it processes.
    - Detection Tools:
        - Platforms like Arize AI and Fiddler AI track changes in data distributions and flag potential drift.
        - Statistical tests and visualization tools help identify when new data deviates significantly from training data.
    - Example: In fraud detection, a model trained on historical data may underperform as fraud tactics evolve. Drift detection tools can identify these changes, prompting model retraining.

2. **Ensuring Robustness**
   - **Definition**: Robustness refers to a model's ability to perform consistently under varying conditions.
   - **Tools**:
     - Stress testing features in platforms like W&B simulate edge cases to evaluate model reliability.
     - Robustness metrics, such as adversarial accuracy, help identify vulnerabilities.
   - **Example**: A self-driving car's AI must remain accurate in diverse weather conditions. Robustness testing ensures the model performs reliably under all scenarios.
3. **Flagging Anomalies**
   - **Definition**: Anomalies are unexpected patterns or deviations in data or model predictions.
   - **Detection Tools**:
     - Real-time monitoring platforms like Arize AI identify anomalies in input data, predictions, or performance metrics.
     - Root cause analysis tools help investigate anomalies and implement corrective actions.
   - **Example**: Anomaly detection in a healthcare AI system can flag unusual patient data, preventing potential misdiagnoses.

CONTINUOUS MONITORING

Continuous monitoring ensures that AI systems remain reliable, accurate, and compliant over time. Real-time dashboards and alert systems are integral to this process.

1. **Real-Time Dashboards**
   - Dashboards provide a centralized view of AI system performance.
   - Features include:
     - Visualizations of key metrics such as accuracy, drift, and fairness.
     - Filters for examining specific datasets or periods.

- Example: A retail company can use dashboards to monitor the performance of its demand forecasting model, ensuring accurate predictions during peak seasons.

2. Alert Systems
   - Alert systems notify stakeholders of significant events or issues in real-time.
   - Features include:
     - Customizable thresholds for triggering alerts.
     - Integration with communication tools like Slack or email.
   - Example: An AI-powered cybersecurity system can alert administrators when it detects unusual login patterns, preventing potential breaches.
3. Governance Oversight
   - Continuous monitoring ensures compliance with ethical and regulatory standards.
   - Monitoring platforms provide audit trails and documentation for governance purposes.
   - Example: A financial institution can use monitoring tools to demonstrate compliance with GDPR and other data protection laws.

CASE STUDY: IMPROVING GOVERNANCE WITH MONITORING TOOLS

Organization: Global Retail Corporation (GRC)
Challenge: GRC deployed an AI system for dynamic pricing but faced issues with model drift and customer complaints about unfair pricing.

Solution:

1. Implementation of Monitoring Tools:
   - GRC adopted Fiddler AI to monitor its pricing model.
   - Drift detection features identified changes in customer purchasing behavior that affected model performance.
2. Bias and Fairness Monitoring:
   - The platform tracked fairness metrics to ensure equitable pricing decisions across customer demographics.

- Root cause analysis tools helped address instances of pricing discrepancies.

3. **Real-Time Alerts:**

    - Custom alerts notified the pricing team when anomalies were detected, enabling swift corrective actions.

4. **Governance Documentation:**

    - Fiddler AI's audit trails provided detailed records of pricing decisions, ensuring compliance with consumer protection regulations.

Outcome:

- GRC improved customer satisfaction by addressing pricing biases and anomalies.
- The organization reduced revenue losses caused by model drift.
- Regulatory audits were completed efficiently, thanks to comprehensive documentation.

13.6 EMERGING TECHNOLOGIES IN AI GOVERNANCE

The rapid evolution of artificial intelligence (AI) has made governance a critical issue. Emerging technologies are subject to governance frameworks and integral to enhancing them. This section explores three key areas: AI-driven governance mechanisms, blockchain for AI governance, and the challenges and opportunities associated with quantum AI governance.

AI-DRIVEN GOVERNANCE

AI itself can play a transformative role in managing governance processes. AI-driven governance leverages machine learning, natural language processing, and predictive analytics to streamline and enhance compliance, risk management, and decision-making processes. Here are some ways AI contributes to governance:

1. **AI for Compliance:**

    - **Regulatory Adherence:** AI tools can monitor vast amounts of data in real-time to ensure organizations comply with regulatory requirements. Natural language processing can analyze legal documents, identify relevant clauses, and compare them against internal policies, reducing human error.
    - **Automated Reporting:** Machine learning algorithms can generate compliance reports, flag anomalies, and suggest corrective actions. This automation not only saves time but also ensures accuracy in documentation.

2. **Risk Prediction and Management:**
   - **Predictive Analytics:** AI models can identify emerging risks by analyzing historical and real-time data patterns. For instance, they can detect potential data breaches, financial fraud, or operational inefficiencies before they escalate.
   - **Scenario Analysis:** AI simulations enable organizations to evaluate the impact of various decisions and prepare for potential risks. For example, AI can simulate the consequences of introducing a new AI model into an existing system, ensuring it aligns with governance standards.
3. **Decision-Making and Transparency:**
   - **Augmented Decision Support:** AI systems can provide decision-makers with data-driven insights, ensuring that governance decisions are based on comprehensive analysis rather than intuition alone.
   - **Explainability:** AI-driven tools are increasingly designed with transparency in mind, offering explanations for their predictions and recommendations. This fosters trust and accountability in governance processes.

By integrating AI into governance, organizations can achieve a more proactive, efficient, and adaptive approach to managing compliance and risks in a dynamic technological landscape.

BLOCKCHAIN FOR AI GOVERNANCE

With its inherent characteristics of decentralization, immutability, and transparency, blockchain technology provides robust solutions for AI governance challenges. It offers a secure and auditable framework for tracking AI processes, ensuring accountability and integrity.

1. **Secure Audit Trails:**
   - **Immutable Records:** Blockchain can create a tamper-proof record of AI training data, model updates, and decision-making processes. This ensures that any changes to an AI system can be traced back to their origin, enhancing accountability.
   - **Transparency in AI Lifecycle:** Organizations can document every stage of an AI model's lifecycle—from development and training to deployment and updates—on a blockchain. This promotes trust among stakeholders, including regulators and end-users.

2. **Data Integrity and Privacy:**
    - **Decentralized Data Verification:** Blockchain's decentralized architecture ensures that the data used to train AI models is authentic and unaltered. This is particularly important when biased or manipulated data could compromise AI outcomes.
    - **Privacy-Preserving Mechanisms:** Blockchain can support privacy-focused governance by enabling techniques like zero-knowledge proofs. These allow organizations to prove compliance without revealing sensitive information.
3. **Smart Contracts for Governance:**
    - **Automated Enforcement:** Smart contracts on blockchain can automate governance protocols, such as granting or revoking access to AI models based on predefined rules. For instance, they can ensure that only authorized entities can modify an AI system.
    - **Real-Time Monitoring:** Blockchain-based smart contracts can continuously monitor AI operations and enforce compliance with governance standards dynamically.

By leveraging blockchain, organizations can address critical concerns about AI transparency, accountability, and data integrity, building trust in AI systems.

FUTURE TRENDS: QUANTUM AI GOVERNANCE

The advent of quantum computing introduces new complexities and opportunities in AI governance. Quantum computing's unparalleled processing power can significantly accelerate AI development, but it also raises unique governance challenges that require innovative solutions.

1. **Quantum AI Challenges:**
    - **Data Security Risks:** Quantum computers can break traditional encryption methods, threatening sensitive AI data's secure storage and transmission. Governance frameworks must evolve to address this risk.
    - **Algorithmic Complexity:** Quantum algorithms used in AI systems are inherently complex and challenging to interpret. Specialized tools and methodologies will be required to ensure explainability and accountability in quantum AI decision-making.
2. **Potential Solutions:**
    - **Post-Quantum Cryptography:** To safeguard AI data and processes, governance frameworks must incorporate cryptographic techniques that are resistant to quantum attacks. Organizations like NIST are already working on standardizing post-quantum cryptographic algorithms.

- **Quantum Transparency Tools:** Developing tools to audit and interpret quantum AI systems is crucial. This may involve creating quantum simulators or hybrid systems that combine classical and quantum computing for enhanced explainability.
- **Ethical Frameworks for Quantum AI:** As quantum AI capabilities expand, ethical considerations will become increasingly important. Governance must address issues such as the potential misuse of quantum AI and the equitable distribution of its benefits.

3. **Collaboration and Standardization:**
   - **Global Standards:** Given the worldwide nature of quantum and AI technologies, international collaboration is essential to establish consistent governance standards.
   - **Interdisciplinary Approaches:** Effective quantum AI governance will require input from diverse fields, including quantum physics, computer science, ethics, and law. This multidisciplinary approach can help anticipate and mitigate emerging risks.

Quantum AI governance represents a frontier that will shape the future of technology and society. By proactively addressing its challenges, organizations can harness the potential of quantum AI while ensuring responsible and ethical development.

CHAPTER 14: TRAINING AND AWARENESS

14.1 INTRODUCTION TO TRAINING IN AI GOVERNANCE

Why Training is Critical

Training in AI governance initiatives is essential for building an organization fully aware of governance principles. As artificial intelligence becomes integral to business operations, organizations must ensure that their teams are equipped with the knowledge to navigate the complexities of ethical, regulatory, and operational frameworks. Training creates a governance-aware culture, empowering employees to make informed decisions while minimizing risks associated with AI adoption.

AI governance training fosters team alignment, ensuring all employees understand and adhere to ethical guidelines, regulatory requirements, and operational expectations. This alignment is critical to mitigate algorithmic bias, non-compliance, and reputational harm. By embedding governance training, organizations can proactively address challenges and build trust with stakeholders, regulators, and customers.

Audience for Training

AI governance training must be tailored to diverse audiences, as individuals across various roles contribute differently to the AI lifecycle. The following groups should be prioritized for training:

1. **Executives and Decision-Makers**: Senior leaders must grasp the strategic importance of AI governance to steer the organization responsibly. Training ensures they can integrate governance principles into organizational goals, allocate resources effectively, and champion a culture of accountability.

2. **Developers and Data Scientists**: These technical teams are at the forefront of AI model development and deployment. Their training focuses on technical aspects, such as identifying and mitigating biases, ensuring transparency, and adhering to ethical AI design practices.

3. **Compliance Officers and Legal Teams** are responsible for regulatory adherence. These professionals require training on the laws, industry standards, and frameworks governing AI systems. This equips them to monitor compliance and advise on risk mitigation strategies.

4. **Operational Teams**: Employees managing AI systems in production need training on monitoring, maintaining, and troubleshooting AI solutions. This includes understanding ethical and operational risks specific to AI technologies.

5. **General Workforce**: All employees need a baseline understanding of AI governance. Training helps them recognize the implications of AI decisions and encourages a shared responsibility for ethical practices within the organization.

Training in AI governance addresses the needs of these diverse groups and ensures a cohesive, organization-wide approach to navigating the complexities of AI while fostering accountability and sustainability.

14.2 DESIGNING AI GOVERNANCE TRAINING PROGRAMS

Creating an effective AI governance training program requires a structured approach to ensure employees understand their roles in fostering responsible AI development and deployment. The program must address the needs of diverse audiences, provide engaging and relevant content, and maintain continuity to adapt to the rapidly evolving AI landscape. This section outlines the essential elements, modules, and tools to build a robust training framework.

KEY ELEMENTS OF EFFECTIVE TRAINING

1. **Customization: Tailoring Training to Different Roles and Departments**

AI governance training must recognize employees' varied responsibilities and expertise within an organization. A one-size-fits-all approach can dilute the program's effectiveness. Customization ensures each role receives targeted information relevant to its function:

- **Executives and Leaders**: Training for this group should emphasize strategic decision-making, risk assessment, and aligning AI governance with organizational objectives.
- **Developers and Engineers**: These teams require technical training on implementing bias detection, ensuring model explainability, and incorporating ethical considerations into AI design.
- **Compliance and Legal Teams**: Training for these roles should focus on understanding legal frameworks, monitoring adherence to regulatory standards, and developing governance policies.
- **Business and Operational** teams need training on the ethical implications of AI for day-to-day operations, risk management, and the long-term sustainability of AI systems.

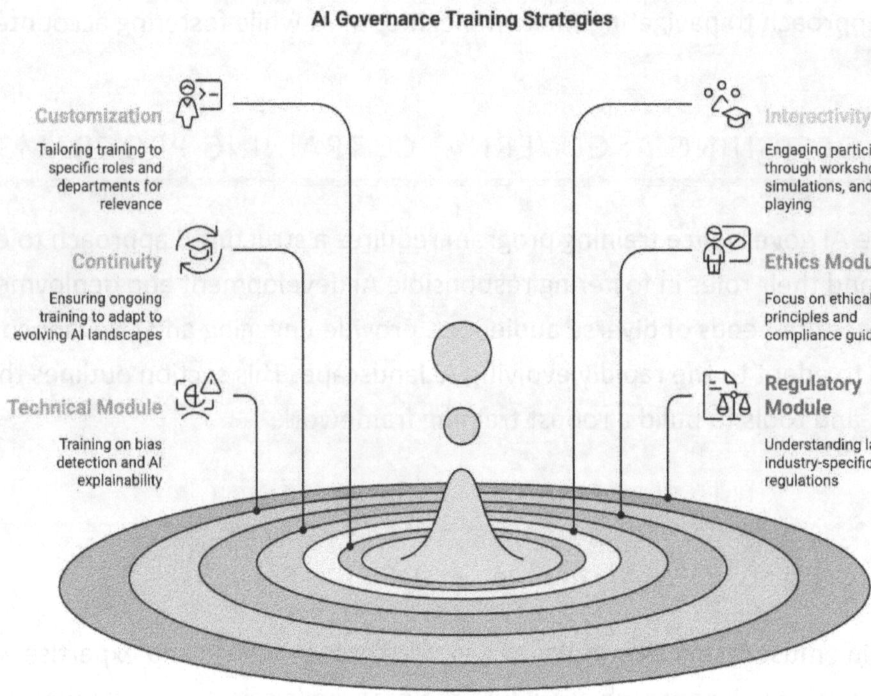

By tailoring content, organizations can maximize the relevance and impact of training for all participants.

2. Interactivity: Workshops, Simulations, and Role-Playing Scenarios

Interactive methods enhance learning by engaging participants actively rather than passively absorbing information. Interactivity fosters a more profound understanding and retention of concepts:

- Workshops: Hands-on workshops allow participants to engage directly with governance challenges. For example, teams can analyze case studies of AI bias or collaborate to draft AI ethics guidelines.
- Simulations: Real-world simulations, such as addressing a regulatory violation or resolving an ethical dilemma in an AI system, prepare employees for practical governance challenges.
- Role-Playing Scenarios: Employees can assume different roles—such as developers, compliance officers, or regulators—to explore various perspectives on governance issues. These exercises promote empathy and a holistic understanding of governance requirements.

Interactive elements ensure the training program resonates with participants, equipping them with actionable skills to address governance challenges.

3. Continuity: Ensuring Training is Not a One-Time Event

AI governance is not static; it evolves with new technological developments, regulations, and ethical considerations. Consequently, training must be an ongoing process:

- Regular Updates: Periodic sessions can address changes in regulatory requirements, new AI tools, and emerging ethical dilemmas.
- Refresher Courses: These help reinforce key concepts and ensure employees remain up-to-date on governance practices.
- Onboarding for New Employees: Governance training should be integrated into onboarding to instill a culture of responsibility from the outset.
- Feedback Loops: Continuous improvement through participant feedback ensures the program stays relevant and practical.

Sustained training efforts help embed governance principles into the organization's culture, making responsible AI practices a natural part of day-to-day operations.

TRAINING MODULES

A comprehensive AI governance training program should include ethical, technical, and regulatory modules. These modules provide employees with a well-rounded understanding of AI governance.

1. Ethics and Compliance

- Core Ethical Principles: Explore principles such as fairness, accountability, transparency, and respect for privacy.
- AI Ethics Frameworks: Introduce widely recognized frameworks, such as those by the IEEE, OECD, and EU.
- Case Studies: Analyze real-world instances of ethical failures in AI systems and their consequences for organizations and society.
- Compliance Guidelines: Teach participants how to align AI practices with organizational values, laws, and industry standards.

2. Technical Aspects

- Bias Detection and Mitigation: Train developers to identify and address biases in datasets, algorithms, and outputs.
- Explainability and Interpretability: Emphasize making AI models understandable to technical and non-technical stakeholders.
- Robustness and Security: Equip teams with tools to enhance the reliability and security of AI systems, reducing the risk of unintended behaviors or adversarial attacks.

- **Monitoring and Auditing**: This section highlights the importance of post-deployment monitoring and periodic audits to ensure ongoing compliance with governance policies.

3. **Regulatory Requirements and Industry-Specific Considerations**

- **Understanding Laws and Regulations**: This section covers global and regional regulations, such as the EU AI Act, GDPR, and industry-specific mandates.
- **Sector-Specific Training**: Tailor content to industries such as healthcare, finance, and manufacturing, addressing unique governance challenges in each sector.
- **Data Governance**: Teach participants how to manage data responsibly, focusing on privacy, security, and ethical use.

Each module should include practical exercises, examples, and tools to help participants apply their knowledge in real-world scenarios.

TOOLS FOR TRAINING DELIVERY

The success of a training program also depends on the effective delivery of content. Organizations should use various delivery methods to accommodate learning styles and logistical needs.

1. **E-Learning Platforms**

E-learning platforms provide a flexible, scalable solution for delivering AI governance training. Key features include:

- **Self-Paced Learning**: Employees can access modules at their convenience, making it easier to balance training with other responsibilities.
- **Interactive Content**: Platforms often include quizzes, videos, and gamified elements to enhance engagement.
- **Analytics**: Track progress, participation rates, and knowledge retention through built-in analytics tools.

Popular platforms like Coursera, Udemy, or custom Learning Management Systems (LMS) can be adapted for governance training.

2. **In-Person Sessions**

In-person training offers direct interaction and fosters collaborative learning. Benefits include:

- **Real-Time Engagement**: Trainers can address participant questions and provide immediate feedback.

- Team-Building Opportunities: Collaborative exercises and discussions build stronger cross-functional relationships.
- Deep Dives: Complex topics like regulatory compliance or ethical dilemmas are more straightforward to explore in a group setting.

Organizations can complement in-person sessions with digital resources to create a blended learning experience.

3. Blended Approaches

Blended learning combines the advantages of e-learning and in-person sessions. This hybrid model is especially effective for organizations with geographically dispersed teams:

- Pre-Learning Modules: Use e-learning for foundational knowledge.
- Workshops and Simulations: Follow up with in-person or virtual interactive sessions to deepen understanding.
- On-Demand Resources: Provide access to recorded sessions, templates, and tools for ongoing learning.

Blended approaches balance flexibility with depth, ensuring employees receive comprehensive training without logistical challenges.

14.3 BUILDING AWARENESS ACROSS THE ORGANIZATION

Building awareness about AI governance across an organization is essential for fostering a culture of responsibility, accountability, and alignment with ethical principles. Awareness ensures that every team member understands their role in implementing governance policies, mitigating risks, and achieving organizational goals. This section explores strategies for running effective awareness campaigns and outlines methods to involve employees at all levels in governance initiatives.

STRATEGIES FOR AWARENESS CAMPAIGNS

Creating awareness about AI governance requires intentional, creative campaigns tailored to an organization's culture and communication dynamics. These campaigns should be designed to engage, educate, and inspire employees to prioritize governance in their daily tasks.

1. Company-Wide Initiatives

Company-wide initiatives ensure that awareness about AI governance reaches all employees, regardless of their role or location. Effective strategies include:

- **Newsletters**: Regular governance-focused newsletters can be a consistent and informative medium for communicating updates, success stories, and best practices. These newsletters can consist of:
    - Updates on regulatory changes or organizational policies.
    - Highlights of successful governance practices within the company.
    - Tips for embedding governance principles into day-to-day operations.
- **Infographics**: Visual content, such as infographics, simplifies complex governance concepts and makes them more accessible. Infographics can be distributed digitally via emails or displayed in common areas like break rooms or intranet portals. Topics might include:
    - Steps to identify and mitigate bias in AI systems.
    - Key principles of ethical AI design.
    - Illustrations of the AI governance lifecycle.
- **AI Ethics Workshops**: Interactive workshops provide an engaging platform for employees to discuss governance principles, ethical dilemmas, and real-world scenarios. Workshops can include:
    - Case studies of governance failures and successes.
    - Group discussions on ethical decision-making.
    - Role-playing exercises to address governance challenges.

These initiatives foster awareness and create opportunities for employees to engage actively with AI governance concepts.

2. **Leveraging Leadership to Champion Governance Awareness**

Leadership is critical in embedding AI governance into an organization's culture. When leaders champion governance initiatives, employees are more likely to recognize and adopt their importance. Key approaches include:

- **Visible Commitment from Executives**: Senior leaders should publicly endorse AI governance initiatives by participating in workshops, addressing employees in town hall meetings, and sharing messages through internal communication channels. This demonstrates that governance is a priority at the highest levels.
- **Governance Ambassadors**: Designating leaders across departments as governance ambassadors can amplify awareness campaigns. These ambassadors can:

    - Act as points of contact for governance-related queries.
    - Share insights during team meetings.
    - Lead discussions on the practical application of governance principles.
- Setting the Tone with Policies: Leadership must also ensure that organizational policies reflect a commitment to governance. Transparent policies with clear expectations signal that ethical AI practices are non-negotiable.

Organizations can effectively leverage leadership to inspire employees to take governance principles seriously and integrate them into their work.

INVOLVING ALL LEVELS OF THE ORGANIZATION

AI governance cannot succeed unless employees embrace it at every organizational level. Awareness campaigns must address each group's unique roles, responsibilities, and concerns to ensure comprehensive engagement.

1. From Executives to Entry-Level Employees

AI governance awareness should be inclusive, covering all employees, from senior executives to entry-level staff. Each level has unique contributions to make, and awareness campaigns must reflect this diversity:

- Executives and Senior Leaders: Awareness efforts for this group should focus on the strategic implications of governance. Executives must understand how governance aligns with organizational goals, manages risks, and enhances stakeholder trust. Awareness campaigns for leaders can include:
    - Executive briefings on emerging regulations and ethical trends.
    - Strategy sessions on integrating governance into business models.
    - Networking events with external governance experts.
- Middle Management: As a bridge between leadership and operational teams, middle managers must be well-versed in governance principles to communicate expectations and provide guidance effectively. Awareness initiatives for managers can involve:
    - Leadership training on governance-related challenges.
    - Guidelines for fostering ethical decision-making within teams.

- **Technical Teams**: Developers, data scientists, and engineers directly interact with AI systems and are responsible for implementing governance measures. Awareness campaigns for these teams should focus on:
    - The technical aspects of governance, such as bias detection and explainability.
    - Case studies of technical failures stemming from poor governance practices.
    - Tools and frameworks for integrating governance into the development lifecycle.
- **Non-Technical Employees**: Marketing, sales, and human resources also play a role in AI governance by ensuring ethical practices in customer communication, hiring, and data handling. Awareness initiatives for these groups can include:
    - Simplified governance concepts are relevant to their work.
    - Discussions on the societal and organizational impact of governance.

Tailoring campaigns to address each group's specific needs and responsibilities ensures that everyone understands their role in upholding governance principles.

2. **Promoting a Culture of Accountability and Responsibility**

Integrating AI governance into an organization's culture requires more than one-off awareness campaigns. It involves cultivating an environment where accountability and responsibility are part of everyday operations. Strategies to achieve this include:

- **Creating Open Channels for Feedback**: Employees should feel empowered to report governance concerns or suggest improvements. Establishing anonymous reporting mechanisms or regular feedback sessions can encourage participation.
- **Recognizing and Rewarding Governance Champions**: Acknowledging individuals or teams that excel in promoting governance can motivate others to follow suit. Recognition programs might include:
    - Awards for innovative solutions to governance challenges.
    - Public acknowledgment during company events or newsletters.
- **Encouraging Cross-Functional Collaboration**: AI governance is inherently interdisciplinary. Encouraging collaboration between technical, legal, operational, and business teams promotes a shared understanding of governance challenges and solutions.
- **Building Governance into Performance Metrics**: Evaluating employees' adherence to governance principles reinforces the importance of ethical practices. For example:

- Technical teams could be assessed on the robustness and fairness of AI systems they develop.
- Leaders could be evaluated on their ability to integrate governance into decision-making.

Organizations can ensure that governance principles are consistently applied and sustained by promoting accountability and responsibility at every level.

14.4 CASE STUDIES: SUCCESSFUL TRAINING PROGRAMS

The success of AI governance training programs is often best demonstrated through real-world examples. This section highlights how two industry leaders—Company A and Company B—designed and implemented effective governance training programs. It also examines the lessons learned from these initiatives, offering insights into what worked, the challenges faced, and the outcomes achieved.

EXAMPLES OF INDUSTRY LEADERS

1. **Company A: Implementing a Governance Training Program for Global Compliance**

Overview:
Company A is a multinational technology enterprise operating in over 40 countries. It develops AI solutions for the healthcare, finance, and logistics sectors. With a diverse workforce and varying regional regulations, Company A recognized the need for a robust governance training program to ensure global compliance.

Training Program Design:

- **Objective**: Align teams across regions with the company's AI governance framework, focusing on regulatory compliance and ethical practices.
- **Customization**: Training content was tailored to specific regions, addressing local regulations, cultural considerations, and industry requirements.
- **Delivery Methods**: A blended approach was adopted, combining:
  - E-learning modules for foundational knowledge.
  - In-person workshops in key regional offices.
  - Webinars for remote teams.
- **Content Focus**: Modules covered critical areas such as data privacy laws (e.g., GDPR), bias mitigation, and explainability of AI models.

Outcomes:

- The program achieved a 95% participation rate among employees.
- Post-training assessments showed a 40% improvement in employees' understanding of regulatory requirements.
- The company avoided legal penalties by proactively addressing compliance issues identified during training.

Key Challenges:

- Coordinating training efforts across multiple time zones required significant logistical planning.
- Tailoring content to diverse cultural and regulatory contexts added complexity.

What Worked:

- Using region-specific case studies helped make the training relatable and actionable for participants.
- Regular feedback loops allowed the company to refine and adapt the program.

2. Company B: Building Team Awareness of Bias and Ethical Considerations

Overview:
Company B, a leading provider of AI-driven marketing solutions, faced criticism for bias in its AI systems. After an internal audit revealed gaps in ethical awareness among its technical teams, the company launched a governance training program focused on bias detection and moral decision-making.

Training Program Design:

- Objective: Equip technical teams with the skills to identify and address AI systems bias while fostering an ethical mindset.
- Interactive Methods:
    - Workshops on bias detection and mitigation, using real-world examples from the company's projects.
    - Role-playing exercises where participants addressed ethical dilemmas in AI deployment.
    - Simulations of algorithmic decision-making processes to highlight unintended consequences.

- Content Focus: Topics included fairness in AI, diverse data sourcing, and the societal impact of biased algorithms.

Outcomes:

- Within six months, the program reduced identified biases across the company's flagship products by 25%.
- Employee surveys indicated a 60% increase in confidence when addressing ethical challenges in AI development.
- The company's reputation improved significantly, with clients citing the program as a key differentiator.

Key Challenges:

- Initial resistance from technical teams who viewed governance as a hindrance to innovation.
- Convincing leadership to allocate resources for an intensive training program must demonstrate its long-term value.

What Worked:

- Emphasizing the tangible business benefits of ethical AI, such as improved customer trust and reduced risk of regulatory penalties, helped secure leadership's support.
- Interactive training methods, such as simulations and role-playing, engaged participants and made abstract ethical concepts more relatable.

LESSONS LEARNED

The experiences of Company A and Company B reveal important lessons for organizations seeking to implement AI governance training programs.

1. What Worked:
    - Customization: Tailoring training content to specific roles, regions, and industries significantly enhanced its relevance and impact. For instance, Company A's region-specific modules addressed local regulatory nuances, making the training practical and actionable.
    - Engaging Delivery Methods: Interactive elements, such as role-playing and simulations, increased engagement and knowledge retention. Company B's real-world examples demonstrated the practical implications of governance principles.

- **Leadership Involvement**: Visible support from leadership was crucial in driving participation and securing resources. Both companies involved executives in program design and delivery, reinforcing the importance of governance.
- **Continuous Improvement**: Regular feedback loops allowed both companies to refine their programs. Participant feedback on content clarity and relevance ensured that the training evolved to meet changing needs.

2. **Challenges Faced**:
   - **Global Coordination**: For Company A, managing a training program across multiple countries required careful planning and significant resources. Overcoming logistical challenges involved leveraging technology, such as e-learning platforms, to ensure accessibility.
   - **Cultural Resistance**: Company B encountered resistance from technical teams who initially viewed governance as an impediment to creativity and efficiency. Addressing these concerns required framing governance as an enabler of long-term success, not a constraint.
   - **Resource Allocation**: Both organizations faced the challenge of convincing leadership to invest in comprehensive training programs. The key to overcoming this challenge was demonstrating the tangible benefits of governance, such as risk mitigation and improved reputation.
3. **Outcomes Achieved**:
   - Both companies saw measurable improvements in governance-related metrics, such as reduced biases in AI systems and increased understanding of regulatory requirements.
   - Survey results and post-training assessments revealed enhanced employee confidence and engagement with governance principles.
   - The initiatives contributed to broader organizational goals, including compliance with regulations, improved product quality, and strengthened customer trust.

14.5 MEASURING TRAINING EFFECTIVENESS

Evaluating the effectiveness of AI governance training programs is critical for ensuring that they meet their objectives, drive meaningful behavioral change, and align employees with organizational goals. Measuring training outcomes provides insights into the program's impact and identifies areas for improvement. This section explores key metrics, feedback mechanisms, and strategies for sustaining the outcomes of governance training initiatives.

Organizations must use quantitative and qualitative metrics to gauge the success of an AI governance training program. These metrics help assess employee participation, knowledge retention, and the extent of behavioral changes.

1. Participation Rates

Participation rates indicate the program's reach and highlight any gaps in engagement. High participation rates ensure that governance principles are understood and adopted across the organization. Metrics to track include:

- Attendance: The percentage of employees attending in-person or virtual training sessions.
- Completion Rates: The percentage of participants who complete online modules or assessments.
- Departmental Engagement: Identifying which teams or roles have low participation to target future outreach efforts.

2. Knowledge Retention

Retention measures whether participants can recall and apply the information shared during the training. Retention is critical to the program's success in imparting key governance concepts. Evaluation methods include:

- Quizzes and Assessments: Short quizzes after each module or session assess immediate knowledge retention.
- Long-Term Testing: Several weeks or months later, follow-up assessments measure whether participants have retained key concepts over time.

3. Behavioral Changes

Behavioral change metrics evaluate whether training translates into improved practices and decision-making. Key indicators include:

- Application of Knowledge: Observing whether employees apply governance principles in their roles, such as integrating bias checks or adhering to ethical guidelines in AI projects.
- Reduction in Governance Risks: Tracking decreases issues such as data misuse, algorithmic bias, or regulatory non-compliance.
- Team Collaboration: Evaluating whether cross-functional teams show better alignment and communication on governance-related projects.

4. **Pre- and Post-Training Assessments**

Pre- and post-training assessments are essential for measuring progress. Organizations can quantify the program's impact by comparing participants' knowledge and skills before and after the training. Assessment methods include:

- **Knowledge Surveys**: Ask employees to rate their understanding of key topics, such as bias detection or regulatory compliance, before and after training.
- **Scenario-Based Evaluations**: Presenting governance-related scenarios before and after training to evaluate how participants' responses evolve.
- **Skills Assessments**: Testing technical teams on their ability to identify and mitigate risks, such as model biases or data security vulnerabilities.

FEEDBACK MECHANISMS

Feedback is vital for continuously improving training programs. Gathering input from participants provides insights into the programs' strengths and areas for improvement.

1. **Participant Surveys**

Surveys conducted immediately after training sessions can capture participants' impressions of the content, delivery, and overall effectiveness. Questions might include:

- Was the training relevant to your role?
- Did the content address real-world governance challenges?
- How engaging were the training methods (e.g., workshops, simulations)?

Surveys can also include open-ended questions, encouraging participants to share specific suggestions for improvement.

2. **Focus Groups**

Focus groups provide a deeper understanding of participants' experiences. These small, interactive sessions allow employees to discuss their perceptions of the training and provide actionable feedback. Focus groups are instrumental for:

- Understanding challenges faced during training.
- Exploring how training concepts are applied in practice.
- Identifying content gaps or areas requiring further detail.

3. **Anonymous Feedback Channels**

Anonymous feedback mechanisms encourage honesty, particularly on sensitive topics. Tools such as anonymous surveys or suggestion boxes can reveal insights participants might hesitate to share in group settings.

4. Trainer Evaluations

Trainers play a crucial role in the effectiveness of governance training. Evaluations can assess:

- Their ability to communicate complex concepts.
- How well they engage participants.
- Their responsiveness to questions and challenges.

Collecting feedback from trainers ensures that future sessions maintain high standards of delivery.

SUSTAINING TRAINING OUTCOMES

Training should not be a one-time initiative; sustaining outcomes requires regular reinforcement to ensure that governance principles remain top-of-mind.

1. Regular Updates

AI governance is an evolving field, with new ethical dilemmas, regulatory changes, and technological advancements emerging frequently. Organizations must provide regular updates to keep employees informed:

- Industry News: Share updates on regulatory developments, such as new compliance requirements or global governance standards.
- Case Studies: Highlight recent examples of successful governance practices or failures to illustrate the importance of training concepts.

2. Refresher Sessions

Periodic refresher sessions help reinforce training concepts and address knowledge gaps. These sessions can take various forms:

- Microlearning Modules: Short, focused lessons that revisit key topics like data privacy or algorithmic transparency.
- Interactive Workshops: In-depth sessions exploring recent governance challenges or emerging risks.
- Pop Quizzes: Brief quizzes on the intranet or learning platform to keep employees engaged.

3. Onboarding for New Employees

AI governance training should be a standard component of new hire onboarding. This ensures that all employees, regardless of tenure, are aligned with the organization's governance principles.

4. **Integration into Performance Reviews**

Incorporating governance-related metrics into performance evaluations reinforces the importance of training outcomes. Examples include:

- Assess technical teams' adherence to ethical AI practices.
- Evaluating leaders on how effectively they promote a culture of accountability and transparency.

5. **Recognition Programs**

Acknowledging employees who excel in applying governance principles fosters motivation and accountability. Recognition methods include:

- Awards for innovative solutions to governance challenges.
- Public acknowledgment during company events or newsletters.
- Incentives tied to governance-related achievements.

CHAPTER 15: CHANGE MANAGEMENT

15.1 INTRODUCTION TO CHANGE MANAGEMENT IN AI GOVERNANCE

WHAT IS CHANGE MANAGEMENT?

Change management refers to the structured approach and practices that transition individuals, teams, and organizations from a current state to a desired future state. In AI governance, change management plays a crucial role in implementing policies, frameworks, and ethical practices that govern AI systems within an organization. Its purpose is to ensure a smooth and effective adoption of governance principles, driving alignment between organizational goals, technological innovation, and ethical responsibilities.

Change management in AI governance involves creating strategies to prepare, support, and guide stakeholders through changes, such as implementing new governance frameworks, establishing data stewardship policies, or adhering to ethical AI standards. Addressing technical and human dimensions ensures AI governance is integrated into organizational culture and daily practices.

WHY CHANGE MANAGEMENT IS CRITICAL FOR AI GOVERNANCE

1. **Addressing Resistance to Governance Practices:** When organizations introduce AI governance practices, resistance is a typical response, especially if stakeholders perceive them as overly restrictive or disruptive. Change management helps address this resistance by fostering understanding, aligning governance with organizational values, and demonstrating the importance of accountability in AI usage. Proactive communication and engagement can transform skeptics into advocates.

2. **Ensuring Smooth Adoption Across the Organization:** Without a structured approach to change, governance initiatives risk fragmented adoption. Change management ensures seamless integration of governance practices by:

    - Identifying key stakeholders.

    - Defining clear roles and responsibilities.

    - Establishing a shared vision for ethical AI practices.

Change management minimizes friction and ensures that governance collaborates across departments through training programs, regular communication, and inclusive policymaking.

1. **Lack of Awareness:** Many stakeholders lack a clear understanding of what AI governance entails or why it is critical. This ignorance can lead to misconceptions and skepticism, making it essential to educating teams about governance principles, their benefits, and how they align with broader organizational objectives.

2. **Conflicting Priorities:** AI governance often competes with organizational priorities such as cost-cutting, rapid product development, or operational efficiency. When governance is seen as a secondary or non-critical priority, securing the resources and attention required for successful implementation can be difficult.

3. **Organizational Inertia:** Organizations often resist change due to deep-rooted behaviors, legacy systems, or an aversion to disrupting the status quo. Overcoming inertia requires leaders to build momentum through small wins, clearly articulate the risks of inaction (e.g., reputational damage or regulatory penalties), and demonstrate tangible benefits of governance efforts.

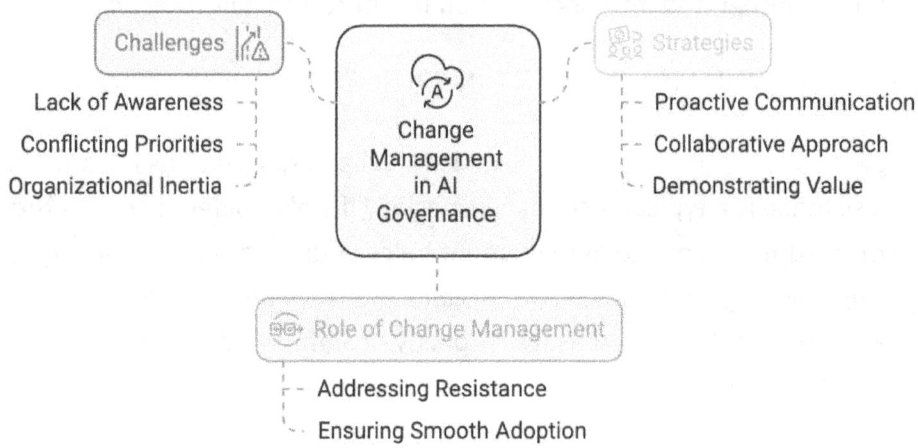

Understanding the role of change management, its criticality, and the challenges involved can help organizations lay a strong foundation for successful AI governance. This enables organizations to comply with regulatory standards and foster a culture of accountability, innovation, and trust in AI systems.

15.2 STRATEGIES FOR OVERCOMING RESISTANCE TO GOVERNANCE

IDENTIFYING SOURCES OF RESISTANCE

Resistance to governance practices in AI is a common obstacle that organizations face when attempting to implement new policies and frameworks. Understanding the root causes of resistance is the first step in overcoming it.

1. Fear of Added Bureaucracy: Many stakeholders, particularly those in fast-paced or innovative environments, may view AI governance as an unnecessary layer of bureaucracy. They fear it could slow decision-making processes, reduce agility, or stifle creativity. This resistance often stems from a misunderstanding of governance as a rigid set of constraints rather than a structured way to ensure accountability and efficiency.

2. Loss of Autonomy: Employees and teams accustomed to making decisions independently may resist governance efforts if they perceive them as limiting their autonomy. For example, data scientists or AI developers might feel that strict governance practices interfere with their ability to innovate or experiment freely.

3. Unclear Benefits: Resistance also arises when stakeholders fail to see the tangible benefits of AI governance. If the value proposition is not communicated, governance may be dismissed as a compliance-driven initiative with little relevance to day-to-day operations.

4. Conflicting Priorities: Organizational teams often have competing objectives, such as meeting tight deadlines, reducing costs, or scaling operations. In such environments, governance can be perceived as a secondary priority, leading to resistance due to time and resource constraints.

5. Organizational Inertia: Legacy systems, entrenched behaviors, and resistance to change are common in organizations with established cultures. Overcoming this inertia requires breaking down long-standing practices and encouraging openness to new frameworks, which is often met with pushback.

ENGAGING STAKEHOLDERS

To overcome resistance, organizations must actively engage stakeholders and create a shared understanding of the need for governance.

1. Proactive Communication: Clear and consistent communication is critical for addressing resistance. Organizations should explain the rationale behind AI governance, emphasizing its role in mitigating risks such as ethical violations, reputational damage, or regulatory penalties. Communication should address organizational goals and individual concerns, demonstrating how governance supports innovation rather than hinders it.

   Effective communication strategies include:

   - Tailoring the message: Customize the message for different stakeholder groups. For instance, executives may need insights into compliance and risk reduction, while technical teams may need guidance on ethical AI implementation.

   - Transparent dialogue: Foster open discussions where stakeholders can voice their concerns, ask questions, and receive honest answers.

- **Highlighting success stories:** Share examples of how governance has benefited other organizations, showcasing its value in driving sustainable innovation.

2. **Collaborative Approach:** Involving stakeholders in the design and implementation of governance practices fosters ownership and reduces resistance. Collaborative efforts should prioritize inclusivity, ensuring input from diverse teams such as developers, legal experts, business leaders, and end-users.

   Key steps in fostering collaboration:

   - **Workshops and focus groups:** Organize sessions where stakeholders can co-create governance policies, aligning them with organizational objectives and addressing specific challenges.
   - **Pilot programs:** Implement governance frameworks on a small scale, allowing teams to provide feedback and refine processes before full-scale adoption.
   - **Empowering champions:** Identify individuals within teams who are enthusiastic about governance and can act as advocates, encouraging their peers to embrace the change.

DEMONSTRATING VALUE

Resistance diminishes when stakeholders see the tangible benefits of governance. Demonstrating the value of AI governance helps shift perceptions from viewing it as a compliance requirement to recognizing it as a strategic enabler.

1. **Using Real-World Examples and Data:** Organizations can build trust in governance by sharing real-world success stories and data illustrating its positive impact. Examples could include:

   - **Reduced risks:** Showcasing how governance has helped mitigate ethical issues or legal challenges in AI applications.
   - **Improved efficiency:** Highlighting how clear governance frameworks streamline decision-making and reduce ambiguity.
   - **Enhanced innovation:** Demonstrating how responsible AI practices build trust among users and stakeholders, driving adoption and growth.

   Data-driven communication is particularly effective for technical teams. Metrics showing reduced error rates in AI models or increased user satisfaction can illustrate the direct benefits of governance.

2. **Quick Wins:** Implementing small, impactful changes early in the process can build momentum and demonstrate the feasibility of governance initiatives. Quick wins help establish credibility, gain stakeholder buy-in, and set the stage for more comprehensive changes.

Examples of quick wins include:

- Creating simple guidelines: Developing straightforward, easy-to-follow policies for AI development and deployment.
- Addressing low-hanging risks: Identifying and mitigating obvious risks in AI systems, such as biased datasets or lack of transparency in model outputs.
- Celebrating early successes: Publicly recognizing teams or individuals who successfully implement governance practices, reinforcing the value of their efforts.

15.3 BUILDING A CULTURE OF RESPONSIBLE AI

LEADERSHIP'S ROLE

Leaders play a pivotal role in building a culture of responsible AI by setting the tone for the entire organization. Their actions, decisions, and communication set examples that resonate with employees, influencing their attitudes toward governance practices.

1. Leading by Example: Leadership must demonstrate a personal commitment to responsible AI practices to inspire employees to follow suit. For instance, when executives consistently adhere to governance principles, such as ensuring transparency in AI decisions or championing ethical AI initiatives, it reinforces the importance of these values across all levels of the organization. Leaders should also actively participate in training sessions and discussions on governance, emphasizing that responsibility is a shared priority.
2. Reinforcing Governance Values: Beyond setting examples, leaders must ensure that governance values are consistently communicated and reinforced. This involves:
   - Strategic Communication: Regularly discussing the importance of responsible AI during team meetings, company-wide events, or official communications. This keeps governance at the top of employees' minds.
   - Vision Alignment: Clearly articulating how governance aligns with the organization's long-term goals, such as innovation, customer trust, or regulatory compliance. By framing governance as a strategic enabler, leaders can foster greater buy-in.
3. Fostering an Ethical Decision-Making Environment: Leaders should empower employees to raise concerns about unethical AI practices. By encouraging open dialogue, actively listening, and promptly addressing issues, leaders build trust and reinforce the organization's commitment to responsible AI.

To truly build a culture of responsible AI, governance must be seamlessly integrated into the organization's identity. It must align with its mission and values while becoming an intrinsic part of daily operations.

1. **Aligning Governance with Mission and Values:** Governance practices must reflect the core values of the organization, such as integrity, fairness, and accountability. When these values are explicitly linked to AI governance, employees are more likely to see governance not as an external imposition but as an extension of what the organization stands for. For example, a company focused on customer-centricity can highlight how responsible AI practices ensure fairness and transparency in AI-driven customer interactions.

   Organizations should also communicate this alignment externally, sharing their commitment to responsible AI with customers, partners, and regulators. This transparency reinforces trust and accountability, further embedding governance into the company's culture.

2. **Making Governance Practices Part of Daily Operations:** Governance should not be seen as a separate function but as a natural part of workflows and decision-making processes. To achieve this:

   - **Operational Integration:** Embed governance checkpoints into key stages of AI development and deployment, such as data collection, model training, and decision-making outputs.
   - **Cross-Functional Collaboration:** Encourage collaboration between technical, legal, and business teams to ensure governance is considered from multiple perspectives.
   - **Accessible Tools and Resources:** Provide teams with tools, frameworks, and guidelines that facilitate compliance with governance practices. For instance, automated tools for bias detection in AI models can streamline compliance efforts.

   Embedding governance into operations ensures that responsibility becomes a habit rather than an afterthought, fostering long-term sustainability in AI governance.

RECOGNITION AND REWARDS

Recognizing and rewarding efforts to embrace responsible AI governance is a powerful way to motivate teams and reinforce desired behaviors.

1. **Incentivizing Teams:** Incentives encourage employees to prioritize governance practices alongside their other responsibilities. These incentives can be both tangible and intangible:

   - **Tangible Rewards:** Bonuses, promotions, or awards for individuals or teams demonstrating exceptional commitment to responsible AI practices.

- Intangible Rewards: Public recognition through company newsletters, team meetings, or official events, where leaders acknowledge contributions to governance efforts.

2. Creating Governance Champions: Recognition programs can identify and elevate "governance champions" within the organization. These champions can be role models, inspiring others to adopt responsible AI practices. For instance, a data scientist who successfully implements a bias mitigation strategy in an AI model can share their approach and results with peers, fostering knowledge-sharing and enthusiasm for governance.

3. Celebrating Success Stories: Sharing success stories about how governance has positively impacted the organization can further reinforce its value. For example, celebrating a project in which adherence to governance principles prevented reputational or legal risks shows employees the tangible benefits of their efforts. These stories also help build a narrative that responsible AI is achievable and rewarding.

15.4 MONITORING AND SUSTAINING CHANGE

CONTINUOUS EVALUATION

Embedding AI governance within an organization does not end with implementation. Continuous evaluation is critical to ensure that governance practices are effectively adopted, sustained, and adapted to meet evolving needs.

1. Monitoring Adoption and Effectiveness of Governance Changes: Organizations must establish mechanisms to monitor their adoption and impact after implementing governance frameworks. This involves:

    - Tracking Metrics: Define and measure key performance indicators (KPIs) that reflect the success of governance changes. Examples include the percentage of AI projects reviewed for ethical compliance, the number of reported governance-related incidents, or employee adherence to governance guidelines.

    - Auditing Processes: Conduct regular audits to evaluate whether governance practices are being followed. This might include reviewing model development workflows, checking for adherence to bias mitigation protocols, or ensuring proper documentation of AI decision-making processes.

    - Stakeholder Engagement: Gather input from employees, customers, and other stakeholders to assess how healthy governance practices are being received and whether they meet organizational goals.

2. Using Feedback to Adjust Strategies as Needed: Governance frameworks must be flexible enough to adapt to new challenges, technological advancements, and organizational needs. Feedback plays a pivotal role in ensuring these frameworks remain relevant and practical:

- **Employee Feedback:** Create channels for employees to share their experiences with governance practices. Anonymous surveys, focus groups, or direct interviews can help identify pain points or areas for improvement.
- **Customer Insights:** For organizations using AI in customer-facing applications, customer feedback can highlight potential governance gaps, such as perceived unfairness in AI decisions or lack of transparency.
- **Iterative Improvements:** Use the collected feedback to refine governance strategies. This iterative approach ensures continuous improvement, addressing weaknesses and building on successes.

Organizations can identify and resolve issues early by continuously monitoring and evaluating governance practices, ensuring their frameworks evolve alongside their business and technological landscape.

MAINTAINING MOMENTUM

Sustaining change requires ongoing efforts to keep governance principles relevant and ingrained within the organizational culture. Initial progress can fade without consistent reinforcement, and governance practices may lose effectiveness.

1. **Regular Training and Awareness Programs:** Training and education are crucial to maintaining a culture of responsible AI governance. Regular programs ensure that employees stay informed about governance principles and understand their importance:
    - **Tailored Training:** Design training programs specific to different roles. For instance, AI developers may need technical training on bias detection, while legal teams may need education on compliance requirements.
    - **Interactive Learning:** Use workshops, simulations, and case studies to make training engaging and practical. This helps employees understand how to apply governance principles in real-world scenarios.
    - **Ongoing Refreshers:** Conduct periodic refresher sessions to reinforce governance knowledge, especially as new technologies, regulations, or organizational priorities emerge.

Training programs build competence and reinforce the message that governance is a priority, ensuring it remains a focus across the organization.

2. **Leadership Updates to Ensure Sustained Focus on AI Governance:** Leaders play a critical role in sustaining momentum by keeping governance at the forefront of organizational priorities:

- Regular Updates: Leadership teams should provide periodic updates on the progress and impact of governance initiatives. Sharing data-driven insights—such as risk reduction efficiency or positive customer feedback—demons—demonstrates governance and motivates continued adherence.
- Celebrating Success: Recognizing and celebrating milestones, such as successfully deploying a responsible AI system, reinforces the importance of governance and encourages employees to stay engaged.
- Strategic Alignment: Leaders must ensure that governance remains aligned with the organization's long-term goals. Integrating governance discussions into broader strategic planning sessions signals its importance as a core element of the organization's future.

CHAPTER 16: MEASURING SUCCESS AND CONTINUOUS IMPROVEMENT

16.1 INTRODUCTION TO MEASURING AI GOVERNANCE SUCCESS

The introduction to measuring AI governance success emphasizes the critical need for organizations to evaluate their governance frameworks, ensuring alignment with organizational goals, regulatory requirements, and emerging technological advancements. This section establishes a foundation for understanding why evaluation and continuous improvement are essential to effective AI governance.

IMPORTANCE OF EVALUATION

As organizations increasingly rely on AI systems, the need for robust governance frameworks has become paramount. These frameworks ensure that AI operates within ethical boundaries, complies with regulations, and aligns with organizational objectives. However, governance frameworks are not static; their effectiveness must be regularly assessed to confirm they address evolving internal and external demands.

1. **Regulatory Compliance:**
   Governments and regulatory bodies worldwide are implementing strict guidelines for AI usage, emphasizing fairness, transparency, and accountability. Evaluation helps organizations ensure compliance with these standards, reducing the risk of legal penalties and reputational damage. For example, frameworks like the EU's AI Act or the U.S. NIST AI Risk Management Framework set clear expectations, making periodic assessments necessary to verify adherence.

2. **Organizational Alignment:**
   AI governance is not just about avoiding risks; it must also drive value. Assessments enable organizations to determine whether their AI governance aligns with strategic goals, such as enhancing operational efficiency, improving customer experience, or driving innovation. For instance, a retail company deploying AI for customer segmentation must evaluate whether the AI's decisions are ethical, unbiased, and effective in achieving targeted business outcomes.

3. **Risk Mitigation:**
   Governance evaluations provide insights into vulnerabilities within AI systems, such as algorithm biases or data security gaps. Identifying these risks early allows organizations to take proactive measures, preventing potential crises.

AI technologies evolve rapidly, often outpacing the frameworks designed to govern them. Continuous improvement ensures that governance remains effective amid these changes. This process is not just about updating frameworks but fostering a culture of adaptability within organizations.

1. Adapting to Technological Advancements:
   With breakthroughs like generative AI, reinforcement learning, and natural language processing, governance frameworks must evolve to address new capabilities and risks. Continuous improvement enables organizations to stay ahead of technological trends, ensuring their frameworks are future-proof.

2. Addressing Emerging Challenges:
   AI systems often face unforeseen ethical dilemmas, such as bias amplification or misuse in decision-making. Regular evaluations help organizations anticipate and address these challenges before they escalate. For example, a financial institution using AI for loan approvals might periodically review its algorithms to ensure they do not inadvertently discriminate against specific demographics.

3. Fostering Stakeholder Trust:
   Continuous improvement reinforces transparency and accountability, essential for maintaining trust among stakeholders, including employees, customers, investors, and regulatory bodies. Regular updates and evaluations demonstrate an organization's commitment to ethical AI practices, enhancing its reputation and stakeholder confidence.

4. Feedback Integration:
   Continuous improvement relies on gathering insights from diverse stakeholders. Feedback mechanisms, such as employee surveys, user feedback, and compliance audits, provide valuable data to refine governance frameworks. For instance, incorporating feedback from end-users of an AI-powered service can uncover usability issues and areas for ethical enhancement.

In conclusion, measuring AI governance success is not a one-time activity but an ongoing journey. By prioritizing evaluation and continuous improvement, organizations can ensure their AI systems remain ethical, compliant, and aligned with their strategic goals. This approach mitigates risks and positions organizations to leverage AI as a transformative force for innovation and growth.

16.2 DEFINING KEY PERFORMANCE INDICATORS (KPIS) FOR AI GOVERNANCE

Key Performance Indicators (KPIs) serve as measurable benchmarks that help organizations assess the effectiveness of their AI governance frameworks. By identifying, categorizing, and continuously monitoring these metrics, organizations can ensure their AI systems operate ethically, efficiently, and in alignment with regulatory requirements. This section delves into selecting relevant KPIs, categorizing them into actionable domains, and establishing baselines to measure progress over time.

SELECTING RELEVANT KPIS

The first step in defining KPIs for AI governance involves aligning them with organizational objectives and regulatory mandates. Effective KPIs should monitor the performance of AI systems and reflect the organization's broader goals, such as enhancing trust, ensuring compliance, and achieving operational efficiency. Here are key considerations:

1. **Alignment with Organizational Objectives:**
   Relevant KPIs should reflect the organization's mission and strategic goals. For example, a healthcare provider implementing AI for patient diagnostics may prioritize accuracy, ethical compliance, and patient satisfaction metrics.

2. **Regulatory Compliance:**
   KPIs must track compliance with applicable laws, regulations, and ethical standards. For instance, the evaluation should include compliance rates with the General Data Protection Regulation (GDPR) or sector-specific guidelines.

3. **Incident Response Times:**
   Measuring the speed at which governance frameworks identify and address incidents, such as algorithmic bias or data breaches, is crucial for minimizing risk and maintaining stakeholder trust.

4. **Stakeholder Satisfaction:**
   Gauging satisfaction among employees, customers, and regulators provides insights into AI systems' perceived fairness, usability, and transparency. Surveys, interviews, and other feedback mechanisms can help capture these metrics.

5. **Scalability and Adaptability:**
   Effective KPIs should also evaluate how well governance frameworks adapt to new challenges, such as evolving technologies or shifting regulatory landscapes.

CATEGORIES OF KPIS

To create a structured approach, KPIs for AI governance can be categorized into three main domains: operational, compliance, and ethical metrics. Each category addresses a distinct aspect of AI governance.

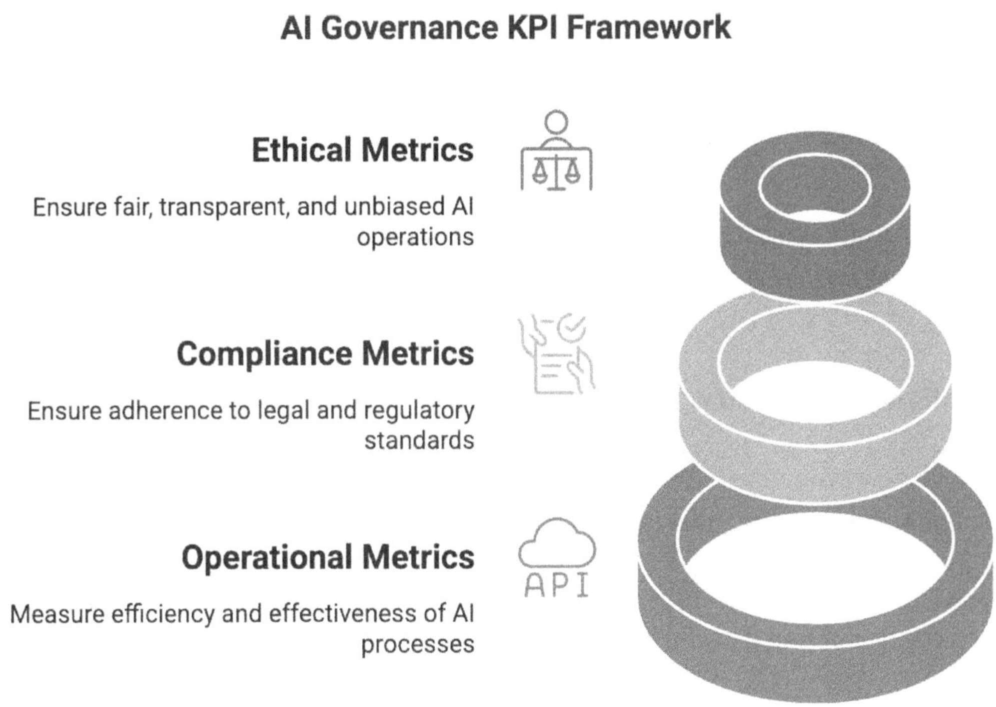

1. **Operational Metrics:**
   These KPIs measure the efficiency and effectiveness of AI processes and systems. They ensure that AI delivers on its intended purpose while maintaining high performance. Examples include:
   - **Accuracy and Precision:** Evaluating the predictive capabilities of AI models.
   - **System Uptime and Availability:** Measuring the reliability of AI systems to ensure uninterrupted operations.
   - **Resource Utilization:** Tracking the computational efficiency of AI, such as memory or energy consumption.
   - **Processing Times:** Monitoring how quickly AI systems can analyze data and generate insights.
2. **Compliance Metrics:**
   Compliance metrics ensure that AI systems adhere to legal, regulatory, and organizational policies. These KPIs are critical for mitigating legal risks and maintaining ethical standards. Examples include:
   - **Regulatory Compliance Rates:** Tracking adherence to GDPR, HIPAA, or AI-specific legislation standards.

- **Audit Completion and Accuracy:** Measuring the thoroughness and timeliness of governance audits.
- **Incident Reporting Rates:** Monitoring the frequency and resolution of non-compliance issues.

3. **Ethical Metrics:**
Ethical KPIs ensure AI systems operate fairly, transparently, and without bias. These metrics help build trust and credibility among stakeholders. Examples include:

   - **Fairness in Outcomes:** Evaluating whether AI systems produce unbiased results across different demographics.
   - **Transparency Levels:** Measuring how AI decision-making processes are explainable and understandable to stakeholders.
   - **Accountability Metrics:** Ensuring that clear lines of responsibility are established for AI-related decisions.
   - **User Satisfaction with Ethical Practices:** Capturing stakeholder feedback on perceived fairness and trustworthiness.

ESTABLISHING BASELINES

Before tracking progress, organizations must establish baselines for their chosen KPIs. Baselines provide reference points to measure the effectiveness of governance practices over time. The process involves several key steps:

1. **Data Collection:**
Collect historical data from existing systems, processes, and governance practices. Organizations can establish benchmarks using system logs, compliance reports, and stakeholder surveys.

2. **Setting Initial Benchmarks:**
Once data is collected, initial benchmarks can be defined for each KPI. For instance, if the average incident response time is 48 hours, this figure becomes the baseline against which improvements will be measured.

3. **Stakeholder Input:**
Engaging stakeholders in the baseline-setting process ensures that metrics are realistic and relevant. For example, employees involved in AI development can provide insights into practical benchmarks for fairness or transparency.

4. **Periodic Reassessment:**
Baselines should not remain static. Organizations must periodically reassess and update their

benchmarks as technologies and governance practices evolve. For instance, a baseline for algorithmic fairness may need adjustment as new datasets and evaluation methods emerge.

5. Comparative Analysis:
   Comparing benchmarks against industry standards and peer organizations can provide additional context. For example, an organization's compliance rate baseline might be evaluated against sector averages to identify gaps or areas for improvement.

IMPLEMENTING KPI FRAMEWORKS

To ensure the successful implementation of KPIs, organizations should:

1. Develop Clear Documentation:
   Documenting each KPI's rationale, methodology, and expected outcomes ensures consistency and clarity.

2. Leverage Technology:
   Employing advanced tools like dashboards, analytics platforms, and AI-powered monitoring solutions can streamline data collection and analysis.

3. Engage Stakeholders:
   Regularly communicating KPI results to stakeholders fosters transparency and collaboration. For example, periodic governance performance reports can highlight progress and areas for improvement.

4. Focus on Continuous Improvement:
   KPIs should measure performance and inform strategies for improvement. If fairness metrics reveal systemic bias, targeted interventions can be implemented, such as retraining models or revising data collection processes.

In conclusion, defining KPIs for AI governance is a multi-faceted process that requires careful alignment with organizational objectives, categorization into actionable domains, and establishing meaningful baselines. By adopting a structured approach, organizations can ensure their AI systems operate responsibly, effectively, and in alignment with evolving expectations.

16.3 DATA COLLECTION AND ANALYSIS FOR GOVERNANCE METRICS

Data collection and analysis are foundational to the success of AI governance. Organizations can ensure that their AI systems align with ethical, operational, and regulatory standards by gathering relevant data, employing analytical tools, and effectively interpreting the results. This section explores the key aspects of data collection and analysis, focusing on data sources, analytical tools, and the interpretation of results.

DATA SOURCES

The quality and relevance of data are critical for effective governance metrics. Organizations must identify and leverage diverse data sources to comprehensively assess AI systems. Key data sources include:

1. **System Logs:**
   System logs capture real-time information about AI systems' behavior and performance. They provide insights into processing times, errors, and decision-making processes, enabling organizations to monitor operational efficiency and detect anomalies. For example, logs from a recommendation engine can reveal patterns in its output and identify potential bias.

2. **Audit Trails:**
   Audit trails document the actions taken by AI systems, including data access, decision rationales, and changes to algorithms or models. These records ensure accountability and traceability, particularly in regulated industries like finance and healthcare. A well-maintained audit trail allows organizations to respond effectively to compliance audits.

3. **User Feedback:**
   Feedback from end-users provides valuable qualitative insights into the performance and impact of AI systems. Surveys, focus groups, and direct user interactions can help organizations understand the system's usability, fairness, and effectiveness. For example, users of an AI-powered chatbot may highlight areas where the system's responses are inadequate or unintuitive.

4. **Compliance Reports:**
   Regular compliance assessments generate reports that highlight adherence to regulatory and ethical standards. These reports often include key metrics such as data privacy violations, bias detection, and adherence to internal policies. Organizations can identify trends and gaps in governance practices by analyzing compliance reports.

5. **External Benchmarks:**
   Comparative data from industry benchmarks and peer organizations can provide context for evaluating governance metrics. For instance, comparing an AI system's fairness metrics against industry averages can help identify areas for improvement.

ANALYTICAL TOOLS

The vast amount of data generated by AI systems necessitates using sophisticated analytical tools to extract actionable insights. These tools enable organizations to effectively process, visualize, and interpret governance metrics. Key types of analytical tools include:

1. **Data Aggregation Tools:**
   These tools collect and consolidate data from multiple sources, providing a unified view of

governance metrics. For example, a centralized dashboard can aggregate data from system logs, audit trails, and user feedback for streamlined analysis.

2. **Visualization Software:**
   Tools like Tableau, Power BI, and Python's Matplotlib enable organizations to create visual representations of data trends. Visualizations such as heatmaps, bar graphs, and line charts make identifying patterns and outliers in governance metrics easier. For instance, a line chart showing monthly compliance rates can highlight periods of underperformance.

3. **AI and Machine Learning Models:**
   Advanced analytical techniques, including machine learning, can identify complex patterns in large datasets. For example, anomaly detection algorithms can flag unusual behaviors in AI systems, such as a sudden spike in error rates.

4. **Natural Language Processing (NLP) Tools:**
   NLP tools analyze textual data, such as user feedback or audit reports, to identify recurring themes and sentiments. Sentiment analysis, for instance, can reveal user perceptions of fairness in an AI-powered service.

5. **Predictive Analytics Tools:**
   Predictive models forecast potential governance challenges based on historical data. For example, they might identify the likelihood of a compliance violation based on past incidents.

6. **Compliance Monitoring Platforms:**
   Specialized platforms like TrustArc and OneTrust provide automated compliance monitoring and reporting capabilities, enabling organizations to stay updated on regulatory adherence.

INTERPRETING RESULTS

Once data has been collected and analyzed, the next step is interpreting the results. This involves understanding the implications of data trends and using these insights to improve governance frameworks. Key considerations for interpreting results include:

1. **Identifying Trends:**
   Analyzing historical data helps organizations identify long-term trends in governance metrics. For example, a steady improvement in fairness metrics might indicate the effectiveness of recent interventions, while recurring drops in compliance rates could signal systemic issues.

2. **Detecting Anomalies:**
   Outliers in governance metrics often point to underlying problems. For instance, a sudden spike in user complaints about bias could indicate flaws in a recent algorithm update. Identifying these anomalies enables organizations to take corrective action promptly.

3. **Assessing Root Causes:**
   Practical interpretation requires delving into the root causes of observed trends or anomalies.

For example, if incident response times are increasing, analyzing system logs and resource allocation might reveal bottlenecks in the escalation process.

4. **Evaluating Governance Effectiveness:**
   Organizations can evaluate the effectiveness of their frameworks by comparing governance metrics against predefined baselines or industry benchmarks. For instance, if an organization's compliance rate consistently exceeds industry averages, it may be a best practice for others.

5. **Prioritizing Improvements:**
   Interpreting results should guide the prioritization of governance enhancements. For example, if ethical metrics reveal significant biases in a specific model, addressing these biases should become a top priority.

6. **Communicating Insights:**
   Clear communication of findings to stakeholders ensures that insights drive actionable decisions. For example, presenting governance metrics through visual dashboards or executive summaries can help stakeholders understand the current state of AI governance and areas requiring attention.

7. **Incorporating Feedback:**
   Data analysis insights should inform updates to governance frameworks. For instance, if user feedback highlights concerns about transparency, organizations might introduce explainability features to improve users' understanding of AI decisions.

16.4 REPORTING AND COMMUNICATING GOVERNANCE PERFORMANCE

Effective reporting and communication are pivotal for the success of AI governance. Transparent, tailored, and comprehensive communication of governance performance ensures that all stakeholders understand the effectiveness of AI systems, the challenges encountered, and the steps taken to overcome them. This section examines developing detailed reports, communicating effectively with diverse stakeholders, and establishing transparency practices to build trust and accountability.

DEVELOPING REPORTS

Reports are the primary medium for documenting and conveying governance performance. They must be comprehensive yet accessible and clearly overview metrics, challenges, and achievements.

1. **Structuring Reports:** A well-structured report should include the following sections:

   - **Executive Summary:** Summarizes key findings, including performance highlights, critical challenges, and recommended actions.
   - **Introduction:** This section provides context, including the report's purpose, the scope of governance activities, and its relevance to organizational objectives.

- Performance Metrics: Details KPIs across operational, compliance, and ethical categories, along with comparative analyses against baselines or benchmarks.
- Challenges and Risks: Identifies issues encountered, such as algorithmic bias, compliance breaches, or stakeholder dissatisfaction.
- Remedial Actions: Outlines corrective measures implemented to address identified challenges.
- Future Recommendations: Suggest strategies for enhancing governance frameworks and addressing emerging risks.

2. Incorporating Data Visualizations: Visual representations such as charts, graphs, and heat maps make complex data more understandable. For example:
   - A bar graph illustrating compliance rates over time can highlight trends.
   - A heatmap showing areas of high-risk incidents can focus attention on priority areas.
   - Pie charts summarizing stakeholder feedback can provide a snapshot of satisfaction levels.
3. Highlighting Achievements: Reports should celebrate successes, such as achieving compliance milestones or improving fairness metrics. Highlighting these accomplishments reinforces the organization's commitment to responsible AI practices.
4. Documenting Challenges: Transparency about challenges—such as audit delays or difficulties addressing bias—adds credibility. Acknowledging shortcomings demonstrates a willingness to improve, and fosters trust.
5. Ensuring Clarity and Accessibility: Use plain language to make reports understandable to non-technical audiences. For instance, instead of using jargon like "model drift," explain it as "changes in AI model performance over time."

STAKEHOLDER COMMUNICATION

Different stakeholders have varying levels of interest, expertise, and influence over AI governance. Tailoring communication to meet these diverse needs ensures effective dissemination of governance performance.

1. Executives and Decision-Makers:
   - Focus Areas: High-level metrics, strategic implications, and ROI.
   - Approach: Provide concise executive summaries with actionable insights. For example, highlight how governance practices have mitigated risks or enabled compliance with new regulations.

- **Mediums:** Board presentations, executive dashboards, and strategic memos.

2. **Regulatory Bodies:**
   - **Focus Areas:** Detailed compliance metrics, audit results, and remediation efforts.
   - **Approach:** Submit formal reports structured to meet regulatory standards. Include supporting documentation, such as audit trails or incident logs.
   - **Mediums:** Compliance submissions, formal audits, and regulatory consultations.

3. **Employees and Internal Teams:**
   - **Focus Areas:** Operational metrics, ethical practices, and transparency.
   - **Approach:** Conduct workshops, internal presentations, or email briefings to inform employees about governance performance and highlight how their roles contribute to achieving governance goals.
   - **Mediums:** Team meetings, intranet updates, and training sessions.

4. **Customers and End-Users:**
   - **Focus Areas:** Transparency, ethical practices, and user impact.
   - **Approach:** Share performance highlights through user-friendly mediums like newsletters, FAQs, or dedicated sections on the company's website.
   - **Mediums:** Public reports, press releases, and social media updates.

5. **Investors and Partners:**
   - **Focus Areas:** Long-term impact, risk mitigation, and competitive advantage.
   - **Approach:** Provide tailored reports showcasing how governance practices align with ESG (Environmental, Social, and Governance) criteria and business sustainability goals.
   - **Mediums:** Investor briefings, annual reports, and partner updates.

TRANSPARENCY PRACTICES

Transparency in AI governance fosters trust, accountability, and collaboration. By openly sharing governance performance, organizations can build credibility with stakeholders and demonstrate their commitment to ethical AI practices.

1. **Publishing Performance Reports:** Regularly publish governance performance reports on public platforms like the company's website or annual ESG reports. Ensure these reports are accessible and include summaries of key findings, progress against benchmarks, and plans.

2. **Engaging in Open Dialogue:** Encourage stakeholder participation by creating forums for feedback and discussion. For instance:
    - Host webinars or Q&A sessions to address stakeholder concerns.
    - Solicit input on governance practices through surveys or advisory panels.
3. **Disclosing Ethical Challenges:** Transparency requires acknowledging ethical dilemmas and outlining steps to address them. For example, if an AI system exhibits bias, report the issue, explain the root cause, and describe corrective actions taken.
4. **Building Explainability into Communication:** Explainability tools can help stakeholders understand how AI systems make decisions. For instance, share case studies or visualizations illustrating how fairness metrics are calculated or how compliance audits are conducted.
5. **Adopting Open Standards:** Collaborate with industry groups to establish and adopt open standards for reporting governance performance. This fosters consistency and comparability across organizations.
6. **Continuous Improvement in Reporting:** Regularly update reporting practices based on stakeholder feedback and evolving standards. For example, if stakeholders find specific metrics unclear, refine how they are presented in future reports.

16.5 IMPLEMENTING CONTINUOUS IMPROVEMENT STRATEGIES

Continuous improvement is essential for maintaining and enhancing the effectiveness of AI governance frameworks. Given the dynamic nature of AI technologies and evolving regulatory landscapes, organizations must proactively refine their governance practices. This section explores the key strategies for implementing continuous improvement, focusing on feedback mechanisms, regular audits and reviews, and adaptive governance.

FEEDBACK MECHANISMS

Feedback is a critical driver of continuous improvement. Establishing robust channels for gathering input from internal and external stakeholders enables organizations to identify gaps, address concerns, and refine their governance frameworks.

1. **Internal Feedback Channels:** Internal stakeholders, including employees, AI developers, and compliance teams, play a vital role in shaping governance practices. Key strategies include:
    - **Employee Surveys:** Conduct regular surveys to gauge employees' perceptions of AI governance effectiveness and identify areas for improvement.
    - **Workshops and Focus Groups:** Hosting interactive sessions to gather insights from teams directly involved in AI development and deployment.

- **Incident Reporting Systems:** Implementing anonymous reporting tools to encourage employees to highlight governance issues, such as potential biases or ethical concerns.

2. **External Feedback Channels:** Input from external stakeholders, including customers, partners, and regulators, provides a broader perspective on governance practices. Effective methods include:

    - **Customer Feedback:** Soliciting input through surveys, focus groups, and online reviews to understand user experiences and ethical concerns.
    - **Regulatory Consultations:** Engaging with regulatory bodies to gain insights into compliance expectations and evolving standards.
    - **Advisory Panels:** Establish panels comprising external experts, academics, and industry leaders to guide governance practices.

3. **Feedback Integration:** Organizations must establish processes to act on feedback promptly and effectively. For example:

    - Develop a centralized system to track and analyze feedback from various channels.
    - Prioritize feedback based on its impact and urgency.
    - Communicate actions taken in response to feedback, fostering trust and transparency.

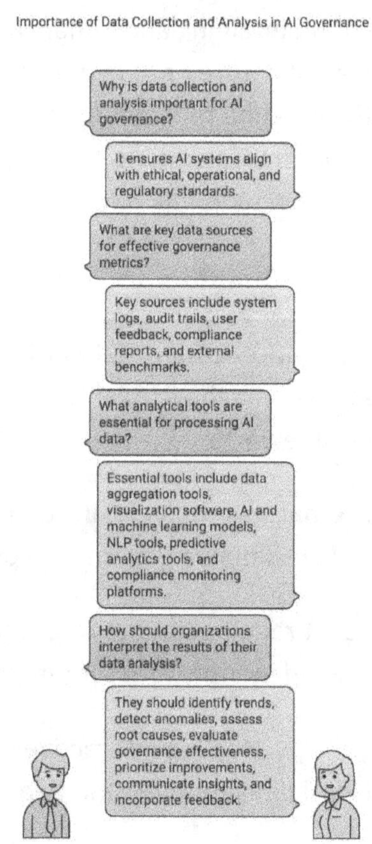

Periodic audits and reviews are indispensable for assessing the effectiveness of governance frameworks and identifying opportunities for improvement. These evaluations provide a structured approach to ensure compliance, address risks, and maintain accountability.

1. **Planning Audits:**
   - Define clear objectives and scope for each audit, such as evaluating compliance rates, detecting biases, or assessing ethical practices.
   - Establish a timeline for regular audits, ensuring they occur frequently enough to capture meaningful insights without overburdening resources.
2. **Conducting Audits:**
   - AI systems are evaluated using automated tools and manual assessments. For instance, bias detection algorithms can complement ethics committees' manual reviews.
   - Collaborate with cross-functional teams, including legal, technical, and operational departments, to ensure comprehensive evaluations.
   - Document findings thoroughly, highlighting both strengths and areas requiring improvement.
3. **Reviewing Governance Frameworks:**
   - Regularly review policies, procedures, and KPIs to ensure alignment with organizational goals and regulatory requirements.
   - Incorporate insights from audits to update governance frameworks, such as revising data handling policies or enhancing transparency mechanisms.
4. **Independent Audits:**
   - Engage third-party auditors to conduct unbiased evaluations. Independent audits add credibility and provide fresh perspectives on governance practices.
5. **Post-Audit Actions:**
   - Develop action plans to address audit findings, specifying timelines, responsibilities, and expected outcomes.
   - Monitor progress on corrective actions and reassess their effectiveness in subsequent audits.

The rapidly changing AI landscape necessitates adaptive governance—a flexible approach to modifying policies and procedures in response to emerging challenges, technological advancements, and regulatory changes.

1. **Monitoring Technological Advancements:**
    - Stay informed about developments in AI technologies, such as generative models, reinforcement learning, or explainable AI.
    - Evaluate how these advancements impact existing governance frameworks and identify necessary adaptations.
    - For example, the rise of generative AI may require enhanced content moderation policies to prevent misuse.
2. **Responding to Regulatory Changes:**
    - Monitor updates to AI-related regulations, such as the EU's AI Act or national data protection laws.
    - Engage with industry groups and regulatory bodies to understand upcoming changes and their implications.
    - Update governance frameworks proactively to ensure compliance with new requirements.
3. **Addressing Emerging Risks:**
    - Identify and mitigate new risks associated with AI systems, such as adversarial attacks, data poisoning, or evolving biases.
    - Use scenario planning and risk assessments to anticipate potential challenges and develop contingency plans.
4. **Incorporating Best Practices:**
    - Learn from industry leaders and organizations recognized for effective AI governance.
    - Adapt and implement proven best practices, such as using open-source tools for bias detection or adopting standardized transparency protocols.

5. **Fostering Organizational Agility:**
    - Cultivate a culture of adaptability, encouraging employees to embrace change and innovate in response to governance challenges.
    - Provide training programs to update teams on the latest AI trends, ethical considerations, and compliance requirements.
6. **Building Iterative Feedback Loops:**
    - Establish mechanisms to continuously gather and analyze data on governance performance, integrating findings into regular updates of policies and procedures.
    - For instance, feedback from audits and user input can be used to refine explainability standards or improve incident response times.

16.6 CASE STUDIES: SUCCESSFUL CONTINUOUS IMPROVEMENT IN AI GOVERNANCE

Real-world examples of successful continuous improvement in AI governance illustrate how organizations can enhance their practices and set benchmarks for responsible AI development. These case studies highlight the strategies employed, challenges overcome, and the impact of adaptive governance practices.

INDUSTRY EXAMPLES

1. **Google's AI Fairness Program:** Google has pioneered addressing bias and fairness in AI systems. Through its "Responsible AI" initiative, the company developed tools like the "What-If Tool" to help engineers visualize and mitigate biases in machine learning models. Regular audits and reviews of these tools have allowed Google to adapt its practices and ensure alignment with fairness goals.
    - **Outcome:** Improved transparency in decision-making processes and increased stakeholder trust.
    - **Key Practices:** Regular bias audits, robust fairness tools, and open dialogue with external experts.
2. **Microsoft's AI Governance Framework:** Microsoft's "AI for Good" program exemplifies adaptive governance. The company established an internal ethics committee, Aether (AI and Ethics in Engineering and Research), to provide continuous feedback on AI development. Through regular audits and stakeholder engagement, Microsoft has integrated ethical considerations into its AI projects, such as accessibility features in its products.

- Outcome: Enhanced ethical standards across AI solutions and compliance with emerging regulations.
- Key Practices: Cross-functional ethics committees, feedback loops, and external collaborations.

3. **IBM's AI OpenScale Platform:** IBM's AI OpenScale platform offers real-time tools for monitoring AI models. It tracks bias, drift, and accuracy, enabling organizations to maintain transparency and accountability. IBM's use of this platform internally has demonstrated how continuous monitoring and iterative feedback improve governance.
    - Outcome: Enhanced model reliability and stakeholder confidence.
    - Key Practices: Real-time monitoring, transparency dashboards, and iterative refinements.

LESSONS LEARNED

1. Prioritize Stakeholder Engagement: Successful organizations emphasize the importance of involving diverse stakeholders in governance processes. Whether through user feedback or advisory panels, continuous dialogue fosters trust and innovation.
2. Adopt Agile Governance: Effective governance frameworks are flexible and responsive to change. For instance, incorporating regular audits and adapting policies in response to emerging risks ensures long-term success.
3. Leverage Technology for Transparency: Tools for real-time monitoring and bias detection, as seen in IBM's AI OpenScale, underscore the role of technology in supporting continuous improvement.
4. Commit to Ethical Accountability: Internal committees like Microsoft's Aether demonstrate the value of dedicated resources to uphold ethical standards and integrate them into operational workflows.

PART V

MEASURING & SCALING GOVERNANCE

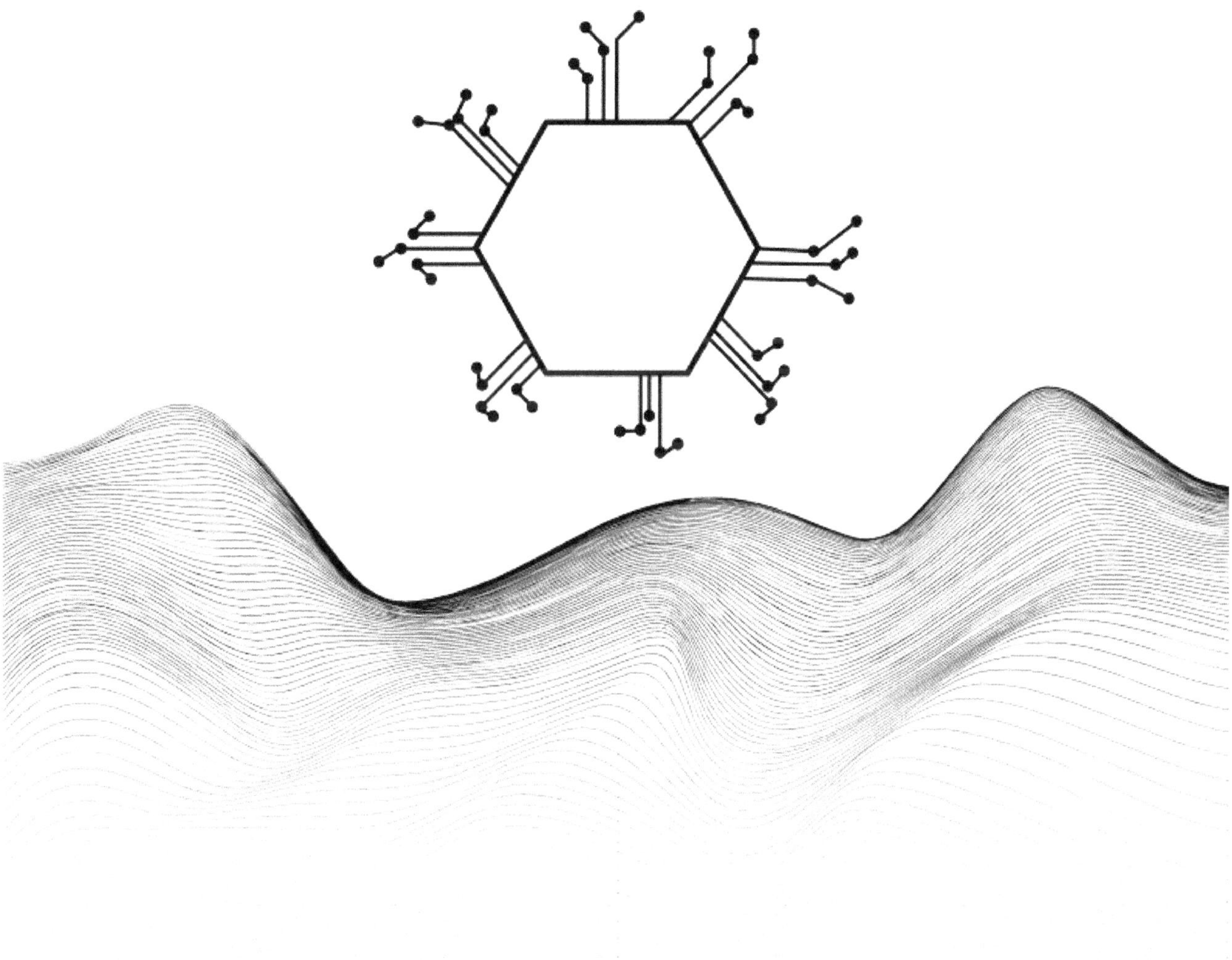

CHAPTER 17: FUTURE TRENDS IN AI GOVERNANCE

17.1 INTRODUCTION TO EMERGING TRENDS

THE EVOLVING LANDSCAPE

The rapid evolution of artificial intelligence (AI) technologies is redefining industries, economies, and governance frameworks at an unprecedented pace. Innovations such as generative AI, autonomous systems, and AI-driven decision-making models are becoming integral to the healthcare and finance sectors. These advancements bring about opportunities for enhanced efficiency, innovation, and problem-solving. However, they also introduce complex challenges that governance systems must address to maintain public trust, promote equity, and ensure responsible use.

One of the most significant trends in this evolving landscape is the emergence of AI models with self-learning capabilities, enabling them to adapt to real-time data and refine their performance over time. This dynamic nature makes them highly valuable and unpredictable, creating risks that current governance practices may be ill-equipped to handle. Furthermore, integrating AI into decision-making processes raises questions about transparency, accountability, and ethical oversight. Without adequate governance mechanisms, the transformative potential of AI could lead to unintended consequences, such as reinforcing biases, breaching privacy, or undermining societal norms.

AI technologies are also becoming more accessible to organizations of all sizes, democratizing their use but amplifying the risks of misuse. While revolutionary for creative applications, generative AI models can be weaponized for disinformation campaigns or intellectual property theft. The dual nature of these tools—both beneficial and potentially harmful—underscores the urgency of adaptive and forward-thinking governance approaches.

IMPORTANCE OF PROACTIVE GOVERNANCE

In this era of rapid technological advancement, reactive governance strategies are no longer sufficient. Proactive governance anticipates challenges before they escalate, ensuring that policies, frameworks, and practices evolve with technological progress. It involves cultivating a deep understanding of emerging technologies, identifying potential risks, and designing strategies to mitigate them effectively.

Proactive governance requires a multi-stakeholder approach, where regulators, industry leaders, technologists, and civil society collaborate to responsibly shape the future of AI. This collaboration is critical as AI systems grow more complex and interconnected, with decisions made in one sector often having cascading effects on others. For instance, AI-driven healthcare solutions must align with regulatory standards for safety and patient data privacy while ensuring accessibility and fairness.

Another critical aspect of proactive governance is its emphasis on building adaptive frameworks. Unlike static policies, these frameworks are designed to evolve in response to new information, technological advancements, and societal expectations. They prioritize flexibility, enabling organizations to navigate uncertainties without compromising ethical standards or innovation potential.

Lastly, proactive governance fosters trust among stakeholders. Organizations committed to transparency, fairness, and accountability can strengthen their relationships with users, regulators, and partners. Trust is a crucial currency in the AI-driven future, and governance proactively addressing emerging trends can help sustain it.

In conclusion, the evolving AI landscape presents both opportunities and challenges for governance. To harness the full potential of these technologies while mitigating risks, organizations must adopt forward-thinking, adaptive, inclusive, and transparent governance strategies. This chapter will explore how these strategies can be implemented and offer insights into the technological, regulatory, and ethical considerations shaping the future of AI governance.

17.2 ADVANCES IN AI TECHNOLOGIES AND THEIR GOVERNANCE IMPLICATIONS

Advances in artificial intelligence (AI) technologies are reshaping industries and raising complex ethical and governance challenges. Generative AI, autonomous systems, and AI-driven decision-making have emerged as transformative yet contentious domains. Each area brings unique opportunities and risks, requiring adaptive, inclusive, and forward-thinking governance frameworks.

GENERATIVE AI

THE RISE OF GENERATIVE MODELS

Generative AI, exemplified by systems like OpenAI's GPT-4 and DALL·E, has revolutionized content creation. These models generate text, images, audio, and even video, producing outputs that impressively mimic human creativity. Trained on vast datasets, generative AI enables marketing, education, and entertainment innovations. However, the rapid growth of these technologies has amplified concerns about misuse and ethical implications.

ETHICAL CONCERNS

1. Content Authenticity:
    - Generative AI can produce highly realistic outputs, making it increasingly difficult to differentiate between actual and AI-generated content.
    - This capability has led to deepfakes—manipulated videos or audio that can mislead viewers, spread misinformation, or tarnish reputations.

- For instance, fake political speeches or fraudulent financial advice created by generative models could have widespread societal and economic impacts.

2. **Intellectual Property (IP) Rights**:

    - Generative AI systems often train on copyrighted materials without explicit permission, leading to disputes about the ownership of AI-generated content.

    - Artists, writers, and content creators argue that their work is being used without compensation or acknowledgment, as seen in recent lawsuits against AI developers.

    - This challenge raises questions about the boundaries of fair use and the need for licensing models that balance innovation with IP protection.

GOVERNANCE IMPLICATIONS

Governance strategies for generative AI must address these ethical concerns while fostering innovation:

- **Data Transparency**:

    - Developers should disclose the sources of their training data and establish agreements to use copyrighted material responsibly.

    - Transparency fosters trust and helps mitigate disputes over IP violations.

- **Content Verification Tools**:

    - Technologies like watermarking AI-generated content and creating detection mechanisms for deepfakes can help ensure authenticity and combat misinformation.

- **Regulatory Guidelines**:

    - Policymakers must establish clear rules governing the use of generative AI, including guidelines for ethical data usage, content ownership, and accountability for misuse.

AUTONOMOUS SYSTEMS

DEPLOYMENT IN CRITICAL SECTORS

Autonomous systems, defined by their ability to operate with minimal human intervention, are gaining traction in healthcare, transportation, and logistics. Examples include surgical robots that enhance precision and self-driving vehicles that promise safer roads by reducing human error. While the potential benefits of these systems are immense, their integration into critical infrastructure introduces significant governance challenges.

GOVERNANCE CHALLENGES

1. **Safety and Reliability**:
    - Ensuring that autonomous systems perform reliably under diverse conditions is a top priority.
    - In healthcare, an error by an autonomous surgical robot could endanger lives, while malfunctions in self-driving vehicles pose risks to passengers and pedestrians.
2. **Accountability and Liability**:
    - Determining responsibility for failures or accidents involving autonomous systems is complex.
    - For instance, if a self-driving car causes an accident, should the manufacturer, software developer, or user be held liable? The absence of clear liability frameworks complicates the adoption of these technologies.
3. **Ethical Dilemmas**:
    - Autonomous systems may encounter situations that require ethical decisions, such as prioritizing lives during unavoidable collisions. Encoding ethical decision-making into algorithms is a contentious and unresolved issue.

GOVERNANCE IMPLICATIONS

Governance strategies for autonomous systems should focus on safety, accountability, and ethical considerations:

- **Rigorous Testing Standards**:
    - Establishing stringent testing protocols to evaluate system performance under real-world conditions is crucial for safety assurance.
- **Legal and Liability Frameworks**:
    - Governments and industries must collaborate to define liability in autonomous systems incidents, providing clarity for developers, manufacturers, and users.
- **Ethical Oversight**:
    - Stakeholders must agree on ethical principles to guide the design and deployment of autonomous systems and ensure they align with societal values.

GROWING ROLE IN ORGANIZATIONS

AI-driven decision-making is transforming how businesses and governments operate. From predictive analytics in supply chain management to algorithmic recommendations in hiring processes, AI systems are entrusted with critical decisions. While these systems enhance efficiency and reduce human bias, they also pose significant challenges to accountability and transparency.

GOVERNANCE CHALLENGES

1. **Accountability**:
   - When AI systems make decisions, it can be challenging to identify who is responsible for their outcomes.
   - For example, determining whether the fault lies with the model or organization is challenging if an algorithm denies a loan application.
2. **Transparency**:
   - Many AI models function as "black boxes," offering little insight into how they arrive at decisions.
   - Lack of transparency erodes trust and makes it difficult for stakeholders to understand or challenge AI-driven outcomes.
3. **Bias and Fairness**:
   - AI systems trained on biased datasets can perpetuate or amplify existing inequalities.
   - For instance, biased hiring algorithms may unfairly disadvantage candidates from underrepresented groups, leading to ethical and legal concerns.

GOVERNANCE IMPLICATIONS

Effective governance of AI-driven decision-making should address these challenges through:

- **Explainability**:
  - Developing explainable AI (XAI) systems that provide clear, interpretable insights into decision-making processes is critical for building trust and accountability.
- **Bias Mitigation**:
  - Organizations must prioritize using diverse, representative datasets and conduct regular audits to identify and address biases in AI systems.

- Stakeholder Engagement:
    - Collaborating with regulators, employees, and affected communities ensures that AI-driven decisions are fair, transparent, and aligned with societal values.

17.3 REGULATORY DEVELOPMENTS ON THE HORIZON

As artificial intelligence (AI) technologies evolve, governments and regulatory bodies intensify efforts to establish legal frameworks and standards to guide their development and deployment. These regulations aim to address the unique challenges posed by AI, including ethical considerations, data privacy, accountability, and security. This section explores global regulatory trends, industry-specific regulations, and compliance strategies to help organizations adapt to emerging legal landscapes.

GLOBAL REGULATORY TRENDS

ANTICIPATED INTERNATIONAL REGULATIONS

AI's transformative nature demands a cohesive global approach to regulation, as its impact transcends national boundaries. Anticipated international regulations shape a framework that balances innovation with ethical and societal concerns.

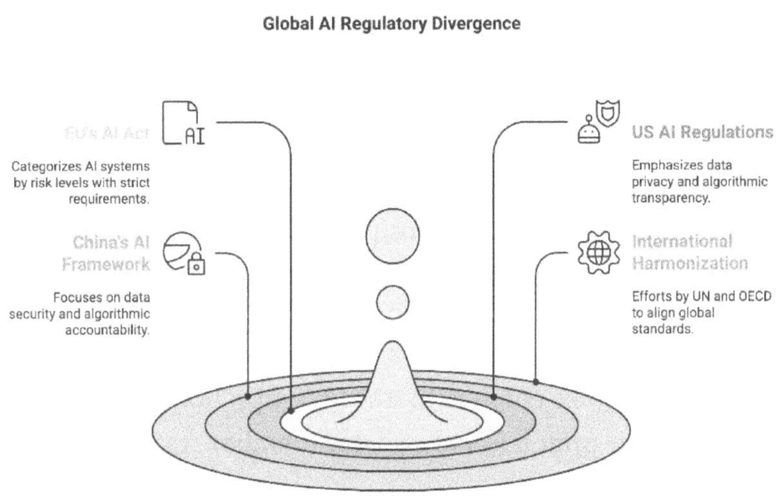

1. European Union's AI Act:
    - The European Union (EU) is leading global efforts with the AI Act, a proposed regulation that categorizes AI systems based on risk levels: unacceptable, high, limited, and minimal.
    - High-risk applications, such as AI in healthcare and law enforcement, are subject to stringent requirements, including transparency, accountability, and data quality standards.

- The AI Act also focuses on banning unacceptable systems, such as those involving government manipulation or social scoring.

2. **United States AI Regulations**:
    - While the United States has historically favored a sector-specific and decentralized approach, recent developments signal a shift toward comprehensive AI regulation.
    - Initiatives like the Blueprint for an AI Bill of Rights emphasize the importance of data privacy, algorithmic transparency, and equitable outcomes.
    - Federal and state-level laws are being developed to address specific concerns, including AI's role in decision-making and its impact on civil liberties.

3. **China's AI Regulatory Framework**:
    - China has introduced robust AI regulations focusing on data security, algorithmic accountability, and content moderation.
    - Its Algorithmic Recommendation Regulations, effective since 2022, mandate transparency in recommendation algorithms and prohibit discriminatory practices.
    - The government emphasizes AI governance to align with national priorities, such as maintaining social stability and ensuring technological leadership.

4. **Harmonization Efforts by International Organizations**:
    - Organizations like the United Nations (UN) and the Organization for Economic Cooperation and Development (OECD) are working to harmonize AI regulations globally.
    - The OECD's AI Principles emphasize transparency, human-centered development, and accountability. They offer a framework for member states to align their policies.
    - The UN's efforts through initiatives like AI for Good seek to establish ethical guidelines that promote sustainable and inclusive AI applications.

IMPLICATIONS FOR AI DEPLOYMENT

Global regulatory trends will significantly influence how AI is developed, deployed, and scaled across borders:

- **Innovation Constraints**: Compliance with stringent regulations may slow the pace of innovation, particularly for smaller organizations with limited resources.

- Market Differentiation: Companies proactively aligning with emerging standards can gain a competitive edge by demonstrating ethical and responsible AI practices.
- Cross-Border Challenges: Differences in regulatory approaches across regions may complicate global AI deployment, necessitating tailored compliance strategies.

INDUSTRY-SPECIFIC REGULATIONS

EMERGING STANDARDS FOR KEY SECTORS

Regulatory bodies also focus on sector-specific standards to address the unique risks and opportunities associated with AI applications in finance, healthcare, and defense industries.

1. Finance:
    - AI is revolutionizing financial services through fraud detection, credit scoring, and algorithmic trading.
    - Regulatory bodies, such as the Financial Stability Board (FSB) and the Basel Committee on Banking Supervision, are developing standards to address AI's impact on financial stability and consumer protection.
    - Key considerations include ensuring transparency in credit decision algorithms, minimizing biases in financial services, and enhancing the security of AI-driven systems.
2. Healthcare:
    - Using AI in diagnostics, treatment planning, and patient care raises critical ethical and safety concerns.
    - Regulations focus on ensuring AI systems' accuracy, reliability, and explainability in healthcare.
    - Organizations like the U.S. Food and Drug Administration (FDA) have introduced frameworks for approving AI-based medical devices, emphasizing post-deployment monitoring and real-world performance evaluations.
3. Defense:
    - AI applications in defense, such as autonomous weapons systems and surveillance tools, pose unique risks to international security and human rights.
    - Regulations aim to establish clear boundaries for using AI in military operations, emphasizing adherence to international humanitarian law.

- Ethical considerations, such as ensuring human oversight of AI systems in combat scenarios, are central to these regulatory efforts.

CHALLENGES AND OPPORTUNITIES

Sector-specific regulations offer both challenges and opportunities for organizations:

- **Customization**: Companies must tailor their AI systems to meet the unique requirements of their respective industries, which may increase development costs and complexity.
- **Risk Mitigation**: Adhering to sector-specific standards helps mitigate risks, such as reputational damage or legal penalties, enhancing long-term sustainability.
- **Innovation Incentives**: Clear regulations provide a roadmap for innovation, encouraging organizations to invest in compliant and ethically sound AI solutions.

COMPLIANCE STRATEGIES

PREPARING FOR AND ADAPTING TO NEW REGULATORY REQUIREMENTS

Organizations must adopt proactive compliance strategies that align with global and industry-specific standards to thrive in an increasingly regulated AI landscape.

1. **Establishing Governance Frameworks**:
   - Companies should develop internal AI governance frameworks that outline compliance policies, roles, and responsibilities.
   - This includes creating cross-functional teams comprising legal, technical, and ethical experts to oversee AI initiatives.
2. **Conducting Regular Audits**:
   - Periodic audits of AI systems are essential to ensure compliance with regulatory requirements and identify areas for improvement.
   - Audits should assess data quality, algorithmic fairness, and system performance under diverse conditions.
3. **Investing in Explainable AI (XAI)**:
   - Explainable AI technologies enable organizations to provide transparent and interpretable insights into their AI systems' decision-making processes.
   - XAI is particularly important for sectors like finance and healthcare, where transparency is a regulatory priority.

4. **Engaging with Regulators and Industry Groups**:
   - Active participation in regulatory discussions and industry groups allows organizations to stay informed about emerging trends and contribute to policy development.
   - Collaboration with regulators can help shape practical and effective AI standards.
5. **Leveraging AI for Compliance**:
   - AI tools can streamline compliance processes, such as monitoring regulatory updates, detecting anomalies in system behavior, and generating compliance reports.
   - For example, natural language processing (NLP) can help organizations analyze complex regulatory documents and extract actionable insights.
6. **Fostering a Culture of Ethical AI**:
   - Beyond legal compliance, organizations should prioritize ethical considerations in their AI strategies.
   - Training programs, ethical guidelines, and leadership commitment to responsible AI development can foster a culture that values long-term societal impact over short-term gains.

17.4 ETHICAL CONSIDERATIONS IN FUTURE AI APPLICATIONS

As artificial intelligence (AI) technologies become more pervasive, their ethical implications demand careful attention. AI systems can enhance efficiency, accuracy, and decision-making, but they also present significant challenges, including algorithmic bias, data privacy concerns, and the dynamics of human-AI collaboration. Addressing these issues requires a comprehensive approach that incorporates ethical principles into designing, developing, and deploying AI systems.

BIAS AND FAIRNESS

THE CHALLENGE OF ALGORITHMIC BIAS

Algorithmic bias arises when AI systems produce outcomes that unfairly disadvantage certain groups or individuals. This bias often stems from biased training data, flawed algorithms, or incomplete representation of diverse populations. Examples include facial recognition systems that misidentify people of certain ethnicities or hiring algorithms that inadvertently favor specific demographics.

Addressing algorithmic bias becomes crucial to ensuring equitable outcomes as AI adoption grows. Bias erodes public trust in AI systems and reinforces systemic inequalities. For example:

- **Healthcare**: AI algorithms used for medical diagnosis or treatment planning may produce biased results if trained on datasets that underrepresent specific demographic groups.
- **Criminal Justice**: Predictive policing systems, if based on historical arrest data, can perpetuate discriminatory practices.
- **Finance**: Credit-scoring algorithms may disadvantage marginalized communities due to biased historical data or unbalanced feature selection.

STRATEGIES TO ENSURE FAIRNESS

1. **Diverse and Representative Data**:
    - Ensuring that AI training datasets are diverse and representative of the population is a critical step toward reducing bias.
    - This involves actively sourcing data from underrepresented groups and mitigating historical biases embedded in datasets.
2. **Bias Detection and Mitigation Tools**:
    - Organizations can use tools like fairness metrics and reweighting techniques to identify and address bias in AI models.
    - Regular audits of algorithms can help identify patterns of unfairness and inform corrective actions.
3. **Regulatory Standards**:
    - Governments and industry bodies should establish guidelines that mandate fairness in AI applications, ensuring compliance with anti-discrimination laws.
    - Transparency in algorithmic decision-making, such as publishing fairness assessments, can help build accountability.

PRIVACY AND DATA PROTECTION

BALANCING DATA UTILIZATION AND PRIVACY RIGHTS

AI systems often rely on vast amounts of data to function effectively. However, collecting, storing, and analyzing personal data raises significant privacy concerns. A key ethical challenge is balancing the use of data for AI advancements with protecting individual privacy.

1. **Privacy Risks in AI**:

- Data Breaches: Centralizing sensitive data in AI systems increases the risk of unauthorized access or cyberattacks.
- Surveillance Concerns: AI-driven surveillance technologies like facial recognition can infringe on individuals' privacy and enable intrusive monitoring.
- Informed Consent: Many individuals are unaware of how AI systems collect and use their data, undermining their ability to provide informed consent.

2. Ethical Implications of Data-Driven AI:
   - Data exploitation without adequate safeguards can erode trust in AI systems and organizations.
   - Excessive data collection and retention can lead to ethical violations, such as profiling or discrimination.

STRATEGIES FOR ETHICAL DATA UTILIZATION

1. Data Minimization:
   - Collecting only the data necessary for a specific purpose reduces privacy risks.
   - Implementing robust data deletion policies ensures that data is not retained longer than required.
2. Privacy-by-Design:
   - Incorporating privacy safeguards into AI system design from the outset ensures compliance with data protection standards.
   - Techniques like differential privacy, federated learning, and encryption can enhance data security while preserving utility.
3. Transparency and Consent Mechanisms:
   - Providing clear information about collecting, using, and sharing data enables individuals to make informed choices.
   - Consent mechanisms should be designed to be accessible and easy to understand, ensuring meaningful participation.
4. Compliance with Legal Frameworks:
   - Organizations must adhere to privacy regulations, such as the EU's General Data Protection Regulation (GDPR) or the California Consumer Privacy Act (CCPA) in the U.S.

- Regular audits and assessments ensure ongoing compliance with evolving legal requirements.

HUMAN-AI COLLABORATION

ETHICAL DYNAMICS OF INTEGRATION

Human-AI collaboration combines the strengths of AI systems—speed, scalability, and data-driven insights—with human intuition, creativity, and ethical judgment. However, integrating AI into decision-making processes introduces ethical questions about roles, accountability, and trust.

1. **Challenges of Human-AI Collaboration**:
   - **Overreliance on AI**: Excessive dependence on AI systems can diminish human oversight and critical thinking, increasing the risk of errors or unintended consequences.
   - **Accountability Gaps**: Shared responsibility between humans and AI can create ambiguity in assigning blame for outcomes, especially in high-stakes domains like healthcare or finance.
   - **Trust Issues**: Building trust between humans and AI requires systems to be transparent, reliable, and explainable.
2. **Ethical Considerations**:
   - AI systems must support, rather than replace, human decision-making, ensuring that final authority remains with humans.
   - The design of AI systems should prioritize user-centric principles, empowering humans to understand and effectively interact with the technology.

FRAMEWORKS FOR ETHICAL COLLABORATION

1. **Explainable AI (XAI)**:
   - AI systems must provide clear, interpretable insights into decision-making, enabling humans to validate and trust outcomes.
   - XAI is particularly important in critical areas like healthcare, where practitioners need to understand AI-driven recommendations.
2. **Clear Role Definitions**:
   - Delineating roles and responsibilities in human-AI collaboration ensures accountability and prevents overreliance on technology.

- Decision-making frameworks should specify when and how human intervention is required.

3. **Ethical Training Programs**:
   - Educating users on the strengths and limitations of AI fosters responsible use and ethical decision-making.
   - Training programs should include scenarios that illustrate potential biases, ethical dilemmas, and best practices for collaboration.

4. **Continuous Monitoring and Feedback**:
   - Establishing mechanisms for monitoring AI performance and soliciting user feedback ensures systems align with human needs and values.
   - Iterative improvements based on real-world interactions enhance the effectiveness and reliability of human-AI collaboration.

17.5 TECHNOLOGICAL SOLUTIONS FOR FUTURE GOVERNANCE CHALLENGES

The increasing integration of artificial intelligence (AI) into societal and organizational functions necessitates robust governance to ensure accountability, transparency, and ethical adherence. Technological solutions, such as Explainable AI (XAI), AI-driven governance tools, and blockchain integration, are emerging as key enablers for addressing the complexities of future governance challenges.

EXPLAINABLE AI (XAI)

THE NEED FOR TRANSPARENCY IN AI DECISION-MAKING

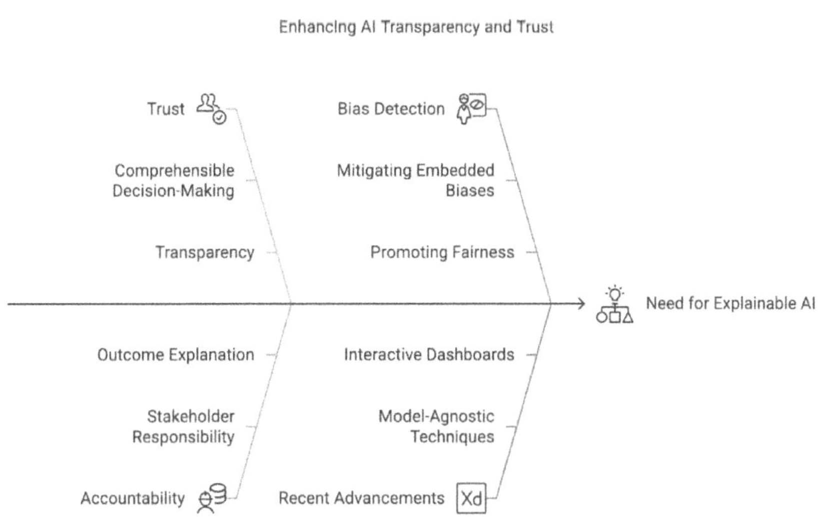

AI systems are often criticized for their "black box" nature, where the logic behind decisions remains opaque. This lack of transparency raises ethical, legal, and operational concerns, particularly in critical healthcare, finance, and criminal justice domains. Explainable AI (XAI) seeks to address these issues by providing insights into how AI models process data and arrive at conclusions.

1. **Importance of XAI:**
   - **Trust**: Transparency builds trust between AI systems and their users by making the decision-making process comprehensible.
   - **Accountability**: Clear explanations enable stakeholders to hold systems accountable for their outcomes.
   - **Bias Detection**: XAI helps identify and mitigate biases embedded in AI models, promoting fairness and equity.
2. **Recent Advancements**:
   - **Model-Agnostic Techniques**: Methods like SHAP (SHapley Additive exPlanations) and LIME (Local Interpretable Model-agnostic Explanations) allow for interpreting predictions made by complex models.
   - **Neural Network Visualization**: Tools that visualize the inner workings of deep learning models, such as saliency maps, highlight the data features influencing specific decisions.
   - **Interactive Dashboards**: User-friendly interfaces allow stakeholders to explore model behavior, analyze potential biases, and simulate decision-making scenarios.

GOVERNANCE IMPLICATIONS OF XAI

By improving transparency, XAI can help organizations address regulatory and ethical challenges:

- **Regulatory Compliance**: Many upcoming AI regulations, such as the EU's AI Act, mandate explainability as a prerequisite for deploying AI in high-risk applications.
- **Operational Risk Management**: Explainability aids in identifying weaknesses in AI models, enabling proactive risk mitigation.
- **Public Confidence**: Transparent AI systems foster public confidence, which is crucial for adoption in sensitive sectors like healthcare and law enforcement.

LEVERAGING AI TO STRENGTHEN GOVERNANCE PRACTICES

AI technologies themselves can play a critical role in enhancing governance frameworks. By automating complex tasks and providing data-driven insights, AI can improve governance systems' efficiency, accuracy, and responsiveness.

1. Applications in Governance:
    - Compliance Monitoring:
        - AI tools can analyze vast volumes of organizational data to ensure adherence to regulatory requirements.
        - For example, natural language processing (NLP) systems can review contracts and policies to identify compliance gaps.
    - Risk Assessment:
        - By analyzing historical data, machine learning models can predict potential risks, enabling organizations to implement preventive measures.
        - In financial governance, AI-driven fraud detection systems can identify suspicious activities in real time.
    - Policy Analysis:
        - AI algorithms can simulate the potential outcomes of policy decisions, helping governments and organizations make evidence-based choices.
        - For instance, predictive models can assess proposed legislation's social and economic impacts.
2. Emerging Innovations:
    - AI-Powered Dashboards: Real-time monitoring platforms powered by AI provide actionable insights into compliance and risk metrics.
    - Behavioral Analytics: AI tools can analyze user behaviors to detect deviations from established norms, aiding cybersecurity and internal governance.
    - Regulatory Intelligence Platforms: These systems use AI to track regulatory changes across jurisdictions, ensuring organizations remain updated on evolving legal landscapes.

CHALLENGES AND OPPORTUNITIES

While AI offers transformative potential for governance, it also introduces challenges:

- **Data Privacy**: The extensive data requirements of AI systems raise concerns about privacy and consent.
- **Algorithmic Bias**: Governance AI tools must be scrutinized for biases to avoid perpetuating unfair practices.
- **Human Oversight**: To ensure accountability, AI-driven governance tools must be used with human expertise, not as standalone decision-makers.

BLOCKCHAIN INTEGRATION

ENHANCING AI GOVERNANCE WITH BLOCKCHAIN

Blockchain technology, known for its immutability and transparency, offers a powerful complement to AI in addressing governance challenges. Blockchain can enhance accountability and trust in AI systems by providing a secure and tamper-proof record of AI-related activities.

1. **Applications of Blockchain in AI Governance**:
    - **Audit Trails**:
        - Blockchain can store detailed logs of AI system operations, creating transparent and immutable records of decisions, data usage, and algorithm updates.
        - This ensures traceability, enabling stakeholders to verify that AI systems comply with governance standards.
    - **Data Integrity**:
        - Blockchain can certify the authenticity and integrity of training datasets, reducing the risk of bias or manipulation.
        - For instance, supply chain AI systems can leverage blockchain to verify the origin and accuracy of data inputs.
    - **Smart Contracts**:
        - Smart contracts can automate governance processes, such as granting or revoking permissions for AI system access based on predefined rules.
        - This enhances security and reduces the potential for human error in compliance enforcement.

2. Real-World Examples:
    - Healthcare:
        - Blockchain-based systems are being used to track the provenance of medical data, ensuring that AI-driven diagnostic tools rely on trustworthy sources.
    - Finance:
        - Blockchain technology helps monitor algorithmic trading systems, providing regulators with clear audit trails to detect fraudulent activities.
    - Education:
        - Academic institutions use blockchain to validate AI-driven grading systems, ensuring that student assessments are accurate and tamper-proof.

BENEFITS AND CHALLENGES

1. Benefits:
    - Enhanced Transparency: Blockchain's distributed ledger ensures all stakeholders access the same information, fostering trust and collaboration.
    - Improved Security: Decentralized storage and encryption make blockchain systems highly resistant to cyberattacks.
    - Regulatory Alignment: Immutable records facilitate compliance with data protection and accountability requirements.
2. Challenges:
    - Scalability: Blockchain systems can struggle with high transaction volumes, limiting their applicability to large-scale governance systems.
    - Interoperability: Integrating blockchain with existing AI systems and governance frameworks requires overcoming technical and organizational hurdles.
    - Energy Consumption: The high energy demands of certain blockchain implementations, such as proof-of-work systems, raise sustainability concerns.

17.6 PREPARING ORGANIZATIONS FOR FUTURE GOVERNANCE NEEDS

As artificial intelligence (AI) technologies evolve rapidly, organizations must proactively prepare to meet the governance demands of an uncertain future. Building adaptive governance frameworks, fostering continuous learning, and engaging with diverse stakeholders are essential strategies for navigating the complexities of AI governance.

BUILDING ADAPTIVE GOVERNANCE FRAMEWORKS

FLEXIBILITY IN POLICY DESIGN

Static governance policies are insufficient in a landscape defined by technological advancements and shifting regulatory requirements. Organizations must prioritize adaptive governance frameworks that can evolve alongside emerging trends.

1. **Core Principles of Adaptive Frameworks**:
    - **Modularity**: Governance frameworks should consist of modular components that can be updated independently as technology or regulations change.
    - **Scenario Planning**: Organizations should anticipate various technological and regulatory scenarios and develop policies that address multiple contingencies.
    - **Iterative Development**: Policies should be regularly reviewed and refined based on feedback to ensure they remain relevant and practical.
2. **Examples in Practice**:
    - **AI Model Lifecycle Governance**: Developing guidelines for every stage of the AI lifecycle—from data collection and model training to deployment and monitoring—ensures comprehensive oversight.
    - **Regulatory Sandboxes**: Establishing sandboxes allows organizations to test innovative AI solutions within controlled environments, fostering experimentation while adhering to governance standards.
3. **Benefits of Adaptability**:
    - Organizations can respond swiftly to new regulations, minimizing compliance risks.
    - Adaptive frameworks encourage innovation by providing a clear structure within which new technologies can be safely explored.

CONTINUOUS LEARNING AND DEVELOPMENT

EMPOWERING TEAMS WITH KNOWLEDGE

The fast-paced nature of AI innovation demands that organizations invest in their teams' continuous learning and development. Keeping employees informed about emerging trends, best practices, and evolving regulations ensures effective governance and fosters a culture of responsibility.

1. Training Programs:
    - Organizations should implement structured training programs tailored to different roles, such as data scientists, compliance officers, and decision-makers.
    - Topics should include ethical AI design, regulatory compliance, and emerging technologies like explainable AI and federated learning.
2. Industry Certifications and Partnerships:
    - Encouraging employees to pursue industry-recognized AI governance and ethics certifications enhances their expertise and credibility.
    - Collaborating with academic institutions and professional organizations can provide access to cutting-edge research and specialized training.
3. Knowledge-Sharing Platforms:
    - Internal knowledge-sharing platforms enable teams to document and share insights gained from real-world projects, ensuring that lessons learned are institutionalized.
4. Fostering a Growth Mindset:
    - Leadership should promote a culture that values continuous improvement and lifelong learning.
    - Rewarding employees committed to staying updated on governance practices can motivate broader participation.

ENGAGING WITH STAKEHOLDERS

COLLABORATION FOR RESPONSIBLE AI GOVERNANCE

Governance challenges often extend beyond organizational boundaries, requiring collective efforts to address them effectively. Engaging with stakeholders—including regulators, industry peers, and the public—ensures that governance frameworks are robust, inclusive, and aligned with societal values.

1. Regulator Collaboration:
    - Proactively engaging with regulators helps organizations stay ahead of new requirements and influence the development of practical policies.
    - Participation in regulatory consultations or advisory committees provides insights into future governance expectations.

2. **Industry Peer Networks**:
   - Collaborating with other organizations within the same industry allows for exchanging best practices and developing sector-specific standards.
   - Joint initiatives, such as creating shared datasets or contributing to open-source governance tools, can advance the collective state of AI governance.
3. **Public Engagement**:
   - Organizations should involve the public in discussions about AI governance to build trust and ensure that policies reflect societal needs.
   - Transparency initiatives, such as publishing AI impact assessments or hosting public forums, encourage accountability and foster dialogue.
4. **Global Partnerships**:
   - Given the cross-border nature of AI applications, international collaboration is essential for harmonizing governance practices.
   - Organizations can participate in global efforts led by bodies like the OECD or the United Nations to shape responsible AI policies.

CHAPTER 18: CASE STUDIES IN AI GOVERNANCE

18.1 INTRODUCTION TO CASE STUDIES

PURPOSE AND IMPORTANCE

Case study analysis is a critical mechanism for advancing knowledge and practices in AI governance. By dissecting real-world applications, organizations and individuals can better understand the complexities and nuances of implementing governance frameworks in various contexts. Case studies provide tangible examples illustrating the challenges and successes associated with governing AI systems, offering valuable insights into practical strategies that may not emerge from theoretical discussions alone.

Case studies primarily aim to bridge the gap between abstract principles and actionable strategies. They help stakeholders, from policymakers to practitioners, grasp the real-world implications of AI governance decisions. Examining how organizations address ethical dilemmas, ensure compliance with regulations, or mitigate risks provides a grounded perspective that fosters informed decision-making. This is particularly important as AI technologies evolve rapidly, posing novel challenges that require adaptive governance frameworks.

Moreover, case studies highlight the impact of governance on trust-building. Whether it is enhancing consumer trust in data privacy or ensuring fairness in algorithmic decisions, the stories of successful governance initiatives inspire confidence among stakeholders. They also underscore the critical role of governance in driving sustainable AI innovation, proving that robust frameworks do not hinder but enable responsible progress in AI development.

SELECTION CRITERIA

To ensure relevance and comprehensive coverage, the industries and organizations featured in this chapter were selected based on their noteworthy AI governance initiatives. The selection criteria considered various factors to highlight diverse approaches and challenges, allowing for a broad exploration of the topic.

1. **Industry Relevance:** Industries were chosen based on their prominence in deploying AI technologies and their unique governance challenges. Healthcare, finance, retail, manufacturing, and public services were prioritized for their critical societal impact and regulatory complexities.

2. **Innovative Practices:** Organizations that have pioneered innovative governance frameworks or tools were included to provide cutting-edge insights. These cases demonstrate how leading entities navigate AI's ethical, legal, and operational challenges.
3. **Geographic and Regulatory Diversity:** A global perspective was ensured by including organizations operating in different regions, reflecting diverse legal and cultural approaches to AI governance. This variety offers readers a comprehensive understanding of how governance strategies must adapt to contextual factors.
4. **Scalability and Transferability:** The selected case studies emphasize governance practices that are effective within their originating contexts and offer transferable lessons for broader application. This ensures that the insights gleaned are valuable to organizations across industries and geographies.

Through this curated approach, the chapter aims to deliver practical insights into real-world AI governance applications, equipping readers with the knowledge to implement effective strategies in their organizational contexts.

18.2 HEALTHCARE INDUSTRY: ENSURING PATIENT PRIVACY AND DATA SECURITY

ORGANIZATION OVERVIEW

The healthcare sector is increasingly leveraging AI to revolutionize patient diagnostics, offering unprecedented precision and efficiency in identifying and managing health conditions. A leading example is MediTrust Health Systems, a globally recognized healthcare provider in over 20 countries. MediTrust employs state-of-the-art AI tools to support diagnostic processes, ranging from early cancer detection to predicting patient outcomes in critical care settings.

MediTrust's AI systems process vast patient data, integrating inputs from electronic health records (EHRs), imaging technologies, and genomic databases. This integration enables clinicians to identify patterns and make data-driven decisions faster and more accurately. For instance, MediTrust's flagship AI-driven diagnostic tool, HealthScan AI, is credited with reducing diagnostic errors by 30% while improving patient outcomes across its network of hospitals and clinics.

Despite these advances, integrating AI technologies in healthcare presents significant governance challenges. MediTrust's efforts to maintain compliance with stringent data protection laws while harnessing the power of AI exemplify the delicate balance required to innovate responsibly in this sensitive domain.

GOVERNANCE CHALLENGES

AI innovation in healthcare intersects with some of the most sensitive and heavily regulated domains of data usage. Patient privacy, data security, and ethical considerations must be meticulously addressed to uphold trust and comply with the Health Insurance Portability and Accountability Act (HIPAA) in the United States and the General Data Protection Regulation (GDPR) in the European Union. MediTrust faced several critical challenges in navigating this landscape:

1. Privacy and Data Protection Compliance: AI tools in healthcare rely on extensive patient data to deliver accurate diagnostics and predictions. However, accessing, processing, and sharing this data requires strict regulatory requirements. MediTrust needed to ensure compliance with HIPAA's rules on patient consent, data storage, and disclosure while avoiding unauthorized access or breaches.

2. Data Anonymization and Re-identification Risks: MediTrust anonymized patient data before utilizing it for AI training to meet privacy requirements. However, advancements in de-anonymization techniques posed a risk of re-identifying individuals, which could lead to privacy violations and reputational damage.

3. Continuous Monitoring and Cybersecurity Threats: Healthcare organizations are frequent targets of cyberattacks. MediTrust's reliance on interconnected AI systems created additional vulnerabilities. Ensuring continuous monitoring and safeguarding of patient data against breaches required robust cybersecurity measures.

4. Balancing Innovation with Ethical Considerations: Deploying AI tools introduced ethical dilemmas, such as ensuring transparency in algorithmic decision-making and mitigating potential biases. MediTrust had to address these issues while fostering innovation and trust.

SOLUTIONS IMPLEMENTED

MediTrust adopted a multifaceted approach to overcome these governance challenges, prioritizing privacy, security, and ethical considerations alongside AI innovation:

1. Robust Data Anonymization Techniques: MediTrust implemented advanced anonymization techniques, such as differential privacy and homomorphic encryption. Differential privacy ensured that patient data remained unidentifiable even when analyzed collectively, while homomorphic encryption allowed AI algorithms to process encrypted data without decrypting it, maintaining confidentiality throughout the process.

2. Continuous Monitoring Systems: MediTrust was developed and deployed to address cybersecurity risks using AI-powered constant monitoring systems. These systems could detect real-time anomalies, identify potential breaches, and implement automated responses to mitigate threats. For example, an AI-driven security tool flagged unusual access patterns, enabling the organization to prevent unauthorized data access proactively.

3. Comprehensive Compliance Frameworks: MediTrust established a centralized compliance team to oversee adherence to privacy regulations across all AI applications. This team

conducted regular audits, updated policies to align with evolving legal requirements, and ensured transparency in data usage.

4. **Ethics Committees and Bias Audits:** To address ethical concerns, MediTrust formed an AI Ethics Committee comprising clinicians, data scientists, ethicists, and patient representatives. The committee evaluated AI models for biases and transparency, ensuring that diagnostic tools provided fair and explainable outcomes. Regular bias audits became a standard practice, reinforcing accountability.

5. **Stakeholder Education and Training:** MediTrust recognized the importance of awareness and initiated training programs for clinicians and staff on AI governance's ethical and regulatory aspects. These programs emphasized the importance of patient consent, data security, and the responsible use of AI tools in clinical settings.

OUTCOMES

The implementation of these measures yielded significant benefits for MediTrust, cementing its reputation as a leader in responsible AI innovation within the healthcare industry:

1. **Enhanced Diagnostic Accuracy:** MediTrust's AI-driven tools demonstrated remarkable improvements in diagnostic precision. For example, the HealthScan AI tool identified early-stage cancers with a sensitivity rate of 95%, compared to 85% for traditional methods. This led to better patient outcomes and reduced healthcare costs.

2. **Strengthened Patient Trust:** MediTrust maintained high patient trust by prioritizing privacy and security. Transparency in data usage and stringent compliance measures reassured patients that their personal information was safeguarded, fostering stronger relationships between patients and healthcare providers.

3. **Regulatory Compliance:** MediTrust successfully navigated the complex landscape of privacy regulations, avoiding penalties and reputational risks associated with non-compliance. Its proactive approach to governance served as a model for other organizations in the healthcare sector.

4. **Operational Resilience:** Continuous monitoring systems enhanced MediTrust's resilience against cyber threats. Over three years, the organization experienced a 40% reduction in attempted breaches, underscoring the effectiveness of its security measures.

5. **Industry Recognition:** MediTrust's governance initiatives earned accolades from industry bodies and regulators, positioning the organization as a thought leader in AI governance. Its practices were featured in several conferences and publications, influencing broader industry standards.

LESSONS LEARNED

MediTrust's experience underscores several key lessons that are broadly applicable to organizations integrating AI into sensitive and regulated industries:

1. Early Integration of AI Governance Frameworks: Establishing governance frameworks at the inception of AI projects is critical. Early integration ensures that privacy, security, and ethical considerations are built into the foundation of AI systems, minimizing the need for costly retrofits or corrective actions.

2. Collaboration Across Disciplines: Effective AI governance requires cooperation among diverse stakeholders, including data scientists, clinicians, ethicists, and legal experts. This interdisciplinary approach ensures that multiple perspectives are considered, leading to more robust solutions.

3. Proactive Compliance and Adaptation: Staying ahead of evolving regulatory landscapes is essential. Organizations must proactively update their policies and practices to reflect changes in laws and technological advancements, avoiding potential compliance gaps.

4. Transparency and Patient Engagement: Open communication about how AI tools are used and how patient data is protected fosters trust and acceptance. Involving patients in governance discussions, such as public consultations or representation on ethics committees, enhances accountability and alignment with societal values.

5. Continuous Improvement and Monitoring: AI governance is not a one-time effort but an ongoing process. Regular audits, performance evaluations, and updates are essential to maintaining the effectiveness and relevance of governance frameworks as technologies and risks evolve.

By addressing these lessons, MediTrust has set a high standard for AI governance in healthcare. It demonstrates that innovation and responsibility can coexist to deliver transformative benefits to patients and society. These insights provide valuable guidance for other organizations seeking to harness AI's potential while safeguarding privacy, security, and ethical integrity.

18.3 FINANCIAL SERVICES: MITIGATING BIAS IN CREDIT SCORING ALGORITHMS

ORGANIZATION OVERVIEW

The financial services industry has been a leader in adopting artificial intelligence (AI) to enhance decision-making and operational efficiency. One prominent example is TrustBank International, a global financial institution with operations in over 30 countries. TrustBank leverages AI for various purposes, including credit risk assessment, fraud detection, and personalized financial services. Its flagship AI system, CreditSmart, evaluates loan applicants' creditworthiness by analyzing diverse data, such as economic history, spending patterns, and employment records.

The introduction of AI has enabled TrustBank to process applications more quickly, reducing approval times from weeks to days. CreditSmart's advanced algorithms can identify nuanced patterns that traditional methods often miss, resulting in more accurate credit risk predictions. However, deploying such AI systems has also presented significant governance challenges, particularly concerning biases that could lead to discriminatory lending practices.

GOVERNANCE CHALLENGES

While AI has immense potential to improve efficiency and fairness in credit scoring, it is not immune to biases inherent in data or design. TrustBank faced several critical governance challenges as it sought to deploy CreditSmart responsibly:

1. **Data Bias and Historical Inequities:** CreditSmart trained its algorithms on historical data, often reflecting past discriminatory practices, such as the systemic exclusion of minority communities from access to credit. As a result, the AI system risked perpetuating these biases, disproportionately disadvantaging underrepresented groups.

2. **Lack of Transparency in Decision-Making:** AI systems like CreditSmart operate as complex, "black-box" models, making it challenging to explain their decisions. This lack of transparency raised concerns among regulators and consumers, who demanded more apparent justifications for credit decisions.

3. **Regulatory Scrutiny and Legal Compliance:** TrustBank had to navigate an evolving regulatory landscape, including laws like the Equal Credit Opportunity Act (ECOA) in the United States, which prohibits discrimination in credit decisions. Ensuring compliance while maintaining AI efficiency posed a significant challenge.

4. **Stakeholder Trust and Reputational Risk:** The potential for bias in AI-driven credit scoring threatened to undermine consumer trust and expose the bank to reputational damage. Addressing these concerns required proactive engagement with stakeholders, including customers, regulators, and advocacy groups.

SOLUTIONS IMPLEMENTED

To address these challenges, TrustBank implemented a series of measures aimed at mitigating bias, enhancing transparency, and fostering trust in its AI systems:

1. **Bias Detection and Mitigation Tools:** TrustBank invested in advanced bias detection tools capable of analyzing CreditSmart's decisions for patterns of unfair treatment. These tools identified potential disparities in how the AI system assessed applicants based on race, gender, or socioeconomic status. When biases were detected, engineers adjusted the algorithms to ensure equitable outcomes.

2. Establishment of an Ethics Review Board: TrustBank recognized the importance of ethical oversight and established an AI Ethics Review Board comprising internal and external experts. The board's mandate included reviewing CreditSmart's design and performance, evaluating its compliance with ethical standards, and providing recommendations for improvement. This collaborative approach ensured diverse perspectives in governance decisions.

3. Transparency Initiatives: To address concerns about the "black-box" nature of AI, TrustBank prioritized explainability in CreditSmart's design. The bank introduced user-friendly tools that provided applicants with clear explanations of how their credit scores were determined. These tools also highlighted actionable steps applicants could take to improve their creditworthiness.

4. Stakeholder Engagement Programs: TrustBank launched initiatives to engage with stakeholders, including community organizations and advocacy groups. These programs facilitated open dialogues about the bank's use of AI, enabling stakeholders to voice concerns and provide feedback. The insights gained from these interactions informed the bank's governance practices and reinforced its commitment to ethical AI deployment.

5. Continuous Monitoring and Audits: TrustBank established a framework for monitoring and auditing CreditSmart's performance on an ongoing basis to ensure long-term accountability. Regular audits assessed the system's compliance with ethical and regulatory standards while monitoring tools tracked its real-time decisions to identify and address any emerging biases.

OUTCOMES

The implementation of these solutions resulted in significant improvements in TrustBank's AI governance and operational outcomes:

1. Enhanced Fairness in Credit Decisions: Deploying bias detection and mitigation tools reduced disparities across demographic groups. CreditSmart's revised algorithms assessed applicants more fairly, contributing to a more inclusive approach to credit access.

2. Increased Regulatory Compliance: TrustBank's proactive efforts to align CreditSmart with regulatory requirements earned praise from regulators. By addressing potential biases and ensuring transparency, the bank avoided legal penalties and strengthened its standing with oversight bodies.

3. Improved Consumer Trust: Transparency initiatives and stakeholder engagement programs fostered trust among customers and communities. Consumers appreciated the clear explanations of credit decisions and viewed TrustBank as a responsible and ethical financial institution.

4. Industry Recognition: TrustBank's leadership in AI governance garnered recognition from industry peers and professional organizations. The bank's initiatives were highlighted as best practices in conferences and publications, setting a benchmark for other financial institutions.

5. **Sustainable Innovation:** By integrating governance frameworks early in CreditSmart's lifecycle, TrustBank established a foundation for sustainable AI innovation. The lessons from this experience informed the development of other AI systems within the organization, ensuring ethical considerations remained central to innovation efforts.

LESSONS LEARNED

TrustBank's journey in mitigating bias in credit scoring algorithms offers several valuable lessons for organizations seeking to deploy AI responsibly:

1. **Ongoing Bias Audits Are Essential:** Bias detection and mitigation cannot be a one-time effort. Continuous audits are necessary to identify and address biases as they emerge, ensuring that AI systems remain fair and equitable over time.

2. **Interdisciplinary Collaboration Strengthens Governance:** Bringing together experts from diverse fields, including data science, ethics, law, and community advocacy, enhances the robustness of AI governance frameworks. Collaboration ensures that multiple perspectives are considered, leading to more comprehensive solutions.

3. **Transparency Builds Trust:** Consumers are more likely to trust AI systems when they understand how decisions are made. Prioritizing explainability enhances trust and aligns AI systems with ethical and legal standards.

4. **Stakeholder Engagement Drives Accountability:** Engaging with stakeholders provides valuable insights into the societal impact of AI systems. Open dialogues and feedback loops enable organizations to address concerns proactively and demonstrate a commitment to ethical practices.

5. **Governance Frameworks Must Evolve with Technology:** The rapid pace of AI innovation requires adaptive governance frameworks that can accommodate new challenges and opportunities. Organizations must remain vigilant and flexible, updating their policies and practices to stay ahead of emerging risks.

By addressing these lessons, TrustBank has set a high standard for ethical AI deployment in the financial services industry. Its experience underscores the importance of integrating governance considerations into every stage of AI development, ensuring that innovation benefits all stakeholders while upholding fairness, transparency, and accountability principles.

18.4 RETAIL SECTOR: PERSONALIZATION VS. CONSUMER PRIVACY

ORGANIZATION OVERVIEW

The retail sector has been transformed by the application of artificial intelligence (AI), particularly in enhancing personalized customer experiences. A leading example is GlobalShop Online, a prominent global e-commerce company with a customer base spanning over 50 countries. Known for its advanced AI-driven personalized marketing strategies, GlobalShop uses algorithms to analyze customer behavior, preferences, and purchase history to tailor product recommendations, dynamic pricing, and targeted advertisements.

GlobalShop's AI systems, such as its flagship marketing tool, ShopAI Insight, have significantly improved customer engagement and sales conversion rates. By predicting individual preferences and anticipating needs, the company delivers highly relevant shopping experiences to millions of customers daily. However, this level of personalization requires extensive data collection and processing, raising critical governance challenges related to consumer privacy.

GOVERNANCE CHALLENGES

AI for personalized marketing introduces a complex interplay between delivering customized experiences and respecting consumer privacy. GlobalShop faced several significant challenges in navigating this dynamic:

1. **Consumer Data Privacy Concerns:** Personalized marketing relies on collecting and analyzing vast customer data, including browsing history, location, purchase behavior, and even inferred preferences. This extensive data usage raised privacy concerns among customers, many of whom felt uncomfortable with the level of surveillance implied by such practices.

2. **Compliance with Data Protection Regulations:** GlobalShop had to ensure adherence to stringent data protection laws such as the General Data Protection Regulation (GDPR) in Europe and the California Consumer Privacy Act (CCPA) in the United States. These regulations impose strict requirements on data collection, storage, usage, and consumer rights, such as the right to access or delete personal data.

3. **Balancing Personalization and Privacy:** Achieving the right balance between offering personalized experiences and respecting privacy posed a significant challenge. Overly intrusive personalization could alienate customers, while insufficient personalization could reduce engagement and sales.

4. **Transparency and Consumer Trust:** Many customers were skeptical about how their data was being used. The lack of transparency in data collection and processing practices eroded trust and called for greater accountability.

5. **Ethical Concerns in AI Usage:** The reliance on AI for personalization also introduced ethical challenges, such as the potential for bias in recommendations or the inadvertent exploitation of consumer vulnerabilities. GlobalShop needed to address these issues to maintain its reputation as an ethical retailer.

SOLUTIONS IMPLEMENTED

To address these challenges, GlobalShop adopted a comprehensive approach that prioritized transparency, compliance, and consumer empowerment:

1. **Transparent Data Usage Policies:** GlobalShop overhauled its privacy policies to ensure clarity and accessibility. Customers were provided with detailed explanations of the collected data, its use, and its purposes. These policies were written in plain language, avoiding technical jargon to ensure consumer understanding.
2. **Opt-In Consent Mechanisms:** The company implemented opt-in consent mechanisms for data collection and personalized marketing. Customers could actively agree to data usage rather than being subjected to default settings. This approach aligned with GDPR requirements and reinforced the principle of informed consent.
3. **AI Ethics and Bias Audits:** To address ethical concerns, GlobalShop conducted regular audits of its AI systems to identify and mitigate biases in recommendations. These audits involved analyzing the algorithms' outputs for patterns of discrimination and ensuring that personalization was fair and inclusive across all demographic groups.
4. **Enhanced Consumer Controls:** GlobalShop introduced a user-friendly data management portal that allows customers to view, modify, or delete their data. The portal also includes features to customize the level of personalization they desire, giving customers greater control over their experiences.
5. **Privacy-by-Design Frameworks:** A privacy-by-design approach embedded privacy considerations into the design and development of AI systems. This proactive framework ensured that data protection measures were integral to every stage of the AI lifecycle, from data collection to algorithm deployment.
6. **Engaging Stakeholders and Building Awareness:** GlobalShop launched educational campaigns to inform customers about the benefits of personalization and the safeguards in place to protect their privacy. By engaging with stakeholders, including advocacy groups and regulators, the company demonstrated its commitment to ethical AI practices.

OUTCOMES

The implementation of these solutions resulted in several positive outcomes for GlobalShop, setting a benchmark for responsible AI deployment in the retail sector:

1. **Increased Customer Trust:** Transparency initiatives and enhanced consumer controls reassured customers that their data was being handled responsibly. Post-implementation trust surveys showed a 25% increase in customer confidence regarding data privacy practices.

2. Improved Personalization and Engagement: By aligning personalization efforts with consumer preferences and consent, GlobalShop achieved a 15% improvement in engagement rates and a 20% increase in sales conversions. Customers appreciated the relevance of product recommendations without feeling intruded upon.

3. Regulatory Compliance: The company's proactive measures ensured full compliance with GDPR, CCPA, and other relevant regulations. GlobalShop maintained its position as a trusted market leader by avoiding legal penalties and reputational risks.

4. More substantial Ethical Standards: Regular AI audits and bias mitigation efforts enhanced the fairness and inclusivity of GlobalShop's personalization strategies. This ethical approach garnered positive feedback from consumers and advocacy groups alike.

5. Industry Recognition: GlobalShop's governance initiatives earned recognition from industry bodies and media outlets. The company received awards for ethical AI practices and was invited to share its experiences at international conferences.

LESSONS LEARNED

GlobalShop's experience highlights several critical lessons for organizations navigating the tension between personalization and privacy:

1. Transparency is Key to Trust: Providing clear and accessible information about data usage fosters consumer trust. Transparency should be a central pillar of any data governance strategy.

2. Empowering Consumers Builds Loyalty: Offering customers control over their data and personalization preferences enhances their sense of agency and strengthens brand loyalty.

3. Compliance Drives Innovation: Adhering to data protection regulations need not stifle innovation. On the contrary, it can drive the development of creative solutions that align with ethical standards.

4. Privacy-by-Design Ensures Sustainability: Embedding privacy considerations into AI systems from the outset reduces risks and ensures that governance frameworks can adapt to evolving regulations and consumer expectations.

5. Ethical AI Practices are Non-Negotiable. Regular audits and proactive bias mitigation are essential to maintaining fairness and inclusivity in AI-driven personalization. Ethical AI practices protect consumers and enhance brand reputation.

6. Stakeholder Engagement is Crucial: Open dialogues with consumers, regulators, and advocacy groups provide valuable insights that inform governance strategies and demonstrate accountability.

By embracing these lessons, GlobalShop successfully navigated the challenges of balancing personalization with privacy, delivering meaningful customer experiences while upholding ethical and regulatory standards. Its approach is a model for other organizations seeking to leverage AI responsibly in the retail sector.

18.5 MANUFACTURING: INTEGRATING AI IN SUPPLY CHAIN MANAGEMENT

ORGANIZATION OVERVIEW

The manufacturing sector has witnessed a transformative shift in adopting artificial intelligence (AI), particularly in optimizing supply chain management. One notable example is GlobalManufacture Corp, a leading multinational manufacturing firm specializing in consumer electronics and industrial machinery. The company operates across 25 countries and relies on a vast and intricate supply chain network to source raw materials, manage inventory, and distribute finished products to global markets.

GlobalManufacture Corp employs cutting-edge AI technologies to address critical supply chain challenges such as demand forecasting, production planning, and logistics optimization. The firm's proprietary AI platform, SupplyChainAI, integrates data from multiple sources, including supplier databases, transportation systems, and market analytics, to provide real-time insights and predictive analytics. This AI-driven approach has enabled GlobalManufacture Corp to enhance operational efficiency, reduce costs, and improve customer satisfaction. However, integrating AI into such a complex and dynamic environment presented several governance challenges that required careful consideration and strategic action.

GOVERNANCE CHALLENGES

Implementing AI in supply chain management introduced a range of governance challenges for GlobalManufacture Corp, including:

1. **Ensuring Data Accuracy and Consistency:** The effectiveness of AI systems depends heavily on the quality of data. In a global supply chain, data is often collected from diverse sources, such as suppliers, warehouses, and logistics providers, leading to inconsistencies and inaccuracies. Ensuring data accuracy and standardization across the supply chain was a significant challenge.

2. **Managing the Complexity of AI Integration:** GlobalManufacture Corp's supply chain involved multiple stakeholders and processes, each with unique requirements and constraints. Integrating AI systems into this complex ecosystem requires careful coordination to avoid disruptions and ensure seamless operation.

3. **Cybersecurity and Data Privacy Risks:** The interconnected nature of AI systems in supply chain management exposed the organization to cybersecurity threats. Protecting sensitive data, such as supplier contracts and customer information, was critical.

4. **Employee Resistance and Skill Gaps:** The introduction of AI systems was met with resistance from employees unfamiliar with the technology or fearing job displacement. Additionally, there was a skills gap in effectively using and managing AI tools.

5. **Compliance with Global Regulations:** Operating in multiple countries meant adhering to varying regulatory requirements for data usage, trade, and labor. Ensuring compliance while implementing AI systems added to the complexity.

SOLUTIONS IMPLEMENTED

To address these challenges, GlobalManufacture Corp adopted a comprehensive strategy that combined technology, governance, and workforce development:

1. **Centralized Data Governance Framework:** The company established a centralized framework to standardize data collection, storage, and usage practices across its supply chain. This framework included:
    - Data validation protocols to ensure accuracy and consistency.
    - Uniform data formats and standards to enable seamless integration across systems.
    - Regular audits to identify and rectify data discrepancies.
2. **AI Integration Roadmap:** GlobalManufacture Corp developed a phased AI integration roadmap to manage complexity and minimize disruptions. The roadmap prioritized:
    - Pilot projects to test AI systems in specific supply chain segments, such as inventory management and logistics.
    - Gradual scaling of successful pilots to other areas of the supply chain.
    - Continuous monitoring and refinement of AI systems based on feedback and performance metrics.
3. **Robust Cybersecurity Measures:** To mitigate cybersecurity risks, the company implemented advanced security protocols, including:
    - Encryption and access controls to protect sensitive data.
    - AI-powered threat detection systems to identify and respond to potential breaches in real-time.
    - Regular cybersecurity training for employees to foster a culture of vigilance.

4. **Employee Training and Engagement Programs:** Recognizing the importance of workforce readiness, GlobalManufacture Corp launched comprehensive training programs to upskill employees. These programs covered:
    - Fundamentals of AI and its applications in supply chain management.
    - Hands-on training on using AI tools and interpreting analytics.
    - Change management workshops to address resistance and build employee buy-in.
5. **Cross-Departmental Collaboration:** The company established cross-departmental teams comprising representatives from procurement, logistics, IT, and operations. These teams:
    - Facilitated communication and coordination during AI implementation.
    - Shared insights and best practices to enhance system performance.
    - Ensured alignment between AI initiatives and organizational goals.

OUTCOMES

The implementation of these solutions delivered substantial benefits for GlobalManufacture Corp, demonstrating the value of AI in supply chain management:

1. **Improved Supply Chain Efficiency:** SupplyChainAI enabled real-time visibility into supply chain operations, reducing delays and inefficiencies. For instance, predictive analytics improved demand forecasting accuracy by 20%, leading to better inventory management and reduced stockouts.
2. **Reduced Operational Risks:** The centralized data governance framework minimized data errors and inconsistencies, reducing risks associated with faulty decision-making. Enhanced cybersecurity measures protected the company from data breaches and related financial losses.
3. **Enhanced Workforce Productivity:** Employee training programs equipped the workforce with the skills to leverage AI tools effectively. As a result, employees became more confident and efficient in their roles, contributing to overall productivity gains.
4. **Cost Savings:** Optimized logistics and inventory management reduced transportation costs by 15% and inventory holding costs by 10%. These savings improved the company's bottom line and freed up resources for further innovation.
5. **Sustainability Improvements:** AI-driven supply chain optimization reduced waste and improved resource utilization, aligning with the company's sustainability goals. For example, optimized routing algorithms lowered fuel consumption in logistics operations.

6. Strengthened Competitive Advantage: By integrating AI into its supply chain, GlobalManufacture Corp. gained a competitive edge in the market. The company's ability to respond quickly to market changes and customer demands enhanced its reputation as a reliable and innovative manufacturer.

LESSONS LEARNED

GlobalManufacture Corp's experience offers valuable lessons for organizations seeking to integrate AI into supply chain management:

1. Data Quality is Paramount: High-quality data is the foundation of effective AI systems. Organizations must invest in robust data governance practices to ensure accuracy, consistency, and reliability.

2. Phased Implementation Minimizes Disruption: A phased approach to AI integration allows organizations to identify and address challenges early, ensuring a smoother transition and reducing risks.

3. Collaboration Drives Success: Cross-departmental collaboration fosters alignment and innovation, enabling organizations to maximize the value of AI systems.

4. Continuous Learning is Essential: AI technologies and supply chain dynamics constantly evolve. Organizations must prioritize ongoing training and development to stay ahead of the curve.

5. Cybersecurity Cannot Be Overlooked: Protecting sensitive supply chain data is critical to maintaining trust and avoiding costly breaches. Proactive security measures are an integral part of AI governance.

6. Sustainability is a Key Consideration: AI can significantly achieve sustainability goals by improving resource efficiency and reducing waste. Integrating sustainability into AI initiatives enhances their long-term value.

Addressing these lessons, GlobalManufacture Corp. has set a benchmark for AI-driven supply chain management. It demonstrates how innovation and governance can work together to deliver transformative results.

18.6 PUBLIC SECTOR: AI IN PUBLIC SERVICES AND ETHICAL CONSIDERATIONS

ORGANIZATION OVERVIEW

In the public sector, AI has become a transformative tool for enhancing service delivery and addressing societal challenges. A leading example is the National Digital Services Agency (NDSA), a government body responsible for implementing AI initiatives to improve public services. NDSA aims to harness AI to streamline processes, reduce costs, and deliver citizen-centric solutions across various domains, such as healthcare, transportation, and social welfare.

One notable project spearheaded by NDSA is the CitizenConnect AI platform, designed to provide personalized assistance to citizens seeking government services. By leveraging natural language processing and machine learning, the platform simplifies access to information and resources, reducing wait times and improving user experiences. While integrating AI into public services offers significant benefits, it also presents ethical challenges and invites public scrutiny, necessitating robust governance mechanisms.

GOVERNANCE CHALLENGES

The deployment of AI in public services involves navigating a complex landscape of ethical considerations and public accountability. NDSA faced several key challenges:

1. **Ethical Concerns:**
    - AI systems deployed in public services must uphold fairness, equity, and transparency principles. The risk of algorithm bias, particularly in areas like welfare allocation or law enforcement, raises concerns about potential discrimination and unequal treatment.
    - Decisions made by AI systems could have far-reaching implications for citizens' lives, making it imperative to ensure accuracy and accountability.
2. **Public Scrutiny and Trust:**
    - Citizens were wary of how their data was used and whether AI systems were making decisions in their best interests. Missteps could erode trust in government institutions and lead to public backlash.
3. **Data Privacy and Security:**
    - The collection and processing of sensitive citizen data raised concerns about privacy violations and potential misuse or unauthorized access.
4. **Regulatory and Legal Compliance:**
    - NDSA had to navigate a complex web of legal frameworks governing data usage, algorithmic transparency, and public accountability, often dealing with overlapping or contradictory requirements.
5. **Lack of Public Awareness:**
    - Many citizens did not understand how AI works and its potential benefits, leading to resistance or skepticism toward its deployment in public services.

To address these challenges, NDSA implemented a comprehensive governance strategy that emphasized ethical principles, transparency, and stakeholder engagement:

1. **AI Ethics Committee:**
   - NDSA established an independent AI Ethics Committee comprising experts from diverse fields, including technology, law, ethics, and social sciences. The committee's mandate was to:
     - Review AI projects to ensure alignment with ethical standards.
     - Evaluate potential biases and recommend measures to mitigate them.
     - Provide ongoing oversight and accountability.
2. **Public Consultation Processes:**
   - Recognizing the importance of public trust, NDSA launched consultation initiatives to involve citizens in developing and deploying AI systems. These processes included:
     - Town hall meetings and online surveys to gather public feedback.
     - Citizen advisory panels to provide insights into community needs and concerns.
3. **Transparency Measures:**
   - To address concerns about the "black-box" nature of AI, NDSA implemented measures to enhance transparency, such as:
     - Publishing detailed reports on AI system design, decision-making processes, and data usage policies.
     - Developing explainable AI models to provide clear and accessible explanations of algorithmic decisions.
4. **Data Privacy and Security Protocols:**
   - NDSA adopted robust data governance frameworks to safeguard citizen data. Key measures included:
     - Encrypting sensitive data and restricting access to authorized personnel.
     - Implementing strict data anonymization techniques to prevent the identification of individuals.

5. **Public Awareness Campaigns:**

   - To build public understanding and acceptance of AI, NDSA launched educational campaigns that:

     - Highlighted the benefits of AI in public services, such as improved efficiency and accessibility.
     - Addressed common misconceptions and emphasized the agency's commitment to ethical practices.

OUTCOMES

The implementation of these solutions delivered significant benefits for NDSA and the communities it served:

1. **Enhanced Public Trust:**

   - Establishing an AI Ethics Committee and transparent practices reassured citizens that ethical considerations were prioritized. Post-implementation surveys showed a 30% increase in public trust toward AI initiatives.

2. **Improved Service Delivery:**

   - The CitizenConnect AI platform reduced response times for service requests by 40%, making government services more accessible and efficient for citizens.

3. **Greater Accountability:**

   - Regular audits and public consultations ensured that AI systems remained accountable to societal values and legal requirements. This proactive approach minimized the risk of ethical lapses and regulatory violations.

4. **Stronger Data Protection:**

   - Robust data governance measures reduced data breaches and incidents of unauthorized access, reinforcing public confidence in the agency's ability to protect sensitive information.

5. **Positive Public Perception of AI:**

   - Educational campaigns increased public awareness of AI's potential benefits, with 65% of respondents expressing support for its continued use in public services.

LESSONS LEARNED

NDSA's experience highlights several critical lessons for integrating AI into public services:

1. Transparency Builds Trust:
   - Open communication about AI systems, their purposes, and their limitations fosters public trust and reduces skepticism. Agencies must prioritize transparency at every stage of AI implementation.
2. Public Engagement is Essential:
   - Involving citizens in decision-making ensures that AI initiatives align with community values and address societal needs. Public consultation fosters a sense of ownership and accountability.
3. Ethics Must Be a Core Priority:
   - Establishing independent oversight mechanisms, such as ethics committees, ensures that AI systems adhere to fairness, equity, and accountability principles.
4. Continuous Monitoring is Crucial:
   - AI systems must be regularly evaluated to identify and address emerging ethical, legal, or operational challenges. Proactive monitoring minimizes risks and enhances system reliability.
5. Education Drives Acceptance:
   - Public awareness campaigns play a vital role in demystifying AI and building acceptance. Educating citizens about the benefits and safeguards of AI systems ensures informed and constructive dialogue.
6. Adaptability is Key:
   - As technology and societal expectations evolve, governance frameworks must be flexible enough to adapt to new challenges and opportunities. For long-term success, policies and practices must be regularly updated.

By embracing these lessons, NDSA has set a benchmark for responsible AI deployment in the public sector. It has demonstrated how ethical governance and public engagement can enhance the societal impact of AI initiatives.

PART VI

CASE STUDIES AND FUTURE INSIGHTS

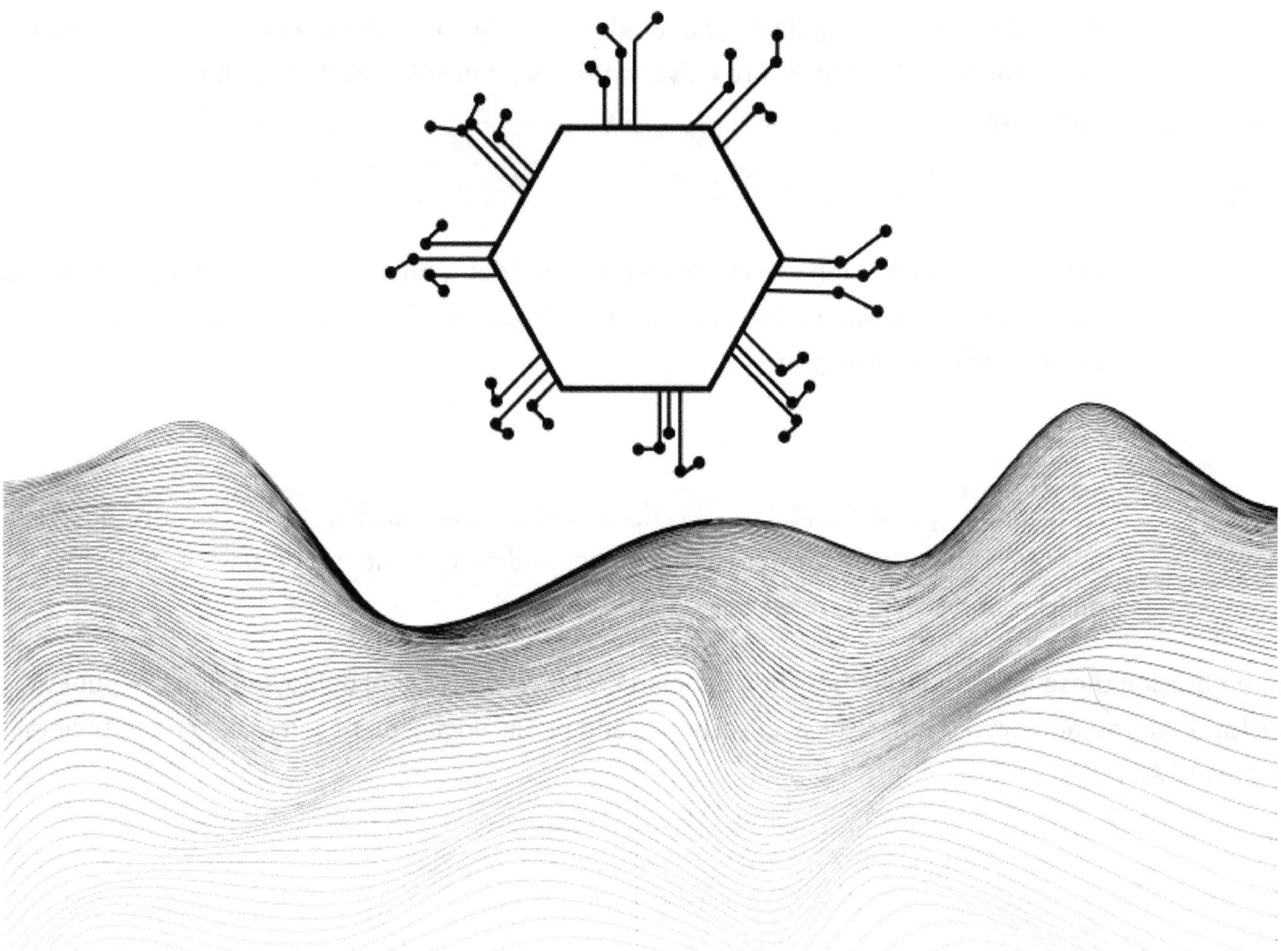

CHAPTER 19: GLOBAL PERSPECTIVES ON AI GOVERNANCE

19.1 INTRODUCTION TO GLOBAL AI GOVERNANCE

IMPORTANCE OF GLOBAL PERSPECTIVES

The rapid advancement of artificial intelligence (AI) technologies has profound implications for societies worldwide, making global AI governance increasingly urgent. AI systems transcend national borders, influencing global markets, international security, and human rights. Effective AI governance, therefore, requires international cooperation to ensure these technologies are developed and deployed responsibly. A global perspective on AI governance fosters collaboration between nations, reducing the risks of fragmented regulations and fostering interoperability across jurisdictions. Countries can address challenges such as bias, privacy breaches, and security vulnerabilities by working together while promoting innovation and equitable access to AI advancements.

Moreover, global AI governance ensures that all nations—regardless of their economic or technological status—have a voice in shaping the future of AI. International cooperation can help prevent a few powerful entities from monopolizing AI technologies, ensuring a fair distribution of benefits. This inclusivity also contributes to building trust and fostering accountability among stakeholders, which are essential for the long-term success of AI governance efforts.

DIVERSE APPROACHES

AI governance strategies vary widely globally due to cultural, economic, and political differences. Each nation's approach reflects its unique priorities, challenges, and values. For example, Western countries often emphasize individual rights, privacy, and ethical AI development. In contrast, nations like China prioritize using AI for economic growth, social governance, and state security. Understanding these diverse approaches is essential for creating frameworks that respect regional differences while promoting shared goals.

Cultural factors play a significant role in shaping AI governance. In some regions, collective societal benefits may take precedence over individual freedoms, leading to policies prioritizing large-scale AI technology implementation for public welfare. On the other hand, areas that value individualism may focus on safeguarding personal data and ensuring transparency.

Economic factors also influence governance strategies. Wealthier nations with advanced technological capabilities may focus on innovation and market leadership. In contrast, developing countries may prioritize using AI to address local challenges, such as improving healthcare, education, and infrastructure. Political systems further shape governance approaches, with democratic nations emphasizing stakeholder engagement and authoritarian regimes favoring top-down regulations.

Recognizing and respecting these diverse approaches is crucial for fostering global cooperation. A one-size-fits-all model is unlikely to succeed in a world marked by such variation. Instead, global AI governance should establish flexible frameworks that accommodate regional differences while adhering to universal fairness, accountability, and transparency principles.

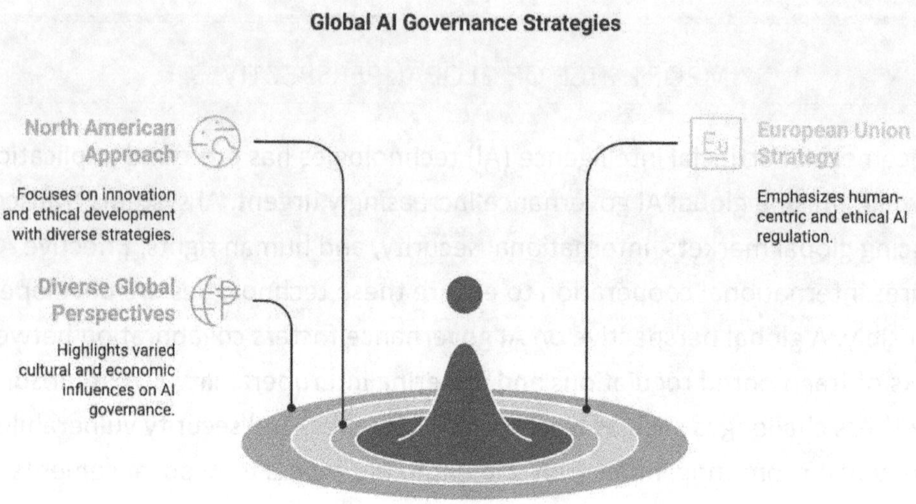

19.2 AI GOVERNANCE IN NORTH AMERICA

North America is a leader in developing and governance artificial intelligence (AI), with the United States and Canada taking unique approaches to managing its impact. The region's strong technological ecosystem, vibrant private sector, and proactive policymaking make it a critical player in the global AI landscape. While the United States and Canada share many goals, their strategies vary, reflecting their cultural, political, and economic differences.

UNITED STATES: OVERVIEW OF FEDERAL AND STATE-LEVEL AI POLICIES

The United States, a global leader in AI innovation, has adopted a decentralized approach to AI governance. Federal initiatives provide a broad framework, while state-level policies often add specific regulations tailored to local needs. This fragmented yet dynamic structure reflects the country's broader governance philosophy of balancing federal oversight with state autonomy.

At the federal level, AI governance has been a strategic focus for several years. The National Artificial Intelligence Initiative Act of 2020 is a cornerstone policy establishing a comprehensive framework to accelerate AI research and development (R&D). It created the National AI Initiative Office to coordinate efforts across federal agencies, including the National Institute of Standards and Technology (NIST), the Department of Defense (DoD), and the Department of Energy (DOE). The Act emphasizes key priorities such as AI safety, workforce development, and global competitiveness.

The National Institute of Standards and Technology (NIST) has played a pivotal role by releasing the AI Risk Management Framework (RMF) to guide organizations in identifying, assessing, and mitigating risks associated with AI systems. This voluntary framework emphasizes transparency, fairness, and accountability, offering a flexible tool that aligns with the U.S.'s market-driven ethos.

State-level initiatives also contribute significantly to the AI governance landscape. For instance, California, home to Silicon Valley, has implemented progressive regulations, including the California Consumer Privacy Act (CCPA). Although not exclusively focused on AI, the CCPA addresses critical concerns such as data privacy, a foundational element of AI ethics. Similarly, Illinois has enacted laws governing AI use in employment decisions, requiring organizations to disclose and audit their algorithms to prevent bias.

The United States has also prioritized AI in defense and national security. The Department of Defense's Joint Artificial Intelligence Center (JAIC) focuses on using AI to enhance military capabilities while adhering to ethical principles. Initiatives like the Blueprint for an AI Bill of Rights highlight federal efforts to establish moral guidelines for AI systems that affect citizens' daily lives.

ROLE OF PRIVATE SECTOR INITIATIVES AND ETHICAL GUIDELINES

The U.S. private sector, driven by industry giants such as Google, Microsoft, and OpenAI, significantly shapes AI governance. These companies invest heavily in AI research and often lead the development of ethical frameworks and best practices. For example:

- Google's AI Principles commit to using AI for socially beneficial purposes and avoiding applications that cause harm.
- Microsoft's Responsible AI Standard outlines fairness, reliability, inclusivity, and transparency guidelines in AI systems.
- OpenAI emphasizes safety and alignment with human values when developing advanced AI technologies like GPT models.

Industry consortia, such as the Partnership on AI, bring together stakeholders from academia, civil society, and business to promote ethical AI practices. These organizations focus on issues such as algorithmic bias, transparency, and accountability, complementing government initiatives by providing practical, industry-driven solutions.

Ethical guidelines developed by the private sector often influence public policy, creating a feedback loop between regulators and innovators. However, this close relationship also raises concerns about regulatory capture, where corporate interests may overshadow public welfare. Balancing innovation with accountability remains a key challenge.

CANADA: EMPHASIS ON ETHICAL AI DEVELOPMENT AND THE PAN-CANADIAN AI STRATEGY

Canada has emerged as a global leader in ethical AI development, leveraging its inclusivity and social responsibility reputation. The Pan-Canadian Artificial Intelligence Strategy guides the country's approach, which was launched in 2017 as one of the world's first national AI strategies. With significant funding from the federal government, the strategy focuses on four pillars:

1. Advancing AI research and talent development.
2. Supporting commercialization and innovation.
3. Promoting policy research on AI ethics, privacy, and governance.
4. Enhancing Canada's international leadership in AI.

The Canadian Institute for Advanced Research (CIFAR) manages the strategy and has fostered collaboration between academia, industry, and government. CIFAR's AI & Society Program explicitly addresses AI's ethical and societal implications, providing a platform for interdisciplinary dialogue.

Ethics are central to Canada's AI governance framework. The Directive on Automated Decision-Making, introduced in 2019, requires federal agencies to assess and mitigate risks associated with AI systems used in public services. This directive prioritizes transparency, accountability, and fairness and mandates that all decisions made by AI systems be explainable and auditable.

Canada also emphasizes the integration of Indigenous perspectives in AI governance, recognizing the need for inclusive policies that respect diverse worldviews. Initiatives such as the First Nations Principles of OCAP® (Ownership, Control, Access, and Possession) have informed guidelines for data governance, ensuring that AI systems do not exploit or marginalize Indigenous communities.

In the private sector, Canadian companies like Element AI (now acquired by ServiceNow) have focused on building AI systems that align with ethical principles. Collaboration between businesses, academia, and non-profits has strengthened Canada's reputation as a hub for responsible AI development.

CHALLENGES AND OPPORTUNITIES

While North America leads in AI governance, the United States and Canada face challenges balancing innovation with regulation and addressing public concerns about privacy and bias.

Balancing Innovation with Regulation

One of the primary challenges in North America is creating policies that foster innovation without stifling progress. Overregulation could hinder the agility of AI startups and deter investment, while underregulation risks the proliferation of harmful or biased AI systems. Striking this balance requires nuanced policies that adapt to the fast-evolving nature of AI technologies.

The decentralized governance structure in the U.S. poses coordination challenges. State-level regulations often differ significantly, creating compliance burdens for companies operating across multiple jurisdictions. For example, privacy laws like California's CCPA and Virginia's Consumer Data Protection Act (CDPA) differ in scope and enforcement, complicating the regulatory landscape.

In Canada, resource constraints can limit the implementation of comprehensive governance measures. Smaller provinces may lack the expertise and funding needed to enforce AI regulations effectively, leading to uneven adoption of national standards.

Addressing Public Concerns About Privacy and Bias

AI systems are increasingly integrated into everyday life, raising public concerns about privacy and bias. In the United States, high-profile incidents of algorithmic discrimination—such as biased hiring tools or racially skewed facial recognition software—have fueled demands for greater accountability. Advocacy groups have called for stricter regulations to ensure that AI systems do not perpetuate systemic inequalities.

Canada faces similar concerns, particularly regarding data privacy. The rise of AI-powered surveillance tools has sparked debates about their impact on civil liberties. The federal government has responded with legislative proposals, such as Bill C-27, which includes provisions for the Artificial Intelligence and Data Act (AIDA). This proposed law aims to regulate high-impact AI systems, protect Canadians from harm, and promote innovation.

Public education is another critical area for improvement. Both countries must invest in initiatives that empower citizens to understand AI's risks and benefits, fostering informed participation in governance discussions.

Opportunities

Despite these challenges, North America has significant opportunities to shape the global AI governance agenda. Collaboration between the U.S. and Canada could lead to harmonized standards that serve as a model for other regions. For instance, joint efforts to address cross-border data flows and cybersecurity risks could strengthen trust in AI systems worldwide.

The region's diverse ecosystem of researchers, policymakers, and industry leaders provides a fertile ground for innovation. By leveraging their strengths, the United States and Canada can create governance frameworks that balance ethical considerations with economic competitiveness, setting a global benchmark for responsible AI development.

CONCLUSION

AI governance in North America reflects the region's diversity and leadership in innovation. The United States emphasizes market-driven approaches and state autonomy, complemented by robust private-sector initiatives. Canada, focusing on ethical AI development and inclusivity, offers a model for balancing innovation with social responsibility. Together, these countries face shared challenges in regulating AI while addressing public concerns about privacy and bias. However, their collaborative potential and commitment to responsible AI development position North America as a critical player in shaping the future of global AI governance. By navigating these complexities thoughtfully, the region can set a precedent for ethical and effective AI policies worldwide.

19.3 AI GOVERNANCE IN EUROPE

Europe has emerged as a global artificial intelligence (AI) governance leader, championing a human-centric and ethical approach. The European Union (EU) and the United Kingdom (UK) have made significant strides in shaping regulatory frameworks that balance innovation with responsibility. However, Europe also faces unique challenges, including harmonizing regulations across diverse legal systems and ensuring competitiveness in the global AI race.

EUROPEAN UNION: THE AI ACT AND ITS IMPLICATIONS FOR MEMBER STATES

The European Union has taken a proactive and ambitious approach to regulating AI, reflecting its commitment to ethical, human-centric development. The cornerstone of the EU's efforts is the **Artificial Intelligence Act (AI Act)**, a landmark legislative proposal introduced in 2021. This regulation establishes a unified framework for AI across all 27 member states, ensuring safety, accountability, and trust in AI systems while fostering innovation.

OVERVIEW OF THE AI ACT

The AI Act adopts a **risk-based approach** to AI governance, categorizing AI systems into four risk levels:

1. **Unacceptable Risk:** AI systems deemed to pose significant threats to fundamental rights or public safety, such as social scoring by governments, are prohibited.

2. **High Risk:** Systems that significantly impact people's lives, such as those used in healthcare, law enforcement, or recruitment, are subject to stringent requirements. Developers must demonstrate compliance with transparency, accountability, and fairness standards.

3. **Limited Risk:** AI applications like chatbots must adhere to transparency obligations, such as informing users they are interacting with AI.

4. **Minimal or No Risk:** Most AI systems, including entertainment applications or spam filters, face no regulatory burden.

The AI Act significantly emphasizes **human oversight, transparency, and accountability**. To build trust among users, developers of high-risk systems must conduct risk assessments, implement robust data governance practices, and ensure explainability.

IMPLICATIONS FOR MEMBER STATES

The AI Act aims to **harmonize the regulatory environment** across the EU, reducing fragmentation and ensuring a level playing field for AI innovators. Member states must establish national supervisory authorities to enforce the Act, which a centralized European Artificial Intelligence Board supports for oversight and coordination.

The Act reinforces Germany's and France's leadership in AI governance by aligning national policies with EU-wide standards. Smaller member states, however, face challenges in implementing the Act due to resource constraints and limited technical expertise. The EU has addressed this disparity through funding initiatives, such as the Digital Europe Programme, which supports AI capacity-building and infrastructure development.

FOCUS ON HUMAN-CENTRIC AND TRUSTWORTHY AI

Central to the EU's AI governance is its human-centric and trustworthy AI emphasis. This approach is rooted in European values, prioritizing protecting fundamental rights and ethical principles over purely economic considerations. The following principles define trustworthy AI:

1. Fairness and Non-Discrimination: Ensuring AI systems do not perpetuate bias or inequality.
2. Transparency and Explainability: Requiring AI decisions to be understandable and auditable.
3. Accountability: Holding developers and users responsible for the outcomes of AI systems.
4. Privacy and Data Protection: Aligning AI governance with the General Data Protection Regulation (GDPR), a global benchmark for data privacy.

This focus on ethics has positioned the EU as a thought leader in AI governance, influencing global discussions on responsible AI development.

UNITED KINGDOM: POST-BREXIT AI STRATEGY AND REGULATORY FRAMEWORK

Following Brexit, the UK has charted its path in AI governance, leveraging its regulatory autonomy to craft a distinctive approach. The country has prioritized flexibility, innovation, and global competitiveness, aiming to become a leader in AI development while maintaining high ethical standards.

POST-BREXIT AI STRATEGY

The UK's National AI Strategy, launched in 2021, outlines a ten-year vision for AI development and governance. The strategy is built around three core pillars:

1. Investing in R&D and Talent Development: The UK government has committed significant funding to AI research, including £46 million for creating Turing AI Fellowships and establishing AI-focused PhD programs.

2. **Promoting Ethical AI:** The UK has established the **Centre for Data Ethics and Innovation (CDEI)** to guide AI ethics, fairness, and accountability. The CDEI works closely with industry and civil society to develop best practices.
3. **Shaping Global AI Governance:** The UK recognizes its role as a global leader and seeks to influence international standards for AI governance through active participation in organizations like the G7 and the OECD.

The UK has also introduced the **Artificial Intelligence Rulebook**, which emphasizes outcome-based regulation. Unlike the EU's prescriptive AI Act, the UK's approach is more flexible, allowing regulators to tailor requirements based on specific industries and use cases.

REGULATORY FRAMEWORK

The UK has adopted a **pro-innovation approach** to AI governance, focusing on enabling experimentation and minimizing regulatory burdens. The **Regulatory Horizons Council** has been tasked with identifying and addressing barriers to innovation, while **sandbox initiatives** allow companies to test AI technologies in controlled environments.

However, the UK remains committed to high ethical standards. The **Alan Turing Institute**, the country's leading AI research center, is pivotal in advancing explainable and responsible AI. Additionally, the UK's regulatory framework aligns closely with GDPR, ensuring continuity in data privacy standards.

Post-Brexit, the UK must maintain regulatory alignment with the EU to facilitate cross-border trade and data flows. To address this, the UK has prioritized bilateral agreements and partnerships, including collaborating with the EU on scientific research through the Horizon Europe program.

CHALLENGES AND OPPORTUNITIES

Europe's leadership in AI governance is not without its challenges. The region must navigate the complexities of harmonizing regulations, promoting innovation, and ensuring global competitiveness while upholding its ethical standards.

HARMONIZING REGULATIONS ACROSS DIVERSE LEGAL SYSTEMS

One of Europe's most significant challenges for AI governance is achieving regulatory harmonization across its diverse legal systems. The EU's 27 member states have distinct legal traditions, political priorities, and levels of technological maturity. While the AI Act aims to create a unified framework, its implementation will require extensive coordination and collaboration.

Smaller member states may struggle to meet the Act's requirements due to resource constraints, potentially creating disparities in enforcement. Additionally, differences in national interpretations of the Act could lead to inconsistent application, undermining the goal of harmonization.

The UK faces challenges aligning its regulatory framework with the EU's. Divergence in AI policies could create trade barriers, complicating cross-border collaboration and market access. Maintaining interoperability between UK and EU regulations will be crucial for fostering innovation and ensuring the smooth flow of AI technologies.

PROMOTING INNOVATION WHILE ENSURING ETHICAL STANDARDS

Balancing innovation with ethical considerations is a delicate task. Strict regulations, while necessary to protect fundamental rights, can sometimes hinder the agility of AI startups and deter investment. Europe must find ways to foster a vibrant AI ecosystem without compromising its commitment to ethics and trustworthiness.

The EU's risk-based approach under the AI Act provides a potential solution by imposing regulatory burdens only on high-risk applications. However, ensuring compliance with these requirements could be costly and time-consuming for smaller companies, potentially stifling innovation.

The UK's pro-innovation approach offers an alternative model, but it risks being perceived as less stringent on ethics than the EU. Striking the right balance between flexibility and accountability will be critical for the UK to maintain its global credibility.

19.4 AI GOVERNANCE IN ASIA

Asia is a powerhouse in artificial intelligence (AI) innovation and governance, with leading countries like China, Japan, and South Korea shaping distinct approaches to AI development. The region's diverse political systems, cultural contexts, and economic ambitions have resulted in varied strategies reflecting unique national priorities. While Asia's rapid advancements in AI offer significant opportunities, they also raise ethical, regulatory, and collaborative challenges.

CHINA: GOVERNMENT-LED AI DEVELOPMENT PLANS AND REGULATORY MEASURES

China has emerged as a global leader in AI, driven by an ambitious, government-led strategy to achieve global AI supremacy by 2030. Its approach is characterized by significant state investment, centralized planning, and a focus on leveraging AI for economic growth and social governance.

GOVERNMENT-LED AI DEVELOPMENT PLANS

In 2017, China launched its **Next Generation Artificial Intelligence Development Plan**, outlining a comprehensive roadmap for AI leadership. The plan has three core phases:

1. **By 2020**: Establish a foundation for AI development, including robust R&D infrastructure and basic regulatory frameworks.

2. **By 2025**, significant breakthroughs in AI technology will be achieved, and AI will be integrated into key industries such as healthcare, education, and transportation.

3. **By 2030**: Become the global leader in AI innovation, surpassing the United States and other competitors.

The Chinese government has invested heavily in AI R&D, establishing innovation hubs and partnering with companies like Baidu, Alibaba, and Tencent. These companies play a dual role: driving technological advancements and aligning their efforts with state goals. Additionally, China has invested in talent development by funding universities' AI education and research programs.

REGULATORY MEASURES

China has implemented a series of regulations to ensure AI's ethical and safe use. In 2021, it introduced guidelines on **algorithmic accountability**, requiring companies to ensure transparency and fairness in AI systems. The **Regulations on Algorithmic Recommendations**, enacted in 2022, mandate that e-commerce and social media algorithms avoid amplifying harmful content or manipulating public opinion.

China also prioritizes AI applications in surveillance and social governance. Technologies like facial recognition and predictive policing are widely deployed, raising privacy and human rights concerns. These tools are integrated into systems like the **Social Credit System**, which uses AI to monitor and influence citizen behavior.

FOCUS ON ECONOMIC GROWTH AND SOCIAL GOVERNANCE

China's AI strategy is deeply intertwined with its broader economic goals. AI technologies are critical drivers of industrial modernization, with applications in manufacturing, agriculture, and urban planning. For example, AI-powered smart cities like Hangzhou utilize real-time data to optimize traffic, energy use, and public services.

Simultaneously, China uses AI as a tool for social governance, enhancing the state's capacity to monitor and manage society. While this approach has led to efficiency gains, it has also sparked debates about authoritarianism and surveillance.

JAPAN: HUMAN-CENTRIC AI PRINCIPLES AND COLLABORATION WITH INDUSTRY

Japan's AI governance framework is guided by a commitment to **human-centric principles**, emphasizing AI's ethical and societal impacts. Unlike China's top-down approach, Japan adopts a collaborative model involving the government, industry, and academia.

HUMAN-CENTRIC AI PRINCIPLES

Japan's approach to AI governance is encapsulated in its **Social Principles of Human-Centric AI**, released in 2019. These principles emphasize:

1. **Human Dignity and Fairness**: AI systems must respect human rights and avoid perpetuating biases.

2. Transparency and Accountability: Decisions made by AI systems should be explainable and auditable.

3. Sustainability: AI should contribute to solving global challenges, such as climate change and aging populations.

These principles align with Japan's cultural emphasis on social harmony and ethical responsibility, distinguishing its approach from more commercially driven models.

COLLABORATION WITH INDUSTRY

Japan's government has partnered closely with industry leaders to advance AI innovation. The Artificial Intelligence Technology Strategy, launched in 2017, outlines priority areas for AI deployment, including healthcare, mobility, and robotics. Initiatives like the Society 5.0 framework aim to integrate AI into every aspect of society, creating a "super-smart" society that balances technological advancements with human welfare.

Industry-academia collaboration is another hallmark of Japan's strategy. Research institutions like the RIKEN Center for Advanced Intelligence Project collaborate with companies like Sony and Toyota to develop AI technologies that comply with ethical guidelines.

AI FOR AN AGING POPULATION

Japan's demographic challenges, particularly its aging population, have shaped its AI priorities. AI-driven healthcare solutions, such as robotic caregivers and telemedicine platforms, are designed to address labor shortages and improve elderly care. This focus on social utility reinforces Japan's commitment to using AI for the public good.

OUTH KOREA: NATIONAL AI STRATEGIES EMPHASIZING INNOVATION AND ETHICS

South Korea has emerged as a significant player in AI, leveraging its advanced technological infrastructure and strong government support. The country's approach combines a focus on innovation with a commitment to ethical AI development.

NATIONAL AI STRATEGIES

South Korea's National AI Strategy, unveiled in 2019, outlines a vision to become one of the top three AI leaders globally by 2030. The strategy focuses on:

1. AI R&D Investment: The government has allocated substantial funding to AI research, including establishing the AI Graduate School Support Program to nurture talent.

2. **Digital Infrastructure**: South Korea's advanced 5G network provides a robust foundation for deploying AI applications in smart cities, autonomous vehicles, and digital healthcare.

3. **Global Collaboration**: South Korea recognizes the importance of international partnerships and actively collaborates with organizations such as the OECD and UNESCO on AI governance.

ETHICAL AI DEVELOPMENT

In 2020, South Korea introduced its **Ethical Guidelines for AI**, emphasizing fairness, transparency, and inclusivity. These guidelines serve as a reference for the public and private sectors and ensure that AI technologies align with societal values.

South Korea has also taken steps to regulate specific applications of AI. For example, the government has issued guidelines for using AI in hiring processes and requires companies to audit algorithms for potential bias.

AI AS AN ECONOMIC DRIVER

AI is central to South Korea's economic strategy, focusing on fostering innovation in key industries such as manufacturing, finance, and entertainment. AI-powered K-pop content and virtual influencers demonstrate the country's creative application of AI in cultural domains.

CHALLENGES AND OPPORTUNITIES

While Asia's AI leadership is impressive, the region faces challenges and opportunities in balancing rapid development with ethical considerations and navigating international collaborations.

BALANCING RAPID DEVELOPMENT WITH ETHICAL CONSIDERATIONS

Asia's rapid AI development often outpaces regulatory frameworks, raising concerns about ethical lapses. In China, AI's widespread surveillance use has sparked global debates about privacy and human rights. Japan and South Korea, despite their moral commitments, face challenges in ensuring that industry practices align with stated principles.

Enforceable regulations that do not stifle innovation remain critical. Striking this balance requires robust stakeholder engagement, precise accountability mechanisms, and continuous updates to governance frameworks.

NAVIGATING INTERNATIONAL COLLABORATIONS AND COMPETITION

Asia's leading AI nations must navigate the complexities of international collaborations and geopolitical competition. China's dominance in AI has prompted concerns among Western countries, complicating global efforts to establish unified AI governance standards. Japan and South Korea, as allies of the United States, face pressure to align their policies with Western norms while maintaining autonomy.

Collaborative initiatives, such as the Global Partnership on AI (GPAI), offer Asian countries opportunities to contribute to global governance discussions. However, achieving consensus on key issues, such as data sharing and algorithmic accountability, remains challenging.

OPPORTUNITIES FOR LEADERSHIP

Despite these challenges, Asia is well-positioned to lead in AI governance. The region's investment in AI R&D and its focus on societal applications provide a strong foundation for responsible innovation. By leveraging their unique strengths, countries like China, Japan, and South Korea can shape global AI norms and drive advancements that benefit humanity.

19.5 AI GOVERNANCE IN AFRICA AND LATIN AMERICA

The global momentum surrounding artificial intelligence (AI) governance has also made its way into the Global South, with Africa and Latin America increasingly recognizing the potential of AI to address regional challenges and drive sustainable development. While these regions are still in the early stages of implementing comprehensive AI strategies, countries like Kenya, Nigeria, Brazil, and Mexico are leading the way in crafting policies that reflect their unique socio-economic contexts. Despite resources, infrastructure, and capacity-building challenges, the commitment to inclusive and regionally relevant AI governance presents significant opportunities for growth and innovation.

AFRICA: EMERGING AI POLICIES AND INITIATIVES

Africa's approach to AI governance is shaped by its pressing development needs and the desire to use technology for societal transformation. While formal AI policies are still emerging, countries like Kenya and Nigeria are taking proactive steps to integrate AI into their broader development agendas.

KENYA: A LEADER IN AI FOR DEVELOPMENT

Kenya has emerged as a regional leader in technology adoption, earning its reputation as the "Silicon Savannah." Its government has recognized AI's potential to address agriculture, healthcare, and education challenges. In 2019, Kenya launched its Digital Economy Blueprint, which includes AI as a key component of its strategy for economic transformation.

AI-driven solutions are being deployed to tackle local issues. For example, machine learning models provide real-time insights into crop diseases and weather patterns. AI-powered platforms like Afya Rekod enable data-driven patient care and remote consultations, especially in underserved areas. These initiatives highlight Kenya's commitment to using AI as a tool for development.

IGERIA: BUILDING AN AI ECOSYSTEM

Nigeria, Africa's largest economy, has also embraced AI as a driver of innovation. The country has seen significant growth in AI-related startups, with companies like Data Science Nigeria and the AI-focused robotics company Arone pushing the boundaries of what is possible. Nigeria's government has recognized the need for policy frameworks and is working toward creating a national AI strategy.

One of Nigeria's notable AI initiatives is its focus on financial inclusion. AI technologies are being used to expand access to banking services in rural areas, enabling millions of unbanked citizens to participate in the formal economy. Additionally, AI-powered fraud detection systems are helping to enhance the security and reliability of financial transactions.

FOCUS ON AI FOR DEVELOPMENT

Across Africa, AI governance is closely tied to the continent's development goals, as outlined in the **African Union's Agenda 2063**. AI is seen as a critical enabler for eradicating poverty, improving healthcare, and providing access to quality education. Countries are leveraging AI to address local challenges, such as using natural language processing (NLP) to create tools for indigenous language translation, thereby improving access to digital content for non-English speakers.

However, the lack of formalized AI policies across much of Africa remains challenging. While countries like Kenya and Nigeria are making strides, many others lack the resources and expertise to implement AI governance frameworks. Regional initiatives like the **Smart Africa Alliance** are working to bridge these gaps by fostering collaboration and knowledge sharing among member states.

LATIN AMERICA: AI STRATEGIES IN BRAZIL AND MEXICO

Latin America has also embraced AI as a driver of socio-economic development. Countries like Brazil and Mexico lead the region in crafting strategies prioritizing inclusivity and regional cooperation.

BRAZIL: A FOCUS ON ETHICS AND INNOVATION

Brazil is one of the most active Latin American countries in AI governance. In 2021, the Brazilian government published its **National Artificial Intelligence Strategy (Estratégia Brasileira de Inteligência Artificial - EBIA)**, which outlines key priorities for AI development, including:

1. **Promoting R&D**: Brazil has invested in AI research, with initiatives such as creating AI research centers in partnership with academic institutions and private companies.

2. **Strengthening Ethics and Regulation**: The EBIA emphasizes the importance of ethical AI development, ensuring transparency, accountability, and the protection of human rights.

3. **Fostering International Cooperation**: Brazil actively collaborates with global organizations such as the OECD to align its AI governance with international standards.

Brazil's AI strategy also focuses on practical applications that address the country's challenges. For example, AI is being used to improve public safety through predictive policing systems, and in healthcare, machine learning models are helping to optimize resource allocation in underserved regions.

MEXICO: DRIVING INCLUSIVE AI DEVELOPMENT

Mexico has taken a proactive approach to AI governance, focusing on inclusivity and regional cooperation. The country was one of the first in the region to develop a national AI strategy, which emphasizes the use of AI for the public good. Key pillars of Mexico's plan include:

1. AI for Social Inclusion: Initiatives aimed at reducing inequality through AI-powered education and healthcare solutions.

2. Strengthening Local Ecosystems: The government fosters collaboration between startups, universities, and public institutions to build a robust AI ecosystem.

3. Transparency and Accountability: Mexico has prioritized the creation of regulatory frameworks that ensure AI systems are transparent and do not perpetuate discrimination.

One notable example of Mexico's AI efforts is its use in disaster management. Given the country's earthquake vulnerability, AI systems are being developed to enhance early warning systems and improve response coordination.

REGIONAL COOPERATION IN LATIN AMERICA

Latin American countries recognize the importance of regional cooperation in advancing AI governance. Organizations like the Inter-American Development Bank (IDB) support countries in developing AI policies and promoting knowledge sharing. For instance, the IDB's AI for Good initiative provides funding and expertise to help countries leverage AI for sustainable development.

CHALLENGES AND OPPORTUNITIES

Africa and Latin America face common challenges and opportunities in pursuing effective AI governance.

CHALLENGES: RESOURCE CONSTRAINTS AND CAPACITY BUILDING

One of the most significant challenges in both regions is the lack of resources and infrastructure needed to support AI development and governance. Many countries face issues such as limited access to high-performance computing, inadequate funding for research, and a shortage of skilled AI professionals. These resource constraints can hinder AI policy implementation and slow innovation.

Capacity building is another critical challenge. Ensuring that governments, businesses, and civil society have the knowledge and expertise to manage AI systems is essential for effective governance. In Africa, initiatives like the **AI4D Africa Program** aim to address this gap by providing training and resources to policymakers and technologists. Similarly, Latin America has seen efforts to expand AI education, but more investment is needed to build a pipeline of AI talent.

OPPORTUNITIES: LEVERAGING AI FOR SUSTAINABLE DEVELOPMENT

Despite these challenges, AI presents immense opportunities for sustainable development in both regions. In Africa, AI can be a game-changer for agriculture, enabling precision farming and improving food security. In healthcare, AI-powered diagnostic tools can help address the shortage of medical professionals, particularly in rural areas.

In Latin America, AI can improve governance and public services. Predictive analytics can enhance urban planning, while AI-driven platforms can increase transparency in government operations. Additionally, the region's strong tradition of regional cooperation provides a unique opportunity to align AI policies and share resources.

Both regions also have the opportunity to shape the global AI agenda by advocating for frameworks that prioritize inclusivity and sustainability. By focusing on AI applications that address their unique challenges, Africa and Latin America can position themselves as leaders in responsible AI development.

19.6 INTERNATIONAL COLLABORATION AND FUTURE DIRECTIONS

Artificial Intelligence (AI) is transforming the global landscape, presenting opportunities and challenges that transcend national borders. International collaboration has become essential as AI systems increasingly influence global economies, governance, and societies. Organizations like the United Nations (UN) and the Organisation for Economic Co-operation and Development (OECD) are pivotal in shaping global AI governance frameworks. However, cross-border issues such as data privacy, security, and ethical discrepancies complicate the path. Future directions must focus on harmonized international standards and collaborative frameworks that promote responsible innovation while addressing pressing concerns.

GLOBAL INITIATIVES: THE ROLE OF INTERNATIONAL ORGANIZATIONS

UNITED NATIONS

The United Nations (UN) has taken a leadership role in advocating for inclusive, ethical, and sustainable AI development. The **UNESCO Recommendation on the Ethics of Artificial Intelligence**, adopted in 2021, is one of the most comprehensive international frameworks for AI ethics. This document outlines transparency, fairness, accountability, and inclusivity principles, guiding member states in developing their national AI strategies. The recommendation emphasizes human rights and sustainability, aligning AI development with the UN's **Sustainable Development Goals (SDGs)**.

The UN has also facilitated dialogues through platforms like the AI for Good Global Summit, hosted by the International Telecommunication Union (ITU). This annual event brings together stakeholders from governments, industry, and academia to discuss AI's potential to address global challenges, such as climate change, healthcare access, and poverty alleviation.

OECD

The OECD has been instrumental in shaping global AI governance. In 2019, it adopted the OECD AI Principles, endorsed by over 40 countries. These principles promote trustworthy AI systems that respect human rights, foster inclusive growth, and encourage innovation. The OECD's emphasis on transparency, accountability, and robustness has set a benchmark for ethical AI governance.

In addition to its principles, the OECD has created the Global Partnership on AI (GPAI), an international initiative that fosters collaboration on AI research and policy. GPAI focuses on practical solutions to pressing challenges, including AI bias, privacy, and the social impact of automation. By pooling resources and expertise, GPAI enables member countries to share best practices and align their regulatory approaches.

OTHER KEY PLAYERS

Other international organizations, such as the European Union (EU), the World Economic Forum (WEF), and the Group of Seven (G7), are also actively involved in global AI governance. For example, the EU's AI Act has influenced international discussions on risk-based regulation, while the G7's Global Data Protection Principles aim to create common standards for cross-border data sharing.

These global initiatives underscore the importance of multilateral cooperation in shaping AI governance. However, their success depends on bridging diverse national priorities and creating inclusive frameworks that reflect the perspectives of developing nations.

CROSS-BORDER CHALLENGES: DATA PRIVACY, SECURITY, AND ETHICAL STANDARDS

While international collaboration is critical, it faces significant challenges, such as differences in legal systems, cultural values, and technological capabilities.

DATA PRIVACY

Data is the lifeblood of AI, but differences in privacy regulations pose a significant barrier to cross-border collaboration. For instance, the European Union's General Data Protection Regulation (GDPR) sets a high standard for data privacy, emphasizing individual consent and data minimization. In contrast, countries like the United States adopt a more fragmented approach, with sector-specific privacy laws that vary by state.

These discrepancies make it difficult to establish seamless data flows across borders, which is essential for training AI models and conducting global research. Developing interoperable frameworks that respect diverse privacy norms is critical to addressing this challenge.

SECURITY

Cyberattacks increasingly target AI systems, including data breaches, adversarial attacks, and model theft. These threats have global implications, mainly affecting critical infrastructure, financial systems, or national security. Cross-border coordination is essential to combat these risks, yet differences in cybersecurity standards and enforcement mechanisms complicate efforts.

International agreements, such as the **Budapest Convention on Cybercrime**, provide a foundation for collaboration. However, broader participation and more robust mechanisms are needed to address AI-specific security threats effectively.

ETHICAL STANDARDS

Ethical AI development requires alignment on fairness, accountability, and transparency. However, cultural and political differences often lead to divergent interpretations of these values. For example, Western countries prioritize individual rights and privacy, while nations like China emphasize collective welfare and state security.

These differences make establishing universal ethical standards for AI challenging. Bridging this gap requires ongoing dialogue and the inclusion of diverse perspectives, particularly from underrepresented regions like Africa and Latin America.

FUTURE DIRECTIONS: TOWARDS HARMONIZED GLOBAL STANDARDS AND COLLABORATIVE FRAMEWORKS

The global community must move towards harmonized standards and collaborative frameworks to address cross-border challenges and harness AI's potential. These efforts should create inclusive, flexible, and adaptive governance models that balance innovation with accountability.

HARMONIZED GLOBAL STANDARDS

Developing global standards for AI governance is essential for fostering trust and interoperability. These standards should address key issues such as data privacy, algorithmic transparency, and bias mitigation. Organizations like the International Organization for Standardization (ISO) and the IEEE are already working on technical standards for AI, but greater alignment with ethical and legal frameworks is needed.

One promising approach is to create **minimum viable standards** that establish baseline requirements while allowing flexibility for regional variations. For instance, a global data privacy standard could outline core principles, such as informed consent and data protection, while leaving room for localized implementation.

COLLABORATIVE FRAMEWORKS

Collaborative frameworks can facilitate knowledge sharing, capacity building, and joint problem-solving. These frameworks should include:

1. Multistakeholder Participation: Governments, industry, academia, and civil society must collaborate to create inclusive governance models. Platforms like GPAI and the AI for Good Global Summit exemplify the benefits of this collaboration.

2. Regional Cooperation: Regional alliances, such as the African Union's AI Working Group or Latin America's Inter-American Development Bank (IDB) initiatives, can address local challenges and align regional strategies with global standards.

3. Public-Private Partnerships: Partnerships between governments and tech companies can accelerate the development of responsible AI. For example, collaborations on cybersecurity can enhance the resilience of AI systems against global threats.

INCLUSIVE GOVERNANCE

Inclusive governance is essential for ensuring that AI benefits all countries, not just those with advanced technological capabilities. Developing nations must be given a voice in global discussions and access to capacity-building resources. Initiatives like the AI4D Africa Program and the IDB's AI for Good platform demonstrate the importance of supporting local innovation and expertise.

ETHICS BY DESIGN

Future frameworks should emphasize ethics by design, integrating ethical considerations into the entire lifecycle of AI systems. This approach ensures that AI systems are designed with fairness, accountability, and transparency from the outset, reducing the risk of harm.

AI FOR GLOBAL CHALLENGES

Finally, international collaboration should prioritize using AI to address global challenges such as climate change, healthcare disparities, and disaster response. The international community can create solutions that benefit humanity by aligning AI development with the UN's SDGs.

CHAPTER 20: THE FUTURE OF AI GOVERNANCE

20.1 INTRODUCTION TO FUTURE TRENDS IN AI GOVERNANCE

EVOLVING LANDSCAPE

Artificial intelligence (AI) continues to grow at an unprecedented rate, with rapid advancements transforming industries, economies, and societies worldwide. From generative AI and autonomous systems to decision-making algorithms, the pace of innovation in AI technologies presents both opportunities and challenges for governance. Emerging AI capabilities are not confined to single domains but span critical sectors such as healthcare, finance, transportation, and defense, further complicating governance efforts.

This evolving landscape necessitates a shift in how we approach AI governance. Traditional methods often struggle to keep pace with the speed of AI development, leading to gaps in regulation and oversight. Without a robust governance framework, risks such as biased algorithms, privacy violations, and lack of accountability could undermine the benefits AI can bring. Additionally, the global nature of AI innovation calls for an international perspective, recognizing that AI's impact transcends borders and requires collaborative governance efforts.

The dual-use nature of AI technologies further compounds governance challenges. While they have transformative potential for the public good, they can also be misused in ways that pose significant risks, such as deepfake content, autonomous weaponry, or pervasive surveillance systems. Addressing these challenges requires a forward-thinking approach, ensuring that governance structures are resilient enough to adapt to this rapidly changing landscape.

IMPORTANCE OF PROACTIVE GOVERNANCE

Proactive governance is essential to anticipate and address the multifaceted challenges of AI's evolution. Waiting to respond until after issues arise often leads to inadequate, reactive measures that fail to contain the broader consequences. In contrast, a proactive approach enables stakeholders to shape the development and deployment of AI technologies in alignment with ethical principles and societal values.

Establishing flexible, adaptive, and inclusive mechanisms is central to proactive governance. These mechanisms should account for technological innovations while embedding safeguards that protect human rights promote fairness, and ensure accountability. One critical element is the development of anticipatory regulatory frameworks that balance innovation with oversight, allowing experimentation and growth without compromising safety or ethical considerations.

Moreover, fostering a culture of collaboration is pivotal. Engaging diverse stakeholders—including governments, industry leaders, academic researchers, and civil society—ensures that governance strategies are comprehensive and represent varied perspectives. This inclusivity helps identify blind spots in policy-making and creates a shared responsibility for AI's societal impact.

Proactive governance also emphasizes capacity-building, equipping organizations and regulators with the tools and knowledge required to oversee emerging technologies effectively. To prepare for governance challenges, investing in education, research, and technology-specific training programs is critical. Furthermore, leveraging AI as a governance tool—such as through explainable AI and blockchain for transparent record-keeping—can bolster governance practices.

In conclusion, the future of AI governance depends on our ability to recognize the implications of the evolving AI landscape and act preemptively. By embracing forward-thinking strategies, we can maximize AI's benefits while mitigating risks, ensuring its development aligns with ethical and societal priorities. This proactive stance is necessary and an opportunity to shape a future where AI serves humanity responsibly and equitably.

20.2 ADVANCES IN AI TECHNOLOGIES AND THEIR GOVERNANCE IMPLICATIONS

GENERATIVE AI

Generative AI represents a revolutionary advancement in artificial intelligence, marked by its ability to create new and original content, such as images, text, music, and videos. Models like OpenAI's GPT, DALL•E, and Google's Imagen have demonstrated remarkable capabilities, enabling applications in areas ranging from creative industries to scientific research. However, this technological progress brings significant governance challenges, especially concerning content authenticity and intellectual property rights.

One of the primary concerns with generative AI is the proliferation of synthetic media, often called deepfakes. These are hyper-realistic audio, video, or image content created with AI that can be indistinguishable from genuine material. While such technologies have beneficial applications, like entertainment or education, they pose risks. Deepfakes can be weaponized to spread misinformation, manipulate public opinion, or harm individuals through identity theft or character defamation. Governance frameworks must address these ethical concerns by ensuring that generative AI outputs are transparent and traceable. For instance, watermarking techniques and blockchain-based provenance tracking can help verify the authenticity of digital content.

Intellectual property (IP) is another critical area of concern. Generative AI systems are often trained on vast datasets that include copyrighted material, raising questions about fair use and ownership. For example, artists have raised alarms about AI models generating content that mimics their styles, potentially devaluing their work and infringing on their rights. Regulatory bodies must establish clear guidelines on data usage and ensure that creators are adequately compensated when their work is used for AI training.

Moreover, generative AI challenges existing notions of authorship and accountability. When AI generates creative work, who owns the rights? Is it the developer, the user, or neither? These unresolved questions necessitate proactive legislative measures to clarify ownership and responsibility. Establishing norms for ethical AI use in journalism, advertising, and content creation will also help mitigate misuse while fostering innovation.

AUTONOMOUS SYSTEMS

Autonomous systems, including self-driving cars, drones, and robotic process automation (RPA), are transforming critical sectors such as healthcare, transportation, and logistics. These systems rely on self-learning algorithms that adapt to real-world scenarios, reducing the need for human intervention. However, their deployment raises complex governance challenges that require urgent attention.

In the healthcare sector, autonomous systems such as robotic surgeons and diagnostic tools powered by AI have shown promise in improving efficiency and outcomes. However, they also pose risks if governance mechanisms are not adequately designed. For instance, if an autonomous system makes an error—such as a misdiagnosis or surgical mishap—it raises questions about accountability. Traditional liability frameworks struggle to address such scenarios, where the fault might lie with the algorithm, the developer, or the healthcare provider. Establishing robust legal frameworks to delineate accountability and ensure patient safety is critical.

In transportation, autonomous vehicles (AVs) are heralded as a solution to reduce traffic accidents and improve mobility. Yet, they also introduce unique governance challenges. One major issue is decision-making in life-or-death scenarios. For example, how does an AV's algorithm decide whom to prioritize for safety in an unavoidable accident? These ethical dilemmas require policymakers to collaborate with technologists and ethicists to establish principles for algorithmic decision-making that align with societal values.

Another challenge is cyber security. Autonomous systems are highly connected and rely on real-time data exchange, making them susceptible to cyberattacks. A hacked AV or drone could cause catastrophic damage, emphasizing the need for stringent cybersecurity standards and continuous monitoring. Governance frameworks must mandate regular updates, vulnerability assessments, and incident response protocols to mitigate these risks.

Furthermore, autonomous systems in critical infrastructure, such as power grids or defense, require specialized governance approaches. These systems must be resilient to both technical failures and malicious attacks. Governments and organizations should adopt a layered approach to security, integrating fail-safes and redundancy measures to ensure reliability.

AI-driven decision-making is increasingly prevalent in organizational contexts, from hiring and performance evaluations to financial predictions and criminal justice. While these systems offer significant advantages in terms of efficiency and scalability, they also raise critical concerns about accountability, transparency, and fairness.

One major challenge is algorithmic bias. AI systems are only as good as the data they are trained on, and if this data is biased, the resulting decisions will be as well. For example, biased hiring algorithms have been found to disadvantage candidates based on gender, race, or age. This undermines fairness and can lead to legal and reputational risks for organizations. Governance strategies must prioritize identifying and mitigating bias through rigorous testing and validation of AI models before deployment. Techniques such as fairness-aware machine learning and diverse training datasets can help address these issues.

Transparency is another critical governance concern. Many AI systems operate as black boxes, making it difficult to understand how they make specific decisions. This lack of explainability poses challenges in sensitive areas such as credit scoring, where individuals have a right to know why they were denied a loan. Organizations should adopt explainable AI (XAI) practices to address this, ensuring that decision-making processes are interpretable and auditable. Regulatory frameworks should also require organizations to disclose the criteria used by AI systems in making decisions, fostering accountability and trust.

Accountability in AI decision-making is further complicated by the involvement of multiple stakeholders, including developers, users, and organizations. For instance, if an AI system used for risk assessment in banking leads to discriminatory outcomes, who is responsible? Governance frameworks should establish clear lines of accountability, ensuring all stakeholders understand their roles and obligations. This includes mandating regular audits and impact assessments to evaluate AI systems' societal and ethical implications.

AI-driven decision-making also necessitates continuous monitoring and adaptation. As AI models evolve through self-learning, their behavior may change, potentially introducing new risks. Governance mechanisms must include provisions for ongoing evaluation and updates to ensure that AI systems remain aligned with organizational goals and ethical standards. Additionally, organizations should foster a culture of ethical AI use by providing training and resources for employees to understand and address AI-related challenges.

The advancements in generative AI, autonomous systems, and AI-driven decision-making represent transformative shifts in how technology interacts with society. However, these developments also underscore the urgent need for robust governance mechanisms to address their ethical, legal, and societal implications. By prioritizing transparency, accountability, and inclusivity, stakeholders can harness the potential of AI technologies while minimizing their risks.

Addressing content authenticity, intellectual property, and authorship issues will be crucial for fostering trust and innovation in generative AI. Establishing clear accountability frameworks, enhancing cybersecurity, and resolving ethical dilemmas will ensure autonomous systems' safe and effective deployment. Similarly, governance strategies for AI-driven decision-making must focus on eliminating bias, improving transparency, and ensuring accountability to build trust among users and stakeholders.

As AI technologies evolve, so must the governance frameworks that regulate them. This dynamic interplay between innovation and regulation will shape the future of AI, determining whether it becomes a force for good or a source of societal disruption. By adopting proactive and forward-thinking approaches, we can ensure that AI serves as a tool for positive transformation, enhancing lives while safeguarding ethical and societal values.

20.3 REGULATORY DEVELOPMENTS ON THE HORIZON

GLOBAL REGULATORY TRENDS

The rapid proliferation of artificial intelligence (AI) technologies has prompted governments and international organizations to consider regulatory frameworks that ensure ethical use, transparency, and accountability. Anticipated global regulatory trends reflect the growing consensus on the need for standardized AI governance while acknowledging regional differences in priorities and values.

One significant trend is the increasing emphasis on harmonizing international AI regulations. Organizations like the United Nations (UN) and the Organization for Economic Co-operation and Development (OECD) are developing guidelines promoting cross-border collaboration. For instance, the OECD's AI Principles aim to encourage the responsible development of AI systems, emphasizing human-centric design and fairness. Similarly, the European Union's Artificial Intelligence Act (AI Act) is a groundbreaking legislative proposal that seeks to classify AI applications into risk categories, with stringent requirements for high-risk systems. The AI Act's extraterritorial provisions could influence global practices, as international companies must comply with its standards.

In contrast, countries like the United States have adopted a sector-specific approach to AI governance, fostering innovation while addressing risks within specific domains such as healthcare and defense. The National Institute of Standards and Technology (NIST) has introduced a risk management framework for AI to guide organizations in implementing trustworthy AI systems. Meanwhile, China has established a unique governance model emphasizing state control and security, reflected in its algorithmic recommendation systems regulations and data protection laws, such as the Personal Information Protection Law (PIPL).

These varying approaches highlight the need for international cooperation to avoid regulatory fragmentation. Disparate regulations can create barriers to innovation and complicate compliance for multinational corporations. To address this, bilateral and multilateral agreements, such as data-sharing pacts and AI ethics compacts, will likely emerge, promoting interoperability and trust among nations.

Global regulatory trends also indicate a growing focus on addressing AI's societal impacts, such as algorithmic bias and privacy violations. Laws mandating algorithmic audits and transparency, such as those proposed in Canada's Artificial Intelligence and Data Act, aim to ensure that AI systems do not perpetuate discrimination or harm marginalized groups. Additionally, environmental considerations are gaining prominence, with discussions on regulating the carbon footprint of AI models to align with global sustainability goals.

INDUSTRY-SPECIFIC REGULATIONS

AI's transformative potential across various sectors necessitates tailored regulatory frameworks that address industry-specific challenges. Key industries such as finance, healthcare, and defense are at the forefront of adopting these targeted regulations.

In finance, AI is revolutionizing fraud detection, credit scoring, and algorithmic trading. However, these applications raise significant governance issues, including transparency, fairness, and accountability. Regulatory bodies such as the UK Financial Conduct Authority (FCA) and the U.S. Securities and Exchange Commission (SEC) are exploring rules that ensure AI-driven financial systems operate ethically. For example, the European Union's AI Act mandates strict oversight for AI applications in creditworthiness assessments, requiring explainability and fairness in decision-making processes.

Healthcare regulations are another critical focus area, given the life-altering implications of AI-driven diagnostics, treatment planning, and patient care. Agencies like the U.S. Food and Drug Administration (FDA) are working on frameworks to evaluate AI-enabled medical devices for safety and efficacy. Adaptive AI systems that continuously learn from real-world data pose unique challenges, necessitating ongoing monitoring and re-certification to ensure compliance. Privacy regulations, such as the Health Insurance Portability and Accountability Act (HIPAA), are also evolving to address AI's role in handling sensitive health data.

The defense industry faces distinct regulatory challenges, notably autonomous weapons and surveillance systems. AI technologies' dual-use nature—applicable for civilian and military purposes—complicates governance efforts. International treaties, such as the United Nations Convention on Certain Conventional Weapons (CCW), explore bans or restrictions on lethal autonomous weapons systems (LAWS). Meanwhile, individual nations are enacting policies to control the development and export of military AI technologies, balancing national security interests with ethical considerations.

Other industries, such as transportation, retail, and education, are also experiencing the emergence of tailored regulations. Autonomous vehicles, for instance, are governed by sector-specific guidelines addressing safety, liability, and data privacy. Similarly, the retail industry is grappling with regulations on AI-driven personalization and biometric surveillance. At the same time, educational institutions face scrutiny over the ethical use of AI in student assessments and learning analytics.

Organizations must adopt proactive compliance strategies as AI regulations evolve to navigate the complex and dynamic regulatory landscape. These strategies combine organizational culture, technological tools, and stakeholder engagement to ensure compliance with legal and ethical standards.

One fundamental strategy is establishing robust governance frameworks within organizations. These frameworks should include policies and procedures for AI development, deployment, and monitoring aligned with applicable regulations. Assigning clear roles and responsibilities for compliance—such as appointing a Chief AI Ethics Officer or establishing an AI ethics committee—can enhance accountability and oversight.

Regular audits and impact assessments are crucial for identifying and mitigating risks associated with AI systems. For example, algorithmic audits can help uncover biases or unintended consequences, ensuring that AI models comply with fairness and non-discrimination requirements. Impact assessments, such as those mandated by the European Union's General Data Protection Regulation (GDPR), evaluate the privacy implications of AI applications and guide organizations in implementing appropriate safeguards.

Another key compliance aspect is investing in explainable AI (XAI) tools that enhance transparency and trust. These tools enable organizations to interpret and communicate the decision-making processes of AI systems, meeting regulatory demands for accountability and user understanding. Incorporating explainability into AI workflows not only aids compliance but also builds public trust in AI technologies.

Continuous training and education are essential to ensure that employees across all levels understand AI's regulatory requirements and ethical considerations. Organizations can develop customized training programs or leverage external resources to build expertise in AI governance. Engaging with external stakeholders, such as regulators, industry associations, and advocacy groups, can provide valuable insights into emerging regulatory trends and best practices.

Technological solutions, such as AI governance platforms, can streamline compliance efforts by automating documentation, monitoring, and reporting processes. These platforms can integrate real-time regulatory updates, helping organizations stay informed and responsive to new requirements. Blockchain technology offers another promising avenue for compliance, enabling immutable records of AI decision-making processes that facilitate audits and accountability.

Another strategic approach to compliance is engaging in advocacy and policy-shaping initiatives. By participating in public consultations, industry forums, and regulatory discussions, organizations can help shape the development of AI regulations and ensure that their perspectives are considered. Collaborating with peers to establish industry standards can also foster a more cohesive approach to compliance.

Finally, organizations must prepare for regulatory enforcement by developing crisis management plans to address potential violations. These plans should include protocols for incident response, communication with regulators, and remediation measures. Proactively addressing compliance gaps and demonstrating a commitment to ethical AI practices can mitigate penalties and reputational damage in case of non-compliance.

20.4 ETHICAL CONSIDERATIONS IN FUTURE AI APPLICATIONS

BIAS AND FAIRNESS

Algorithmic bias represents one of the most pressing ethical concerns in AI development and deployment. Bias in AI systems often stems from training data that reflects historical inequalities or social prejudices. Left unaddressed, these biases can result in unfair treatment of certain groups, undermining trust in AI technologies and perpetuating systemic discrimination.

A notable example of bias in AI is in recruitment tools, where algorithms trained on historical hiring data favored male candidates over equally qualified female candidates. Such biases arise because the training data reflects historical gender imbalances in the workplace. Similarly, facial recognition systems have been criticized for lower accuracy rates in identifying individuals with darker skin tones than those with lighter skin tones. These disparities raise serious questions about fairness and equity in AI outcomes.

Developers and organizations must adopt a multifaceted approach to address algorithmic bias. One critical step is ensuring diversity in training datasets. Inclusive data that accurately represents various demographics can help mitigate the risk of bias. For example, datasets used in facial recognition should encompass a broad range of ethnicities, ages, and genders to improve accuracy across diverse populations.

Another approach is fairness-aware machine learning, which incorporates fairness constraints into the design and training of AI models. These methods help ensure that AI systems produce equitable outcomes by explicitly accounting for potential biases during development. Regular auditing and impact assessments of AI systems can also identify biases and unintended consequences post-deployment, enabling corrective actions.

Transparency and accountability are also vital for ensuring fairness. Organizations should disclose how their AI systems are trained, and decisions are made. Open-source initiatives and independent reviews can provide additional layers of scrutiny, fostering stakeholder trust. Furthermore, involving ethicists, sociologists, and community representatives in the AI development process ensures that diverse perspectives are considered, reducing the likelihood of biased outcomes.

PRIVACY AND DATA PROTECTION

AI's reliance on vast amounts of data raises significant privacy concerns. While data utilization is essential for training robust AI models, it often conflicts with individuals' privacy and protection rights. Navigating this balance is a critical ethical challenge in future AI applications.

One prominent concern is the potential misuse of personal data. AI systems collect and analyze sensitive information to deliver personalized services, particularly those used in advertising, healthcare, and social media. However, this level of personalization can infringe on privacy rights, leading to issues such as unauthorized data sharing or surveillance. For instance, location-based AI-powered services can track individuals' movements, raising questions about consent and data ownership.

Regulatory frameworks, such as the General Data Protection Regulation (GDPR) in the European Union, provide a foundation for addressing these concerns. The GDPR mandates that organizations obtain explicit consent for data collection and ensure data subjects can access, correct, or delete their information. Adherence to such regulations can help organizations balance leveraging data and respecting privacy rights.

Adopting privacy-preserving technologies is essential for ethical AI applications beyond compliance. Techniques such as differential privacy, federated learning, and homomorphic encryption allow organizations to use data without compromising individual privacy. For example, federated learning enables AI models to be trained on decentralized data sources, ensuring that sensitive information remains on users' devices rather than being stored centrally.

Ethical considerations also extend to transparency in data handling. Organizations should provide clear and accessible explanations of how data is collected, processed, and used in AI applications. Empowering users with greater control over their data—through opt-in mechanisms and granular privacy settings—can foster trust and ensure compliance with ethical standards.

HUMAN-AI COLLABORATION

Integrating AI into human decision-making processes offers tremendous opportunities to enhance productivity, accuracy, and innovation. However, it also raises ethical questions about the nature of human-AI collaboration and the potential for unintended consequences.

One key concern is the risk of over-reliance on AI systems. Decisions informed by AI algorithms can significantly impact lives in critical domains such as healthcare, finance, and criminal justice. While AI can assist by providing data-driven insights, over-reliance may lead to diminished human oversight and critical thinking. For example, a healthcare professional might defer entirely to an AI diagnostic tool, potentially overlooking unique patient circumstances that the algorithm cannot account for.

To address this, ethical frameworks must emphasize the complementary roles of humans and AI. AI should be designed to augment human capabilities rather than replace them. For instance, AI-powered tools in healthcare should assist practitioners by analyzing complex datasets and highlighting potential diagnoses while leaving the final decision to medical experts. This collaborative approach ensures that human judgment remains central, with AI as a supportive tool.

Another ethical challenge is ensuring transparency in human-AI interactions. Users must understand how AI systems make recommendations or decisions, particularly in high-stakes scenarios. Explainable AI (XAI) plays a crucial role in this context, enabling users to interpret and validate AI-driven outcomes. For example, an XAI-enabled loan approval system can provide applicants with a clear explanation of why their application was accepted or rejected, enhancing accountability and trust.

The ethical design of human-AI collaboration also involves addressing issues of accountability. Determining responsibility for AI errors can be challenging, especially when multiple stakeholders—developers, operators, and users—are involved. Clear guidelines for assigning accountability are essential to ensure that individuals or organizations can be held responsible for the consequences of AI-driven decisions.

Moreover, fostering trust in human-AI collaboration requires ongoing education and training. Users must understand AI systems' capabilities and limitations to make informed decisions. For example, in the legal field, lawyers who leverage AI tools for case analysis must be trained to critically evaluate the AI's recommendations rather than accept them at face value. This collaborative mindset empowers humans to harness AI's strengths while mitigating risks.

20.5 TECHNOLOGICAL SOLUTIONS FOR FUTURE GOVERNANCE CHALLENGES

EXPLAINABLE AI (XAI)

Explainable AI (XAI) has emerged as a critical solution to address transparency and accountability challenges in AI systems. Understanding how these systems make decisions is paramount as AI technologies become increasingly complex. XAI seeks to create AI models that are more interpretable, enabling stakeholders to trust and validate AI-driven outcomes.

One key advancement in XAI is the development of model-agnostic techniques, such as LIME (Local Interpretable Model-agnostic Explanations) and SHAP (SHapley Additive explanations). These tools provide insights into the decision-making process of AI models by identifying the contribution of each input feature to a specific outcome. For example, in a credit scoring model, SHAP can explain why a loan application was approved or rejected by highlighting the influence of factors like income, credit history, and employment status. Such transparency enhances user trust and ensures compliance with regulatory requirements, particularly in sectors like finance and healthcare.

Neural networks, often criticized for their black-box nature, are becoming more interpretable through innovations such as attention mechanisms and visualization techniques. Attention mechanisms, commonly used in natural language processing, enable models to focus on relevant portions of input data, making their decision-making process easier to trace. On the other hand, visualization tools allow users to observe how neural networks process images or text, offering a clearer understanding of their inner workings.

Another area of progress in XAI is the integration of counterfactual explanations. Counterfactuals describe how a different input could have led to a different outcome, providing actionable insights for users. For instance, in an AI-driven hiring platform, a counterfactual explanation might suggest that a candidate would have been shortlisted if they had additional experience in a specific skill. Such explanations foster transparency and empower users to make informed decisions based on AI outputs.

XAI is also instrumental in ethical AI development. By enabling audits and validations of AI models, it helps identify biases and ensure fairness in decision-making. This is particularly crucial in applications that impact marginalized communities, where biased algorithms can exacerbate existing inequalities. Regulators and organizations are increasingly mandating using XAI to ensure accountability, making it a cornerstone of future governance frameworks.

AI FOR GOVERNANCE

AI can be a powerful tool for enhancing governance practices offering innovative solutions for compliance monitoring, risk assessment, and decision-making. Organizations can streamline operations and respond proactively to regulatory requirements by leveraging AI-driven insights.

One significant application of AI in governance is compliance monitoring. Regulatory environments are becoming increasingly complex, requiring organizations to track and adhere to numerous laws and standards. AI tools can automate this process by scanning legal documents, identifying relevant regulations, and monitoring organizational activities for compliance. For example, natural language processing (NLP) algorithms can analyze contracts to ensure they align with regulatory guidelines, reducing non-compliance risk.

Risk assessment is another area where AI is transforming governance. Machine learning models can analyze large datasets to identify patterns and anomalies, enabling organizations to predict and mitigate potential risks. In the financial sector, AI systems can detect fraudulent transactions in real-time, safeguard assets, and ensure compliance with anti-money laundering (AML) regulations. Similarly, in healthcare, AI tools can assess risks associated with medical devices or treatment protocols, ensuring patient safety and regulatory adherence.

AI-driven decision-making tools also enhance governance by providing data-backed insights. Predictive analytics can help organizations anticipate market trends, assess the impact of policy changes, and optimize resource allocation. For example, governments can use AI to model the potential outcomes of proposed regulations, enabling evidence-based policymaking. This improves governance efficiency and fosters public trust by ensuring that decisions are transparent and well-informed.

Moreover, AI can facilitate stakeholder engagement and collaboration in governance processes. AI-powered chatbots and virtual assistants can provide citizens with real-time information, enhancing accessibility and transparency. For instance, an AI-powered chatbot might guide individuals through tax filing processes or answer questions about local regulations, making governance more user-friendly and inclusive.

To maximize AI's potential in governance, organizations must address challenges such as data privacy, algorithmic bias, and the risk of overreliance on automated systems. Establishing clear guidelines for AI use, investing in ethical AI practices, and fostering a culture of accountability are essential steps toward leveraging AI for effective governance.

BLOCKCHAIN INTEGRATION

Blockchain technology offers a robust solution for ensuring security and transparency in AI governance. By creating immutable and decentralized records, blockchain can address critical challenges such as data integrity, traceability, and accountability.

One of the most promising applications of blockchain in AI governance is maintaining audit trails. Blockchain's ability to record every transaction or decision made by an AI system ensures its actions are traceable and verifiable. For example, in healthcare, blockchain can log every instance of AI-driven diagnostics or treatment recommendations, providing a transparent record for audits and investigations. This not only enhances accountability but also fosters trust among stakeholders.

Blockchain can also address issues of data integrity and provenance. AI systems rely on vast data for training and operation, making data quality and authenticity critical. By storing data on a blockchain, organizations can ensure it remains tamper-proof and traceable. For instance, in supply chain management, blockchain can verify the origin and authenticity of goods, ensuring that AI-driven logistics systems operate based on reliable information.

Smart contracts, a key feature of blockchain technology, further enhance AI governance. These self-executing contracts automatically enforce predefined rules and conditions, ensuring compliance without manual intervention. For example, smart contracts could regulate the distribution of renewable energy credits based on AI-driven consumption forecasts in the energy sector, ensuring fairness and transparency.

Another application of blockchain in AI governance is identity management. As AI systems increasingly interact with individuals and organizations, verifying identities becomes crucial to prevent fraud and ensure accountability. Blockchain-based identity solutions can provide secure and decentralized identity verification, safeguarding user data while enabling seamless interactions with AI systems.

However, integrating blockchain with AI governance is not without challenges. Scalability remains a significant concern, as blockchain networks often struggle to handle large volumes of transactions at high speeds. Additionally, the energy consumption associated with some blockchain platforms raises environmental concerns. Organizations are exploring energy-efficient consensus mechanisms and hybrid solutions that combine blockchain with other technologies to address these issues.

Despite these challenges, blockchain's potential to enhance AI governance is undeniable. By ensuring transparency, security, and accountability, blockchain can serve as a foundational technology for AI systems' ethical and responsible deployment.

20.6 PREPARING ORGANIZATIONS FOR FUTURE GOVERNANCE NEEDS

BUILDING ADAPTIVE GOVERNANCE FRAMEWORKS

As artificial intelligence (AI) technologies continue to evolve, organizations must develop governance frameworks that are flexible and adaptive to new advancements. Traditional, static policies often fail to address AI systems' dynamic and rapidly changing nature, leaving organizations vulnerable to compliance risks and ethical dilemmas. An adaptive governance framework ensures policies remain relevant, effective, and aligned with technological progress.

Adaptive governance begins with a foundation of principles rather than rigid rules. Organizations can create a governance structure that accommodates innovation while safeguarding ethical standards by focusing on core values such as transparency, fairness, accountability, and inclusivity. For example, organizations can establish decision-making guidelines that allow for case-by-case assessments based on overarching principles instead of prescribing specific rules for all possible scenarios.

Scenario planning and foresight exercises are crucial components of adaptive governance. These approaches enable organizations to anticipate challenges and opportunities associated with emerging AI technologies. For instance, a financial institution might explore scenarios involving quantum computing's impact on encryption algorithms, allowing it to prepare for future regulatory shifts and technological disruptions.

Furthermore, adaptive governance frameworks should include mechanisms for regular review and revision. Establishing governance councils or committees tasked with monitoring technological trends and updating policies ensures that governance frameworks evolve with advancements. These bodies should incorporate diverse perspectives, including technologists, ethicists, legal experts, and end-users, to address the multifaceted nature of AI governance.

Technology can also contribute to adaptive governance. AI-driven tools can monitor regulatory changes, assess compliance risks, and recommend policy updates. For example, natural language processing (NLP) algorithms can analyze legislative texts to identify relevant regulatory developments, streamlining the process of updating governance frameworks. Such tools enable organizations to respond promptly to evolving requirements, reducing non-compliance risk.

CONTINUOUS LEARNING AND DEVELOPMENT

The fast-paced evolution of AI technologies demands that organizations invest in continuous learning and development to keep their teams informed about emerging trends, best practices, and regulatory requirements. A well-informed workforce is better equipped to navigate the complexities of AI governance and ensure that organizational practices align with ethical and legal standards.

One key aspect of continuous learning is providing specialized training for employees across all levels of the organization. This includes technical training for developers and data scientists on topics such as fairness-aware machine learning and explainable AI, as well as broader education for executives and policymakers on AI's ethical and societal implications. By tailoring training programs to different roles, organizations can build a technically proficient and ethically aware workforce.

Partnering with academic institutions, industry associations, and professional organizations can enhance learning initiatives. Collaborative programs like workshops, certifications, and knowledge-sharing forums allow employees to stay updated on the latest advancements and regulatory trends. For example, an organization might collaborate with a university to offer courses on AI ethics or participate in an industry consortium focused on developing best practices for AI governance.

Another essential component of continuous learning is fostering a culture of curiosity and critical thinking. Encouraging employees to question assumptions, explore new ideas, and engage in open discussions about AI-related challenges can lead to more innovative and responsible governance solutions. For instance, regular brainstorming sessions or hackathons focused on AI ethics can help teams develop creative approaches to addressing governance concerns.

Continuous learning should also extend to leadership. Executives and decision-makers must remain informed about the strategic implications of AI technologies to guide their organizations effectively. Executive education programs, such as AI strategy seminars or regulatory trends briefings, can help leaders make informed decisions that balance innovation with ethical considerations.

Finally, leveraging AI itself for learning and development can enhance training programs. AI-powered learning platforms can personalize educational content, recommend relevant resources, and track progress, ensuring employees receive targeted and practical training. For example, an AI-driven training platform might recommend courses on data privacy regulations to employees working in data-intensive roles, enabling them to address compliance challenges proactively.

ENGAGING WITH STAKEHOLDERS

Effective AI governance requires collaboration among stakeholders, including regulators, industry peers, academic researchers, and the public. Engaging with these groups ensures that governance frameworks are comprehensive, inclusive, and aligned with societal values.

Collaborating with regulators is essential for shaping policies that promote responsible AI development. Organizations can participate in public consultations, provide feedback on proposed regulations, and share insights into the practical implications of policy decisions. For instance, a healthcare company might work with regulatory bodies to establish guidelines for the ethical use of AI in medical diagnostics, ensuring that policies balance innovation with patient safety.

Engagement with industry peers fosters the development of shared standards and best practices. Participating in industry associations or consortia can help organizations contribute to initiatives addressing common challenges, such as algorithmic bias or data privacy. Collaborative efforts, such as the Partnership on AI, demonstrate the value of collective action in advancing responsible AI governance.

Academic partnerships also play a crucial role in stakeholder engagement. Researchers can provide valuable insights into emerging trends, ethical considerations, and technological advancements, helping organizations stay ahead. For example, an organization might collaborate with a university research center to explore the implications of generative AI for intellectual property rights, which would inform the development of governance policies.

Public engagement is equally important for building trust and ensuring that AI governance aligns with societal needs. Organizations should actively seek input from diverse communities, particularly those most affected by AI systems. Public forums, town hall meetings, and online surveys allow individuals to voice their concerns and expectations. Transparent communication about how AI is used and governed can further enhance public trust and acceptance.

Stakeholder engagement also involves fostering partnerships with civil society organizations, such as advocacy groups and non-profits, to address ethical and social challenges. For instance, an organization might collaborate with a human rights group to ensure that AI systems used in law enforcement do not perpetuate discrimination or infringe on individual rights.

Organizations should establish dedicated teams or roles focused on outreach and collaboration to facilitate effective stakeholder engagement. These teams can coordinate interactions with regulators, industry groups, and the public, ensuring that diverse perspectives and expertise inform governance efforts.

Preparing organizations for future governance needs requires a proactive and comprehensive approach that combines adaptive frameworks, continuous learning, and stakeholder engagement. By building flexible governance structures, investing in education and training, and collaborating with diverse groups, organizations can navigate the complexities of AI governance while fostering innovation and ethical practices.

Adaptive governance frameworks ensure that policies remain relevant and practical despite technological advancements. Continuous learning equips teams with the knowledge and skills to address emerging challenges. Engaging with stakeholders fosters inclusivity and trust, ensuring that governance efforts align with societal values and regulatory requirements.

As AI technologies continue to shape industries and societies, organizations prioritizing these strategies will be better positioned to lead responsibly, mitigate risks, and contribute to developing a sustainable and equitable AI ecosystem.

CHAPTER 21: AI GOVERNANCE IN THE PUBLIC SECTOR

21.1 INTRODUCTION TO AI IN THE PUBLIC SECTOR

ROLE OF AI IN GOVERNMENT

Artificial Intelligence (AI) transforms the public sector by enhancing efficiency, transparency, and decision-making processes. Governments increasingly leverage AI to optimize public services, streamline administration, and craft data-driven policies.

One of the most visible applications is in public service delivery, where AI-powered systems enable faster and more accurate processing of citizen requests. For instance, chatbots and virtual assistants handle real-time inquiries, reducing human operators' workload. In addition, AI supports urban planning and infrastructure development through predictive analytics, allowing governments to anticipate future needs and allocate resources more effectively.

AI is also pivotal in policy-making. By analyzing vast datasets, AI tools uncover trends and insights that inform healthcare, education, and environmental sustainability policies. Predictive models help governments simulate the potential impact of policy changes, ensuring that decisions are grounded in evidence rather than conjecture. Furthermore, AI aids in detecting fraud, optimizing tax collection, and enhancing overall efficiency of administrative tasks.

However, deploying AI in sensitive areas like law enforcement and immigration has sparked debates. AI-powered surveillance systems and predictive policing tools have raised concerns about privacy and potential misuse, necessitating robust governance to safeguard civil liberties.

IMPORTANCE OF GOVERNANCE

As AI becomes integral to government operations, ensuring its ethical and transparent use is paramount. AI-driven initiatives must align with principles of accountability and public trust, which are essential for maintaining legitimacy in a democratic society.

Transparency is a cornerstone of effective AI governance. Governments must ensure that AI systems are explainable and auditable, especially those affecting citizens' lives. Citizens have a right to understand how decisions impact them, mainly when automated systems are involved. For instance, algorithms used in welfare eligibility determinations or predictive policing must be transparent to avoid potential biases or errors.

Accountability is equally critical. Public sector AI systems must have clear lines of responsibility to address potential grievances. When errors or unintended consequences arise, governments need mechanisms to rectify them promptly. Establishing oversight committees or regulatory bodies can provide additional scrutiny to prevent misuse.

Building public trust is another key governance objective. Trust hinges on demonstrating that AI systems are deployed ethically, with safeguards to protect citizens' data and privacy. Regular engagement with stakeholders, including civil society, academia, and private sector experts, ensures that AI initiatives reflect diverse perspectives and societal values.

Moreover, effective governance requires governments to proactively address AI risks, such as algorithmic bias, lack of fairness, and unintended socioeconomic consequences. Governments can mitigate these risks by implementing frameworks that prioritize inclusivity and fairness while maximizing AI's benefits.

In conclusion, AI offers transformative potential for the public sector, enhancing service delivery and policy-making. However, without robust governance, its adoption risks eroding public trust and exacerbating existing inequalities. Transparent, accountable, and citizen-centric governance frameworks are essential to harnessing AI's power responsibly and equitably.

21.2 REGULATORY FRAMEWORKS AND COMPLIANCE

EXISTING REGULATIONS

As governments increasingly adopt Artificial Intelligence (AI) to enhance efficiency and decision-making, regulatory frameworks are critical in ensuring its responsible use. Current laws and policies governing AI in the public sector vary widely across regions and jurisdictions, reflecting differences in priorities, legal traditions, and levels of technological adoption.

The proposed AI Act in the European Union represents one of the most comprehensive attempts to regulate AI. This legislation introduces a risk-based approach, categorizing AI applications into high-risk, limited-risk, and minimal-risk groups with corresponding regulatory requirements. For instance, AI systems used in biometric identification, healthcare, and law enforcement are subject to stringent oversight. The General Data Protection Regulation (GDPR) also significantly influences AI governance, particularly ensuring data privacy and protecting individual rights.

AI regulation remains fragmented in the United States, with initiatives at the federal and state levels addressing specific aspects. Federal guidelines, such as the National Institute of Standards and Technology (NIST) AI Risk Management Framework, provide voluntary standards for trustworthy AI. Meanwhile, state-level efforts like California's Consumer Privacy Act (CCPA) impact AI systems handling personal data. Sector-specific regulations, such as those governing healthcare and finance, also shape AI deployment in these industries.

International organizations such as the OECD and UNESCO have proposed guidelines for ethical AI use globally, emphasizing transparency, accountability, and fairness. However, these initiatives lack enforceable mechanisms, highlighting the need for harmonized regulatory frameworks that transcend national boundaries.

Despite these developments, gaps persist in existing regulations. Many laws were designed for traditional technologies and struggle to address the unique challenges posed by AI, such as algorithmic bias, lack of transparency, and the rapid pace of innovation. Consequently, governments must continually update and refine their policies to remain relevant in this evolving landscape.

COMPLIANCE CHALLENGES

Navigating the complex regulatory landscape is a significant challenge for public sector organizations adopting AI. Governments must balance compliance with legal standards while fostering innovation and ensuring ethical deployment.

One primary challenge is the lack of uniformity in regulations. Divergent frameworks across regions and industries create a fragmented compliance environment, making it difficult for organizations to navigate requirements. For instance, an AI system used in healthcare may need to comply with data protection laws and medical device regulations, each with distinct mandates.

Another issue is the interpretability of existing laws. Many regulations lack clarity on how they apply to specific AI applications, leaving public sector entities uncertain about compliance obligations. For example, while the GDPR mandates data minimization and purpose limitation, its application to AI's data-intensive processes often raises questions about feasibility.

Resource constraints further complicate compliance efforts. Public sector organizations may lack the expertise, funding, or infrastructure to implement robust governance mechanisms. This is particularly true for smaller municipalities or developing countries, where access to AI expertise and resources is limited.

Monitoring and enforcement present additional challenges. Ensuring compliance requires regular audits, impact assessments, and accountability mechanisms, which can be resource-intensive. Moreover, the opacity of many AI systems, often called "black-box" algorithms, complicates efforts to assess their adherence to regulatory requirements.

Finally, ethical considerations pose a unique challenge. Beyond legal compliance, public sector organizations must ensure that AI systems align with societal values and do not exacerbate existing inequalities. This requires embedding ethical principles into AI development and deployment processes, a task often overlooked in favor of technical and operational priorities.

DEVELOPING NEW POLICIES

Governments must craft adaptive, inclusive, and forward-looking policies to address the limitations of existing regulations and compliance challenges. These policies should address current issues and anticipate future developments in AI technology and its societal impacts.

One approach is to adopt a risk-based regulatory framework similar to the EU's AI Act. Governments can allocate oversight resources more effectively by categorizing AI applications based on their potential impact. High-risk applications, such as those affecting critical infrastructure or individual rights, should be scrutinized, while low-risk applications may require lighter regulation to encourage innovation.

New policies should be centered on transparency and accountability. Governments must mandate that AI systems used in the public sector be explainable, allowing stakeholders to understand their decision-making processes. This includes requiring developers to document algorithms, data sources, and potential biases. Policies should also establish precise accountability mechanisms, assigning responsibility for AI outcomes to specific entities or individuals.

Ethical considerations must be embedded into policy frameworks. Governments should prioritize fairness, inclusivity, and human-centric design in AI deployment. For example, policies could require impact assessments to evaluate potential biases and their implications for marginalized communities. Public consultations and stakeholder engagement should be integral to policy-making, ensuring that diverse perspectives inform regulatory decisions.

Collaboration is another key element. Developing effective AI policies requires coordination across government agencies, private sector actors, academia, and civil society. Multi-stakeholder partnerships can provide valuable insights into technical, ethical, and societal considerations, ensuring practical and comprehensive policies.

To keep pace with technological advancements, governments must adopt agile policy-making approaches. This includes regular regulation updates, pilot programs to test new governance models, and continuous learning initiatives to build AI literacy among policymakers. For instance, regulatory sandboxes can provide a controlled environment for testing AI applications and refining compliance requirements before broader implementation.

International cooperation is also crucial. Given AI's global nature, harmonizing regulatory standards across borders can reduce fragmentation and facilitate collaboration. Forums such as the G20 or the United Nations can foster dialogue and develop consensus on global AI governance principles.

In conclusion, regulatory frameworks and compliance are fundamental to the responsible adoption of AI in the public sector. While existing regulations provide a foundation, addressing their gaps and challenges requires a proactive, collaborative, and adaptive approach. Governments can harness AI's potential while safeguarding public trust and societal values by crafting policies prioritizing transparency, accountability, and ethical considerations.

21.3 ETHICAL CONSIDERATIONS AND PUBLIC TRUST

ETHICAL FRAMEWORKS

Deploying Artificial Intelligence (AI) in the public sector requires robust ethical frameworks to ensure responsible use and safeguard societal values. Ethical guidelines serve as a blueprint for designing, implementing, and operating AI systems that align with fairness, accountability, transparency, and inclusivity principles.

One critical component of ethical frameworks is ensuring that AI systems prioritize human-centric values. This involves embedding principles such as respect for individual rights, privacy, and autonomy into the design and operation of AI technologies. Ethical frameworks must establish data collection and usage standards, ensuring that data is obtained with consent, stored securely, and used in ways that do not harm individuals or communities.

Transparency is another cornerstone of ethical AI. Public-sector AI systems must be designed to be explainable and understandable to non-technical stakeholders. For example, algorithms used in welfare distribution or public health decision-making should be accompanied by documentation detailing their purpose, functioning, and potential limitations. This ensures stakeholders, including policymakers and citizens, can trust the technology.

Accountability mechanisms are also crucial. Ethical frameworks should define roles and responsibilities for all parties involved in AI deployment, from developers to administrators. When AI systems make decisions with unintended consequences, processes must be established to review and address these outcomes. This includes setting up audit trails, impact assessments, and recourse mechanisms for affected individuals.

Ethical AI requires incorporating diverse perspectives. Governments should engage with stakeholders from various backgrounds, including marginalized communities, civil society organizations, and domain experts, to ensure that AI systems reflect multiple values and priorities. This participatory approach helps identify potential ethical challenges early in the development process, reducing the risk of harm.

BUILDING PUBLIC TRUST

Public trust is foundational to successfully adopting AI in the public sector. Citizens may resist AI initiatives without trust, undermining their effectiveness and potential benefits. Building and maintaining trust requires proactive engagement, transparency, and accountability.

Engaging with communities is a key strategy for fostering trust. Governments should involve citizens and stakeholders in discussions about AI initiatives from the outset. Public consultations, town hall meetings, and online forums allow individuals to voice their concerns, ask questions, and offer feedback. This two-way communication educates the public about AI's capabilities and limitations and demonstrates a commitment to inclusivity and responsiveness.

Transparency is equally critical. Governments must communicate clearly and consistently about how AI systems are used, the objectives they aim to achieve, and the safeguards in place to protect citizens' rights. For example, publishing detailed reports on the performance and impact of AI systems can enhance public confidence in their reliability and fairness.

Accountability mechanisms further reinforce trust. Citizens need assurance that public sector organizations are accountable for AI-driven decisions. Establishing independent oversight bodies, ombudspersons, or review boards can provide additional scrutiny and recourse for grievances. These mechanisms ensure that AI initiatives operate within ethical and legal boundaries, enhancing their legitimacy.

Another critical aspect of building trust is addressing fears and misconceptions about AI. Misinformation about AI's capabilities, such as fears of job displacement or surveillance, can erode public confidence. Governments should invest in public education campaigns to demystify AI, highlighting its benefits while honestly and transparently addressing potential risks.

ADDRESSING BIAS AND FAIRNESS

Bias and fairness are among the most significant ethical challenges in AI deployment. AI systems often rely on historical data, which can contain biases reflecting societal inequalities. If not addressed, these biases can perpetuate or even exacerbate disparities, leading to unjust outcomes.

To ensure fairness, governments must implement rigorous processes for identifying and mitigating bias in AI systems. This begins with data governance. Public-sector organizations should audit datasets used to train AI models, ensuring they are representative and free from discriminatory patterns. For example, datasets used in criminal justice applications should reflect diverse demographic groups to prevent over-policing of marginalized communities.

Algorithmic fairness must also be prioritized. Developers should employ bias detection and correction techniques, fairness constraints, and adversarial testing to identify and address potential disparities in AI outcomes. Tools like fairness metrics and explainability frameworks can help assess whether AI systems treat all individuals equitably.

Beyond technical solutions, addressing bias requires an organizational commitment to fairness and inclusivity. Public sector organizations should establish ethics committees or advisory boards to oversee AI projects, ensuring that fairness considerations are integrated at every stage. These bodies can guide ethical dilemmas, assess potential risks, and recommend strategies for promoting equitable outcomes.

Collaboration with external stakeholders is also essential. Partnering with academic researchers, advocacy groups, and industry experts can provide valuable insights into best practices for mitigating bias. For example, universities and research institutions often develop innovative tools and methodologies for fairness in AI that can be applied in public-sector contexts.

Transparency is critical to addressing bias. Governments must disclose information about how AI systems are developed and evaluated, including the steps to ensure fairness. This includes publishing algorithmic audits, impact assessments, and case studies demonstrating efforts to mitigate bias.

Education and training are additional components of addressing bias. Public sector employees involved in AI projects should receive training on ethical considerations, including the impact of prejudice and the importance of fairness. This ensures that teams have the knowledge and skills to design and deploy equitable AI systems.

In conclusion, ethical considerations and public trust are fundamental to the responsible adoption of AI in the public sector. Governments can ensure that AI systems align with societal values and promote equitable outcomes by implementing robust ethical frameworks, engaging with communities, and addressing bias and fairness. These efforts enhance the legitimacy of AI initiatives and maximize their potential to improve public services and policy-making.

21.4 CASE STUDIES: AI GOVERNANCE IN GOVERNMENT INITIATIVES

SMART CITIES: GOVERNANCE OF AI IN URBAN PLANNING AND PUBLIC SERVICE DELIVERY

Smart cities represent a transformative approach to urban development. They leverage Artificial Intelligence (AI) to enhance infrastructure, optimize resource management, and improve residents' quality of life. However, integrating AI in smart cities requires robust governance to address ethical, legal, and operational challenges.

One notable case is the city of Barcelona, which has implemented AI-driven solutions for traffic management, energy efficiency, and public service delivery. The city's intelligent traffic systems use AI algorithms to analyze real-time data from sensors and cameras, optimizing traffic flow and reducing congestion. This approach has resulted in lower emissions and improved commute times. Governance mechanisms ensure data transparency, with public dashboards displaying traffic patterns and system performance metrics to promote accountability.

Singapore's Smart Nation initiative exemplifies AI governance in public service delivery. AI monitors urban infrastructure, predicts maintenance needs, and streamlines government services. For instance, the Municipal Services Office employs AI to efficiently track and address citizen complaints. The government has implemented data protection laws to ensure trust and compliance and regularly engages with stakeholders through public consultations. These measures foster transparency and inclusivity, addressing concerns about data privacy and algorithmic biases.

However, challenges persist. The deployment of facial recognition systems for security purposes in cities like London has sparked debates about surveillance and privacy. While these systems enhance public safety, they also raise concerns about potential misuse and the erosion of civil liberties. To address these issues, governance frameworks must include rigorous oversight, precise accountability mechanisms, and ethical guidelines that balance technological benefits with residents' rights.

HEALTHCARE: MANAGING AI APPLICATIONS IN PUBLIC HEALTH SYSTEMS

AI applications have significantly advanced the healthcare sector, particularly in diagnostics, patient care, and resource management. While these technologies can potentially revolutionize public health, their adoption necessitates careful governance to address data privacy, ethical use, and equitable access.

One example is the use of AI in disease prediction and prevention. During the COVID-19 pandemic, South Korea utilized AI-driven tools to analyze infection patterns, identify hotspots, and allocate resources effectively. The government's transparent communication and adherence to data protection laws helped build public trust in these initiatives. Ethical frameworks ensured that AI applications prioritized public health benefits while safeguarding individual rights.

AI has been integrated into public health systems in the United States to enhance diagnostic accuracy. For example, AI algorithms analyze medical imaging data for early signs of diseases such as cancer. Studying in this context requires rigorous validation to ensure that AI systems meet clinical standards. Regulatory bodies like the Food and Drug Administration (FDA) oversee the approval and monitoring of AI-based medical devices, ensuring their safety and effectiveness.

Despite these successes, challenges remain. Data privacy is a critical concern in AI-driven healthcare systems. Sensitive medical information must be collected and analyzed using stringent safeguards to prevent misuse. Governments must enforce robust data protection laws, such as the Health Insurance Portability and Accountability Act (HIPAA) in the United States, and ensure compliance through regular audits.

Ethical considerations also play a crucial role. AI systems must be designed to avoid biases that lead to unequal patient treatment. For instance, disparities in training data can result in diagnostic errors for underrepresented populations. Healthcare organizations should adopt diverse datasets and conduct regular bias audits to address this. Public engagement and education are vital to building trust and ensuring AI applications align with societal values.

LAW ENFORCEMENT: OVERSIGHT OF AI TOOLS IN POLICING AND CRIMINAL JUSTICE

The use of AI in law enforcement has become increasingly prevalent, offering tools for crime prediction, facial recognition, and data analysis. While these technologies enhance efficiency and effectiveness, they raise significant ethical, legal, and social concerns. Effective governance is essential to ensure AI tools in policing and criminal justice uphold human rights and promote fairness.

One prominent case is the implementation of predictive policing systems in the United States. These systems analyze historical crime data to identify areas at higher risk of criminal activity, enabling law enforcement to allocate resources more effectively. While predictive policing has shown potential in reducing crime rates, it has also been criticized for perpetuating systemic biases. Reliance on biased historical data can disproportionately target minority communities, exacerbating social inequalities. To address this, governance frameworks must include transparency requirements, independent audits, and mechanisms for community oversight.

Facial recognition technology is another area of concern. Cities like San Francisco have banned law enforcement from using facial recognition due to privacy and accuracy issues. Misidentification, particularly of women and people of color, has highlighted the need for stricter standards and accountability. In contrast, countries like China have extensively deployed facial recognition for public safety, raising questions about the balance between security and civil liberties. Effective governance requires clear legal frameworks, regular evaluations, and public dialogue to address these concerns.

Ethical oversight is also crucial in the criminal justice system. AI tools used for sentencing recommendations or parole decisions must be transparent and free from bias. For instance, the COMPAS algorithm in the United States faced scrutiny for allegedly producing racially biased risk assessments. Such cases underscore the importance of rigorous testing, algorithmic transparency, and accountability measures to ensure fairness and justice.

Collaboration between stakeholders is key to improving AI governance in law enforcement. Governments should engage with civil society, academia, and technology developers to establish best practices and ethical standards. Public consultations can address community concerns and foster trust in AI initiatives. Additionally, investments in training and education for law enforcement personnel are necessary to ensure responsible and effective use of AI tools.

The case studies of smart cities, healthcare, and law enforcement illustrate AI's transformative potential in the public sector. However, they also highlight the critical importance of governance in addressing ethical, legal, and operational challenges. Governments can harness AI's benefits while safeguarding public trust and societal values by implementing robust regulatory frameworks, promoting transparency and accountability, and engaging with diverse stakeholders.

Governance frameworks must evolve to keep pace with technological advancements, ensuring that AI initiatives are equitable, inclusive, and aligned with public interests. As these case studies demonstrate, effective governance is not a one-size-fits-all approach but requires tailored strategies that reflect each application area's unique contexts and challenges. Through proactive governance, governments can maximize AI's potential to improve public services and policy-making while upholding the principles of fairness, transparency, and accountability.

21.5 CHALLENGES AND OPPORTUNITIES

RESOURCE CONSTRAINTS: ADDRESSING LIMITATIONS IN FUNDING, EXPERTISE, AND INFRASTRUCTURE

Adopting Artificial Intelligence (AI) in the public sector offers immense potential, but significant resource constraints often hinder it. Limited funding, a shortage of expertise, and inadequate infrastructure present substantial challenges that governments must address to implement and govern AI initiatives effectively.

Funding constraints are among the most prominent barriers. Implementing AI systems requires substantial investment, from acquiring cutting-edge technologies to maintaining and updating systems. Many government agencies struggle to allocate sufficient budgets for AI projects, particularly those in developing countries or underfunded sectors. This lack of funding often results in reliance on outdated technologies or incomplete implementation of AI solutions, reducing effectiveness and undermining public trust.

The scarcity of AI expertise further compounds the problem. Governments often compete with the private sector, which offers higher salaries and more attractive incentives to skilled AI professionals. This talent gap leaves many public sector organizations without the expertise to design, deploy, and manage AI systems effectively. Training existing employees or partnering with academic institutions can help bridge this gap, but these solutions require time and additional resources.

Infrastructure limitations also pose challenges. Many public-sector agencies lack the advanced computing resources and robust data management systems to support AI applications. Outdated IT infrastructure and fragmented data systems hinder the integration of AI technologies and the sharing insights across departments. Investing in modern infrastructure and adopting cloud-based solutions can help overcome these barriers, enabling governments to deploy AI at scale.

Addressing resource constraints also presents opportunities for innovation despite these challenges. Public-private partnerships can help governments access funding, expertise, and infrastructure while fostering collaboration between sectors. For example, technology companies can provide AI solutions and training programs to support public sector initiatives, ensuring that governments benefit from cutting-edge advancements.

INTERAGENCY COLLABORATION: FOSTERING COOPERATION AMONG VARIOUS GOVERNMENT ENTITIES FOR COHESIVE AI GOVERNANCE

Effective AI governance requires seamless collaboration among government entities, yet interagency cooperation often faces challenges due to bureaucratic silos, conflicting priorities, and communication gaps. Addressing these barriers is critical to ensuring cohesive and efficient AI governance.

One challenge lies in the fragmented nature of government operations. Different agencies often operate independently, with limited coordination or information sharing. This fragmentation can lead to duplicative efforts, inefficiencies, and inconsistencies in AI governance frameworks. For example, one agency may develop AI standards that conflict with those established by another, creating confusion and hindering compliance.

Governments must establish centralized coordination mechanisms to foster collaboration. Dedicated bodies or task forces responsible for AI governance can help align agencies' policies, standards, and practices. For instance, a national AI council could oversee the development of unified guidelines and facilitate interagency communication, ensuring consistency in AI deployment and regulation.

Data sharing is another critical aspect of interagency collaboration. Many AI applications rely on large, diverse datasets to deliver accurate insights. However, agencies often face legal, technical, or cultural barriers to sharing data. Implementing data governance frameworks prioritizing security and privacy while enabling collaboration can address these challenges. Secure data platforms and federated learning can facilitate data sharing without compromising sensitive information.

Collaboration also extends to partnerships with external stakeholders. Engaging with academia, industry, and civil society organizations can bring diverse perspectives and expertise to AI governance efforts. For example, partnerships with universities can provide access to cutting-edge research, while collaborations with technology companies can ensure that public sector AI initiatives benefit from the latest advancements.

INNOVATION VS. REGULATION: BALANCING THE NEED FOR INNOVATION WITH THE IMPERATIVE OF REGULATION AND OVERSIGHT

One of the most significant challenges in AI governance is balancing the need for innovation with the imperative of regulation and oversight. Fostering innovation is essential to harnessing AI's potential to improve public services and policy-making, while regulation is critical to ensuring that AI systems operate ethically, transparently, and safely.

Overregulation can stifle innovation by creating bureaucratic hurdles that discourage experimentation and slow the adoption of new technologies. For example, overly stringent AI development and deployment requirements may deter startups or small businesses from entering the public sector market. To avoid this, governments should adopt agile regulatory frameworks that provide flexibility for innovation while maintaining oversight.

Regulatory sandboxes offer a practical solution to this challenge. These controlled environments allow developers to test AI applications under real-world conditions while remaining within regulatory boundaries. By providing a space for experimentation, sandboxes enable innovation while ensuring emerging technologies comply with ethical and legal standards. For instance, the UK's Financial Conduct Authority has successfully used regulatory sandboxes to encourage innovation in the financial technology sector.

Conversely, underregulation can lead to significant risks, including privacy violations, algorithmic bias, and lack of accountability. Without proper oversight, AI systems may exacerbate societal inequalities or cause harm to vulnerable populations. For example, an unregulated facial recognition system used in law enforcement could result in wrongful arrests or surveillance abuses, eroding public trust in government initiatives.

To strike the right balance, governments must adopt a principles-based approach to regulation. Instead of prescribing specific technical requirements, principles-based frameworks emphasize overarching goals such as transparency, accountability, and fairness. This approach allows for flexibility in implementing regulations, enabling innovation while ensuring ethical AI deployment.

Public engagement is also vital to balancing innovation and regulation. Involving citizens and stakeholders in discussions about AI policies ensures that governance frameworks reflect societal values and priorities. By fostering dialogue and incorporating diverse perspectives, governments can build trust and create regulations that support innovation and public interest.

21.6 FUTURE DIRECTIONS FOR PUBLIC SECTOR AI GOVERNANCE

ADAPTIVE GOVERNANCE MODELS: DEVELOPING FLEXIBLE FRAMEWORKS THAT CAN EVOLVE WITH TECHNOLOGICAL CHANGES

The rapid evolution of Artificial Intelligence (AI) necessitates governance models that are not only robust but also adaptable. Traditional governance frameworks designed for static technologies struggle to keep pace with AI development's dynamic and iterative nature. To address this, governments must embrace adaptive governance models that can evolve alongside technological advancements while safeguarding ethical and legal standards.

Adaptive governance emphasizes flexibility and responsiveness. Instead of rigid, one-size-fits-all regulations, it promotes a modular approach that can be updated as new challenges and opportunities emerge. For instance, governments could establish baseline principles—such as transparency, accountability, and fairness—while allowing specific rules and guidelines to be revised based on technological and societal changes. This approach ensures that regulations remain relevant without stifling innovation.

One example of adaptive governance is iterative policy development, where governments pilot new regulations in controlled environments before scaling them. Regulatory sandboxes, for instance, allow AI developers to test applications under real-world conditions while adhering to provisional rules. Lessons learned from these experiments can inform broader regulatory frameworks, ensuring they are practical and effective.

Another critical aspect of adaptive governance is foresight planning. Governments must invest in scenario analysis and predictive modeling to anticipate future trends in AI technology and its societal impact. By proactively identifying potential risks and opportunities, policymakers can craft regulations that address emerging issues before they escalate.

Public engagement is essential to adaptive governance. Regular consultations with citizens, industry stakeholders, and academia ensure that governance models reflect diverse perspectives and societal values. This participatory approach enhances the legitimacy of regulations and builds public trust in AI initiatives.

INTERNATIONAL COLLABORATION: ENGAGING IN GLOBAL DIALOGUES TO HARMONIZE AI GOVERNANCE STANDARDS

AI is a global phenomenon, with technologies and data often crossing national borders. Therefore, effective governance requires international collaboration to harmonize standards, share best practices, and address transnational challenges. Without coordinated efforts, fragmented regulatory approaches could lead to inconsistencies, conflicts, and missed opportunities for collective progress.

International organizations, such as the United Nations, the Organisation for Economic Co-operation and Development (OECD), and the Global Partnership on AI, play a pivotal role in fostering dialogue among nations. These forums provide platforms for governments to exchange ideas, align on ethical principles, and develop common frameworks for AI governance. For example, the OECD's AI Principles emphasize human-centric design, transparency, and accountability, offering a foundation for global cooperation.

Bilateral and multilateral agreements are also critical. Governments can work together to establish cross-border data-sharing agreements, ensuring data flows comply with privacy and security standards. Collaborative efforts in cybersecurity, algorithmic fairness, and intellectual property protection can address shared concerns and promote mutual benefits.

One challenge to international collaboration is the varying levels of AI maturity and regulatory capacity across countries. Developed nations often lead AI innovation, while developing countries may lack the resources or expertise to participate fully in global discussions. Addressing this disparity requires capacity-building initiatives, such as training programs, funding support, and knowledge sharing, to empower all nations to contribute to and benefit from AI governance.

Another challenge is reconciling cultural and legal differences. AI governance must account for diverse societal values and norms, which can influence perspectives on privacy, surveillance, and algorithmic bias. Open, inclusive dialogues help bridge these gaps and foster mutual understanding.

CONTINUOUS LEARNING: INVESTING IN TRAINING AND DEVELOPMENT TO BUILD AI LITERACY AMONG PUBLIC SECTOR EMPLOYEES

As AI becomes increasingly integrated into government operations, building AI literacy among public-sector employees is essential. Continuous learning initiatives ensure employees have the knowledge and skills to design, deploy, and manage AI systems effectively and ethically.

AI literacy encompasses understanding the basics of AI technology, its potential applications, and its ethical implications. Employees must also know relevant regulations, data management practices, and risk assessment methodologies. This foundational knowledge enables public servants to make informed decisions about AI adoption and governance.

Training programs should be tailored to different roles within the public sector. For instance, policymakers need a broad understanding of AI's societal impact and governance requirements, while technical staff require more specialized training in AI development and deployment. Customized programs can address the unique needs of various job functions, ensuring that all employees are equipped to contribute effectively to AI initiatives.

Partnerships with academic institutions and industry organizations can enhance training efforts. Universities can provide certification programs or workshops on AI ethics, data science, and governance, while private sector experts can offer insights into the latest technological advancements. Online learning platforms and Massive Open Online Courses (MOOCs) are valuable resources for scaling training initiatives across large public sector workforces.

Mentorship and peer learning programs can further support skill development. Pairing experienced AI practitioners with less experienced employees fosters knowledge transfer and builds organizational capacity. Collaborative projects and cross-agency working groups can also facilitate learning by exposing employees to diverse perspectives and use cases.

Fostering a culture of continuous learning is vital in addition to formal training. Governments should encourage employees to stay updated on AI trends and developments through conferences, webinars, and industry publications. Access to research papers, case studies, and toolkits ensures employees can deepen their expertise over time.

Governments must also address the ethical dimension of AI literacy. Employees should be trained to recognize and mitigate biases, evaluate the fairness of AI systems, and engage with stakeholders transparently. Ethical training helps ensure public sector AI initiatives align with societal values and promote equitable outcomes.

Investing in AI literacy benefits individual employees and the broader public sector. A skilled workforce enhances the government's ability to harness AI for the public good, from improving service delivery to addressing complex societal challenges. It also builds public trust by demonstrating a commitment to responsible and informed AI adoption.

The future of public sector AI governance depends on proactive and forward-thinking strategies. This vision is essential to adaptive governance models, international collaboration, and continuous learning. By embracing flexibility, fostering global cooperation, and building AI literacy, governments can navigate the complexities of AI while maximizing its potential to serve society.

Adaptive governance ensures that regulatory frameworks remain relevant despite rapid technological change, balancing innovation with oversight. International collaboration promotes harmonized standards and collective problem-solving, addressing AI's global nature. Continuous learning empowers public-sector employees to deploy AI responsibly and effectively, enhancing their capacity to deliver equitable and impactful outcomes.

As AI continues to evolve, so must the approaches to its governance. By prioritizing adaptability, inclusivity, and education, governments can create a resilient foundation for AI governance that reflects societal values and meets future challenges.

PART VII

TEMPLATES AND FRAMEWORKS

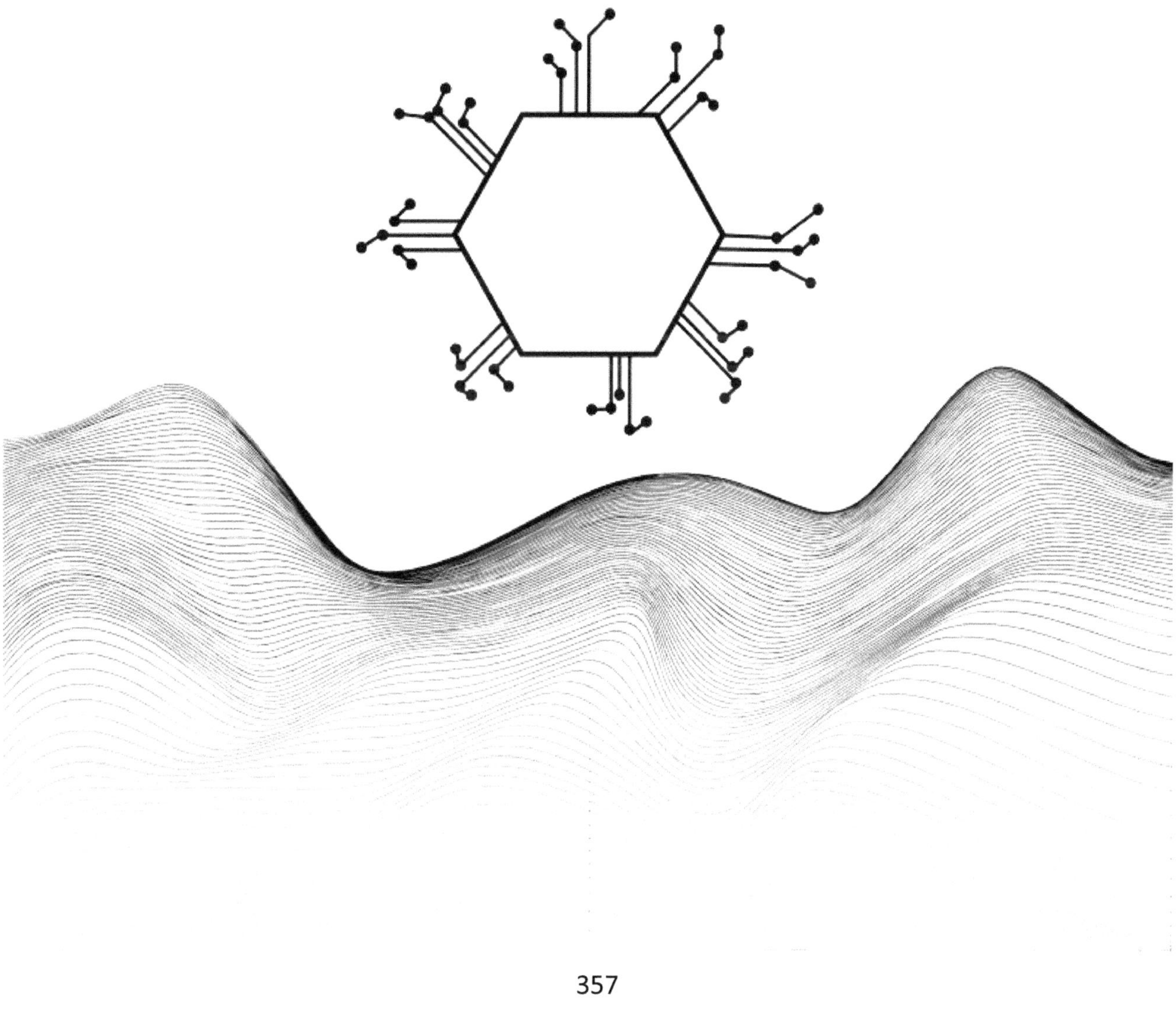

CHAPTER 22: PRACTICAL RESOURCES FOR AI GOVERNANCE

22.1 INTRODUCTION TO PRACTICAL RESOURCES

In the evolving domain of AI governance, theoretical understanding lays the groundwork, but applying these concepts drives meaningful outcomes. Practical resources are the critical bridge between governance theory and actionable practice, enabling organizations to implement effective frameworks, achieve compliance, and foster trust and accountability.

WHY PRACTICAL RESOURCES MATTER

Governance is inherently multifaceted, requiring a balance between regulatory adherence, ethical principles, and operational efficiency. While theoretical models provide direction, organizations often struggle to translate these ideas into day-to-day practices. This gap underscores the need for practical resources that simplify complex governance principles into actionable tools. Templates, checklists, and frameworks are indispensable as they provide a starting point for organizations, irrespective of their size or maturity level in AI governance.

Moreover, practical resources enhance consistency and clarity across teams by standardizing approaches to risk management, compliance tracking, and ethical decision-making. By leveraging these tools, organizations can move beyond ad hoc responses to challenges and adopt a proactive stance toward governance. This ensures they meet regulatory requirements and foster innovation in a controlled and ethical environment.

WHAT THIS CHAPTER OFFERS

This chapter aims to provide readers with a comprehensive toolkit to operationalize AI governance. Each section focuses on a specific type of resource designed to address common governance challenges:

1. **Templates:** Predefined structures for governance frameworks that can be adapted to various industries and organizational contexts. These templates simplify the creation of policies, procedures, and role assignments tailored to specific needs.

2. **Checklists:** These detailed lists ensure compliance with key governance areas, including regulatory standards, ethical principles, and risk mitigation strategies, are audited.

3. **Frameworks:** Holistic models that integrate governance components into a cohesive structure. Frameworks provide a roadmap for organizations to align their governance initiatives with strategic objectives.

This chapter collects tools and provides a guide to their practical application. Alongside these resources, you will find instructions, examples, and best practices demonstrating how organizations have successfully utilized these tools to strengthen their AI governance practices.

By the end of this chapter, readers will have a clear understanding of how to deploy practical resources to achieve robust governance outcomes. Whether you are leading a multinational corporation, a public institution, or a startup, this chapter equips you with the actionable tools needed to navigate the complexities of AI governance.

22.2 GOVERNANCE FRAMEWORK TEMPLATES

Governance frameworks provide a structured approach to ensuring AI systems are developed, deployed, and managed responsibly. These frameworks are essential for organizations to address regulatory compliance, ethical considerations, and operational risks. In this section, we delve into examples of AI governance frameworks, their core components, usage scenarios, and practical steps for customization to meet diverse organizational needs.

CORE FRAMEWORKS

EXAMPLES OF AI GOVERNANCE FRAMEWORKS

AI governance frameworks vary widely depending on the size and industry of an organization. Below are examples tailored to different contexts:

1. **For Small and Medium Enterprises (SMEs):**
    - A lightweight governance framework focusing on essential compliance and ethical standards.
    - Example: A startup developing a recommendation system can use a streamlined framework that includes policies for data privacy, regular algorithm audits, and a simple escalation process for ethical concerns.
2. **For Multinational Corporations (MNCs):**
    - A comprehensive governance structure integrating global regulatory requirements and ethical guidelines.
    - Example: A multinational financial institution implementing AI for fraud detection could establish a framework incorporating cross-border data-sharing policies, detailed risk management protocols, and specialized roles for compliance officers in each region.
3. **For Public Institutions:**
    - A governance framework prioritizing transparency, accountability, and public engagement.

- Example: A government agency deploying AI for public health monitoring might focus on open data policies, public consultation mechanisms, and rigorous bias assessment procedures.

OVERVIEW OF COMPONENTS

Effective governance frameworks are built on several core components:

1. **Policies:**
   - Clearly defined rules governing the ethical and legal use of AI.
   - Examples include policies on data protection, algorithm transparency, and decision-making accountability.
2. **Procedures:**
   - Step-by-step instructions for implementing policies.
   - These include processes for conducting impact assessments, reviewing AI models, and reporting incidents.
3. **Roles and Responsibilities:**
   - Assigned roles to ensure accountability.
   - Key roles may include data stewards, compliance officers, risk managers, and AI ethics boards.
4. **Monitoring and Evaluation:**
   - Mechanisms to track the performance and compliance of AI systems.
   - Tools such as dashboards and periodic audits ensure ongoing alignment with governance objectives.

USAGE SCENARIOS

ADAPTING TEMPLATES FOR DIFFERENT ORGANIZATIONS

Governance templates are not one-size-fits-all; they need to be tailored to an organization's unique characteristics. Below are strategies for adapting templates to various contexts:

1. **Small and Medium Enterprises (SMEs):**
   - **Challenges:** Limited resources and expertise.
   - **Adaptation Strategies:**

        - Use simplified templates focusing on high-priority areas such as data privacy and algorithm fairness.
        - Leverage open-source tools and community resources to implement governance practices cost-effectively.

2. **Multinational Corporations (MNCs):**
    - **Challenges:** Complex organizational structures and diverse regulatory environments.
    - **Adaptation Strategies:**
        - Develop modular templates that accommodate regional variations in laws and cultural expectations.
        - Implement a tiered governance structure with global, regional, and local layers.

3. **Public Institutions:**
    - **Challenges:** Balancing public accountability with operational efficiency.
    - **Adaptation Strategies:**
        - Emphasize transparency and stakeholder engagement in governance templates.
        - Incorporate feedback mechanisms to address public concerns and enhance trust.

STEP-BY-STEP GUIDE

CUSTOMIZING FRAMEWORKS TO MEET ORGANIZATIONAL NEEDS

To effectively implement governance frameworks, organizations should follow a structured customization process. Below is a step-by-step guide:

1. **Assess Organizational Needs:**
    - Conduct a thorough assessment of your organization's AI use cases, regulatory obligations, and risk exposure.
    - Example: A healthcare provider deploying AI for diagnostics would prioritize patient privacy and model explainability.

2. **Define Objectives:**
    - Clearly articulate the goals of your governance framework.
    - Example: A retail company might aim to ensure its AI systems enhance customer experience while avoiding discriminatory outcomes.

3. **Select a Template:**
    - Choose a governance template that aligns with your organization's size, industry, and maturity level.
    - Example: SMEs might opt for a minimalistic template, while MNCs require comprehensive frameworks.
4. **Customize Policies:**
    - Modify the policies in the template to reflect your specific regulatory and ethical requirements.
    - Example: A financial institution might include policies on algorithmic trading to comply with sector-specific regulations.
5. **Develop Procedures:**
    - Create detailed procedures for implementing the customized policies.
    - Example: A logistics company could establish a procedure for auditing route optimization algorithms for bias.
6. **Assign Roles and Responsibilities:**
    - Clearly define who is responsible for each aspect of governance.
    - Example: Appoint a Chief AI Officer to oversee governance implementation.
7. **Implement Monitoring Mechanisms:**
    - Set up tools and processes for ongoing monitoring and evaluation.
    - Example: Use dashboards to track compliance with governance metrics such as bias detection and model performance.
8. **Train Stakeholders:**
    - Provide training to ensure all stakeholders understand their roles and responsibilities.
    - Example: Train data scientists on ethical AI principles and compliance requirements.
9. **Pilot the Framework:**
    - Test the customized framework on a small scale before full implementation.
    - Example: A retail company could apply the framework to a single product line to identify potential issues.

10. **Refine and Scale:**

   - Use feedback from the pilot phase to refine the framework and scale it across the organization.
   - Example: Incorporate lessons learned from pilot audits to improve risk management protocols.

Governance frameworks are indispensable tools for navigating the complexities of AI implementation. Providing a structured approach to policies, procedures, roles, and monitoring enables organizations to align their AI initiatives with ethical and regulatory standards. Whether you are a startup, a global corporation, or a public institution, this section equips you with the knowledge and tools to customize governance frameworks that meet your unique needs. The following sections will delve into complementary resources such as compliance checklists and risk assessment tools, further enhancing your ability to operationalize AI governance.

22.3 COMPLIANCE CHECKLISTS

Compliance checklists ensure that AI systems adhere to regulatory, ethical, and operational standards. They provide a structured method for auditing AI implementations, identifying potential gaps, and maintaining accountability throughout the AI lifecycle. This section explores checklists for key governance areas, their integration into regular practices, and real-world examples of their application.

CHECKLISTS FOR KEY GOVERNANCE AREAS

REGULATORY COMPLIANCE

1. **General Data Protection Regulation (GDPR):**

   - Confirm data minimization practices to avoid unnecessary data collection.
   - Verify user consent mechanisms for data collection and processing.
   - Ensure proper data anonymization and encryption methods are implemented.
   - Maintain records of processing activities for transparency and accountability.

2. **AI Act (Proposed by the European Union):**

   - Assess AI systems against risk categories outlined in the AI Act.
   - Validate conformity assessments for high-risk AI systems.
   - Confirm that AI models meet transparency requirements, such as disclosing interactions with AI.
   - Ensure post-deployment monitoring mechanisms for continuous compliance.

3. **Sector-Specific Regulations:**
   - Financial Services: Adhere to anti-money laundering (AML) and algorithmic trading guidelines.
   - Healthcare: Validate compliance with HIPAA or equivalent standards for patient data privacy.
   - Manufacturing: Ensure AI systems comply with safety standards for automated equipment.

ETHICAL CONSIDERATIONS

1. **Bias and Fairness:**
   - Evaluate datasets for representation across demographics.
   - Implement bias-detection tools during model development.
   - Establish review processes to assess fairness in AI decision-making.
2. **Transparency:**
   - Ensure the explainability of AI model outcomes for end-users and stakeholders.
   - Provide detailed documentation of AI algorithms, datasets, and training processes.
   - Disclose AI use in customer interactions to maintain trust.
3. **Accountability:**
   - Assign clear ownership for AI system development and operation.
   - Implement incident reporting mechanisms for ethical concerns or regulatory breaches.

RISK MANAGEMENT AND MITIGATION

1. **Risk Identification:**
   - Conduct initial assessments to identify operational, ethical, and compliance risks.
   - Categorize risks based on severity and likelihood.
2. **Mitigation Strategies:**
   - Develop contingency plans for high-risk scenarios.
   - Implement automated monitoring systems to flag potential issues in real-time.
3. **Periodic Review:**

- Schedule regular reviews of risk mitigation measures.
- Update strategies based on new threats or regulatory changes.

HOW TO USE CHECKLISTS

INTEGRATING THESE TOOLS INTO REGULAR AUDITS AND EVALUATIONS

1. **Establish a Compliance Audit Schedule:**
    - Define a timeline for routine audits, ensuring they align with organizational milestones and regulatory deadlines.
    - Example: Conduct GDPR audits quarterly to align with data protection obligations.
2. **Incorporate Stakeholder Input:**
    - Engage cross-functional teams, including legal, technical, and ethical experts, to review checklist items.
    - Example: Include data scientists and ethicists in fairness and bias audits.
3. **Automate Wherever Possible:**
    - Use compliance tools that integrate with AI workflows to monitor real-time adherence.
    - Example: Leverage platforms like Power BI or Tableau to track compliance metrics.
4. **Document Findings:**
    - Maintain comprehensive records of audit results, including areas of non-compliance and corrective actions taken.
    - Example: Use version-controlled documentation for audit reports to ensure traceability.
5. **Close the Loop:**
    - Ensure follow-up actions are completed for all issues identified during audits.
    - Example: After identifying a fairness issue, retrain models using diverse datasets.

CASE EXAMPLES

DEMONSTRATING HOW ORGANIZATIONS HAVE UTILIZED CHECKLISTS EFFECTIVELY

1. **Tech Startup Leveraging GDPR Compliance Checklists:**
    - **Scenario:** A startup specializing in AI-driven marketing used a GDPR checklist to audit its data processing activities.

- **Outcome:** Identified gaps in user consent mechanisms and updated their website forms and workflows to comply fully with GDPR. Regular audits ensured sustained compliance as their customer base grew.

2. **Healthcare Provider Addressing Ethical AI Concerns:**
   - **Scenario:** A hospital deploying AI for diagnostics used ethical checklists to evaluate transparency and bias.
   - **Outcome:** By implementing explainability protocols and auditing model predictions for biases, the hospital improved patient trust and met ethical standards for AI in healthcare.
3. **Financial Institution Managing Risk with Checklists:**
   - **Scenario:** A global bank used risk management checklists to assess its AI-powered fraud detection system.
   - **Outcome:** By integrating risk identification and mitigation tools, the bank reduced false positives and strengthened regulatory compliance, avoiding potential penalties.
4. **Government Agency Enhancing Transparency:**
   - **Scenario:** A public sector organization used transparency checklists to audit AI systems deployed for citizen services.
   - **Outcome:** Introduced public disclosure reports and stakeholder consultations, which improved public trust and reduced complaints.

22.4 RISK ASSESSMENT TOOLS

Risk assessment is a critical component of AI governance, ensuring organizations can proactively identify, evaluate, and mitigate risks associated with AI systems. Organizations can safeguard against operational, ethical, and compliance challenges by employing structured tools and methodologies. This section explores risk identification and management templates, provides guidelines for practical application, and highlights real-world examples of organizations that have strengthened their governance through robust risk assessments.

TEMPLATES FOR RISK IDENTIFICATION AND MANAGEMENT

IDENTIFYING OPERATIONAL, ETHICAL, AND COMPLIANCE RISKS

1. **Operational Risks:**
   - **System Failures:** Assess the reliability and robustness of AI systems.
   - **Performance Variability:** Identify scenarios where the AI model's performance could degrade (e.g., in different datasets or environments).

- **Scalability Issues:** Evaluate whether AI systems can handle increased workloads or diverse use cases.

2. **Ethical Risks:**
    - **Bias in Decision-Making:** Review datasets and algorithms for potential biases that could lead to unfair outcomes.
    - **Lack of Transparency:** Identify areas where the system's decisions or processes are opaque to users or stakeholders.
    - **User Harm:** Evaluate scenarios where AI outputs could harm individuals (e.g., misinformation or unintended consequences).
3. **Compliance Risks:**
    - **Regulatory Violations:** Check for alignment with data protection laws, such as GDPR or the AI Act.
    - **Inadequate Documentation:** Ensure sufficient documentation exists to meet audit and reporting requirements.
    - **Cross-Border Data Transfers:** Identify risks related to data movement across jurisdictions with varying regulations.

EVALUATING THE LIKELIHOOD AND IMPACT OF RISKS USING A MATRIX

A risk matrix is an effective tool for prioritizing risks based on their likelihood and impact:

1. **Likelihood Levels:**
    - Low: Rarely occurs under normal circumstances.
    - Medium: Occurs occasionally but not frequently.
    - High: Frequently occurs or is almost inevitable.
2. **Impact Levels:**
    - Low: Minimal effect on operations or stakeholders.
    - Medium: Moderate disruption or reputational damage.
    - High: Significant harm, financial loss, or regulatory penalties.
3. **Risk Categorization:**
    - Map risks onto the matrix to determine priority levels.

- Example: A high-likelihood, high-impact risk (e.g., algorithmic bias in hiring) should be addressed immediately.

GUIDELINES FOR APPLICATION

TIPS FOR INTEGRATING RISK ASSESSMENT TOOLS INTO GOVERNANCE WORKFLOWS

1. **Embed Risk Assessment into AI Development Lifecycles:**
   - Conduct risk assessments during key stages of the AI lifecycle: development, deployment, and monitoring.
   - Example: Use risk assessment tools during model training to identify biases early.
2. **Leverage Cross-Functional Expertise:**
   - To provide diverse perspectives engage teams across disciplines, including data science, legal, ethics, and operations.
   - Example: Include ethicists and compliance officers in risk identification workshops.
3. **Automate Risk Monitoring:**
   - Use AI-powered tools to monitor and flag potential risks in real time continuously.
   - Example: Implement anomaly detection systems to identify unusual patterns that may indicate operational issues.
4. **Establish Clear Accountability:**
   - Assign ownership of risk assessment processes to specific roles or teams.
   - Example: Designate a Risk Manager responsible for overseeing assessments and mitigation efforts.
5. **Regularly Update Risk Assessment Frameworks:**
   - Periodically review and refine risk assessment tools to align with evolving regulations, technologies, and organizational priorities.
   - Example: Update risk criteria to include new regulatory guidelines, such as changes in the AI Act.

ORGANIZATIONS THAT IMPROVED GOVERNANCE BY IMPLEMENTING STRUCTURED RISK ASSESSMENTS

1. **Financial Services Firm:**
    - **Challenge:** A bank deploying an AI-based credit scoring system faced bias and regulatory non-compliance risks.
    - **Solution:** Implemented a risk assessment framework that evaluated data sources, algorithm transparency, and model outputs.
    - **Outcome:** Reduced bias in credit decisions, ensuring compliance with anti-discrimination laws and improving customer trust.
2. **Healthcare Provider:**
    - **Challenge:** A hospital using AI for patient diagnostics encountered ethical concerns about model explainability.
    - **Solution:** Conducted ethical risk assessments, focusing on transparency and user education.
    - **Outcome:** Enhanced patient trust and improved acceptance of AI-driven diagnostic tools.
3. **E-Commerce Platform:**
    - **Challenge:** An online retailer leveraging AI for personalized recommendations faced operational risks related to scalability.
    - **Solution:** Deployed risk assessment tools to evaluate system performance under varying loads and scenarios.
    - **Outcome:** Improved system robustness and ensured consistent user experience during peak demand periods.
4. **Public Sector Agency:**
    - **Challenge:** A government agency using AI for resource allocation must address unfair distribution risks.
    - **Solution:** Used a risk matrix to prioritize ethical risks and implemented mitigation strategies such as regular audits.
    - **Outcome:** Ensured equitable resource distribution and strengthened public confidence in AI use.

Monitoring and reporting dashboards are vital tools in AI governance. They enable organizations to track real-time performance, compliance, and other key metrics. These dashboards provide a centralized view of governance data, promoting transparency and supporting informed decision-making across teams. This section explores examples of dashboards, tips for implementation, and the benefits they bring to organizations.

Dashboard Examples

Effective dashboards visualize key governance metrics in a clear and actionable manner. Here are examples of metrics commonly included:

1. **Compliance Rates:**
    - Tracks adherence to regulatory frameworks such as GDPR, HIPAA, or the AI Act.
    - Example: A dashboard displaying the percentage of AI models certified compliant with data protection regulations.
2. **Model Performance:**
    - Monitors metrics like accuracy, precision, recall, and false-positive rates.
    - Example: A dashboard highlighting performance trends over time, segmented by use case or dataset.
3. **Audit Outcomes:**
    - Summarizes the results of internal and external audits.
    - Example: Visualizing areas of non-compliance, pending actions, and audit completion rates.
4. **Ethical Metrics:**
    - Tracks fairness, bias, and explainability of AI systems.
    - Example: A dashboard showing demographic parity across AI-driven decisions.
5. **Risk Indicators:**
    - Highlights operational, ethical, and compliance risks.
    - Example: A risk heatmap identifying high-priority issues needing immediate attention.

Implementation Tips

Setting up dashboards requires careful planning and the right tools to ensure effectiveness. Below are steps for successful implementation:

1. **Define Key Metrics:**
   - Collaborate with stakeholders to identify metrics that align with governance objectives.
   - Example: Compliance officers may prioritize regulatory metrics, while data scientists focus on model performance.
2. **Choose the Right Tools:**
   - Select tools like Tableau, Power BI, or custom software based on organizational needs and technical capabilities.
   - Example: Tableau offers powerful visualization capabilities, while Power BI integrates seamlessly with Microsoft tools.
3. **Integrate Data Sources:**
   - Ensure dashboards pull data from diverse sources, including AI systems, compliance records, and audit reports.
   - Example: Connect APIs to automate real-time data updates.
4. **Design User-Friendly Interfaces:**
   - Create intuitive layouts with clear visualizations and minimal clutter.
   - Example: Use color-coded indicators to highlight areas of concern.
5. **Train Stakeholders:**
   - Provide training to ensure teams can interpret and act on dashboard insights effectively.
   - Example: Conduct workshops for compliance teams on navigating and customizing dashboards.

Benefits

Dashboards deliver significant advantages for AI governance:

1. **Continuous Monitoring:**
   - Dashboards enable real-time tracking of governance metrics, allowing for prompt identification and resolution of issues.
2. **Enhanced Transparency:**

- Centralized data visualization fosters accountability and improves communication across teams.

3. **Data-Driven Decisions:**
    - Provides actionable insights that help organizations prioritize governance initiatives and allocate resources efficiently.
4. **Regulatory Compliance:**
    - Facilitates compliance by offering clear, real-time evidence of adherence to standards.
5. **Improved Collaboration:**
    - Dashboards are shared resources aligning cross-functional teams toward common governance goals.

In summary, monitoring and reporting dashboards are indispensable for modern AI governance. They provide the clarity and insights necessary for responsible AI management.

22.6 ADDITIONAL RESOURCES AND REFERENCES

This section provides a curated list of resources to help organizations and individuals deepen their understanding of AI governance and implement effective practices. By exploring the recommended reading materials, leveraging online tools, and engaging with professional communities, readers can stay informed and connected in the rapidly evolving field of AI governance.

READING LISTS

1. **Books:**
    - "AI SUPERPOWERS" BY KAI-FU LEE: Explores the global AI landscape with a focus on ethics and governance.
    - "WEAPONS OF MATH DESTRUCTION" BY CATHY O'NEIL: A critical look at the societal impact of biased algorithms.
    - "ETHICS OF ARTIFICIAL INTELLIGENCE AND ROBOTICS" BY VINCENT C. MÜLLER: Discusses foundational and emerging ethical challenges in AI.
2. **Articles and White Papers:**
    - "THE FUTURE OF AI GOVERNANCE" by the World Economic Forum: Offers insights into global governance frameworks.
    - "ETHICAL AI: BALANCING INNOVATION AND RESPONSIBILITY" by McKinsey & Company provides practical strategies for implementing ethical AI.

- The European Commission's "Guidelines for Trustworthy AI" outline principles for creating AI systems aligned with ethical and legal standards.

ONLINE TOOLS

1. **Free Tools:**
   - **AI Fairness 360 (IBM):** Open-source toolkit for detecting and mitigating bias in AI models.
   - **Lime and SHAP:** Tools for explainability and interpreting model predictions.
   - **Google's What-If Tool:** A visualization tool for exploring model performance and fairness.
2. **Paid Tools:**
   - **DataRobot:** Comprehensive platform for AI lifecycle management, including governance features.
   - **H2O.ai:** Offers tools for compliance tracking and model interpretability.
   - **OneTrust AI Governance:** Specializes in managing AI compliance and risk assessment.

CONTACTS AND COMMUNITIES

1. **Organizations:**
   - **Partnership on AI:** A multi-stakeholder organization focusing on AI ethics and best practices.
   - **OpenAI Ethics Committee:** Provides resources and guidelines for responsible AI use.
   - **AI Global:** Supports the development of ethical AI systems through frameworks and certification programs.
2. **Forums and Networks:**
   - **LinkedIn Groups:** Join groups like "AI Ethics and Governance" for discussions and updates.
   - **AI Now Institute:** A research institute focused on the social implications of AI.
   - **IEEE Global Initiative on Ethics of Autonomous and Intelligent Systems:** Offers resources and opportunities to participate in standards development.

By engaging with these resources, tools, and communities, readers can expand their knowledge and maintain an active role in advancing responsible AI governance practices.

REFERENCE AND BIBLIOGRAPHY

- Future of Life Institute. (2017). ASILOMAR AI PRINCIPLES. Retrieved from https://futureoflife.org/ai-principles
- European Union. (2018). GENERAL DATA PROTECTION REGULATION (GDPR). Retrieved from https://eur-lex.europa.eu/eli/reg/2016/679
- UNESCO. (2021). RECOMMENDATION ON THE ETHICS OF ARTIFICIAL INTELLIGENCE. Retrieved from https://en.unesco.org/artificial-intelligence/ethics
- Organisation for Economic Co-operation and Development. (2019). OECD AI PRINCIPLES. Retrieved from https://oecd.ai
- United Nations Economic Commission for Europe (UNECE). (2020). GUIDELINES FOR AUTONOMOUS VEHICLES SAFETY. Retrieved from https://unece.org
- California State Legislature. (2018). CALIFORNIA CONSUMER PRIVACY ACT (CCPA). Retrieved from https://leginfo.legislature.ca.gov/faces/codes_displayText.xhtml?lawCode=CIV&division=3.&title=1.81.5.&part=4.
- Partnership on AI. (n.d.). BEST PRACTICES FOR AI GOVERNANCE. Retrieved from https://partnershiponai.org
- National Institute of Standards and Technology. (2019). Study on facial recognition accuracy. NIST. Retrieved from https://www.nist.gov
- European Union. (2016). General Data Protection Regulation (GDPR) (Regulation (EU) 2016/679). Retrieved from https://gdpr-info.eu
- Amazon. (n.d.). AI hiring tool controversy. Retrieved from https://www.amazon.com (if specific URL is known)
- Partnership on AI. (n.d.). Promoting responsible AI development. Retrieved from https://www.partnershiponai.org
- Google. (n.d.). AI principles: Fairness, privacy, and security. Retrieved from https://ai.google/principles
- Clearview AI. (n.d.). Facial data collection controversy. Retrieved from https://clearview.ai (if specific URL is known)
- OpenAI. (n.d.). Energy consumption in AI training: GPT series. Retrieved from https://www.openai.com
- Microsoft. (n.d.). Responsible AI principles. Retrieved from https://www.microsoft.com/en-us/ai/responsible-ai
- IBM. (n.d.). Watson OpenScale platform. Retrieved from https://www.ibm.com/cloud/watson-openscale
- European Commission. (2021). PROPOSAL FOR A REGULATION OF THE EUROPEAN PARLIAMENT AND OF THE COUNCIL LAYING DOWN HARMONISED RULES ON ARTIFICIAL INTELLIGENCE (ARTIFICIAL INTELLIGENCE ACT). Retrieved from https://eur-lex.europa.eu/legal-content/EN/TXT/?uri=CELEX:52021PC0206
- European Union. (2016). GENERAL DATA PROTECTION REGULATION (GDPR). Retrieved from https://gdpr-info.eu/
- California State Legislature. (2020). CALIFORNIA PRIVACY RIGHTS ACT (CPRA). Retrieved from https://oag.ca.gov/privacy/ccpa
- Illinois General Assembly. (2008). BIOMETRIC INFORMATION PRIVACY ACT (BIPA). Retrieved from https://www.ilga.gov/legislation/ilcs/ilcs3.asp?ActID=3004
- Virginia General Assembly. (2021). CONSUMER DATA PROTECTION ACT (CDPA). Retrieved from https://law.lis.virginia.gov/vacode/title59.1/chapter52/
- International Organization for Standardization (ISO) & International Electrotechnical Commission (IEC). (2020). ISO/IEC 22989: ARTIFICIAL INTELLIGENCE – CONCEPTS AND TERMINOLOGY. Retrieved from https://www.iso.org/standard/74296.html
- International Organization for Standardization (ISO) & International Electrotechnical Commission (IEC). (2020). ISO/IEC 23053: FRAMEWORK FOR AI SYSTEMS. Retrieved from https://www.iso.org/standard/74297.html

- Institute of Electrical and Electronics Engineers (IEEE). (2019). ETHICALLY ALIGNED DESIGN: A VISION FOR PRIORITIZING HUMAN WELL-BEING WITH AUTONOMOUS AND INTELLIGENT SYSTEMS. Retrieved from https://ethicsinaction.ieee.org/
- National Institute of Standards and Technology (NIST). (2023). ARTIFICIAL INTELLIGENCE RISK MANAGEMENT FRAMEWORK. Retrieved from https://www.nist.gov/itl/ai-risk-management-framework
- China State Council. (2017). NEXT GENERATION ARTIFICIAL INTELLIGENCE DEVELOPMENT PLAN. Retrieved from http://www.gov.cn/zhengce/content/2017-07/20/content_5211996.htm
- Government of India. (2020). NATIONAL STRATEGY FOR ARTIFICIAL INTELLIGENCE. Retrieved from https://niti.gov.in/national-strategy-ai
- U.S. White House. (2022). BLUEPRINT FOR AN AI BILL OF RIGHTS. Retrieved from https://www.whitehouse.gov/ostp/ai-bill-of-rights/
- European Parliament. (2016). General Data Protection Regulation (GDPR). Official Journal of the European Union. Retrieved from https://gdpr-info.eu
- California Legislature. (2018). California Consumer Privacy Act (CCPA). Retrieved from https://oag.ca.gov/privacy/ccpa
- Ribeiro, M. T., Singh, S., & Guestrin, C. (2016). "Why Should I Trust You?" Explaining the Predictions of Any Classifier. Proceedings of the 22nd ACM SIGKDD International Conference on Knowledge Discovery and Data Mining. Retrieved from https://arxiv.org/abs/1602.04938
- Lundberg, S. M., & Lee, S.-I. (2017). A Unified Approach to Interpreting Model Predictions. Advances in Neural Information Processing Systems. Retrieved from https://arxiv.org/abs/1705.07874
- European Commission. (2021). Proposal for a Regulation on Artificial Intelligence (Artificial Intelligence Act). Retrieved from https://digital-strategy.ec.europa.eu/en/policies/european-approach-artificial-intelligence
- Google AI. (n.d.). Federated Learning: Collaborative Machine Learning without Centralized Training Data. Retrieved from https://research.google/pubs/federated-learning/
- Apple. (n.d.). Differential Privacy. Retrieved from https://www.apple.com/privacy/
- Basel Committee on Banking Supervision. (2020). Principles for Operational Resilience. Bank for International Settlements. Retrieved from https://www.bis.org/bcbs/index.htm
- General Data Protection Regulation (GDPR). (2018). REGULATION (EU) 2016/679 OF THE EUROPEAN PARLIAMENT AND OF THE COUNCIL. Retrieved from https://gdpr-info.eu
- National Institute of Standards and Technology (NIST). (2021). NIST AI RISK MANAGEMENT FRAMEWORK. U.S. Department of Commerce. Retrieved from https://www.nist.gov/itl/ai-risk-management-framework
- Organisation for Economic Co-operation and Development (OECD). (2019). OECD PRINCIPLES ON ARTIFICIAL INTELLIGENCE. Retrieved from https://www.oecd.org/going-digital/ai/principles/
- Microsoft Corporation. (2023). RESPONSIBLE AI STANDARD. Retrieved from https://www.microsoft.com/ai/responsible-ai
- Health Insurance Portability and Accountability Act (HIPAA). (1996). HIPAA PRIVACY RULE. U.S. Department of Health and Human Services. Retrieved from https://www.hhs.gov/hipaa/index.html
- California Consumer Privacy Act (CCPA). (2018). CALIFORNIA CIVIL CODE SECTION 1798.100 ET SEQ. Retrieved from https://oag.ca.gov/privacy/ccpa
- U.S. Securities and Exchange Commission (SEC). (2020). REGULATION BEST INTEREST AND FORM CRS. Retrieved from https://www.sec.gov
- Food and Drug Administration (FDA). (2021). GUIDANCE ON AI/ML-BASED SOFTWARE AS A MEDICAL DEVICE. Retrieved from https://www.fda.gov/medical-devices

- European Union. (2021). ARTIFICIAL INTELLIGENCE ACT: A LEGAL FRAMEWORK FOR AI IN EUROPE. Retrieved from https://digital-strategy.ec.europa.eu/en/policies/european-approach-artificial-intelligence
- General Data Protection Regulation (GDPR). (2018). Regulation (EU) 2016/679. Retrieved from https://gdpr-info.eu/
- IBM. (n.d.). AI FAIRNESS 360: AN OPEN-SOURCE TOOLKIT FOR DETECTING AND MITIGATING BIAS IN MACHINE LEARNING MODELS. Retrieved from https://aif360.mybluemix.net/
- Lundberg, S. M., & Lee, S.-I. (2017). A unified approach to interpreting model predictions. ADVANCES IN NEURAL INFORMATION PROCESSING SYSTEMS, 30. Retrieved from https://github.com/slundberg/shap
- Ribeiro, M. T., Singh, S., & Guestrin, C. (2016). "Why Should I Trust You?": Explaining the predictions of any classifier. PROCEEDINGS OF THE 22ND ACM SIGKDD INTERNATIONAL CONFERENCE ON KNOWLEDGE DISCOVERY AND DATA MINING. Retrieved from https://github.com/marcotcr/lime
- U.S. Equal Employment Opportunity Commission. (n.d.). ARTIFICIAL INTELLIGENCE AND ALGORITHMIC FAIRNESS IN EMPLOYMENT. Retrieved from https://www.eeoc.gov/
- National Institute of Standards and Technology (NIST). (2022). AI RISK MANAGEMENT FRAMEWORK. Retrieved from https://www.nist.gov/ai
- OECD. (2021). OECD PRINCIPLES ON ARTIFICIAL INTELLIGENCE. Retrieved from https://www.oecd.org/going-digital/ai/principles/
- General Data Protection Regulation (GDPR). (2016). Regulation (EU) 2016/679 of the European Parliament and of the Council of 27 April 2016. Retrieved from https://eur-lex.europa.eu
- Health Insurance Portability and Accountability Act (HIPAA). (1996). U.S. Department of Health and Human Services. Retrieved from https://www.hhs.gov/hipaa/
- GDPR: General Data Protection Regulation. (n.d.). Retrieved from https://gdpr-info.eu
- California Consumer Privacy Act (CCPA). (2018). Retrieved from https://oag.ca.gov/privacy/ccpa
- IBM AI Fairness 360. (n.d.). Retrieved from https://aif360.mybluemix.net
- Google What-If Tool. (n.d.). Retrieved from https://pair-code.github.io/what-if-tool
- IEEE Global Initiative on Ethics of Autonomous and Intelligent Systems. (n.d.). Retrieved from https://ethicsinaction.ieee.org
- Health Insurance Portability and Accountability Act (HIPAA). (1996). Retrieved from https://www.hhs.gov/hipaa
- SMOTE: Synthetic Minority Over-sampling Technique. (n.d.). Retrieved from https://imbalanced-learn.org/stable/references/generated/imblearn.over_sampling.SMOTE.html
- OneTrust
  OneTrust. (n.d.). PRIVACY, SECURITY, AND GOVERNANCE PLATFORM. Retrieved from https://www.onetrust.com
- TrustArc
  TrustArc. (n.d.). PRIVACY AND COMPLIANCE SOLUTIONS. Retrieved from https://www.trustarc.com
- IBM AI Fairness 360
  IBM. (n.d.). AI FAIRNESS 360: AN OPEN-SOURCE TOOLKIT. Retrieved from https://aif360.mybluemix.net
- Fairlearn
  Microsoft. (n.d.). FAIRLEARN: A TOOLKIT FOR ASSESSING AND IMPROVING FAIRNESS. Retrieved from https://fairlearn.org
- SHAP (SHapley Additive ExPlanations)
  Lundberg, S. M., & Lee, S.-I. (2017). A UNIFIED APPROACH TO INTERPRETING MODEL PREDICTIONS. In Proceedings of the 31st International Conference on Neural Information Processing Systems (pp. 4765–4774). Retrieved from https://github.com/slundberg/shap

- LIME (Local Interpretable Model-Agnostic Explanations)
  Ribeiro, M. T., Singh, S., & Guestrin, C. (2016). "WHY SHOULD I TRUST YOU?": EXPLAINING THE PREDICTIONS OF ANY CLASSIFIER. Proceedings of the 22nd ACM SIGKDD International Conference on Knowledge Discovery and Data Mining, 1135–1144. Retrieved from https://github.com/marcotcr/lime

- Fiddler AI
  Fiddler Labs. (n.d.). EXPLAINABLE MONITORING FOR AI MODELS. Retrieved from https://www.fiddler.ai

- Arize AI
  Arize AI. (n.d.). PERFORMANCE MONITORING AND BIAS DETECTION FOR MACHINE LEARNING MODELS. Retrieved from https://arize.com

- Weights & Biases
  Weights & Biases. (n.d.). EXPERIMENT TRACKING, MODEL MONITORING, AND COLLABORATION. Retrieved from https://wandb.ai

- Google's Explainable AI Platform
  Google Cloud. (n.d.). EXPLAINABLE AI: TOOLS TO EXPLAIN AND INTERPRET MACHINE LEARNING MODELS. Retrieved from https://cloud.google.com/explainable-ai

- LogicGate
  LogicGate. (n.d.). RISK AND COMPLIANCE MANAGEMENT PLATFORM. Retrieved from https://www.logicgate.com

- NIST Post-Quantum Cryptography
  National Institute of Standards and Technology (NIST). (n.d.). POST-QUANTUM CRYPTOGRAPHY PROJECT. Retrieved from https://csrc.nist.gov/Projects/Post-Quantum-Cryptography

- European Commission. (n.d.). THE EU AI ACT: REGULATION FOR ARTIFICIAL INTELLIGENCE. Retrieved from https://digital-strategy.ec.europa.eu/en/policies/eu-ai-act

- National Institute of Standards and Technology (NIST). (2021). AI RISK MANAGEMENT FRAMEWORK. Retrieved from https://www.nist.gov/ai

- Google. (n.d.). WHAT-IF TOOL: RESPONSIBLE AI INITIATIVE. Retrieved from https://pair-code.github.io/what-if-tool

- Microsoft. (n.d.). AI FOR GOOD AND THE AETHER COMMITTEE. Retrieved from https://www.microsoft.com/en-us/ai/ai-for-good

- IBM. (n.d.). AI OPENSCALE PLATFORM: REAL-TIME AI MONITORING. Retrieved from https://www.ibm.com/cloud/ai-openscale

- General Data Protection Regulation (GDPR). (2016). Regulation (EU) 2016/679 of the European Parliament and of the Council of 27 April 2016. Retrieved from https://eur-lex.europa.eu/

- Health Insurance Portability and Accountability Act (HIPAA). (1996). U.S. Department of Health & Human Services. Retrieved from https://www.hhs.gov/hipaa/

- National Artificial Intelligence Initiative Act of 2020. (2020). Comprehensive framework for AI research and development. Retrieved from https://www.congress.gov/bill/116th-congress/house-bill/6216

- National Institute of Standards and Technology (NIST). (2021). AI Risk Management Framework (RMF). Retrieved from https://www.nist.gov/artificial-intelligence

- California Consumer Privacy Act (CCPA). (2018). Privacy rights and data regulations in California. Retrieved from https://oag.ca.gov/privacy/ccpa

- Blueprint for an AI Bill of Rights. (2022). Ethical guidelines for AI systems affecting daily life. Retrieved from https://www.whitehouse.gov/ostp/ai-bill-of-rights/

- Directive on Automated Decision-Making. (2019). Guidelines for federal AI use in Canada. Retrieved from https://www.canada.ca/en/government/system/digital-government/directive-automated-decision-making.html

- Artificial Intelligence Act. (2021). European Union's risk-based AI governance framework. Retrieved from https://eur-lex.europa.eu/legal-content/EN/TXT/?uri=CELEX%3A52021PC0206
- Social Principles of Human-Centric AI. (2019). Japan's ethical guidelines for AI development. Retrieved from https://www.soumu.go.jp/main_sosiki/joho_tsusin/eng/presentation/pdf/Japan_2019.pdf
- Next Generation Artificial Intelligence Development Plan. (2017). China's roadmap for AI leadership by 2030. Retrieved from http://english.www.gov.cn/
- Pan-Canadian Artificial Intelligence Strategy. (2017). Canada's framework for ethical AI development. Retrieved from https://www.cifar.ca/ai/pan-canadian-artificial-intelligence-strategy
- UNESCO Recommendation on the Ethics of Artificial Intelligence. (2021). International framework for ethical AI. Retrieved from https://en.unesco.org/artificial-intelligence/ethics
- U.S. Department of Health & Human Services. (1996). Health Insurance Portability and Accountability Act (HIPAA). Retrieved from https://www.hhs.gov/hipaa/
- United Nations. (n.d.). Convention on Certain Conventional Weapons (CCW). Retrieved from https://www.un.org/disarmament/ccw/
- Partnership on AI. (n.d.). About Partnership on AI. Retrieved from https://www.partnershiponai.org/
- Ribeiro, M. T., Singh, S., & Guestrin, C. (2016). "Why Should I Trust You?": Explaining the Predictions of Any Classifier. Retrieved from https://arxiv.org/abs/1602.04938
- Nakamoto, S. (2008). Bitcoin: A Peer-to-Peer Electronic Cash System. Retrieved from https://bitcoin.org/bitcoin.pdf
- European Union. (n.d.). PROPOSAL FOR A REGULATION LAYING DOWN HARMONIZED RULES ON ARTIFICIAL INTELLIGENCE (ARTIFICIAL INTELLIGENCE ACT). Retrieved from https://eur-lex.europa.eu
- General Data Protection Regulation (GDPR). (2016). REGULATION (EU) 2016/679 OF THE EUROPEAN PARLIAMENT AND OF THE COUNCIL. Retrieved from https://gdpr-info.eu
- National Institute of Standards and Technology (NIST). (n.d.). AI RISK MANAGEMENT FRAMEWORK. Retrieved from https://www.nist.gov
- California Consumer Privacy Act (CCPA). (2018). CALIFORNIA CIVIL CODE TITLE 1.81.5. Retrieved from https://oag.ca.gov/privacy/ccpa
- Organisation for Economic Co-operation and Development (OECD). (2019). OECD AI PRINCIPLES: RECOMMENDATION OF THE COUNCIL ON ARTIFICIAL INTELLIGENCE. Retrieved from https://oecd.ai/en/dashboards
- UNESCO. (2021). RECOMMENDATION ON THE ETHICS OF ARTIFICIAL INTELLIGENCE. Retrieved from https://unesdoc.unesco.org
- Financial Conduct Authority (FCA). (n.d.). REGULATORY SANDBOX. Retrieved from https://www.fca.org.uk/firms/innovation/regulatory-sandbox
- Health Insurance Portability and Accountability Act (HIPAA). (1996). PUBLIC LAW 104-191. Retrieved from https://www.hhs.gov/hipaa
- Global Partnership on Artificial Intelligence (GPAI). (n.d.). WORKING TOWARDS RESPONSIBLE AI. Retrieved from https://gpai.ai
- United Nations (UN). (n.d.). THE UN ACTIVITIES ON ARTIFICIAL INTELLIGENCE. Retrieved from https://www.un.org/en/artificial-intelligence
- City of Barcelona. (n.d.). SMART CITY INITIATIVE. Retrieved from https://ajuntament.barcelona.cat/digital/en/smart-city
- Singapore Government. (n.d.). SMART NATION SINGAPORE. Retrieved from https://www.smartnation.gov.sg
- South Korean Government. (n.d.). AI USE IN PUBLIC HEALTH DURING COVID-19 PANDEMIC. Retrieved from https://www.mohw.go.kr

- United States Food and Drug Administration (FDA). (n.d.). AI/ML-BASED SOFTWARE AS A MEDICAL DEVICE (SAMD). Retrieved from https://www.fda.gov
- San Francisco Board of Supervisors. (2019). ORDINANCE BANNING FACIAL RECOGNITION TECHNOLOGY. Retrieved from https://sfbos.org
- U.S. Department of Justice. (n.d.). USE OF AI IN PREDICTIVE POLICING. Retrieved from https://www.justice.gov

Books

- Lee, K.-F. (2018). AI SUPERPOWERS: CHINA, SILICON VALLEY, AND THE NEW WORLD ORDER. Houghton Mifflin Harcourt. Retrieved from https://www.amazon.com/dp/132854639X
- O'Neil, C. (2016). WEAPONS OF MATH DESTRUCTION: HOW BIG DATA INCREASES INEQUALITY AND THREATENS DEMOCRACY. Crown. Retrieved from https://www.amazon.com/dp/0553418815
- Müller, V. C. (2020). ETHICS OF ARTIFICIAL INTELLIGENCE AND ROBOTICS. Routledge. Retrieved from https://www.routledge.com/Ethics-of-Artificial-Intelligence-and-Robotics/Muller/p/book/9781138744650

Articles and White Papers

- World Economic Forum. (2020). THE FUTURE OF AI GOVERNANCE. Retrieved from https://www.weforum.org
- McKinsey & Company. (2020). ETHICAL AI: BALANCING INNOVATION AND RESPONSIBILITY. Retrieved from https://www.mckinsey.com
- European Commission. (2019). GUIDELINES FOR TRUSTWORTHY AI. Retrieved from https://ec.europa.eu

Online Tools

- IBM. (n.d.). AI FAIRNESS 360. Retrieved from https://aif360.mybluemix.net
- Lime and SHAP. (n.d.). TOOLS FOR EXPLAINABILITY AND INTERPRETING MODEL PREDICTIONS. Retrieved from https://github.com
- Google. (n.d.). WHAT-IF TOOL. Retrieved from https://pair-code.github.io/what-if-tool/

Paid Tools

- DataRobot. (n.d.). AI LIFECYCLE MANAGEMENT. Retrieved from https://www.datarobot.com
- H2O.ai. (n.d.). AI GOVERNANCE TOOLS. Retrieved from https://www.h2o.ai
- OneTrust. (n.d.). AI GOVERNANCE AND RISK ASSESSMENT. Retrieved from https://www.onetrust.com

Organizations

- Partnership on AI. (n.d.). Retrieved from https://www.partnershiponai.org
- OpenAI Ethics Committee. (n.d.). Retrieved from https://www.openai.com
- AI Global. (n.d.). Retrieved from https://www.ai-global.org

Forums and Networks

- LinkedIn Groups. (n.d.). AI ETHICS AND GOVERNANCE GROUP. Retrieved from https://www.linkedin.com
- AI Now Institute. (n.d.). Retrieved from https://ainowinstitute.org
- IEEE Global Initiative on Ethics of Autonomous and Intelligent Systems. (n.d.). Retrieved from https://ethicsinaction.ieee.org

www.ingramcontent.com/pod-product-compliance
Lightning Source LLC
LaVergne TN
LVHW060021210926
848481LV00013B/3756
* 9 7 9 8 3 4 8 5 3 0 0 7 5 *